The Arts

a visual encyclopedia

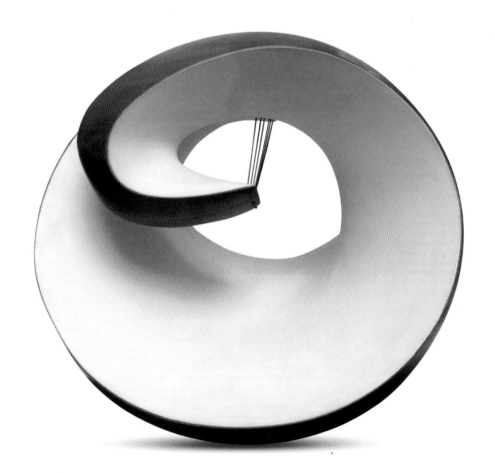

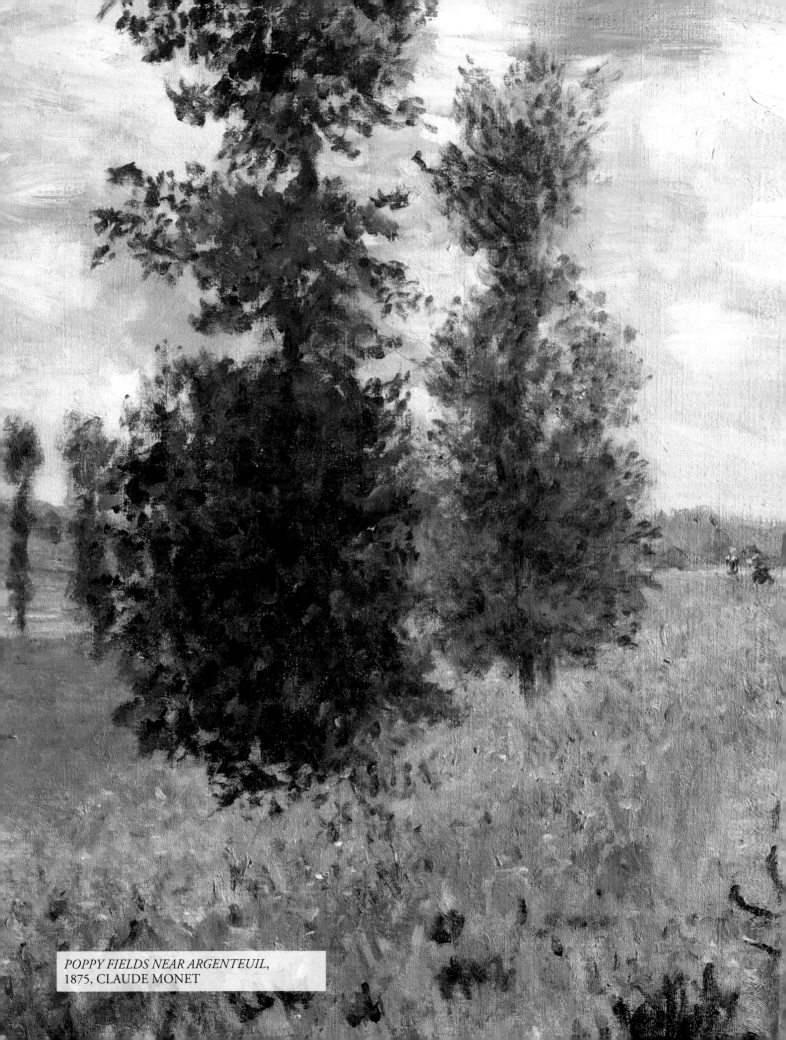

POPPY FIELDS NEAR ARGENTEUIL,
1875, CLAUDE MONET

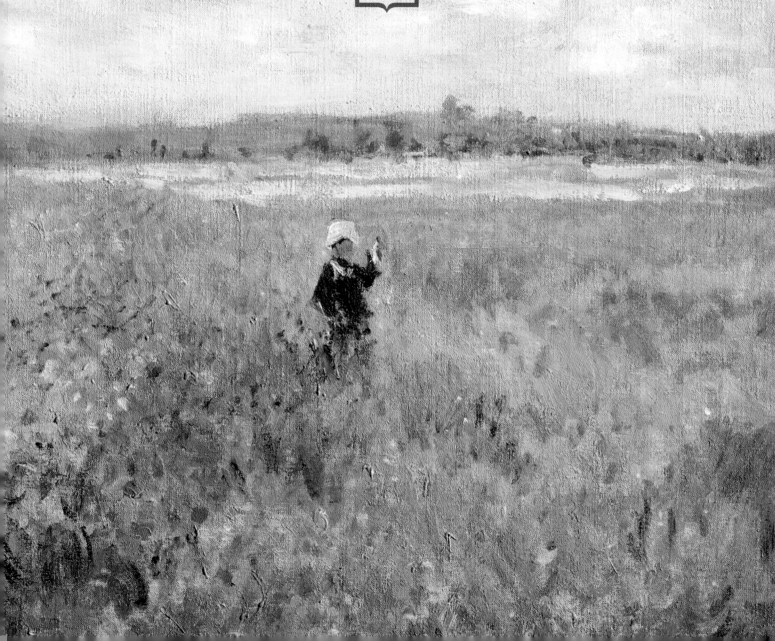

The Arts

a visual encyclopedia

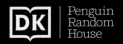

DK Penguin Random House

Author (Painting and Sculpture) Susie Hodge
Author (Photography) David Taylor
Author (Music) Joe Fullman
Author (Dance) Peter Chrisp

Project Editor Ashwin Khurana
US Editors Shannon Beatty, Karyn Gerhard
Senior Art Editor Spencer Holbrook
Managing Editor Francesca Baines
Managing Art Editor Philip Letsu
Producers, Pre-production David Almond, Robert Dunn
Senior Producer Gary Batchelor
Jacket Designers Dhirendra Singh, Surabhi Wadha
Senior DTP Designer Harish Aggarwal
Jackets Editor Claire Gell
Jackets Editorial Coordinator Priyanka Sharma
Jacket Design Development Manager Sophia MTT
Publisher Andrew Macintyre
Art Director Karen Self
Associate Publishing Director Liz Wheeler
Design Director Phil Ormerod
Publishing Director Jonathan Metcalf

Tall Tree Ltd
Editors Rob Colson, David John
Designer Ben Ruocco

First American Edition, 2017
Published in the United States by DK Publishing
1450 Broadway, Suite 801, New York, NY 10018

A catalog record for this book is available from
the Library of Congress.
ISBN: 978-1-4654-6178-0 (Paperback)
ISBN: 978-1-4654-6290-9 (ALB)

DK books are available at special discounts when purchased in
bulk for sales, promotions, premiums, fund-raising, or educational use.
For details, contact: DK Publishing Special Markets,
1450 Broadway, Suite 801, New York, NY 10018
SpecialSales@dk.com

Printed and bound in China

All images © Dorling Kindersley Limited
For further information see: www.dkimages.com

For the curious
www.dk.com

MIX
Paper from
responsible sources
FSC™ C018179

This book was made with Forest
Stewardship Council™ certified
paper – one small step in DK's
commitment to a sustainable future.
For more information go to
www.dk.com/our-green-pledge

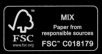

Contents

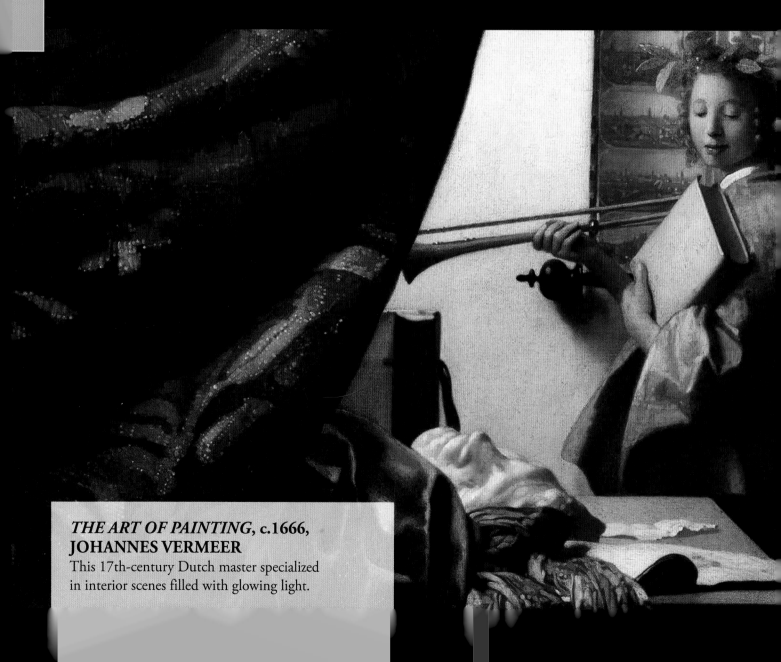

PAINTING

***THE ART OF PAINTING*, c.1666, JOHANNES VERMEER**
This 17th-century Dutch master specialized in interior scenes filled with glowing light.

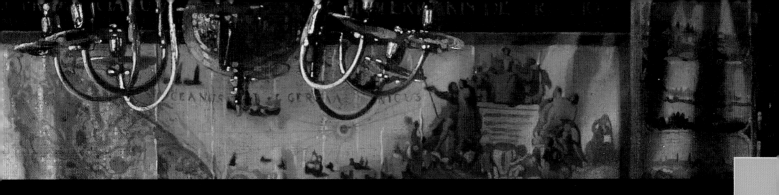

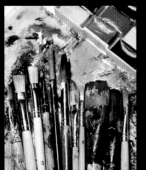 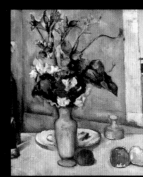 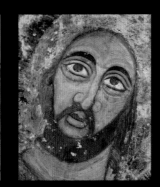

Human beings have been painting for thousands of years, using surfaces of all kinds for their works— including cave walls, church ceilings, wooden panels, paper, and canvases.

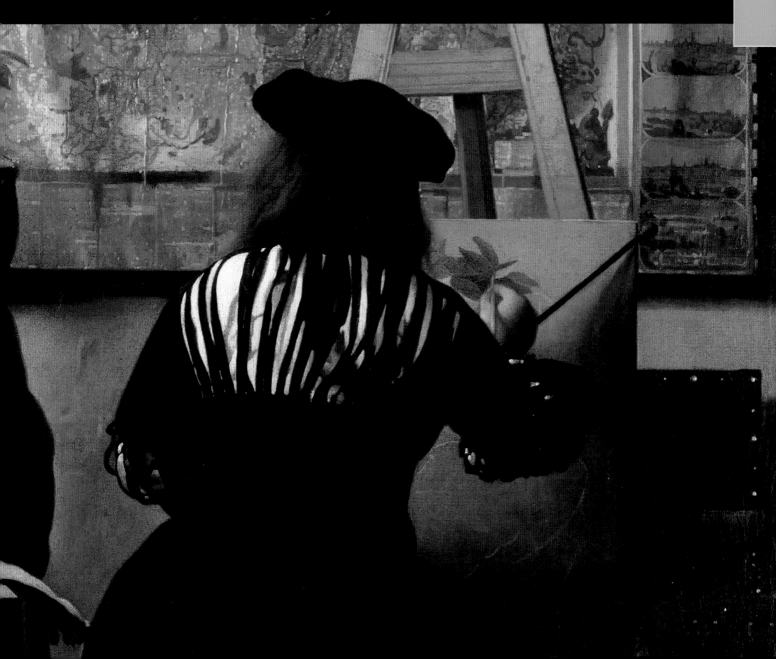

Subject and composition

Artists paint about all manner of subjects and for many different reasons. Some paintings tell stories, or honor people or events, while others get you to feel differently about a subject by delighting or provoking you. Many artists paint to inform viewers, or to get them to think about issues in unexpected ways.

▼ *PARK NEAR LUCERNE*, 1938, PAUL KLEE
This abstract work was inspired by the strolls that Klee enjoyed with his wife Lily near Lucerne, Switzerland. In it, paths criss-cross between trees with colorful foliage.

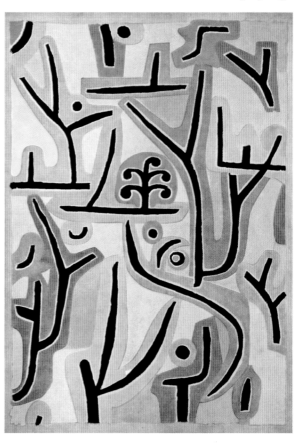

SUBJECT AND STYLE

The list of subjects explored by artists is endless—people, landscapes, love, war, to mention just a few. Usually, these subjects are depicted in a representative (realistic) style. In the 20th century, however, some artists began making paintings where the subjects are often unrecognizable. This style, known as abstract art, uses shapes or colors to convey feelings or ideas.

SHAPE AND COMPOSITION

The shape of a painting is known as its format. The two most common formats are portrait (vertical) and landscape (horizontal). But artists do not just make pictures to hang in frames; they also paint on walls and ceilings, which are known as frescoes. The way the artist chooses to arrange the subject matter within the format is called its composition.

◄ *APPLES, PEACHES, PEARS, AND GRAPES*, 1880, PAUL CÉZANNE
A composition of a group of objects, such as this bowl of fruit, is called a still life.

IMPACT AND REACTION

Artists want their works to create an impact and to draw a reaction, whatever their subject. Picture stories are usually composed so the viewer can follow the sequence of events, while landscapes often have a foreground, middle ground, and background, designed to lead you through the picture. Portraits will usually feature their subjects in powerful close-up.

In early Western Europe—when few people could read—bible stories were told through paintings.

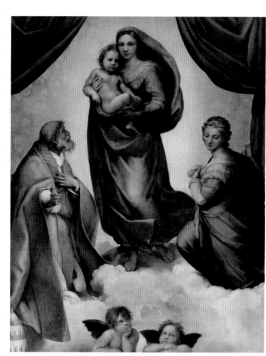

▶ *SISTINE MADONNA*, 1512, RAPHAEL
The large central figures of Mary and the baby Jesus dominate this painting. Two saints kneel at Mary's feet, with one looking down, drawing attention to the two angels.

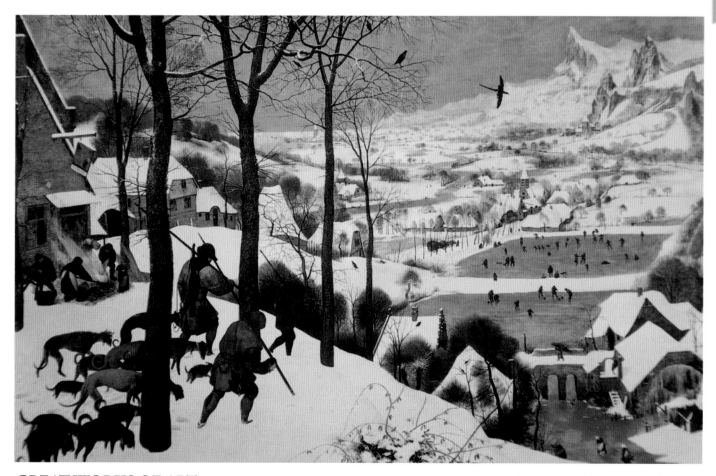

GREAT WORKS OF ART

Great paintings, by artists talented in their chosen style, continue to fascinate people long after they were made. Despite the passing of time, there is something unique about the subject and composition of a great work of art that continues to draw viewers in, making them see the world in a new or slightly different way.

▲ *HUNTERS IN THE SNOW*, 1565, PIETER BRUEGEL THE ELDER
Hunters trudge through the snow, leading us into a wintery landscape that is full of details of peasant life in Northern Europe almost 500 years ago.

Perspective

Artists use a technique called perspective to create an illusion of the real, three-dimensional world on flat surfaces, such as paper or canvas. Objects that are far away are made to appear smaller and closer together than objects that are nearby. Artists also vary the amount of light and shade in their works to create the appearance of depth.

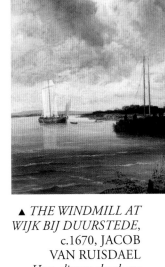
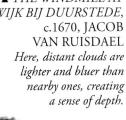

▲ *THE WINDMILL AT WIJK BIJ DUURSTEDE*, c.1670, JACOB VAN RUISDAEL
Here, distant clouds are lighter and bluer than nearby ones, creating a sense of depth.

LINEAR PERSPECTIVE

In the early 15th century, the Italian architect Filippo Brunelleschi developed mathematical rules for drawing perspective. Called linear perspective, Brunelleschi's system uses straight lines that meet in the far distance at a place called a vanishing point.

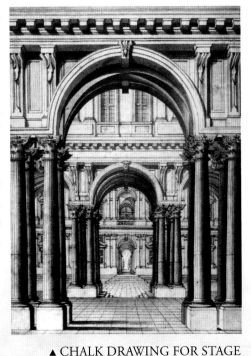

▲ CHALK DRAWING FOR STAGE DESIGN, 1700s, TORINESE SCHOOL
In this perspective drawing, the vanishing point is through the most distant arch.

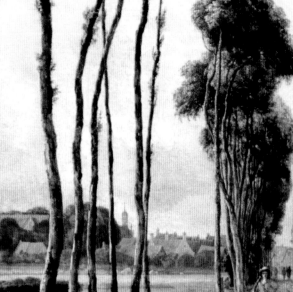

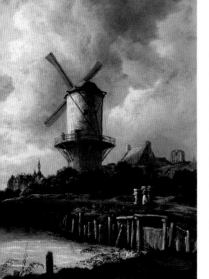

AERIAL PERSPECTIVE

Artists can also create illusions of space and distance using color, a method known as aerial, or atmospheric, perspective. In real life, due to the Earth's atmosphere, objects that are far away appear lighter, bluer, and less detailed. Italian artist Leonardo da Vinci described these effects: "Colors become weaker in proportion to their distance from the person who is looking at them."

The highest viewpoint is a bird's-eye view, in which the artist looks straight down on the landscape.

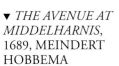

▼ *THE AVENUE AT MIDDELHARNIS,* 1689, MEINDERT HOBBEMA
This avenue of trees follows lines of perspective toward a vanishing point on the horizon.

VANISHING POINTS AND VIEWPOINTS

Vanishing points are the places where parallel lines appear to meet in a perspective drawing. They are normally found on the horizon. The position of vanishing points in a picture changes depending on the artist's viewpoint: high, low, or in the middle. The closer objects are to a vanishing point, the smaller they appear in the painting.

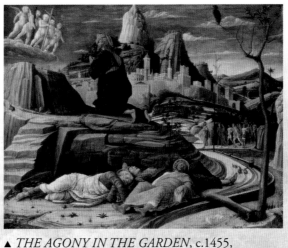

FORESHORTENING

If an object is close to us, its shape will appear distorted through an effect called foreshortening. This makes the closest parts of the object seem large, while parts that are further away look smaller and shorter. Artists use foreshortening to increase the illusion of depth.

▲ *THE AGONY IN THE GARDEN,* c.1455, ANDREA MANTEGNA
The feet of the figure at the front of this painting appear larger and longer than his head due to foreshortening.

▲ *TOUR EIFFEL*, 1926, ROBERT DELAUNAY
French artist Delaunay painted many versions of this iconic structure.
This one uses complementary colors to create a bright effect.

Color and tone

Some artists paint using natural colors from the world around them, while others use colors taken from their imaginations. Color can be used to create different moods and to express emotions. Tone recreates the way light and shade fall on objects, and helps give a picture depth.

COLOR CONTRASTS

When colors directly opposite each other are placed next to each other, they appear brighter. These are known as complementary colors and always consist of a primary and a secondary color. Complementary colors are: red and green, blue and orange, yellow and violet. Artists often use these combinations to make their works look vivid.

In the 19th century, Impressionist painters experimented with scientific color theories to create new shades and tones.

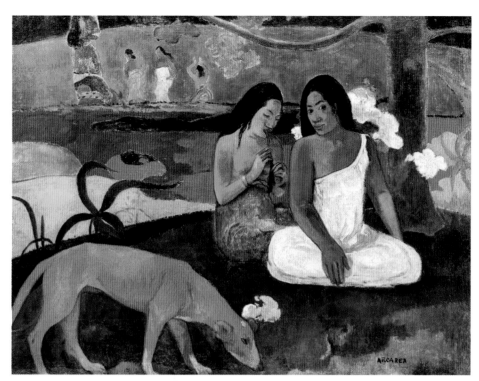

COOL AND WARM COLORS

Blue, green, and violet are cool colors. These colors tend not to catch the eye and are often used in the background. The warm colors, such as red, orange, and yellow, make objects stand out. Color can also convey a mood, such as anger, jealousy, or sadness.

◄ *AREAREA*, 1892, PAUL GAUGUIN
French painter Gauguin used bright colors to recreate the strong light and lavish flora of the South Pacific.

LIGHT AND SHADE

Tone refers to the way artists create light and shade in a painting. A range of tones helps to make flat pictures look three-dimensional. Highlights are where the light is strongest, while shadows are the darker areas of tone. Where there is a greater contrast between light and shade, the illusion becomes more apparent.

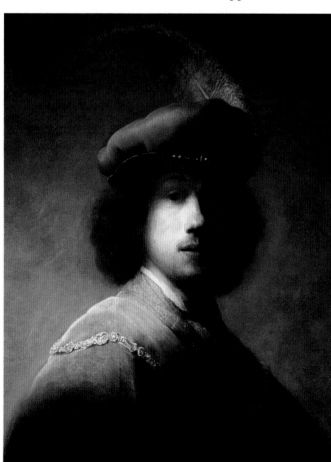

◄ *SELF-PORTRAIT, AGED 23*, 1629, REMBRANDT VAN RIJN
The method of painting in bright highlights and dark shadows to create dramatic effects is called chiaroscuro.

THE COLOR WHEEL

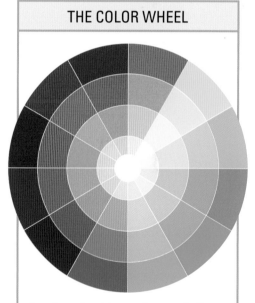

A color wheel is made up of all the colors of the rainbow. It shows primary colors (red, yellow, and blue), secondary colors (orange, green, and violet), and tertiary colors (such as red-orange and blue-green). In the 19th century, French chemist Michel Eugène Chevreul created a color wheel to show how placing different colors side-by-side can make them brighter or duller.

Prehistoric art

Pictures have been telling stories for far longer than written language. We cannot be completely sure of the purpose of prehistoric art because there is no written record to tell us. However, it is thought that the earliest artworks were perhaps part of a religious ritual. Prehistoric art was made throughout the world at different times.

The hand prints left behind by prehistoric artists show that many of them were women.

CAVE ART

No one knows when the first paintings were made. The oldest found to date were made about 40,000 years ago in Indonesia, and about 30,000 years ago in Europe and Australia. They were painted on rocks inside caves. Experts think it is likely that there is more prehistoric art in the world, but that it has not yet been found.

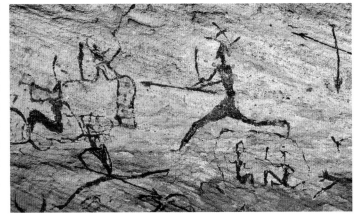

◄ ACACUS MOUNTAINS, LIBYA, c.12,000 BCE
In the Sahara Desert, Africa, giraffes, camels, elephants, and people have been depicted in rock paintings.

HAND PAINTINGS

The earliest rock drawings are called petrograms (which means rock art). Some were made by blowing charcoal through hollow bones over hands that were pressed against cave walls. Others were made by people putting their hands in charcoal and then pressing them on the walls.

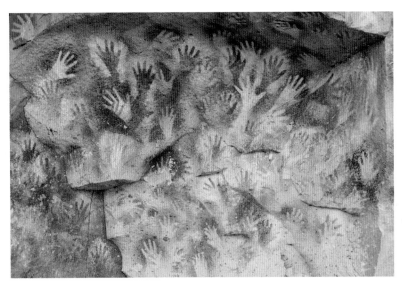

◄ CUEVA DE LOS MANOS, c.7300 BCE
This cave in Santa Cruz, Argentina, is famous for its hand paintings and prints made by men, women, and children.

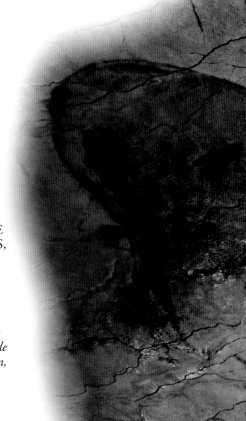

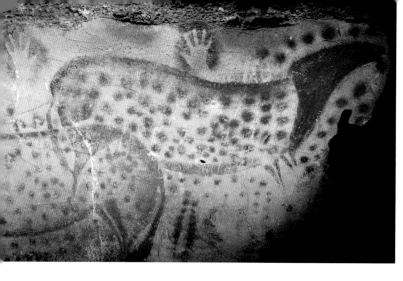

IN THE DARK

Some of the most famous prehistoric paintings have been found in southwestern France and northern Spain, deep inside caves where few people would have seen them. This suggests that they were not made for everyday enjoyment. Rather, it is likely that they were used as part of a religious ceremony to bring success in hunting.

◄ GROTTE DU PECH MERLE, c.16,000 BCE
Created in dark caves in southern France, these animals were not painted from observation, but from memory.

PAINTING AND DRAWING MATERIALS

Prehistoric artists used materials they found around them. They applied color with sticks, stones, bones, or their fingers. Black was made from charcoal, white from chalk, browns from different types of earth, and red by adding blood. These were crushed into powder and used either dry or mixed with water or animal fat.

▼ ALTAMIRA, c.15,000 BCE
These prehistoric paintings were discovered in a group of caves in Altamira, Spain, in 1879 by a nine-year-old girl.

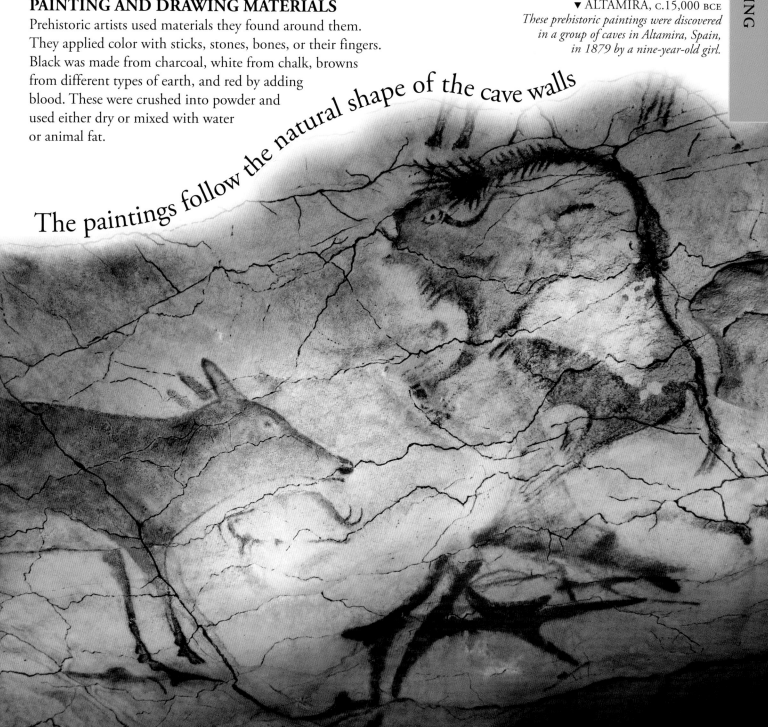

The paintings follow the natural shape of the cave walls

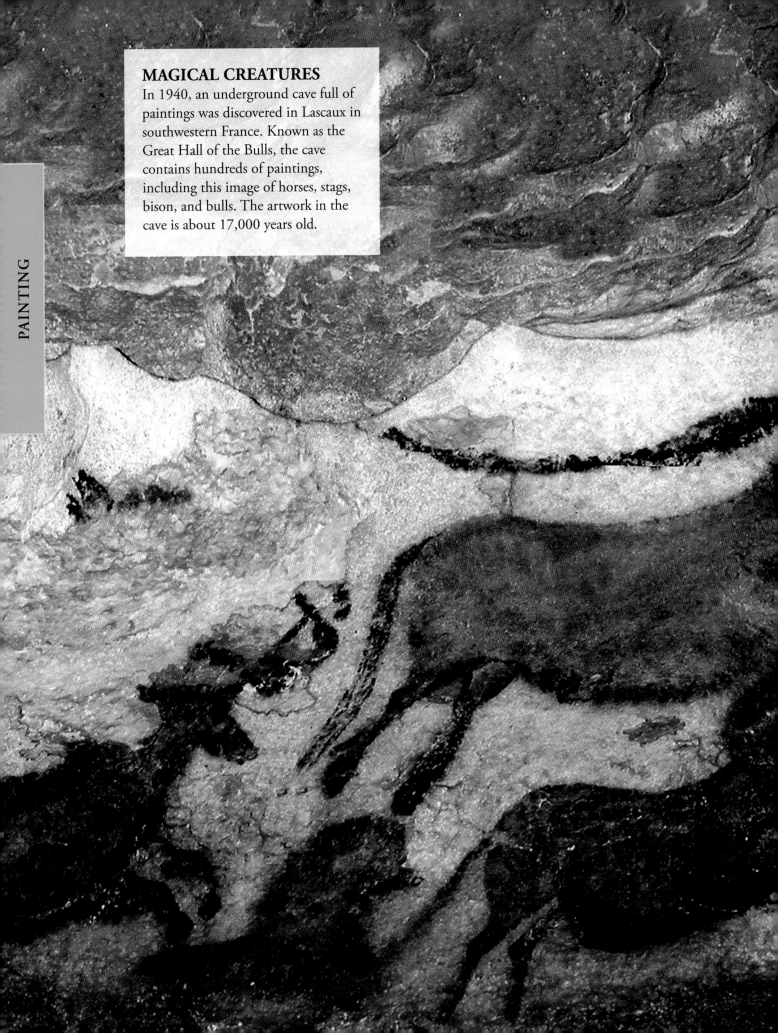

MAGICAL CREATURES
In 1940, an underground cave full of paintings was discovered in Lascaux in southwestern France. Known as the Great Hall of the Bulls, the cave contains hundreds of paintings, including this image of horses, stags, bison, and bulls. The artwork in the cave is about 17,000 years old.

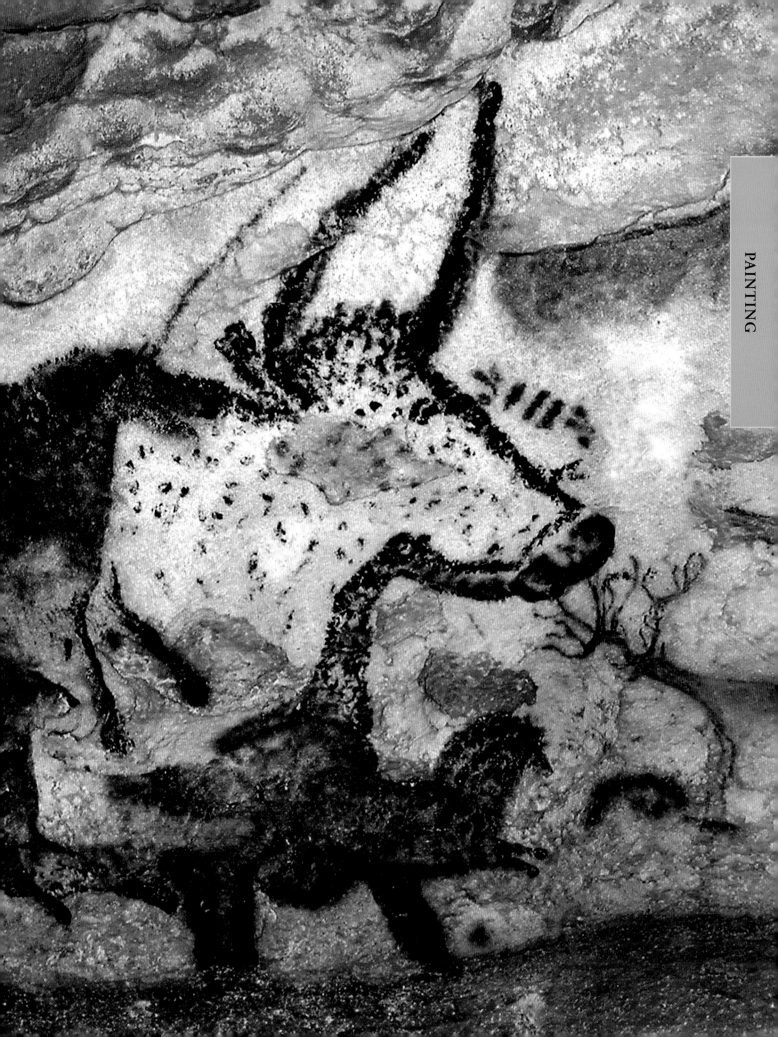

Standard of Ur

In 1927, the fragments of what was later pieced together to form this ornate box were discovered at the site of the ancient city of Ur. Ur was a Sumerian metropolis in Mesopotamia, which is modern-day Iraq. About 4,500 years old, the fragments were found in a royal tomb. The Sumerians were an advanced civilization who built some of the world's first cities.

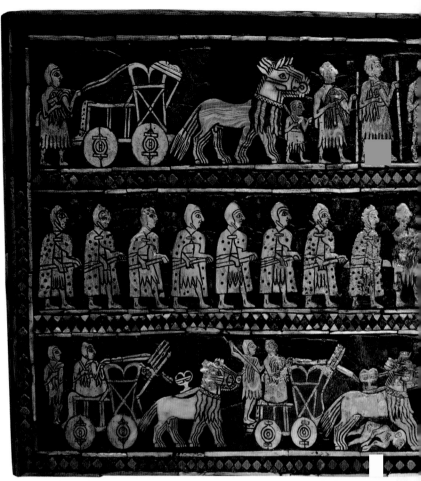

DECORATED BOX
The box is made of wood, decorated with mosaics of shell, limestone, and lapis lazuli. It measures 8½ x 19½ in (21.6 x 49.5 cm).

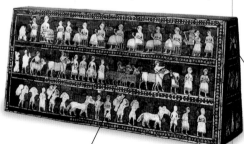

The reverse side depicts scenes of wartime.

This side depicts scenes of peacetime.

MUSICAL INSTRUMENT
The British archaeologist Sir Charles Leonard Woolley named the box the Standard of Ur. He thought it was a "standard" (royal emblem) carried on a long pole. However, it is now thought to be a sound box for a musical instrument.

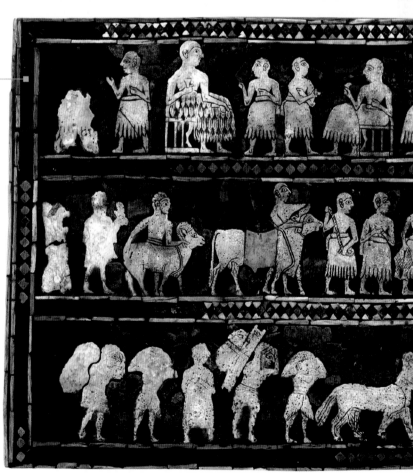

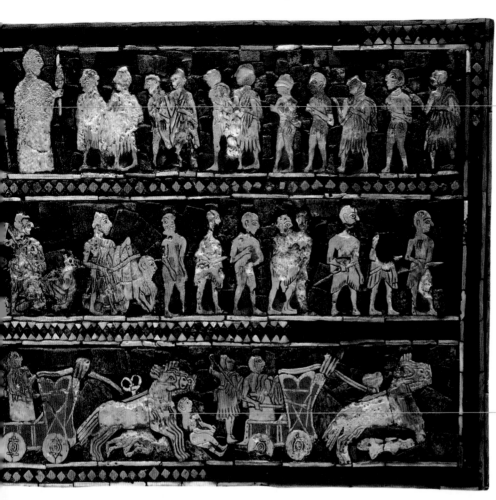

WAR AND PEACE
Historians believe that the two larger sides of the box tell one story: a war is fought, and then peace is celebrated. The scenes read from bottom to top. A king appears on both sides, larger in scale than the other figures.

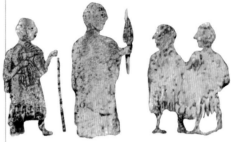

BATTLE SCENES
A Sumerian army with donkey-drawn chariots and infantry attacks an unidentified enemy. Naked prisoners stand before the soldiers. Another chariot waits nearby to take the prisoners away.

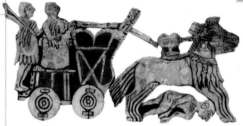

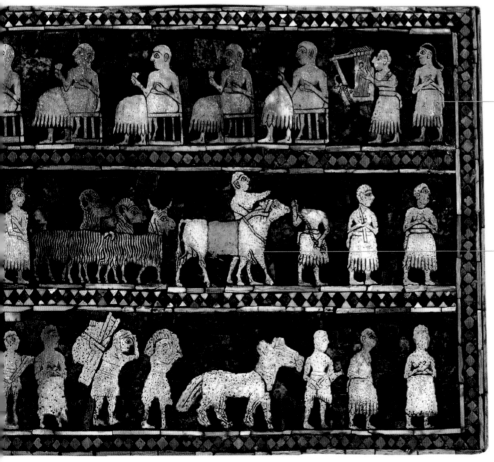

ENTERTAINERS
To celebrate peace, a singer and a man playing a lyre (a kind of small harp) entertain the king and other important figures.

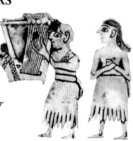

A GREAT BANQUET
On the reverse side of the box, men lead bulls, sheep, and goats to a large banquet for the nobility. Many of the men depicted carrying goods are slaves.

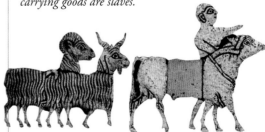

Ancient Egyptian art

About 5,000 years ago, the Egyptians began creating their own distinctive style of art, and for the next 3,000 years, their art hardly changed at all. Most ancient Egyptian art was connected to the Egyptians' belief in the afterlife. Art was made to provide instructions to the gods so that they could look after the dead.

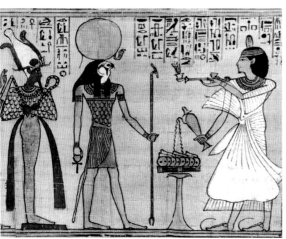

◄ SUN GOD, c.1000 BCE
In this scene from the Book of the Dead, *the Sun god Ra-Harakhti is receiving a sacrifice. He has the body of a man, but the head of a falcon.*

THE BOOK OF THE DEAD
In ancient Egypt, important people were buried with wall paintings and statues that celebrated their afterlife. From about 1550 BCE, they were also laid to rest with papyrus scrolls featuring pictures inscribed with spells that helped them navigate their way to land of the dead. One type of these scrolls is known as the *Book of the Dead.*

◄ PRACTICE SKETCH, c.1500 BCE
An artist named Nebnefer drew this practice sketch of a goddess. As paintings were for the gods, it was important to get them right.

ARTISTIC TRAINING
Artists began their training at the age of nine, and had to follow strict rules. They drew every feature from the angle that best displayed it, so chests and eyes were shown from the front, but heads, legs, feet, and arms from the side. Everything was painted to look flat.

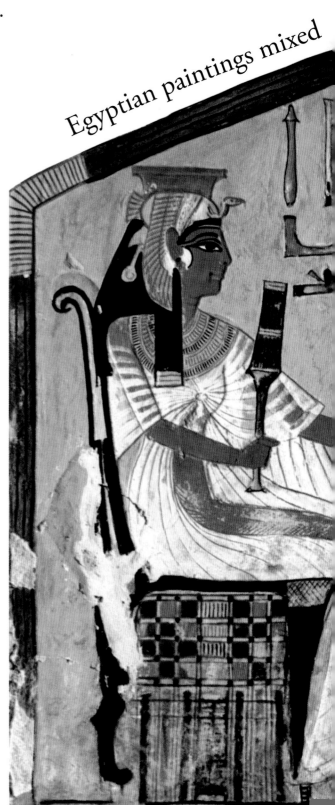

Egyptian paintings mixed

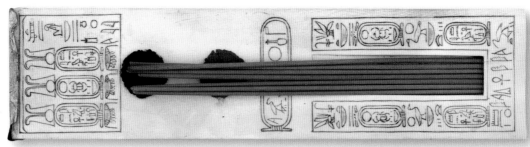

▶ IVORY PALETTE,
c.1330 BCE
This palette holds reed pens for writing hieroglyphs and pots for colored pigments. Each hieroglyph was itself a work of art that followed precise proportions.

PLANNING A PAINTING

Egyptian wall paintings were made following careful plans. First the wall was smoothed with white plaster. Then a grid was drawn using string dipped in red paint. Copying from a small picture on papyrus, artists drew the scene following the grid lines and used reed pens or small brushes for the hieroglyphs. The outlines were then colored in from a palette of different pigments.

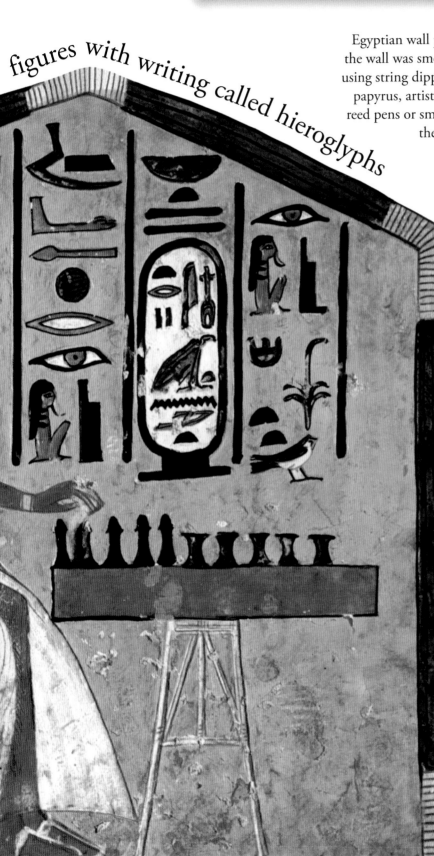

figures with writing called hieroglyphs

Egyptian paintings depict men with darker skin than women, as they were considered spiritual opposites.

THE AFTERLIFE

The afterlife was believed to be a continuation of life on Earth, reached after a dead person had been judged in a place called the Hall of Truth. Paintings were included in tombs to inform the gods how the dead people had lived so that they could carry on these lifestyles in the afterlife. The paintings might show the dead person at work or playing one of their favorite games.

◀ PLAYING GAMES
In fine clothes and jewels, Queen Nefertari, the favorite wife of Pharaoh Ramesses II, plays an ancient board game called senet.

Tomb of Sennedjem

This wall painting was found in the tomb of an ancient Egyptian master craftsman called Sennedjem. He lived in Deir el-Medina on the west bank of the Nile river around 1300 BCE. The painting was made to create a spell to ensure that Sennedjem and his wife Iy-neferti would always have enough to eat in the afterlife.

HARVESTING WHEAT

Sennedjem cuts the ears of wheat stalks with a curved wooden sickle. Iy-neferti follows him, collecting the ears of wheat in a basket. They wear their finest clothes and wigs, which indicates that this is a spell and not a real event.

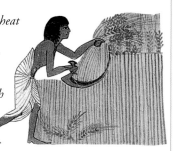

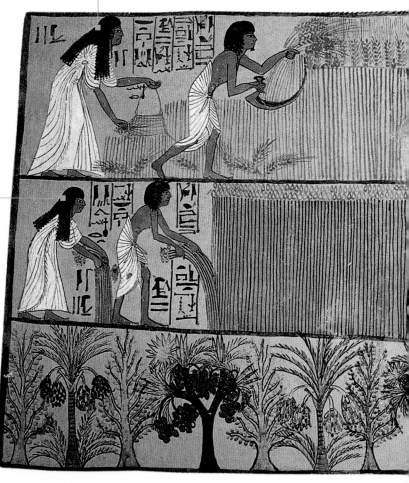

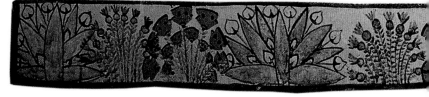

FARMING LIFE

In the Fields of Iaru, Sennedjem and Iy-neferti are shown sharing a happy life sowing, plowing, and reaping a harvest, surrounded by the waters of the Nile river.

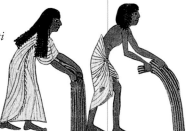

SERVANT IN THE PLACE OF TRUTH

Sennedjem's official title was "Servant in the Place of Truth." He was buried in his tomb with his family. Many paintings covered the walls of Sennedjem's tomb. They were all made to show the gods how Sennedjem spent his life so that they would know what he needed in the afterlife.

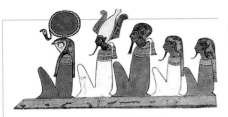

PRAYING TO THE GODS
Five gods, including Ra, Osiris, and Ptah, listen to the prayers of Sennedjem and Iy-neferti, who are kneeling before them.

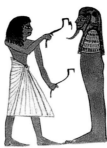

OPENING OF THE MOUTH
At the end of the story, Sennedjem's son touches his dead father's mouth with special tools so that he may breathe, eat, and drink in the afterlife.

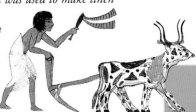

PLOWING
Below the wheat scene, Sennedjem harvests flax, a plant that was used to make linen and produce oil. Next, Sennedjem pushes a plow pulled by two oxen.

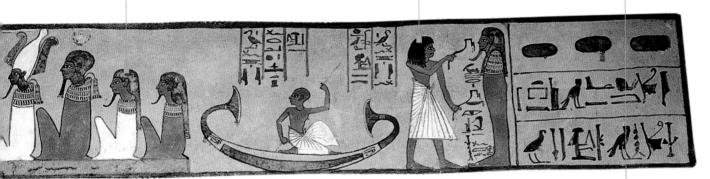

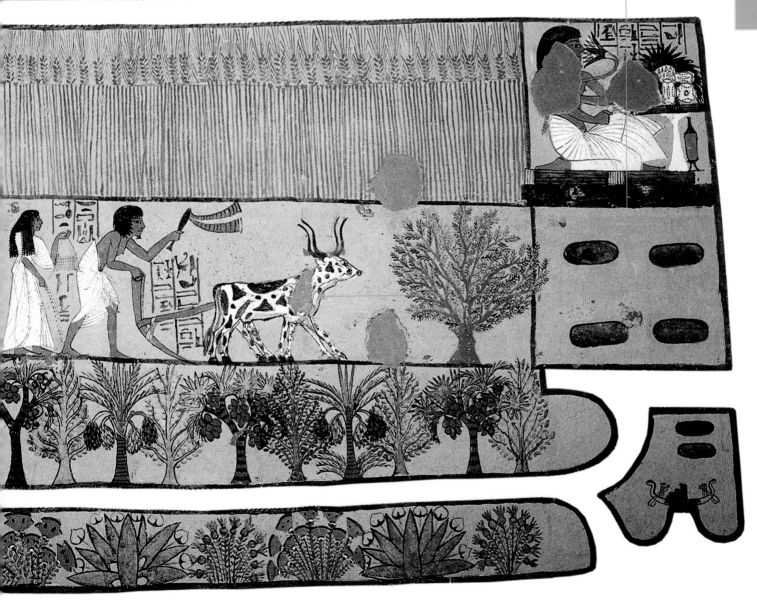

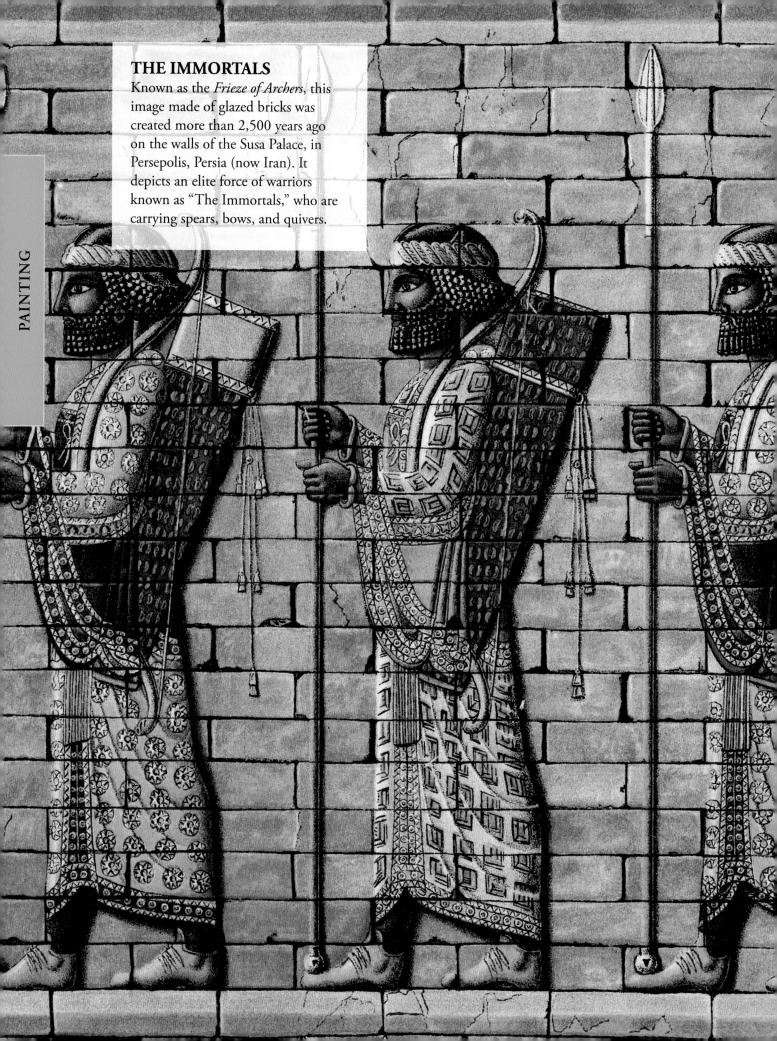

THE IMMORTALS

Known as the *Frieze of Archers*, this image made of glazed bricks was created more than 2,500 years ago on the walls of the Susa Palace, in Persepolis, Persia (now Iran). It depicts an elite force of warriors known as "The Immortals," who are carrying spears, bows, and quivers.

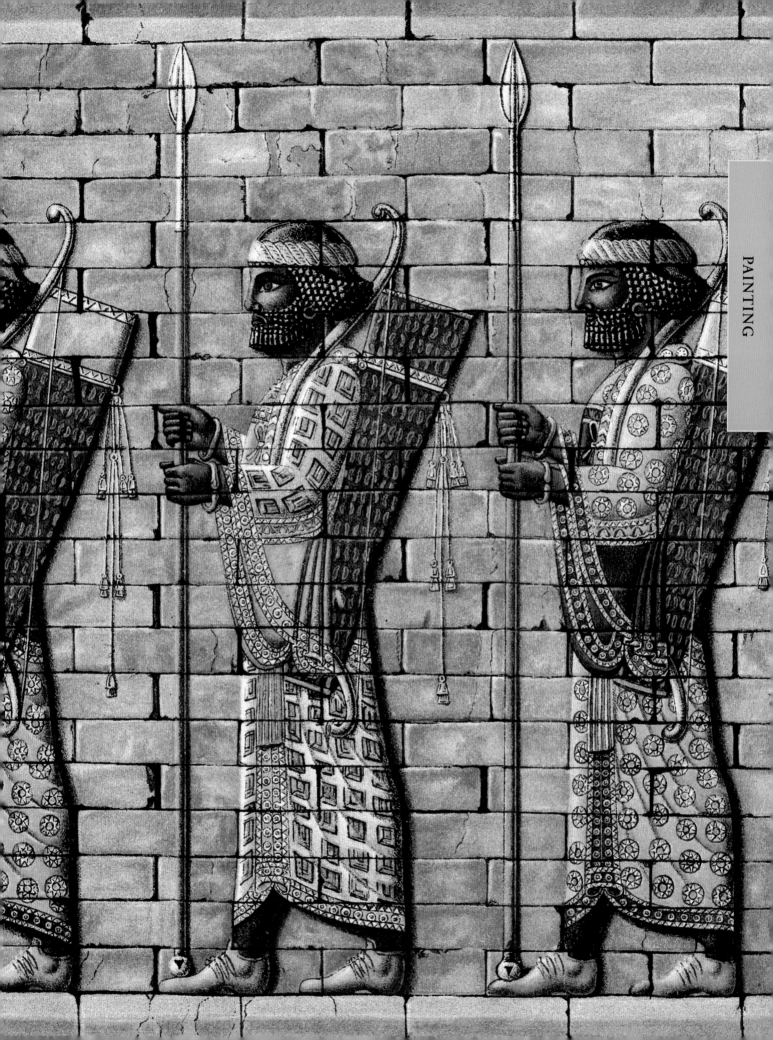

Minoan, Greek, and Roman art

The ancient Egyptians passed on their artistic skills to other people who lived around the Mediterranean Sea. The Minoans, who lived on the island of Crete and in some other parts of Greece from about 3000 BCE to 1380 BCE, created art that showed clear Egyptian influences, including ways of drawing people and the use of bright colors. These painting styles spread across Greece and eventually to Rome.

▼ VILLA OF THE MYSTERIES, 1ST CENTURY CE
This fresco in a Roman villa near Pompeii in Italy depicts rituals carried out during a religious festival.

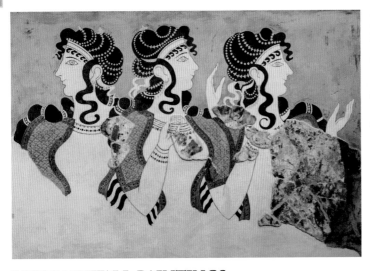

◄ LADIES IN BLUE AT KNOSSOS, c.1500 BCE
This Minoan painting portrays three ladies in flat profile, showing a clear Egyptian influence.

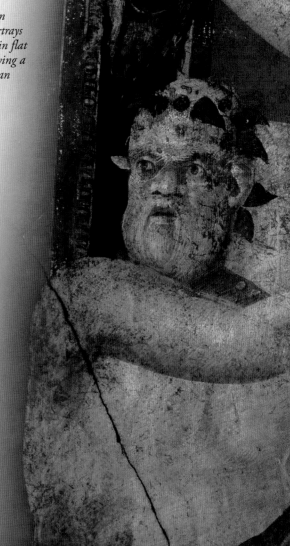

MINOAN WALL PAINTINGS

The Minoans painted on walls while the plaster was still wet. As the paint and plaster dried, they fused together. This technique was later called *fresco*, which means fresh in Italian. Minoan artists did not use grids, so their pictures are not as rigid as Egyptian art. Most of their work was displayed in palaces, to be looked at by people rather than gods.

ROMAN CHARACTERS

The Romans added their own ideas to older artistic traditions. They liked the perfection of Greek art, but they also liked to portray things more realistially, such as people aging. Artists worked throughout the Roman Empire, making art to honor their gods, celebrate achievements, and proclaim their power.

LOST WORKS

Very few Greek paintings have survived. The damp climate of Greece rotted paintings that had been made on wooden panels, and most ancient buildings are long gone. However, we have learned much about ancient Greek painting from the painted pottery they produced. Greek artists were also employed by the Romans. Some Roman art painted by Greek artists provides clues as to what the style of Greek paintings may have been like.

◄ PANATHENAIC AMPHORA, c.500 BCE
A large type of Greek vase was awarded as a prize in sporting contests. This one is decorated with an image of a chariot racer, in a style known as black figure.

LIFELIKE SCENES

By 100 CE, the Romans ruled over a huge empire, across which Roman, Egyptian, and Greek artists produced all sorts of art, including frescoes, panel paintings, and mosaics. Over time, new ideas evolved and spread, and much of the art in the Roman Empire became increasingly lifelike in style.

► FRESCO, 1ST CENTURY CE
Aeneas, a legendary Trojan warrior, is shown lifelike and vulnerable as his wounds are treated.

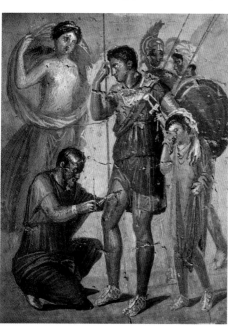

Romans rubbed wax over the surface of painted frescoes to preserve them and make them shine.

27

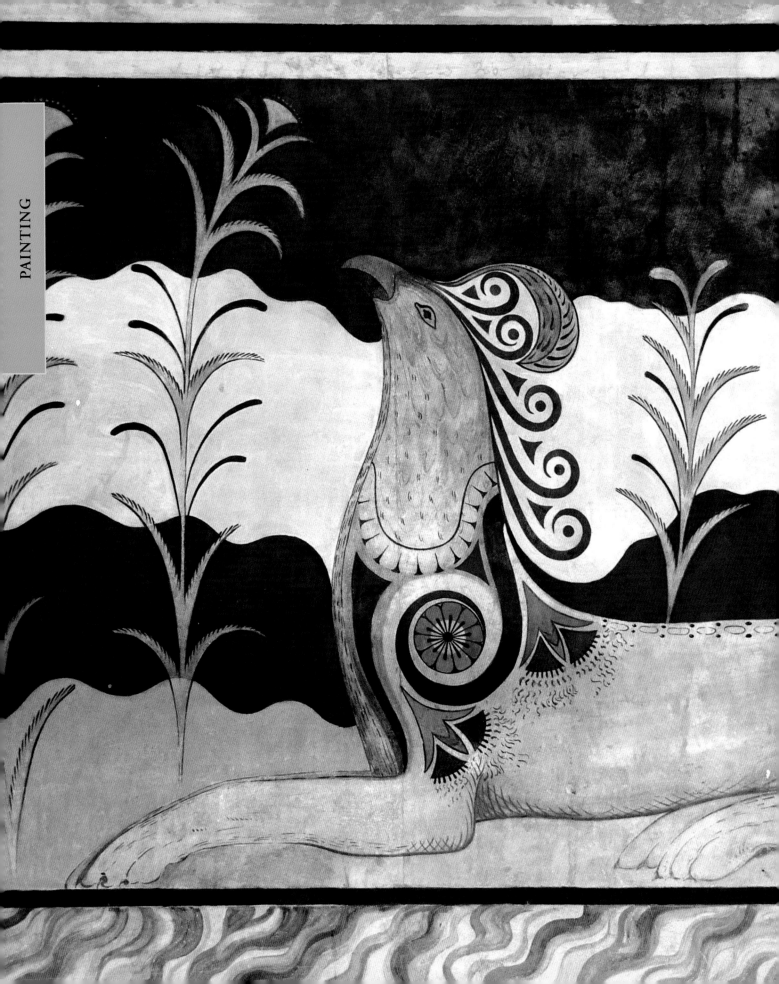

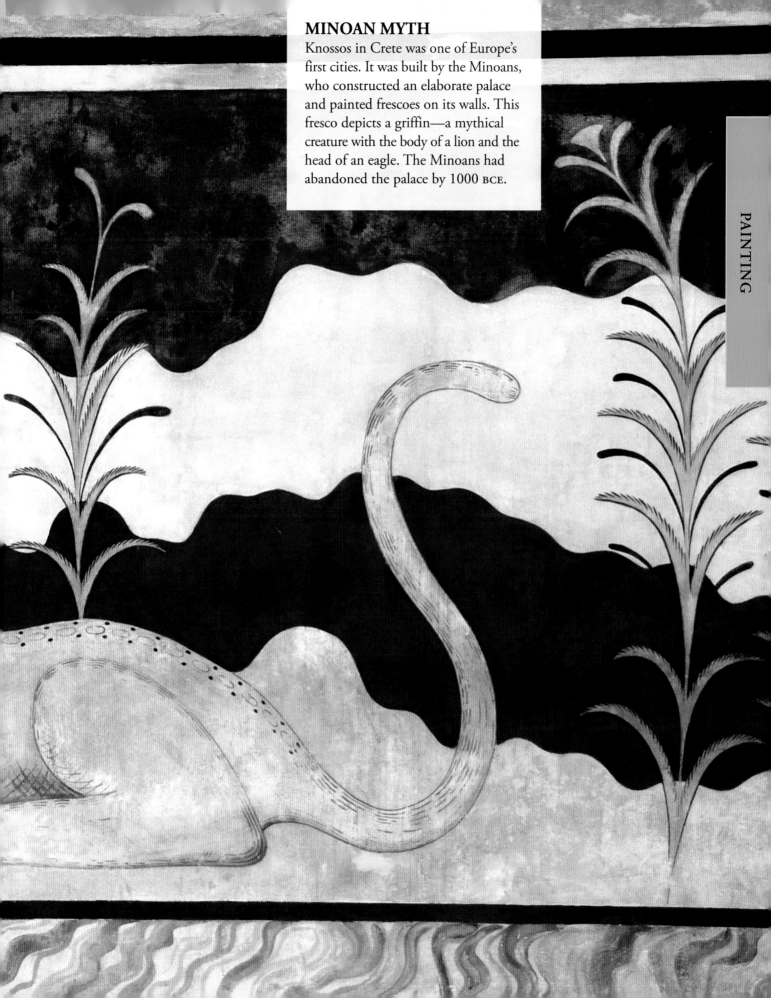

MINOAN MYTH

Knossos in Crete was one of Europe's first cities. It was built by the Minoans, who constructed an elaborate palace and painted frescoes on its walls. This fresco depicts a griffin—a mythical creature with the body of a lion and the head of an eagle. The Minoans had abandoned the palace by 1000 BCE.

PAINTING

Greek painting and mosaics

Like the Minoans, the ancient Greeks highly valued painting. Early Greek art was flat-looking, mainly featuring symbols and patterns. Later, artists sought to create art that was more lifelike and in beautifully balanced proportions. Ancient Greek art is divided by art historians into four stylistic periods: the Geometric, Archaic, Classical, and Hellenistic.

Krater

A vessel used for diluting wine with water

- **Date** 8th century BCE
- **Medium** Terra-cotta pot

The earliest stylistic period was the Geometric period, which lasted from about 1100 to 800 BCE. It began in Athens and spread throughout the cities of the Aegean Sea. The art of this time featured patterns using straight lines and simple shapes. However, by the end of the Geometric period, the designs had become more intricate and figures of people and animals, such as the horses on this krater, were more common.

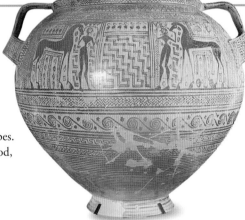

Battling warriors

Terra-cotta neck amphora

- **Date** c.500–480 BCE
- **Medium** Terra-cotta pot

In the Archaic period (800–480 BCE), artists followed set rules. They painted flat-looking pictures on their pottery using a mixture of clay, water, and wood ash, and left backgrounds bare. When the clay was fired, the pictures and patterns turned black, but the backgrounds stayed red. This was called black figure style pottery.

Dionysus and his thiasos

The thiasos were followers of the Greek god Dionysus

- **Date** 525–500 BCE
- **Medium** Terra-cotta vessel

The ancient Greeks often told stories about their gods and goddesses in pictures on pottery. This late-Archaic example depicts Dionysus, the god of wine and the grape harvest, with all his followers. By the period in which this pot was made, artists began their training from a young age and worked together in workshops. Often, art and craft skills were passed down through families, usually from father to son.

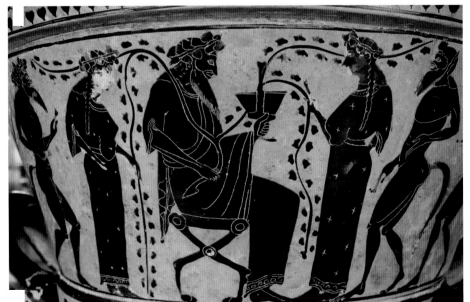

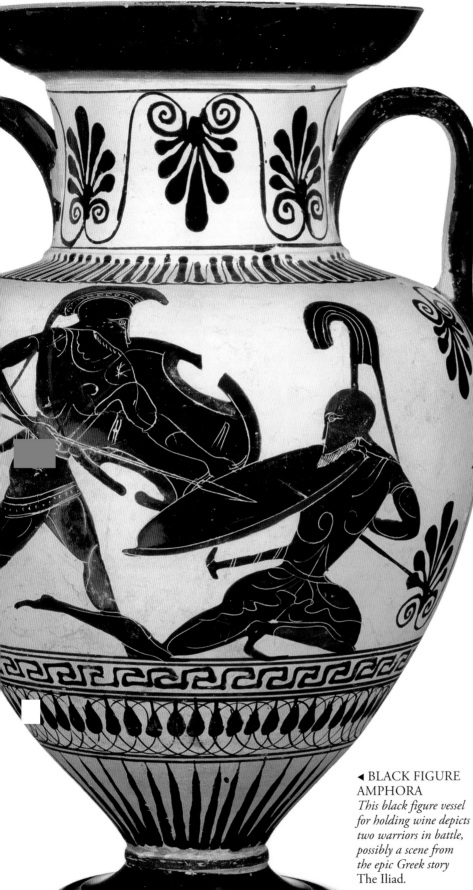

The Diver
An ancient Greek tomb painting

■ **Date** c.470 BCE
■ **Medium** Fresco

Only a few ancient Greek wall paintings survive. This one, of a man diving into a pool, is in a building known as the Tomb of the Diver. The image is simple and only uses brown paint, but it is lifelike and easily understood. It was made around the start of the Classical period (480–323 BCE), when Greek art became more natural-looking.

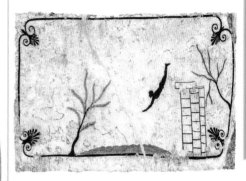

Sappho
A mosaic of a famed female Greek poet

■ **Date** 3rd–4th century CE
■ **Medium** Stone and glass

At first, Greek mosaics were only made to cover floors, but later they were made on walls as well. Following drawn plans, the artists cut stones into tiny squares, and then stuck them into a mixture of lime and sand. This example was made in the earlier style of the Hellenistic period in Greek art (c.323–100 BCE), during which artists further developed greater mosaic-making skills.

◄ BLACK FIGURE AMPHORA
This black figure vessel for holding wine depicts two warriors in battle, possibly a scene from the epic Greek story The Iliad.

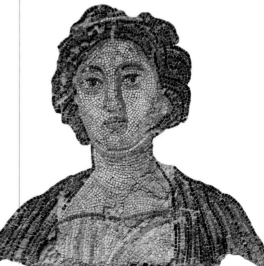

31

Roman frescoes and mosaics

Although only a small number of Roman panel paintings have been found, many mosaics survive. Several Roman frescoes were preserved under ash when the volcano Vesuvius erupted in 79 CE, covering the nearby city of Pompeii, Italy. They show that Roman artists enjoyed creating realistic-looking scenes of the world around them.

Fayum mummy portrait
A coffin decorated with precious stones

- **Date** 1st–3rd century BCE
- **Medium** Wax and pigment on wood

By the 1st century CE, the Roman Empire extended to Egypt. In Fayum, near modern-day Cairo, realistic-looking portraits of the dead were painted on wooden boards that were attached to their mummy cases (coffins). Many of these remarkably realistic paintings have survived, and they suggest that other Roman paintings from that time may have been just as lifelike.

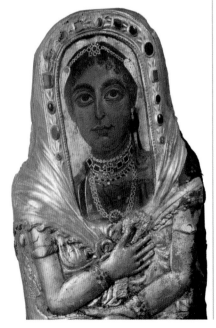

Villa Boscoreale
A Roman villa that was preserved by ash

- **Date** c.50–40 BCE
- **Medium** Fresco

More wall paintings survive than any other kind of painting from ancient Rome. However, frescoes such as this one, found under the volcanic ash of Vesuvius in 1900, were not considered the highest form of painting by the Romans. After sculpture, the most prestigious form of art was panel painting, but most of the wooden panels have long since rotted away. A sense of depth is created in this scene by the use of color, but it does not use the techniques of true linear perspective, which were invented much later.

Pompeii landscape
A decoration in a Roman home

- **Date** 1st century CE
- **Medium** Fresco

Romans were the first Western artists to develop landscape painting, using their own form of perspective and shading to make things look realistic. Some landscapes were gardens with flowers, birds, and trees, while others depicted farms with animals. Sometimes they featured buildings that look three-dimensional, with painted angles and shading. Many landscapes were painted to seem as if they were views seen through windows, rather than paintings.

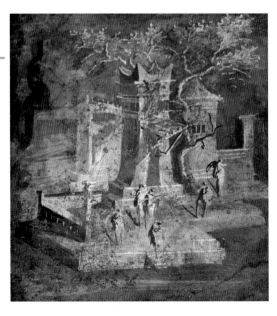

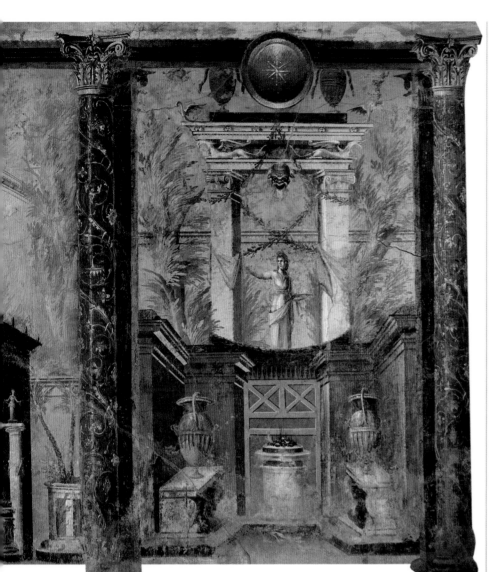

Plato and his pupils

A finely detailed Roman mosaic at Pompeii

- **Date** 1st century BCE
- **Medium** Mosaic

Roman mosaics were made with tiny black, white, and colored squares (tesserae) of marble, glass, pottery, stone, or shells. These were pressed into wet cement and any gaps between them filled with more cement. Many wealthy Romans had mosaics in their homes. They also appeared in public buildings across the Roman Empire. Many tell stories, such as this scene from the life of the Greek philosopher Plato, shown teaching at his famous academy. They also show us what everyday items, such as clothes and tools, looked like.

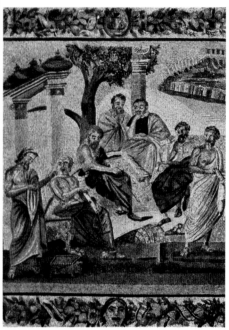

▲ BEDROOM FRESCO AT BOSCOREALE
Without techniques of perspective, a sense of depth can be created by using cold blues for the background and warm reds for the foreground.

The Garden of Livia

Fresco in an underground vault of a villa near Rome

- **Date** 1st–3rd century CE
- **Medium** Fresco

The Villa of Livia belonged to Livia Drusilla, the wife of the Roman emperor Augustus. The walls of the underground rooms are decorated with a beautiful garden scene. The plants are painted with a high degree of realism and detail. However, they have come into flower and fruit at the same time, which cannot happen in real life. This creates a dreamlike feeling to the work, and it shows that Roman artists were not always primarily concerned with portraying real life, but rather an idealized version of it.

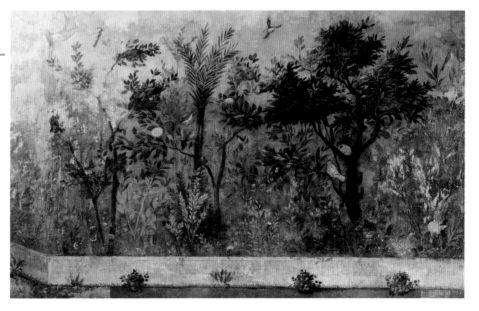

Ancient Asian art

Across the vast continent of Asia, art was influenced by a wide range of religious beliefs and mythical traditions. These ideas were expressed by local artists in various styles, depicting their stories and myths. In China and India, many great works of art were inspired by the Buddhist religion.

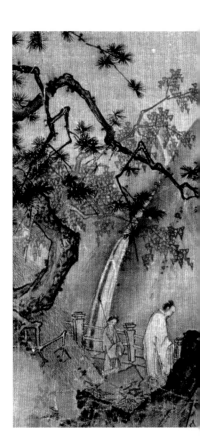

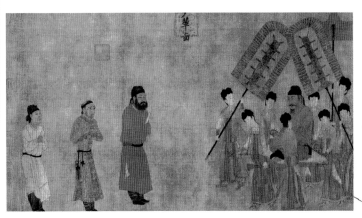

◀ TANG COURT IN THE 7TH CENTURY
This painting, by court artist Yan Liben, depicts the second Tang emperor, Taizong (seated), granting an audience to the ambassador of the Tibetan Empire (in red).

CHINESE "GOLDEN AGE"

The Tang dynasty ruled over the Chinese Empire between 618 and 906 CE. Trade, literature, and art flourished during this period, which is often described as China's "Golden Age." Calligraphy (decorative writing) expressed Buddhist and Taoist beliefs, while painters captured the rich splendors of court life.

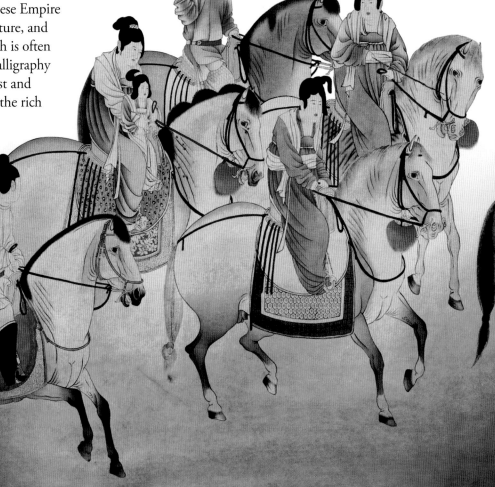

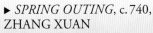

▶ *SPRING OUTING*, c. 740, ZHANG XUAN
Well-dressed people of the court embark on a journey. The smooth lines of the figures were achieved with fine brushes.

PAINTING EMOTIONS

During the Tang dynasty, landscape painting, called *shanshui hua* (mountain-water paintings), became extremely popular in China, where landscapes were seen as the highest form of artistic achievement. Artists did not create realistic views, as they were more interested in conveying emotion or atmosphere. They achieved this by painting with delicate brushstrokes that resembled calligraphy.

▲ *WATERFALL,*
c. 1200, MA YUAN
This picture was painted using ink on silk, and shows a scholar gazing into a bubbling waterfall.

The finest mountain-water paintings were mounted on scrolls, which could be hung on walls or rolled up.

BUDDHIST CAVES

India is a vast country with diverse local traditions and beliefs, and many different styles of art have developed there. Some of the finest examples of early Indian art are found in the Ajanta caves in Maharashstra state. Created between 200 BCE and 650 CE, these include rock carvings and murals that celebrate the Buddhist religion.

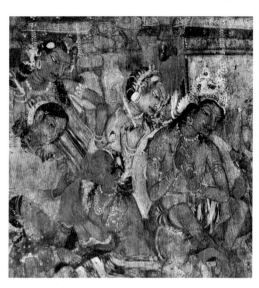

▲ BUDDHIST MURAL
This mural in the Ajanta caves depicts a story from The Jataka Tales, *which recounts Buddha's past lives.*

FINE TECHNIQUE

Tang artists painted with inks and watercolors on paper or silk. Usually, they outlined their pictures with fine black lines first, then filled them with color. They held their brushes vertically, painting with the tip of the brush to create flowing lines.

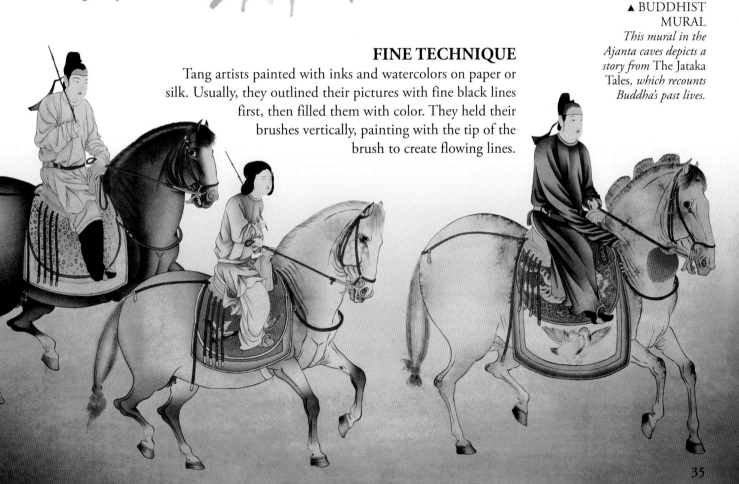

Early Christian art

Christianity grew from a small sect into a popular religion during the three centuries after the death of Jesus. At first, the Romans banned the religion, so Christians met secretly in tunnels and tombs below ground, known as catacombs. On the tomb walls, they painted scenes from the Bible. Later, it became the official religion of the Roman Empire, and Christian art flourished in the open.

THE EMPIRE MOVES EAST

By 313 CE, Christianity had become so popular that Roman emperor Constantine stopped trying to suppress it. He also transferred the capital city of his Empire from Rome to Byzantium (now Istanbul), renaming it Constantinople after himself. In 380, shortly after Constantine's death, Christianity became the official religion of the Roman Empire, and Christian artists no longer had to work in secret.

Rich with mosaics, Hagia Sophia in Istanbul, built in 537, was the biggest church in the world for 1,000 years.

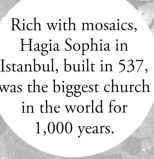

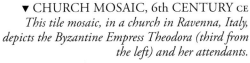

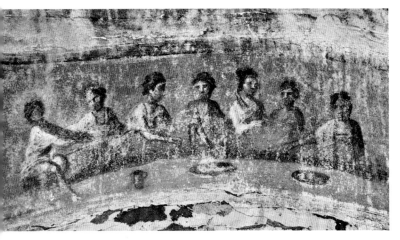

▲ *THE BREAKING OF BREAD*, 2nd CENTURY CE,
This image of Jesus (center) is a very early example of Christian art, painted in secret in an underground chapel in Rome.

▼ CHURCH MOSAIC, 6th CENTURY CE
This tile mosaic, in a church in Ravenna, Italy, depicts the Byzantine Empress Theodora (third from the left) and her attendants.

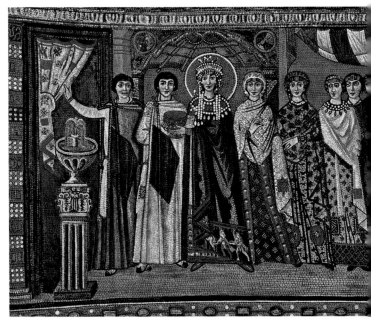

AVOIDING REALISM

Between around 330 and 1453, a distinct style of art developed in Constantinople, which we now call Byzantine art. It was made to tell Bible stories, and also to depict powerful people. Unlike older Greek and Roman styles, Christian art did not try to be realistic, as this was considered to be sinful.

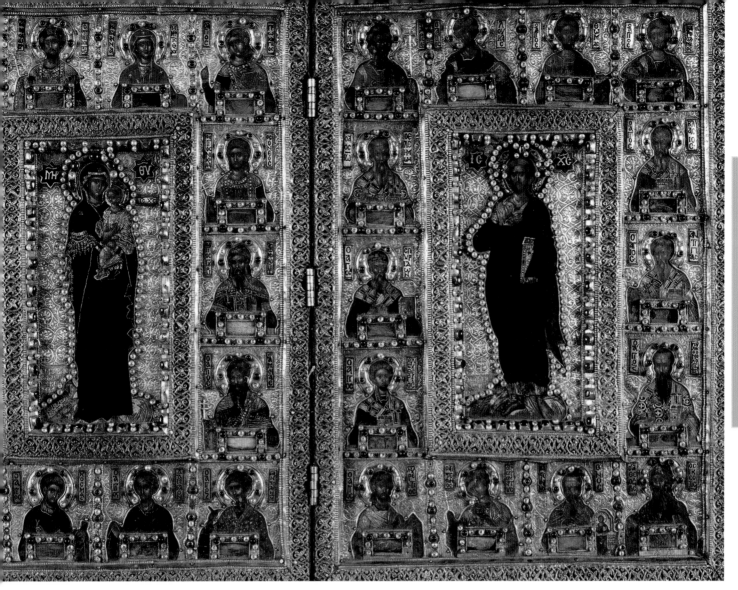

▲ *RELIQUARY OF THE*
HOLY DESPOTS, c.1370
These richly decorated panels,
embossed with silver, were made
in Spain. They are an example
of late-period Byzantine art.

WORDS AND IMAGES

Byzantine artistic styles spread across Europe, from Spain in the west to Russia in the east. Illuminated manuscripts of holy texts were made, but most churchgoers were illiterate, so large frescoes and mosaics were created for the new churches to inform people about the Bible through art.

STORY OF A CONQUEST

The Bayeux Tapestry is a huge embroidery with over 70 scenes illustrating the story of the Battle of Hastings in 1066, in which the Norman William the Conqueror defeated the English king Harold.
Although not overtly religious, the work was displayed in Bayeux Cathedral, France, and may have been intended to give a divine justification for William's conquest of England.

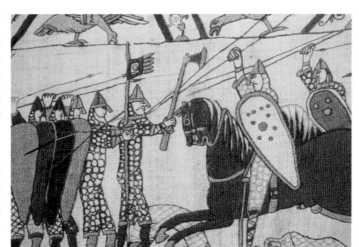

◄ BAYEUX
TAPESTRY,
c.1070
In this scene,
Normans on
horseback
attack English
footsoldiers.

Icons of the Church

The word "icon"—from the Greek *eikon*—describes a work of art that represents a holy person, created for people to contemplate as they prayed. Icons were made mainly in Christian areas, including Rome, Greece, Turkey, Sicily, and Russia. The names of the artists who created them are usually unknown.

Christ the Merciful

Decorative icon for private worship

- ■ **Date** 1100–1150
- ■ **Medium** Glass and stone

Glass and stone mosaic icons were often made for churches, where they would glitter in the candlelight. However, this example, from Byzantium (present-day Istanbul), was made for worship in a private home. Its owner was probably rich, as most other icons for private prayer were made from wood. Jesus, his mother Mary, the saints, and angels were the most typical subjects for private icons.

◄ PORTABLE ICON
This mosaic icon of Jesus is 24 in (60 cm) long, small enough to be carried from room to room.

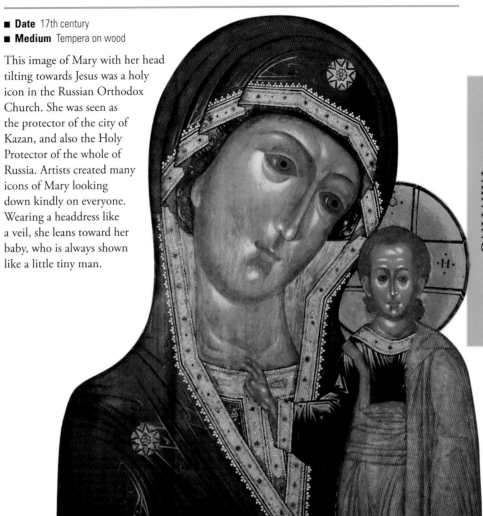

Our Lady of Kazan
The Protector of Russia

- **Date** 17th century
- **Medium** Tempera on wood

This image of Mary with her head tilting towards Jesus was a holy icon in the Russian Orthodox Church. She was seen as the protector of the city of Kazan, and also the Holy Protector of the whole of Russia. Artists created many icons of Mary looking down kindly on everyone. Wearing a headdress like a veil, she leans toward her baby, who is always shown like a little tiny man.

St George and the Dragon
Mythical story of extreme bravery

- **Date** 15th century
- **Medium** Gesso on wood

George was a soldier in the Roman army, who was later worshipped as a saint in the Catholic, Anglican, Eastern Orthodox, and Oriental Orthodox churches. The tale of St George and the Dragon was first told in Europe by Crusaders—soldiers returning from the Holy Land in the 11th century. The story often appeared in icons from then on. This painting shows St George's bravery in killing the dragon to save a princess.

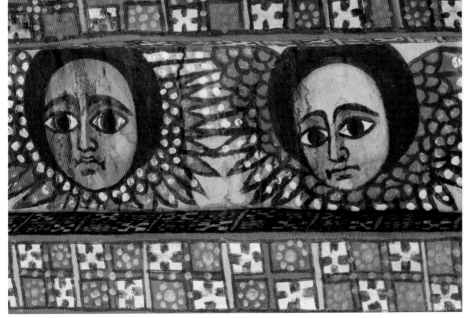

Angels
Ornate decoration for an Ethiopian church

- **Date** 19th century
- **Medium** Fresco

These icons appear in a church built by the Ethiopian Emperor Eyasu II. The church was named Debre Birhan, or "Mountain of Light," after the emperor's nickname. Inside, the walls and ceiling are covered with icons, including 135 of these angel faces—or winged cherubs—which cover the ceiling. With their huge black eyes, they represent God's presence everywhere. In other parts of the church (not shown), three identical men with halos around their heads are icons of the Holy Trinity: the Father, the Son, and the Holy Spirit.

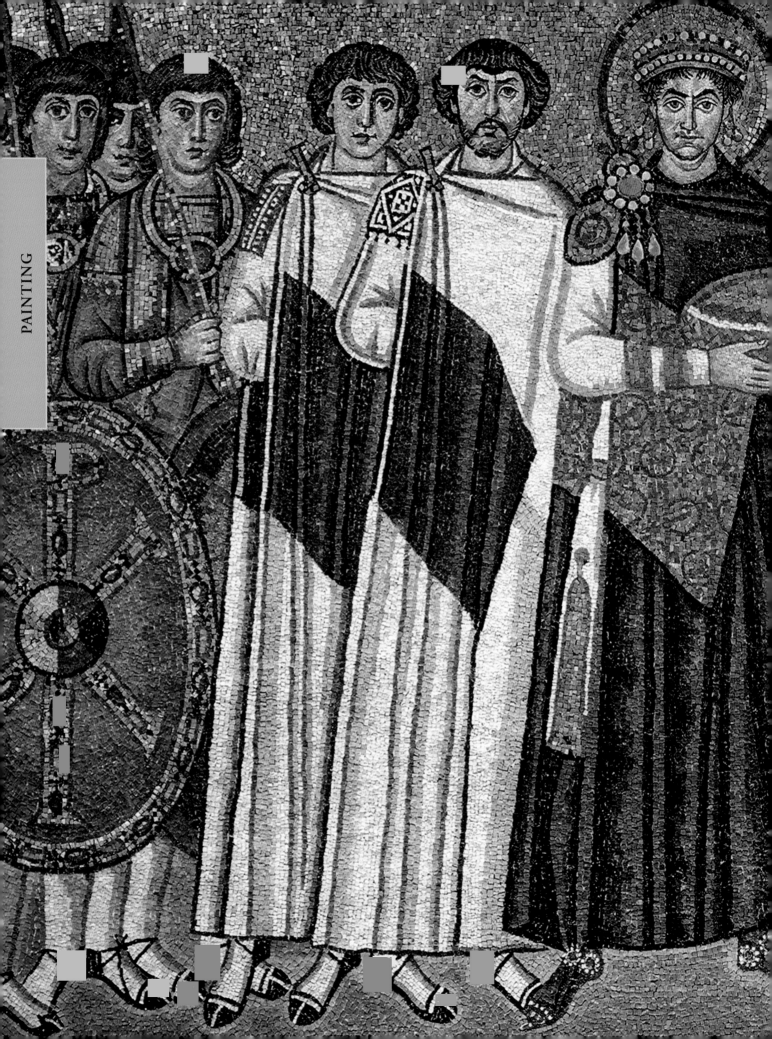

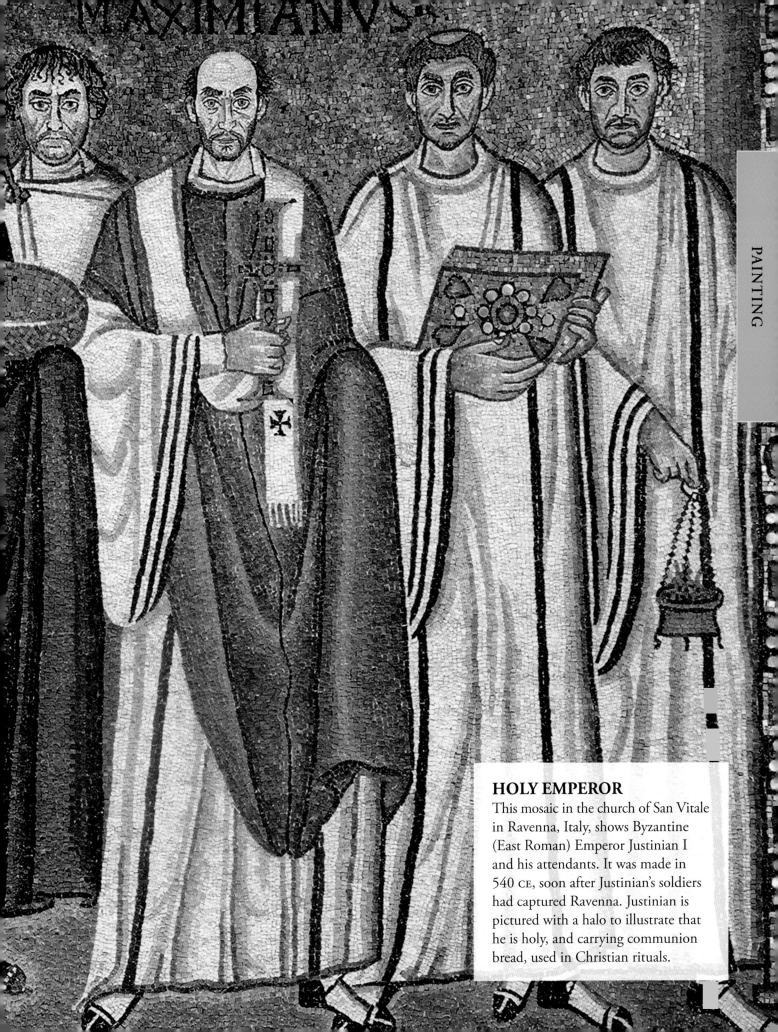

HOLY EMPEROR

This mosaic in the church of San Vitale in Ravenna, Italy, shows Byzantine (East Roman) Emperor Justinian I and his attendants. It was made in 540 CE, soon after Justinian's soldiers had captured Ravenna. Justinian is pictured with a halo to illustrate that he is holy, and carrying communion bread, used in Christian rituals.

Early Islamic art

The religion of Islam was established in Medina (in modern-day Saudi Arabia) by the prophet Muhammad in 622 CE. Through the seventh century, the faith spread to Asia, Africa, and Europe. Various artistic influences, from early Persian to Christian art, merged to create a distinct Islamic artistic style.

▼ GEOMETRIC TILE, 13TH CENTURY
Islamic art was often mixed with older Persian styles, as seen on this tile, which features a phoenix and calligraphy.

BEAUTIFUL PATTERNS

Magnificent mosaics were created to decorate mosques and other religious buildings. Islamic art is different from most Western and Asian art, as it rarely shows people or other living creatures. Instead, it often features calligraphy and geometric or floral patterns.

MAJOR DEVELOPMENTS

Great advances in art, architecture, science, medicine, mathematics, and astronomy were made in the area where the Islamic faith was first practiced, from North Africa in the west to the Persian Gulf in the east. Art was often religious, but non-religious art, such as enameled glass and patterned carpets, was also highly valued in Islamic societies.

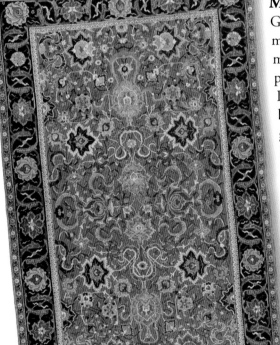

▲ PERSIAN RUG, 16TH CENTURY
Many parts of the Islamic world became reonowned for decorative arts. Persia (modern-day Iran) produced fine rugs.

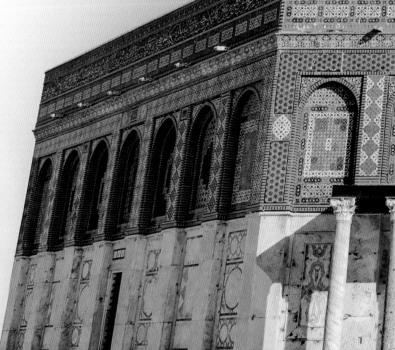

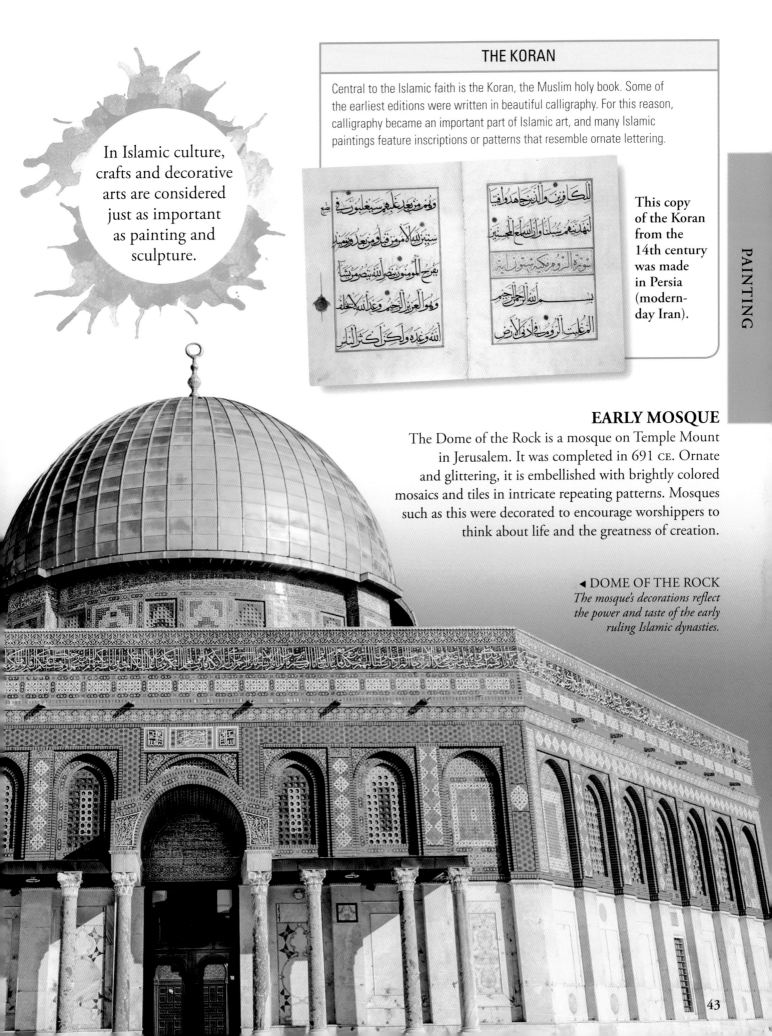

In Islamic culture, crafts and decorative arts are considered just as important as painting and sculpture.

THE KORAN

Central to the Islamic faith is the Koran, the Muslim holy book. Some of the earliest editions were written in beautiful calligraphy. For this reason, calligraphy became an important part of Islamic art, and many Islamic paintings feature inscriptions or patterns that resemble ornate lettering.

This copy of the Koran from the 14th century was made in Persia (modern-day Iran).

EARLY MOSQUE

The Dome of the Rock is a mosque on Temple Mount in Jerusalem. It was completed in 691 CE. Ornate and glittering, it is embellished with brightly colored mosaics and tiles in intricate repeating patterns. Mosques such as this were decorated to encourage worshippers to think about life and the greatness of creation.

◄ DOME OF THE ROCK
The mosque's decorations reflect the power and taste of the early ruling Islamic dynasties.

PAINTING

The Book of Kells

The Book of Kells is an illuminated manuscript—an illustrated, handwritten book. It contains the four Gospels from the Bible's New Testament, telling the story of the life of Jesus. It includes 10 full-page illustrations such as this one. The book is thought to have been made by Celtic monks on the Scottish island of Iona in the 8th century.

FOUR EVANGELISTS

These are the four men who wrote the Gospels of the New Testament: Matthew, Mark, Luke, and John. Each man had his own symbols so that readers could identify him. For example, Mark's symbol was the lion.

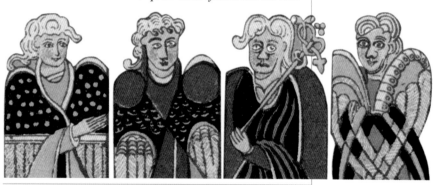

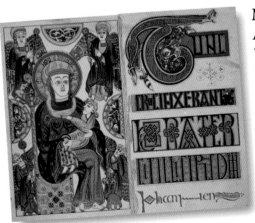

MADONNA AND CHILD

This page features the first ever picture of the Madonna and Child in a Western manuscript. On the opposite page, the Latin words tell another part of Christ's story. They translate as: "Then two thieves were crucified with Christ."

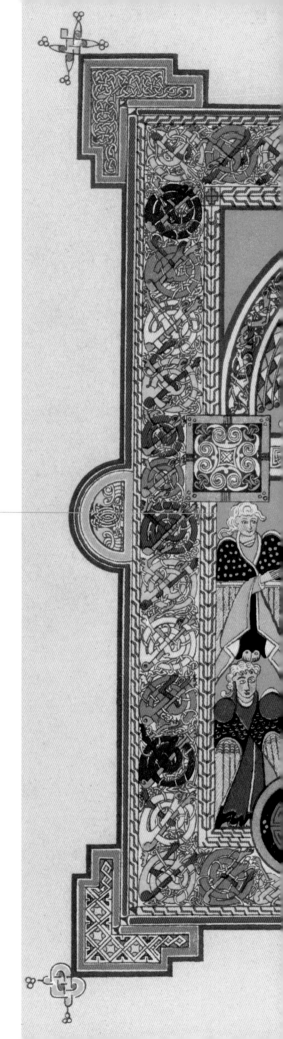

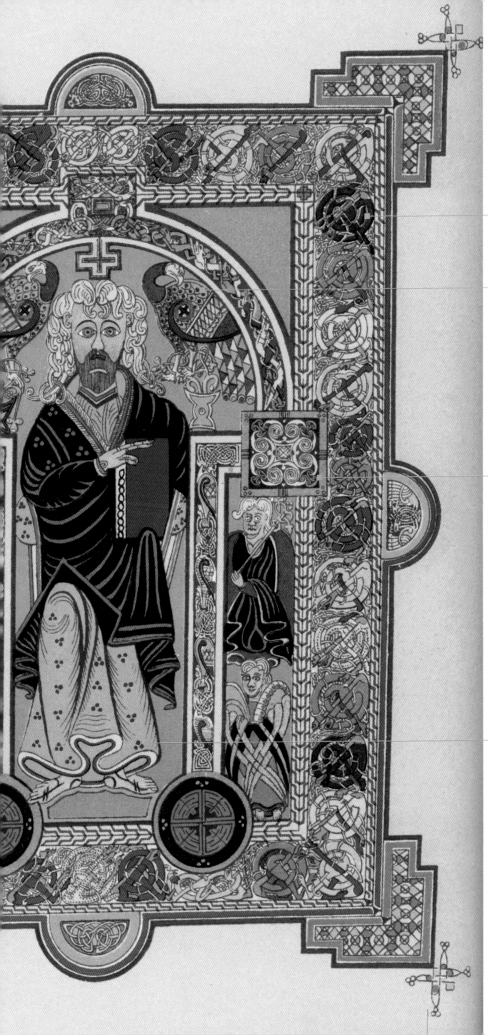

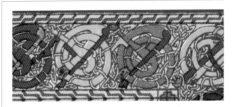

VIVID COLORS

At least three monks copied the words of the Gospels, then other monks drew the illuminations, using brilliantly colored inks. Some were made from rare dyes.

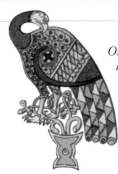

THE PEACOCKS

On either side of Christ is a peacock. The bird was a symbol of his resurrection as it was believed that the peacock's flesh never decayed.

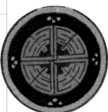

CELTIC DETAILS

Patterns and pictures appear in the elaborate lettering. Sometimes these are cats or mice, other times human figures. The curls, knots, and twists are all part of the Celtic art style.

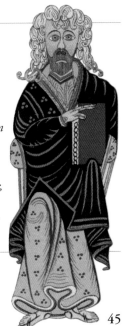

CHRIST ENTHRONED

Jesus is depicted sitting on a throne to show that he is ruler of the world. This was a common image in early Christian art. Jesus was always placed in the center, surrounded by other sacred figures.

Rise of Italy

From about 1290, art in Italy began to change, a process that is now known as the Pre-Renaissance or Proto-Renaissance. Christian art of the Byzantine Empire—centered around modern-day Turkey— had been flat and unrealistic. These Italian artists painted the same religious subjects as the Byzantines, but made their paintings more lifelike.

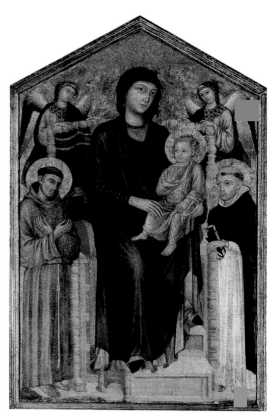

REALISTIC PROPORTIONS

Although little is known of his life, the Florentine artist Cimabue may have been the first Italian artist to break away from some of the styles of Byzantine painting. Although he used Christian imagery that was similar to Byzantine painters, he created more lifelike proportions and shading.

▲ *MADONNA ENTHRONED*, 1280–1285, CIMABUE
This resembles a Byzantine composition but with a more lifelike figure of Jesus.

A MORE NATURAL LOOK

Florence-born Giotto di Bondone painted pictures that looked more natural and realistic than the stylized Byzantine paintings. He did this through his use of light and dark tones, by making his figures overlap, and by adding facial expressions to convey emotions.

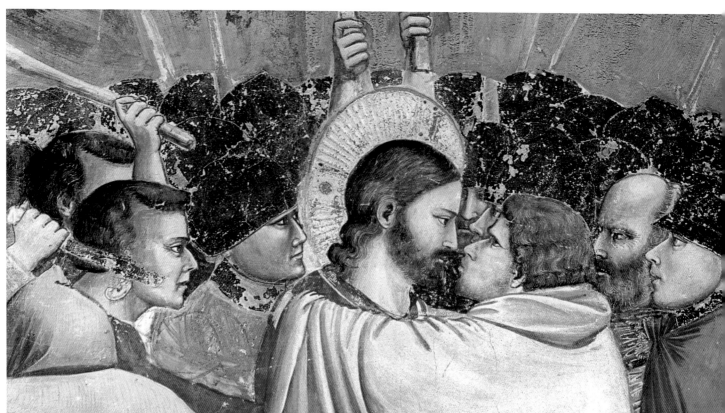

RICH COLOR

The artist Duccio di Buoninsegna lived and worked in the Italian city of Siena. He ran a large workshop, creating expressive and delicate paintings that emphasized color and harmony. In contrast to the sharp lines of Byzantine art, Duccio painted soft figures in warm colors.

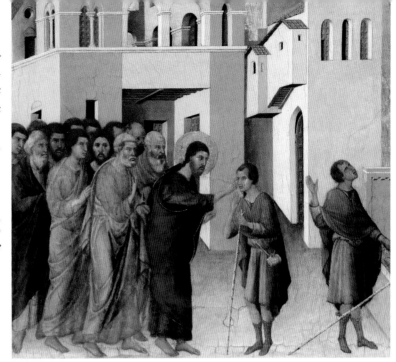

▶ *HEALING THE MAN BORN BLIND,*
1307–1311, DUCCIO
*This soft, colorful painting shows the
story of Jesus performing a miracle.*

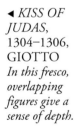

In this period, Italy was divided into city-states, whose artists would compete with each other.

TEMPERA AND FRESCO

Italian artists of this period painted with two types of paint. One was tempera, a dry powdered pigment (color) mixed with egg. Tempera paint could be brightly colored, but it dried quickly, so artists had to work quickly. Some artists also painted on freshly plastered walls using the fresco technique that the ancient Minoans had used from about 2000 BCE.

◀ *KISS OF JUDAS,*
1304–1306,
GIOTTO
In this fresco, overlapping figures give a sense of depth.

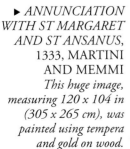

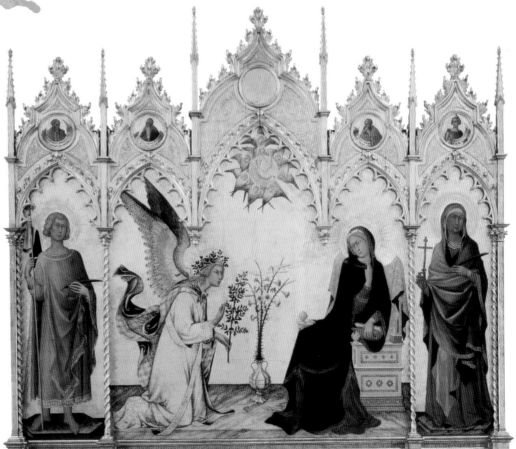

▶ *ANNUNCIATION
WITH ST MARGARET
AND ST ANSANUS,*
1333, MARTINI
AND MEMMI
This huge image, measuring 120 x 104 in (305 x 265 cm), was painted using tempera and gold on wood.

Gothic art

From the 12th century, great churches and cathedrals were built across Europe. Artists decorated them with brightly colored paintings, often featuring slightly elongated, elegant figures and intricate details. Lavish illustrations for illuminated manuscripts were also made. This artistic style later became known as International Gothic.

The Wilton Diptych
An exquisitely decorated double panel

- **Artist** Unknown
- **Date** c.1395
- **Medium** Tempera on two panels

The Wilton Diptych is a painting of King Richard II of England kneeling before Mary and Jesus. Behind him stands Saint John the Baptist and the saints Edward the Confessor and Edmund the Martyr. It is made with gold leaf and blue lapis lazuli. Consisting of two hinged panels, it is called a diptych, from Greek words meaning "two" and "fold."

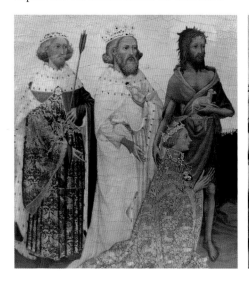
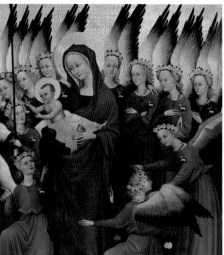
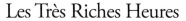

Les Très Riches Heures
One of a series of book illustrations

- **Artist** Limbourg brothers
- **Date** 1412–1416
- **Medium** Gouache on parchment

As pictures in illuminated manuscripts became more sophisticated, some of the artists' names became known and celebrated. Among them were the Limbourg Brothers of France, who produced this work for the Duke of Berry. They created detailed scenes for every month of the year, painted in vivid colors. This outdoor scene represents the month of April.

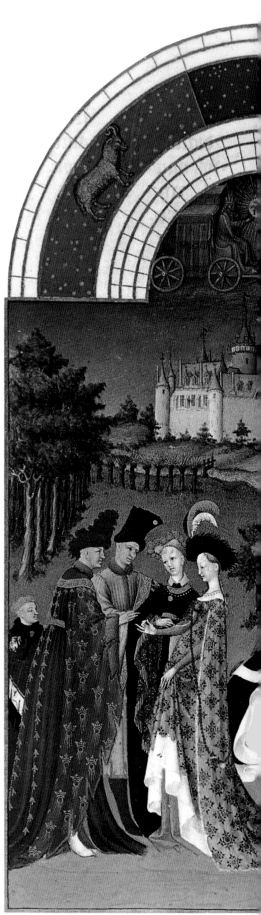

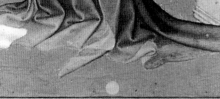

Adoration of the Magi

A public display of wealth and piety

- **Artist** Gentile da Fabriano
- **Date** 1423
- **Medium** Tempera on a wooden panel

International Gothic art first developed in the courts of France and Italy, and then spread across Europe. Much of the art was commissioned by royal and noble families, who wanted to show how religious and rich they were. This lavish picture was featured on an altarpiece, painted by the Italian artist Gentile da Fabriano. It depicts the Three Wise Men worshipping the baby Jesus and giving him gifts. The three men also represent old age, middle age, and youth.

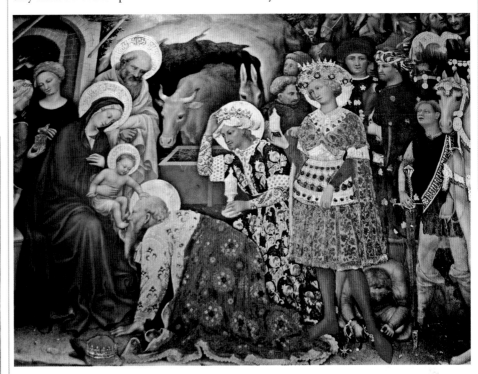

Presentation in the Temple

A painting for a private home

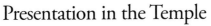

- **Artist** Stefan Lochner
- **Date** 1447
- **Medium** Oil on a wooden panel

International Gothic artists were often commissioned to paint small wooden panels for people to pray in front of in their homes. This example, by the German painter Stefan Lochner, depicts a Bible story in which Mary presents her baby at the Temple of Jerusalem. Lochner filled his backgrounds with elaborate detail, and used overlapping figures to create a sense of depth. The lavish use of blue and gold makes the painting look like an ornament. It would have glittered like a jewel in the candlelight of a church.

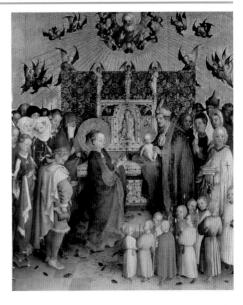

European Renaissance

From the 15th century, in parts of Italy a new interest grew in the art and science of ancient Greece and Rome. Ambitious painters mixed these ideas with those they had seen in the work of Pre-Renaissance artists, such as Giotto, and tried to make the most lifelike art they could. This period later became known as the Renaissance.

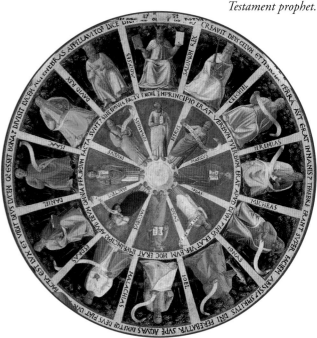

▼ *THE MYSTIC WHEEL,*
1451–1452, FRA ANGELICO
This ambitious work uses an unusual circular composition to show a vision of Ezekiel, a Christian Old Testament prophet.

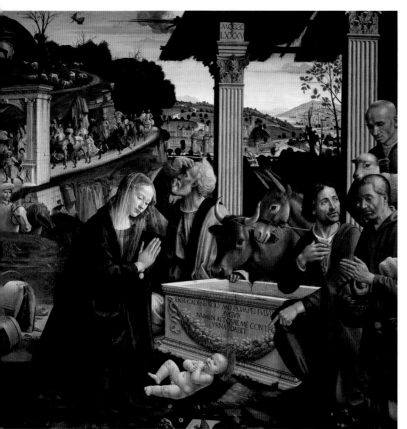

A NEW DIRECTION

The period between the 15th and 17th centuries was given the name Renaissance—which means "rebirth" in French—in the 19th century. This movement spread across Europe, as Renaissance artists used skills and ideas that had been neglected since Roman times, adding new methods, such as linear perspective, to make their art even more realistic.

◄ *ADORATION OF THE SHEPHERDS,* 1485, DOMENICO GHIRLANDAIO
This large altarpiece was made for a church in Florence.

The Renaissance was the first time since ancient Rome that European art looked three-dimensional.

FUNDING THE ARTS

The powerful rulers of Italian cities such as Florence, Milan, Siena, and Venice used the wealth they had made through trade and banking to fund the arts. These rich patrons commissioned artists to produce large paintings and sculptures for churches, palaces, and public buildings.

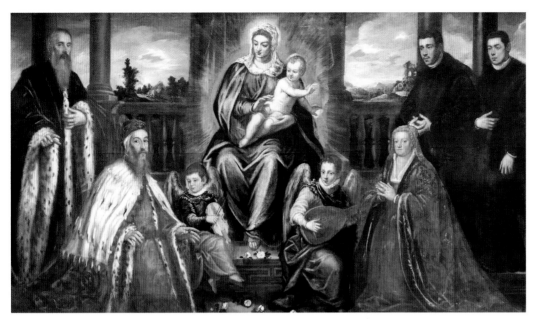

VENETIAN COLOR

By the 16th century, Renaissance artists in different cities had begun to develop their own distinctive styles. Artists of the Venetian school, such as Titian and Tintoretto, experimented with oil paint. They found that they could use this new paint to create rich and glowing color effects.

▲ *DOGE ALVISE MOCENIGO AND FAMILY BEFORE THE MADONNA AND CHILD*, 1573, TINTORETTO
Rich patrons were often depicted in Renaissance paintings. The Doge Mocenigo, a prominent Venetian leader, is shown here in glowing oil-paint colors, kneeling at the front left.

STYLIZED FIGURES

In the 16th century, painters such as the Spanish artist El Greco moved away from realistic paintings to exaggerate and elongate their figures—a style known as Mannerism. This means that their paintings often appear out of proportion, with awkward poses, unusual perspective effects, and unnatural lighting and color.

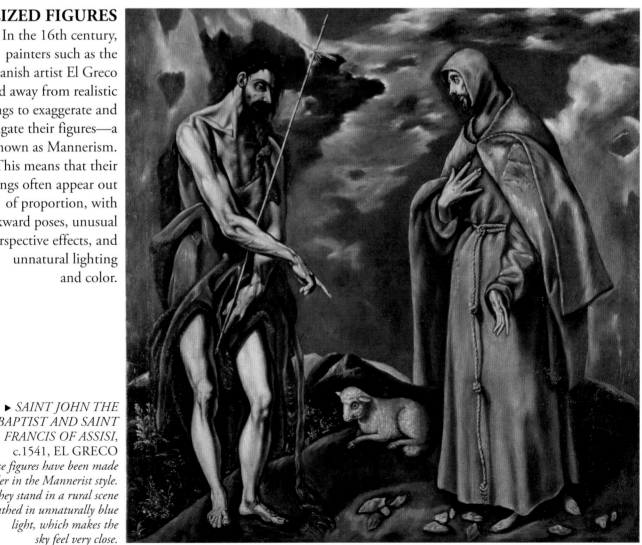

▶ *SAINT JOHN THE BAPTIST AND SAINT FRANCIS OF ASSISI*, c.1541, EL GRECO
These figures have been made taller in the Mannerist style. They stand in a rural scene bathed in unnaturally blue light, which makes the sky feel very close.

Florentine art

The period from the end of the 14th century to the end of the 15th century is usually called the Early Renaissance. Many of the new developments of this time in the arts were centered around the Italian city-state of Florence in the region of Tuscany.

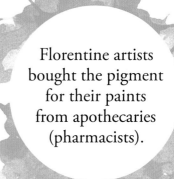

Florentine artists bought the pigment for their paints from apothecaries (pharmacists).

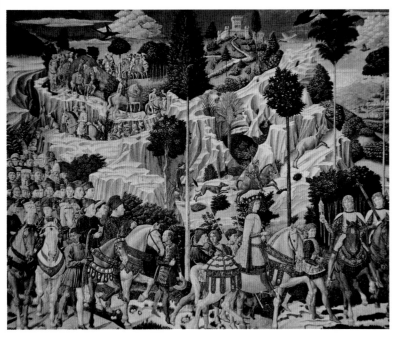

FLORENCE FLOURISHES

Governed by the powerful Medici family, Florence grew and prospered during the 15th century, and the city took the lead in many new developments, particularly in art. As a result, many great artists lived and worked there, and Florence became known as "the cradle of the Renaissance."

◄ *PROCESSION OF THE MAGI*,
1459, BENOZZO GOZZOLI
The three kings of the nativity story are shown riding to Bethlehem. The landscape is Tuscan in appearance.

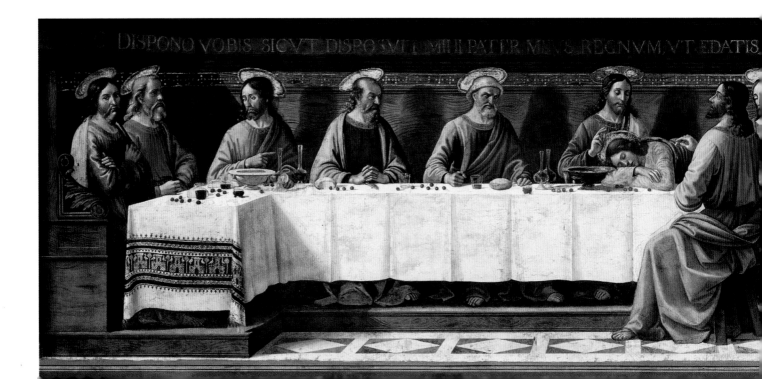

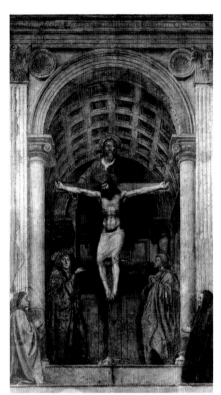

◄ *THE HOLY TRINITY,*
c.1427, MASACCIO
To draw the lines needed to achieve perspective, the artist stuck a nail in the base of the cross and attached radiating strings from it.

▼ *THE BIRTH OF VENUS*, 1486, SANDRO BOTTICELLI
Botticelli painted the Roman goddess Venus as a symbol of divine love.

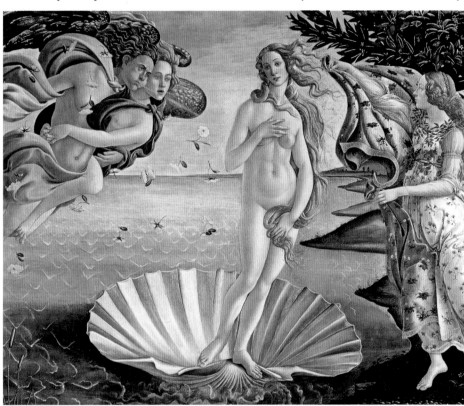

BREAK FROM TRADITION

An idea called humanism developed during the Early Renaissance. This was the belief that everyone should be educated, that art should be lifelike, and that religion did not have to be the only subject in art. Many Florentine artists began to paint subjects related to Greek and Roman myth, rather than Christianity.

PAINTING

RULES OF PERSPECTIVE

Although some artists had created a sense of distance by drawing certain things smaller than others, they did this by instinct. In about 1420, the architect Filippo Brunelleschi worked out mathematical rules for drawing perspective accurately, and the artists of the Renaissance soon began using his method.

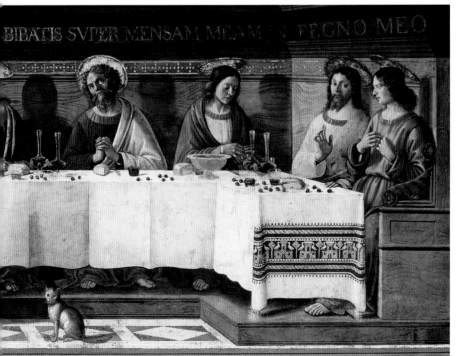

ARTISTIC INVESTIGATION

Early Renaissance painters studied the natural world so that they could accurately represent the human body, plants, textures, light, and movement. New buildings were built in rich cities such as Florence, and this gave artists the opportunity to adorn them with large new works, with plenty of space to explore their ideas.

◄ *THE LAST SUPPER*, 1480, DOMENICO GHIRLANDAIO
This lifelike painting of a scene from the Bible was painted to adorn the refectory of a monastery, where it could be contemplated by the monks.

Renaissance invention

Believing that ancient Greek and Roman artists had produced the greatest art ever, early Renaissance painters blended ideas from the Classical world with their own humanist ideas, and developed skills in the use of linear perspective. This led to a distinct and innovative style of art.

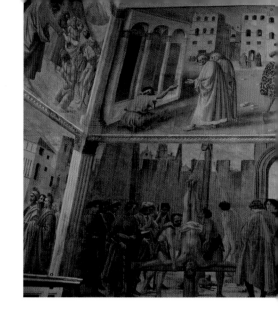

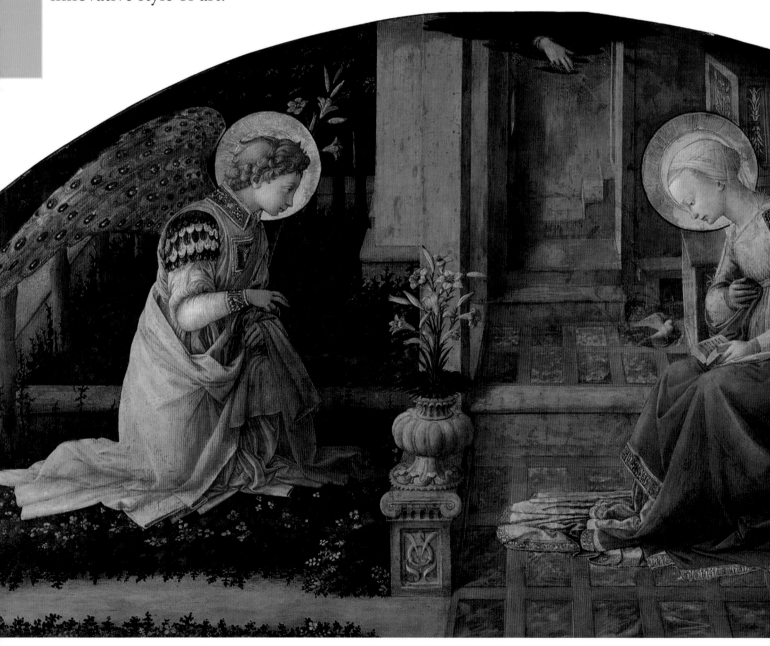

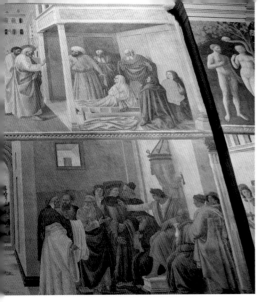

The Brancacci Chapel
Decorations for a private chapel

- **Artist** Masaccio and Masolino
- **Date** c.1424–1427
- **Medium** Fresco

In about 1424, two artists began painting frescoes depicting the life of Saint Peter in the Brancacci family's chapel at the Carmelite Church in Florence. Both artists were named Tommaso, so they were nicknamed Masaccio and Masolino—"Clumsy Tom" and "Little Tom." Masaccio's work, in particular, demonstrated an understanding of anatomy, perspective, foreshortening, and color.

The Baptism of Christ
A mathematically balanced composition

- **Artist** Piero della Francesca
- **Date** 1450s
- **Medium** Tempera on wooden panel

Piero was both an artist and a mathematician, who wrote works on geometry and perspective. Using his mathematical knowledge, he produced geometric shapes to create harmonious compositions. In this work, he has made a composition that is arranged around perfectly balanced shapes, with the dove directly above Christ's head.

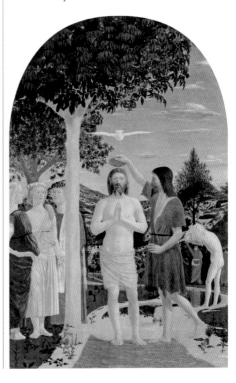

▼ THE ANNUNCIATION
Lippi used expensive gold and blue lapis lazuli pigment to make this painting look rich. He made the biblical figures look like wealthy people from Florence so viewers would relate to them.

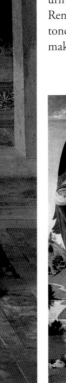

The Annunciation
Decoration for the Palazzo Medici, Florence

- **Artist** Fra Filippo Lippi
- **Date** c.1450–1453
- **Medium** Tempera on wooden panel

Fra Filippo Lippi painted gentle-looking figures, richly decorated surfaces, and textures in soft colors to express both his artistic skills and his devotion to Christianity. This work was probably commissioned by the powerful Florentine Medici family, whose emblem of a diamond ring and feather can be seen on the wall below the urn of lilies. Lippi demonstrates a skill that Renaissance painters perfected: showing tone by using light and dark shading to make pictures look solid.

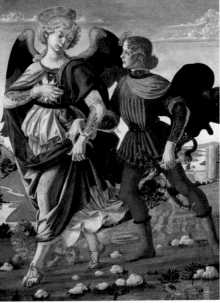

Tobias and the Angel
A piece created by an artist's assistants

- **Artist** Workshop of Andrea del Verrocchio
- **Date** c.1470–1475
- **Medium** Tempera on wood

Renaissance artists learned their skills by training with master artists. When they had gathered sufficient experience, they were allowed to paint some of the artist's paintings. This work was painted by several assistants and apprentices in the workshop of the Florentine artist Andrea del Verrocchio. It depicts a scene from the Old Testament Book of Tobit, in which Tobias is instructed by an angel on how to deal with a fish that has tried to swallow his foot.

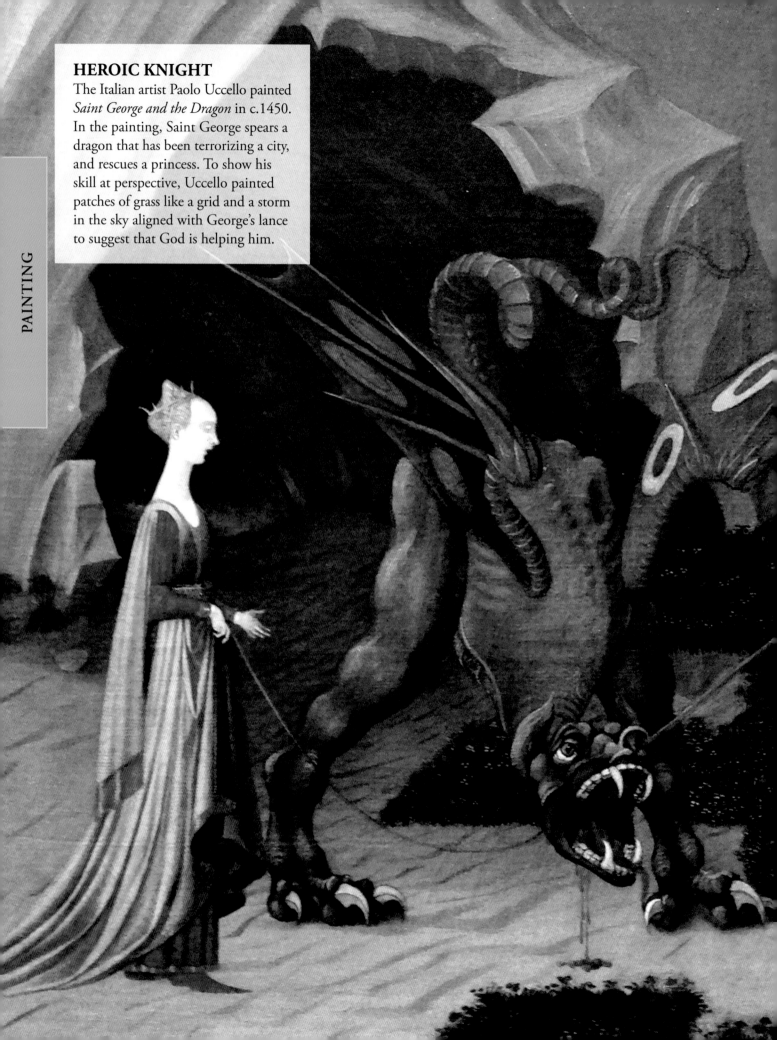

HEROIC KNIGHT

The Italian artist Paolo Uccello painted *Saint George and the Dragon* in c.1450. In the painting, Saint George spears a dragon that has been terrorizing a city, and rescues a princess. To show his skill at perspective, Uccello painted patches of grass like a grid and a storm in the sky aligned with George's lance to suggest that God is helping him.

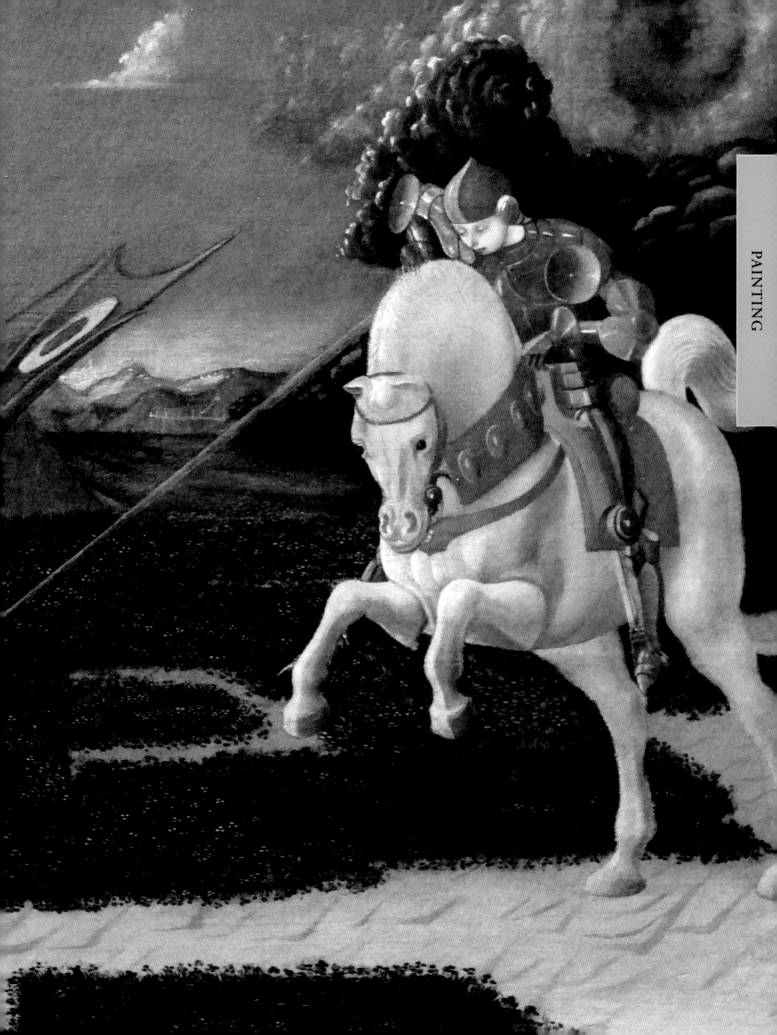

Primavera

Mixing Greek and Roman mythology with Christian themes, *Primavera* (*Spring*) was painted in 1482 by Florentine artist Sandro Botticelli. He was adored by some of the greatest patrons of the Early Renaissance, including the Pope. This work was made for the rich and powerful Medici family, who ruled Florence at the time.

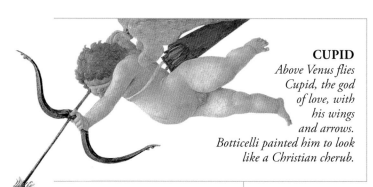

CUPID
Above Venus flies Cupid, the god of love, with his wings and arrows. Botticelli painted him to look like a Christian cherub.

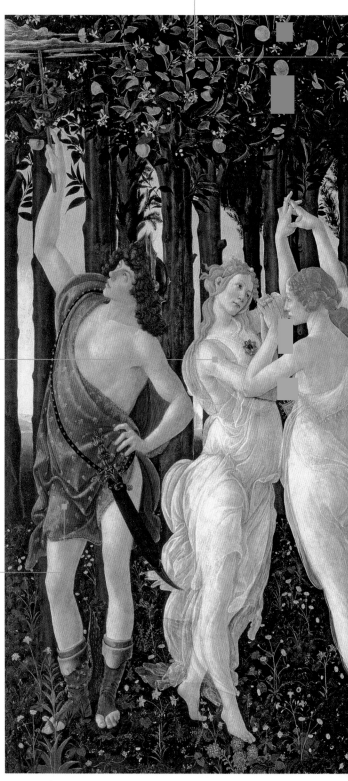

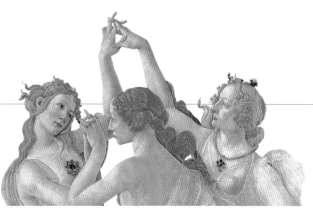

THE THREE GRACES
Dancing together in a circle are the Three Graces, daughters of Zeus, the king of the gods. In Greek mythology, they were created to fill the world with happy moments and feelings. They also symbolize beauty and the happiness of spring.

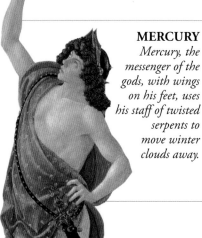

MERCURY
Mercury, the messenger of the gods, with wings on his feet, uses his staff of twisted serpents to move winter clouds away.

NATURAL WORLD
Botticelli painted almost 500 different kinds of plants here. In this, his painting style resembles the tapestries that were often hung in wealthy Florentine homes.

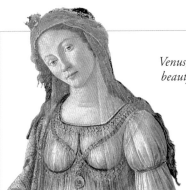

VENUS

Venus, the Roman goddess of love and beauty, stands in a garden. Under an arch of fruit trees, she resembles popular representations of the Virgin Mary, but she wears the headdress of a respectable married Florentine woman.

FLORA

Zephyr, the West Wind, is chasing a nymph called Chloris. A nymph is a beautiful young woman, but not a goddess. In the Greek myth, Zephyr turns Chloris into Flora, the goddess of flowers and spring.

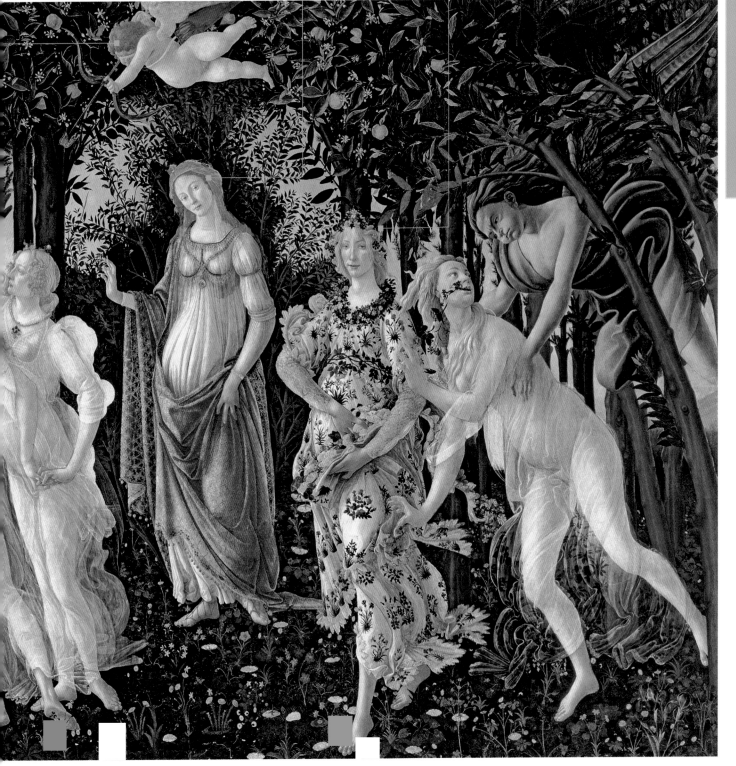

Master artists

Between 1490 and 1527, Italian artists—especially those based in Rome—began painting more realistically than ever before. Perspective and shading techniques became more sophisticated and images of people and nature even more lifelike. Painters focused on making compositions with harmony and balance. This period is known as the High Renaissance.

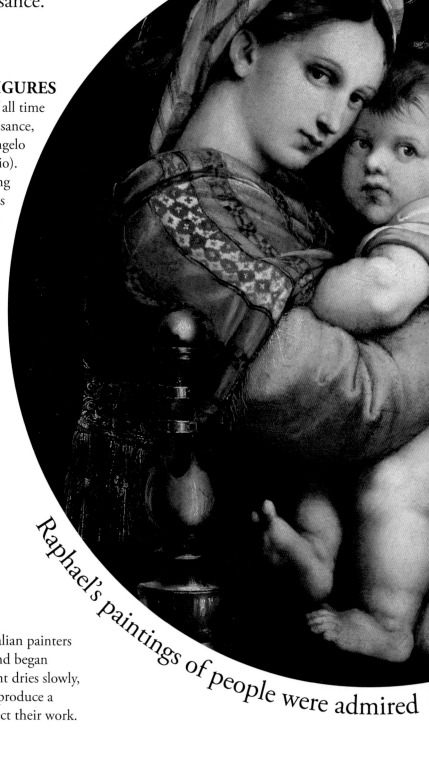

MAJOR FIGURES

Some of the most famous painters of all time were working in Rome during the High Renaissance, including Leonardo da Vinci, Michelangelo Buonarroti, and Raphael (born Raffaello Sanzio). These great artists gained enormous fame during their lifetimes and received many invitations to work in cities across Italy.

▼ *MADONNA OF THE HARPIES,* 1517, ANDREA DEL SARTO
Del Sarto was able to create a wide palette of rich colors for this picture by using oil paints.

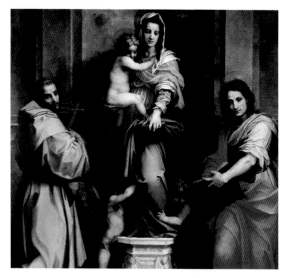

SWITCHING TO OIL PAINTS

Learning from northern European artists, most Italian painters stopped using tempera in the High Renaissance and began mixing their powdered pigments with oil. Oil paint dries slowly, giving artists more time to blend their colors and produce a greater variety of tones, and to add details or correct their work.

Raphael's paintings of people were admired

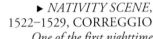

▼ *MADONNA OF THE CHAIR*, c.1513–1514, RAPHAEL
In this warm image, the Virgin Mary cuddles her baby while a young John the Baptist looks on.

When Raphael died in 1520 at the age of just 37, huge crowds lined the streets of Rome for his funeral.

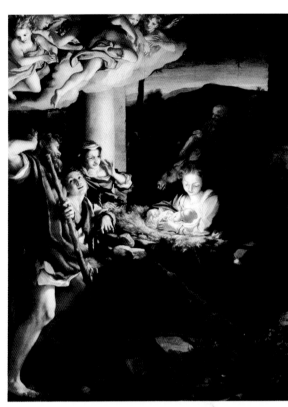

▶ *NATIVITY SCENE*, 1522–1529, CORREGGIO
One of the first nighttime paintings, this dramatically lit picture seemed to viewers to glow with a mystical light.

CLOSE OBSERVATIONS

Like the ancient Greeks, the artists of the High Renaissance aimed for idealism—or to show nature as perfectly as possible. To do this, they strove for beauty, balanced proportions, and harmonious colors. They closely observed the world around them, using the extra painting time provided by oil paints to include the tiniest details and create the impression of depth and light.

for their realistic look

▶ *MYSTIC MARRIAGE OF ST CATHERINE*, 1512, FRA BARTOLOMEO
This Dominican friar worked in Florence, Venice, and Rome. Here, he has depicted Mary and Jesus for a church altarpiece.

THE SPREAD OF NEW IDEAS

As the Renaissance gathered pace, many of the ideas that had started in Florence or Rome spread across Italy and the rest of Europe. Rich patrons who paid for works to be made admired individuality and inventiveness, so artists produced ever more grand and sumptuous paintings.

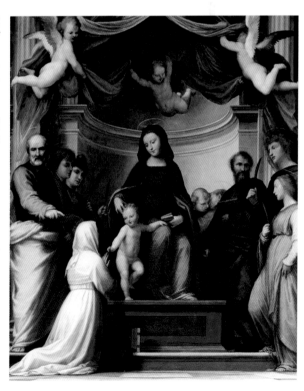

Leonardo da Vinci

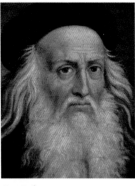

A painter, sculptor, architect, engineer, inventor, scientist, and musician, Leonardo was a master in many areas. He is widely considered the greatest genius of the Italian Renaissance, and is called a "Renaissance man" for his many talents. He was named "da Vinci," meaning "of Vinci," after the town in Italy near which he was born.

A 19th-century painting of Leonardo

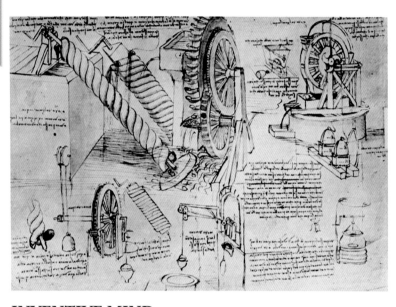

◄ WATER RAISING DEVICE
Leonardo designed the parts and workings of this machine that would help to irrigate and drain canals.

► *MONA LISA*, c.1504
In this work—his most famous—Leonardo applied thin layers of translucent (semi-transparent) oil paint, picking out delicate details and creating soft-looking highlights and shadows.

INVENTIVE MIND

Leonardo wrote and drew in thousands of notebooks on subjects including geology, anatomy, flight, gravity, and optics. He also worked as a military engineer, and came up with ideas for a tank, a bicycle, a parachute, a submarine, and flying machines hundreds of years before they were actually made.

WORLD-FAMOUS PAINTING

Sitting high on a balcony, smiling slightly with her mouth but not with her eyes, the woman in the *Mona Lisa* has captivated people for more than 500 years. Leonardo produced her glowing skin and lifelike features using a special method of soft, natural-looking shading called sfumato. In the background is a misty landscape featuring lakes and the Alps mountains. The identity of the model is uncertain, but it is possible that she was Lisa Gherardini, the wife of a wealthy Florentine banker.

LIFE STORY

1452–1471	1472–1475	1476–1481	1482–1489
Leonardo is born in 1452. At 15, he enters the workshop of the Italian artist Andrea del Verrocchio in Florence.	The 20-year-old Leonardo is accepted into the prestigious painters' guild of Florence. In 1473, he draws a landscape in ink, his earliest known drawing.	Leonardo sets up his own workshop and begins filling notebooks with his ideas and works for the powerful Medici family.	He moves to Milan and works for Ludovico Sforza as an engineer, architect, painter, and sculptor. In 1489, he begins a huge horse sculpture.

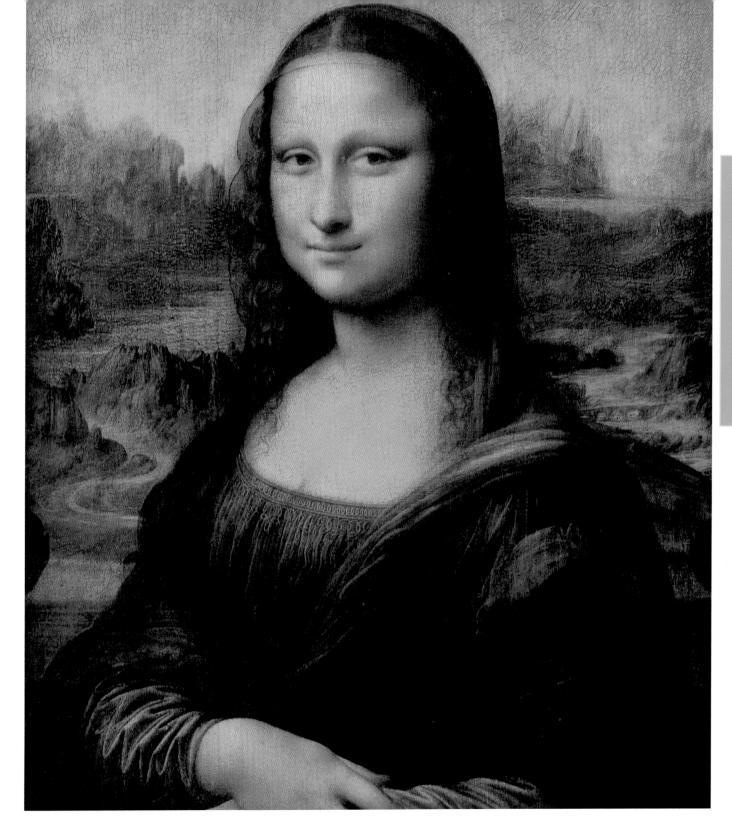

1490–1501	1502–1503	1504–1512	1513–1519
After designing scenery and stage costumes, in 1495 Leonardo begins *The Last Supper*. Four years later, he moves to Mantua.	Working in Florence as a senior military engineer and architect, Leonardo makes plans to divert the Arno river. He produces some of the first accurate maps.	Leonardo designs a flying machine. He completes the *Mona Lisa* and returns to Milan. He becomes the King's Painter to Louis XII of France.	In 1515, Leonardo makes a mechanical lion for the new French king, François I, and moves to the French court. He dies in 1519.

Renaissance masterpieces

Many artists in the High Renaissance strove to imitate the masters of the era—Leonardo, Michelangelo, and Raphael. During this period, these three great painters produced some of the most famous paintings of all time, including Michelangelo's epic works that cover the ceiling of the Sistine Chapel in Rome.

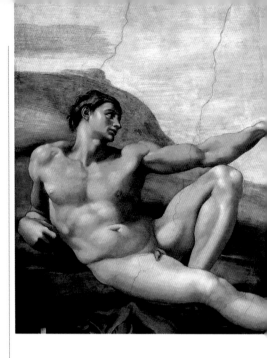

The Sistine Madonna (detail)
A large church altarpiece

- **Artist** Raphael
- **Date** 1512
- **Medium** Oil on canvas

Commissioned by Pope Julius II, this was the last of Raphael's Madonna paintings, made for the high altar of the church of Saint Sixtus in Piacenza, Italy. Below is a detail from the bottom of the painting. A pair of cheeky cherubs, or *putti*, look up at the adult figures above them (not shown), balancing the painting and giving it an extra human touch.

Portrait of Francesco delle Opere
Painted by the teacher of Raphael

- **Artist** Pietro Perugino
- **Date** 1494
- **Medium** Oil on panel

This Florentine artist has painted his friend at a three-quarter angle. In his right hand, Francesco holds a metal name plate inscribed with the words *Timete Devm* (Latin for "Beware of God"). Perugino was one of the most successful artists in the 1480s and 1490s. He ran a studio in Florence, where Raphael was an apprentice.

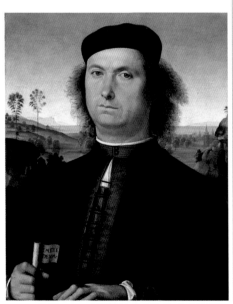

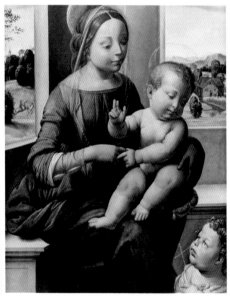

Madonna and Child with the Young St John the Baptist
Delicate work showing the influence of the masters

- **Artist** Fra Bartolomeo
- **Date** c.1497
- **Medium** Oil and gold on wood

Bartolomeo painted this work shortly before he became a Dominican friar. It shows the influence of Leonardo and Raphael through the delicate faces and graceful poses of the holy figures, who are bathed in a soft light. Bartolomeo renounced painting on becoming a friar, only to resume a few years later at the request of his holy order.

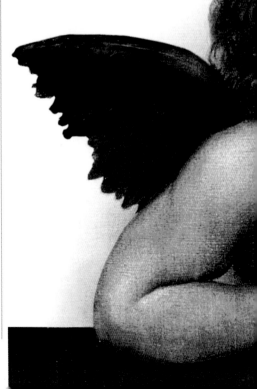

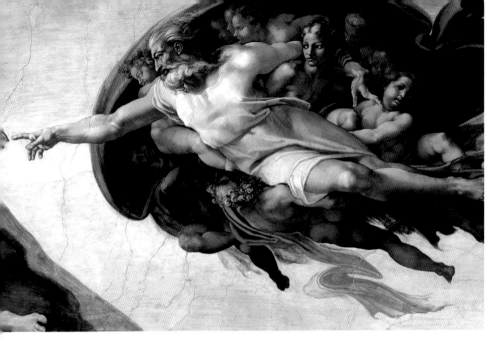

The Creation of Adam
Masterpiece of the Sistine Chapel

- **Artist** Michelangelo
- **Date** 1508–1512
- **Medium** Fresco

Michelangelo's works were so admired that he was nicknamed *Il Divino* ("The Divine One"). His style was described in Italian as his *terribilità*, which translates as "awe-inspiring grandeur." In 1508, he was commissioned by Pope Julius II to paint the Sistine Chapel ceiling in Rome. Over the next four years, he covered the vast ceiling with scenes from the Old Testament. One of the most well-known is his painting of God giving life to Adam, the first human.

Portrait of a Young Man
By a Renaissance artist overshadowed by his peers

- **Artist** Andrea del Sarto
- **Date** c.1517–1518
- **Medium** Oil on linen

Although greatly admired during his lifetime, del Sarto was almost forgotten after his death because Leonardo, Michelangelo, and Raphael became so famous. The turning man in this painting has not been identified. Light shines down from high above him to the left, highlighting his white shirt and throwing parts of his head into strong shadow.

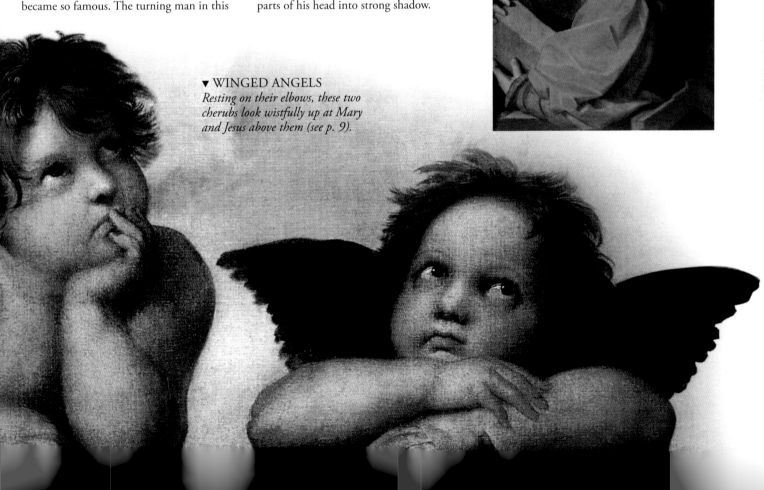

▼ WINGED ANGELS
Resting on their elbows, these two cherubs look wistfully up at Mary and Jesus above them (see p. 9).

The School of Athens

PAINTING

The son of a painter and influenced early on by his teacher Pietro Perugino, Raphael studied the art of Leonardo and Michelangelo, and became a great master himself. In 1509, in Rome, he painted 12 frescoes for Pope Julius II. This is one of them, showing an imagined scene in which the great thinkers of history have gathered together in the same room.

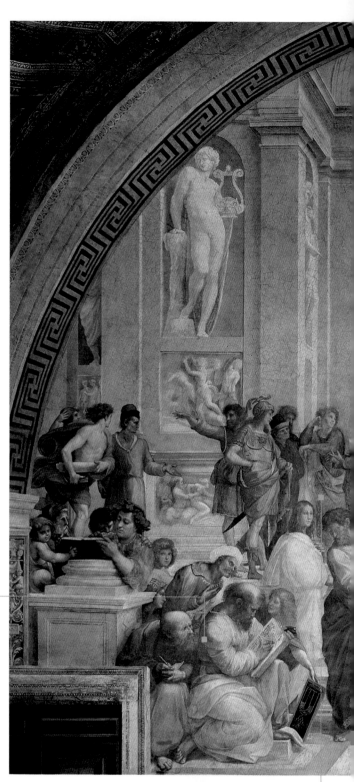

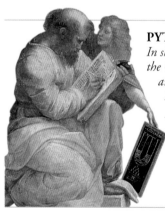

PYTHAGORAS
In skillfully painted robes, the Greek philosopher and mathematician Pythagoras writes his famous theorem about triangles in a book, while one of his pupils shows him a diagram on a chalkboard.

RAPHAEL'S ROOMS

The Stanze di Raffaello (Raphael's Rooms) were four rooms in the Vatican. Each room represented a different concept, which was illustrated by four of Raphael's frescoes. The Stanza della Segnatura, which was originally intended as the library, was decorated with frescoes representing four branches of humanist learning: theology, philosophy, law, and poetry. *The School of Athens* represents philosophy, featuring thinkers from ancient Greece.

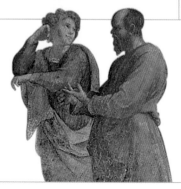

ALEXANDER AND SOCRATES
Alexander the Great, the King of Macedonia and a pupil of Aristotle, listens to the philosopher Socrates, who counts on his fingers as he talks.

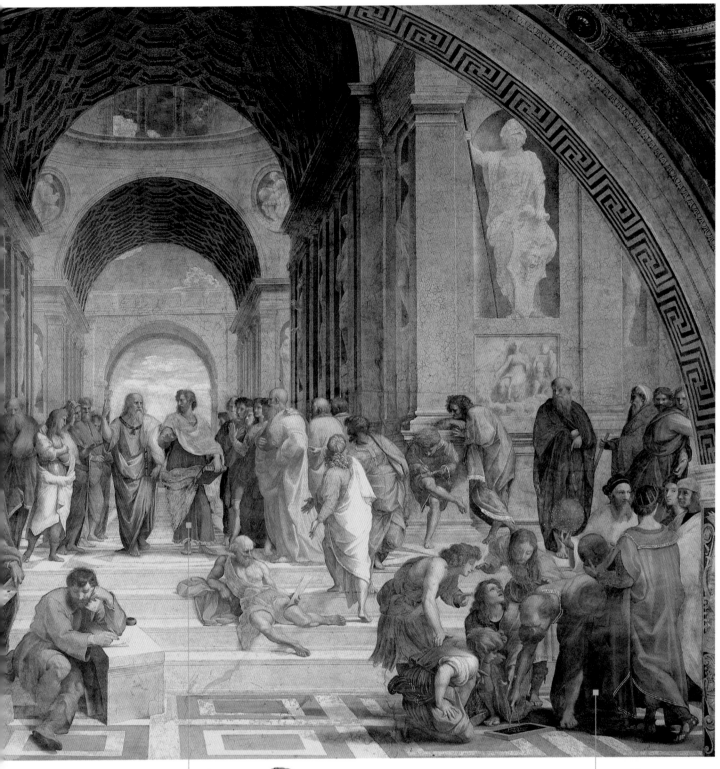

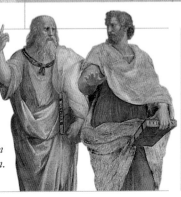

PLATO AND ARISTOTLE

The Greek philosopher Plato (who was modeled on Leonardo) points to the sky, while Aristotle points to the ground, suggesting Plato's idealism and Aristotle's realism.

EUCLID TEACHING

Bending to draw with his compasses and demonstrate to pupils around him is the ancient Greek mathematician Euclid. Raphael's model for Euclid was the Renaissance architect Donato Bramante.

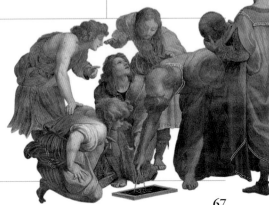

The art of Venice

At the time of the Renaissance, Venice was linked to many major trade routes. This meant that Venetian artists were in a unique position to gather new ideas. They obtained pigments for their paints through trade, and they learned new ideas from foreign merchants. Their own sailors also returned from distant lands with fresh ideas.

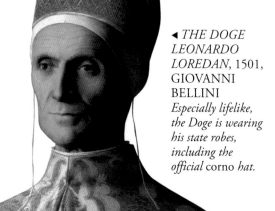

◄ *THE DOGE LEONARDO LOREDAN*, 1501, GIOVANNI BELLINI
Especially lifelike, the Doge is wearing his state robes, including the official corno *hat.*

BEAUTIFUL BUILDINGS

Proud of their city built on a lagoon, the Venetians constructed beautiful palaces and public buildings, which artists embellished lavishly. Venice was ruled by the Doge, an elderly, elected statesman who ruled for life. The Doge's Palace in Saint Mark's Square was decorated by the greatest Venetian painters, including Titian, Tintoretto, and Paolo Veronese.

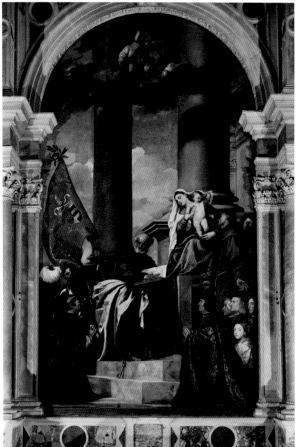

◄ *PESARO MADONNA*, 1519–1526, TITIAN
Here, Titian played with traditional composition. It was unusual to paint the Virgin Mary off-center.

VISITORS FROM FAR AND WIDE

By the 15th century, Venice had become one of the richest city-states in Italy. Through its trading success, it had links to the east with the Islamic world and as far as China, and to the north with Germany and the Netherlands. Visitors brought with them new ideas about painting, such as methods of showing perspective and using oil paint, and painters experimented with these ideas.

Venetian painters layered and blended their colors to achieve the glowing, rich appearance for which they were famed.

► *THE THREE PHILOSOPHERS*, c.1506, GIORGIONE
There is much debate as to who these figures are. They may represent three different ages: from the right, the Classical world, the Islamic world, and the modern European world.

LIGHT AND SPARKLE

Perhaps inspired by light on the canals and lagoons, and by the glittering mosaics in Saint Mark's Cathedral, Venetian painters were especially skilled in painting surface patterns and light. On a smooth white paint base, they blended brilliantly colored oil paints. Bellini, Giorgione, and Titian sometimes also added ground glass to their pigments for added sparkle.

LEONARDO IN VENICE

By 1500, the Christian Byzantine Empire in the Eastern Mediterranean had been overthrown by the Muslim Ottoman Empire. Venice was at war with the Ottomans, and the Doge employed Leonardo da Vinci to work on methods of defending the city from naval attack. During his stay, Leonardo's ideas about art, such as sfumato (see p. 62), greatly influenced Venetian painters.

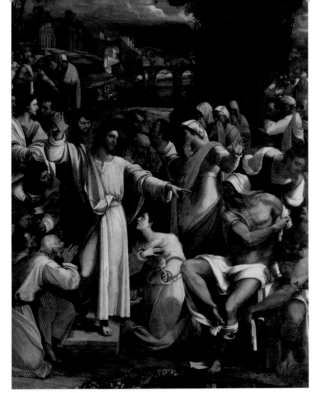

▲ *THE RAISING OF LAZARUS,*
1519, SEBASTIANO DEL PIOMBO
Using the bright colors typical of Venetian art, Sebastiano depicts the biblical miracle in which Jesus raises Lazarus from the dead.

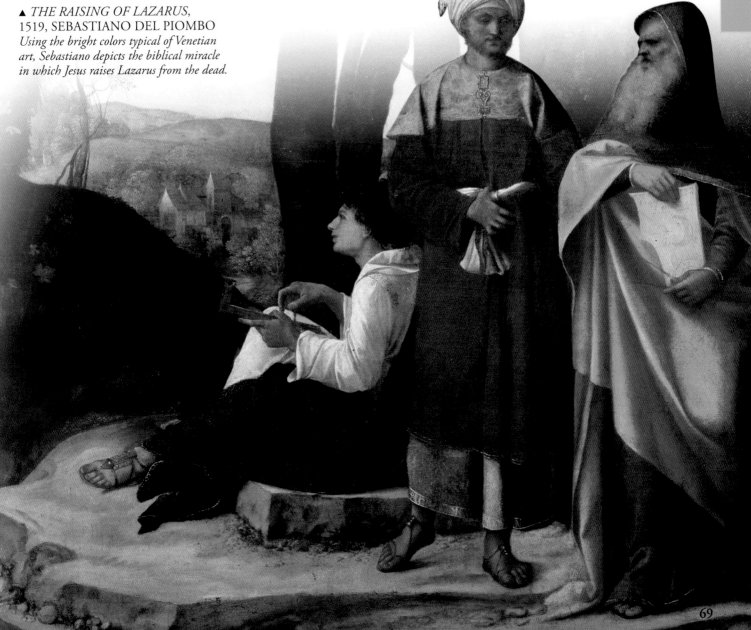

Venetian masters

Venetian Renaissance artists all took ideas from one another. The most influential artists were the Bellini family: Jacopo and his sons Gentile and Giovanni. Many of the Venetian masters, including Titian, Sebastiano, and possibly Giorgione, started their careers as apprentices to Giovanni Bellini, who taught them to make rich colors with slow-drying oil paint.

PAINTING

The Virgin Annunciate

A portrait by the first Italian to use oil paint

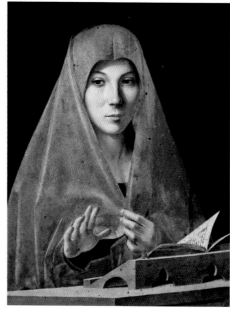

- **Artist** Antonello da Messina
- **Date** c.1476
- **Medium** Oil on wood

The Sicilian-born artist da Messina has been credited with introducing oil paint to Italy. He visited Venice in 1475–1476 and it is believed that while he was there, he showed Venetian painters the possibilities of oil painting. This work shows the Virgin Mary being interrupted while she is reading by the angel Gabriel, who tells her she will be the mother of Christ. This was a common theme for paintings, known as "the Annunciation."

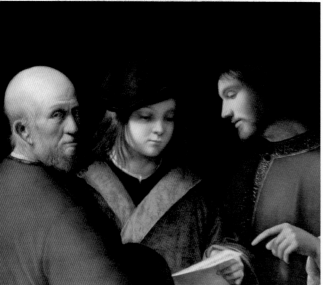

The Singing Lesson

Three generations of men

- **Artist** Giorgione
- **Date** c.1500–1501
- **Medium** Oil on canvas

In this work, often called *The Three Ages of Man*, the identity of the characters is unclear. The picture may represent an emperor or it may show a biblical story. Giorgione was a highly successful artist, but his career was cut short when he died in his early 30s. Along with Titian and the Bellinis, Giorgione established the Venetian Renaissance style.

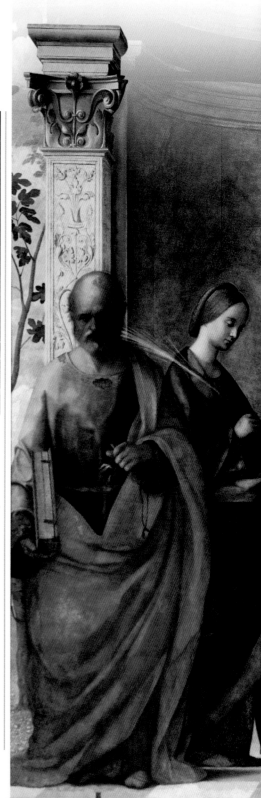

San Zaccaria Altarpiece

A huge, sculpture-like composition

- **Artist** Giovanni Bellini
- **Date** 1505
- **Medium** Oil on panel

Giovanni Bellini inspired many other Venetian Renaissance painters with his brilliant colors, glowing light, and the sculptural appearance of his figures. This altarpiece in a church in Venice is an example of a *sacra conversazione*, or "sacred conversation:" a picture of the Virgin and Child among saints from different periods in history.

▼ A GATHERING OF SAINTS
Around the Madonna and Child on a throne are an angel musician and four saints: Peter, Catherine, Lucy, and Jerome.

Mary Magdalene Reading

A work by a later Venetian master who blended styles

- **Artist** Tintoretto
- **Date** 1582–1587
- **Medium** Oil on canvas

Often classed as both a Renaissance and Mannerist painter, Tintoretto's work usually includes muscular figures, dramatic poses, bold perspective, and intense color and light. Alone in a wood, this woman is Mary Magdalene, a repentant sinner who is forgiven by Jesus in the New Testament. She sits by a tree reading, illuminated by a radiant light—an effect that shows the influence of Northern Renaissance styles.

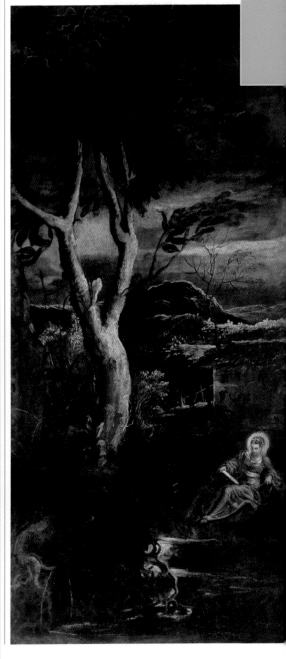

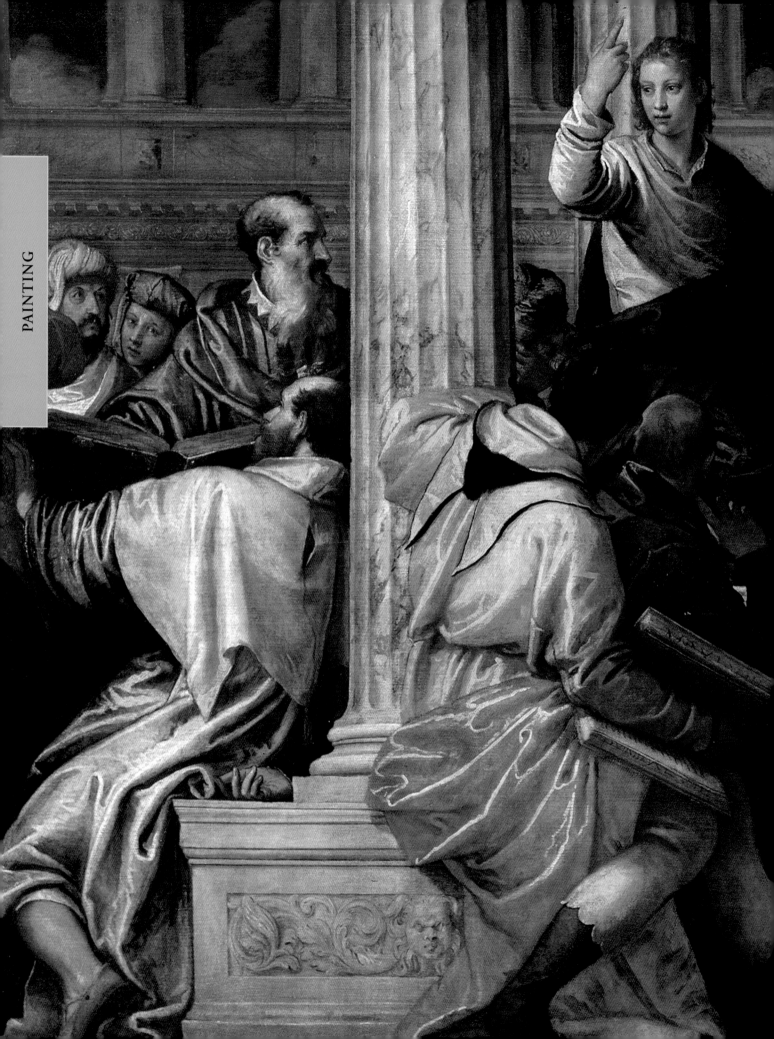

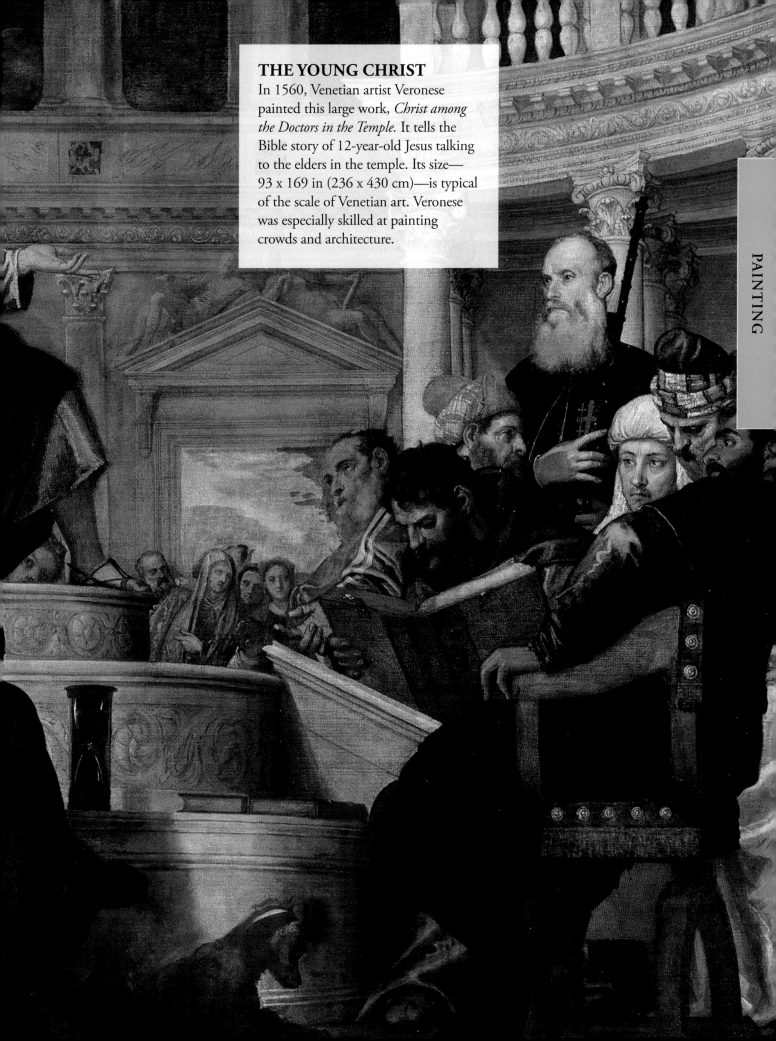

THE YOUNG CHRIST
In 1560, Venetian artist Veronese painted this large work, *Christ among the Doctors in the Temple*. It tells the Bible story of 12-year-old Jesus talking to the elders in the temple. Its size— 93 x 169 in (236 x 430 cm)—is typical of the scale of Venetian art. Veronese was especially skilled at painting crowds and architecture.

PAINTING

Northern directions

Art developed in a distinct way during the Renaissance in northern Europe. Exploration by intrepid sailors opened up new trade routes, increasing prosperity and providing fresh approaches to art. Meanwhile, new ideas about Christianity challenged northern European artists to approach religious themes in new ways.

Northern Renaissance artists painted sharp details, smooth contours, and the effects of clear light.

NEW WEALTH AND NEW COMMISSIONS

In northern Europe, artists were less dependent on the Church than their southern counterparts. Unlike the Catholic south, large frescoes were not needed for the Protestant churches of the north. Instead, artists were often commissioned by ordinary people who had become wealthy through trade and wanted smaller images for their homes. These newly wealthy people commissioned both religious and non-religious works.

▼ *CHILDREN'S GAMES*, 1560, PIETER BRUEGEL THE ELDER
In this scene of everyday life, children of all ages play with toys, roll hoops, stilt-walk, ride hobby horses, and perform handstands.

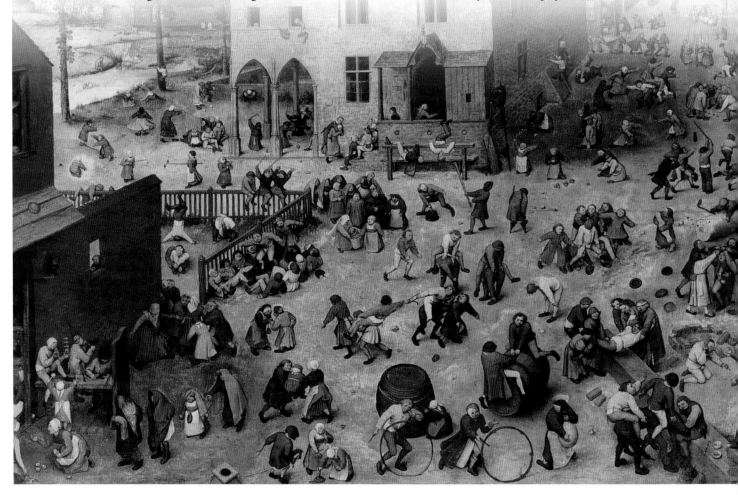

RELIGIOUS ART IN A MODERN SETTING

Unlike Italian painters, Northern Renaissance artists were not rediscovering the art of ancient Greece and Rome, but remained inspired by the International Gothic style (see pp. 48–49). Northern artists were also affected by the ideas of religious reformers, who questioned the way Christianity was being interpreted. As a result, they often depicted holy figures as wealthy, middle-class people in contemporary domestic settings.

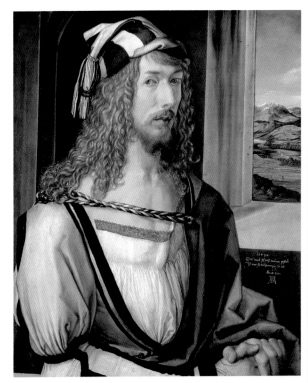

▲ *SELF PORTRAIT*, 1498, ALBRECHT DÜRER
One of the most skillful artists of the time, the German artist Dürer paints himself, age 26.

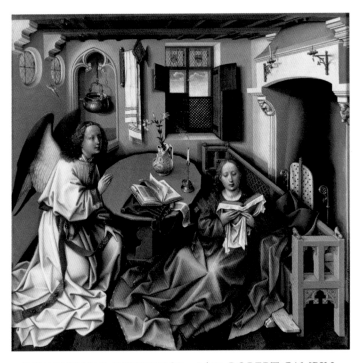

▲ *THE MERODE ALTARPIECE*, c.1430, ROBERT CAMPIN
The Dutch painter Campin has set his Gothic-style scene of the angel Gabriel visiting the Virgin Mary in an ordinary home.

SKILL AND DETAIL

The best northern Renaissance artists were outstandingly skillful, using the new oil-based paints with confidence to depict closely observed details in their works, which were often made on wooden panels rather than canvas. With greater freedom to choose their subject matter, artists experimented with self-portraits, landscapes, and scenes from everyday life, in addition to religious stories.

THE FIRST OIL PAINTS

No one knows when oil paints were first used or who originally invented them, but some time during the 15th century, artists in the Netherlands mixed dry powered pigments with oil instead of egg. Oil paints have a slight sheen, are easy to spread, and dry slowly, so artists had time to make adjustments to their works and add details.

▶ *CHRIST CARRYING THE CROSS*, 1475–1480, MARTIN SCHONGAUER
This is a detail from a larger altarpiece, showing the rich color range of oil paints.

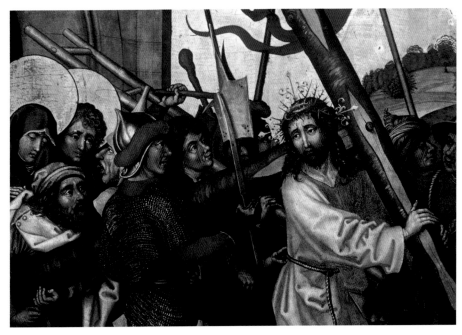

Jan van Eyck

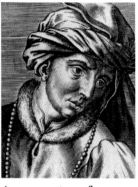

An engraving of
van Eyck c.1425

Flemish artist Jan van Eyck had become a master
painter by the age of 30, running a workshop in
The Hague with his older brother, Hubert. After
Hubert's death, Jan was hired by the powerful Duke
of Burgundy, for whom he worked for the rest of his
life, developing new techniques for oil painting and
producing incredibly lifelike works.

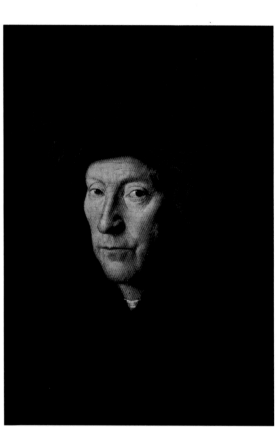

◄ MAN IN A
TURBAN, 1433
Van Eyck's skill as
a portrait painter
can be seen in
this lifelike study,
which many believe
is a self-portrait.

DIPLOMATIC PAINTER

Van Eyck worked in Lille and Bruges for most of
his life, for private patrons as well as the Duke
of Burgundy. A well-educated man, he was sent by
the Duke on several diplomatic missions abroad.
Renowned for his skill as a portrait painter, he traveled
to Lisbon to paint the portrait of the Duke's future
wife, Isabella of Portugal. This was sensitive work,
as the Duke did not know what Isabella looked like.

METICULOUS DETAILS

Although only about 23 paintings have been
confirmed as by van Eyck alone, his influence
on other artists was huge. Many tried to copy
his lifelike, meticulous details, clear colors,
precise perspective, and brilliant light effects.
He finely layered translucent oil paints, which
he made by mixing pigments with linseed oil.
At the time, oil paints were revolutionary.
Van Eyck used them to paint with almost
invisible brushmarks.

LIFE STORY

1390–1395	1396–1421	1422–1425	1426–1430
Jan van Eyck is born in Maaseik, Belgium. His older brother, Hubert van Eyck, is about five years older than Jan.	Little is known about his childhood, but van Eyck learns to write in Latin, Greek, and Hebrew. He has two younger siblings, Lambert and Margareta.	Working in The Hague with his brother Hubert, van Eyck is employed by John of Bavaria as a court painter. From 1425, he works for Philip the Good, Duke of Burgundy.	Hubert van Eyck dies. From 1426 to 1429, Jan van Eyck undertakes secret commissions for Philip as an envoy of his court, for which he is paid well.

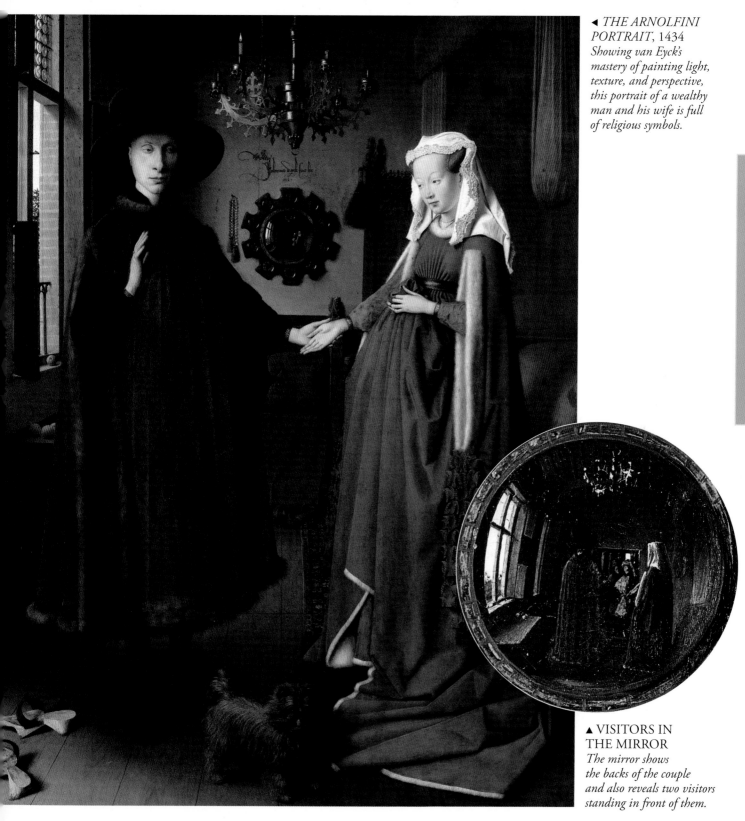

◄ THE ARNOLFINI
PORTRAIT, 1434
*Showing van Eyck's
mastery of painting light,
texture, and perspective,
this portrait of a wealthy
man and his wife is full
of religious symbols.*

▲ VISITORS IN
THE MIRROR
*The mirror shows
the backs of the couple
and also reveals two visitors
standing in front of them.*

1431–1432	1433–1434	1435–1436	1437–1441
In Philip's employ, van Eyck earns enough to run his own workshop. In 1432, he completes the Ghent Altarpiece started by Hubert.	Van Eyck develops new oil painting methods. In 1433, he completes *Man in a Turban,* and in 1434, *The Arnolfini Portrait.*	With his lifelike, detailed paintings, van Eyck becomes widely admired and achieves great fame. In 1435 and 1436, he produces some of his best work.	Van Eyck becomes a member of the prestigious Guild of St Luke in Tournai and runs a busy workshop in Bruges, but he dies soon after in 1441.

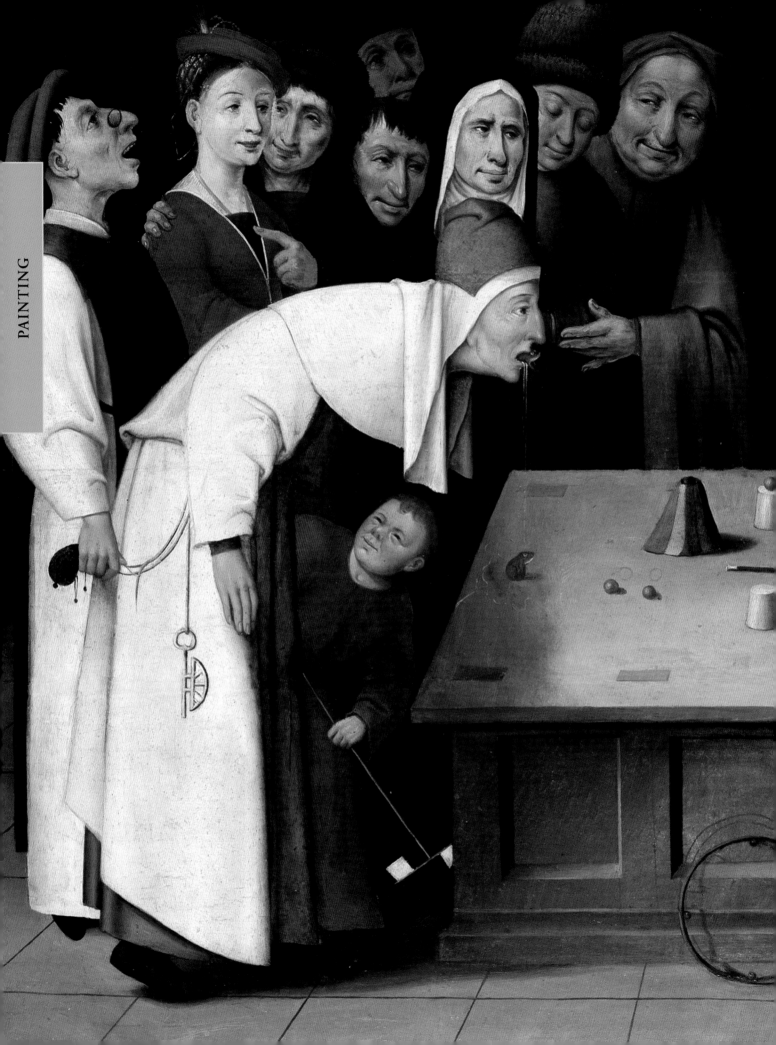

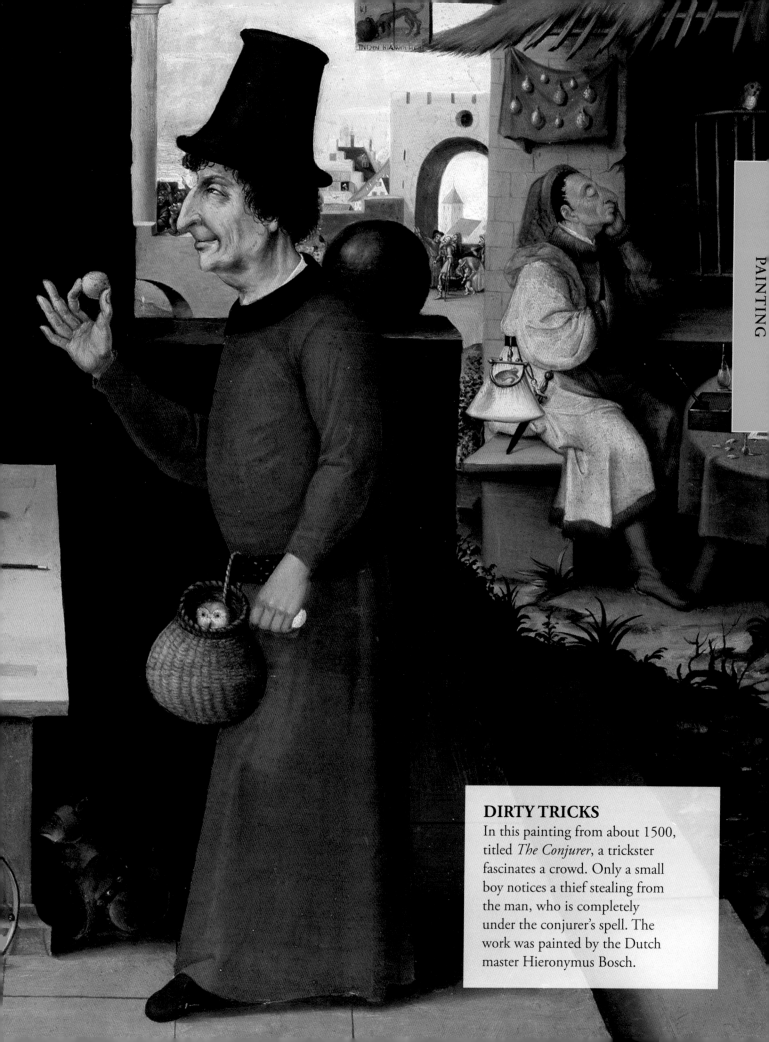

DIRTY TRICKS
In this painting from about 1500, titled *The Conjurer*, a trickster fascinates a crowd. Only a small boy notices a thief stealing from the man, who is completely under the conjurer's spell. The work was painted by the Dutch master Hieronymus Bosch.

CLOSER LOOK

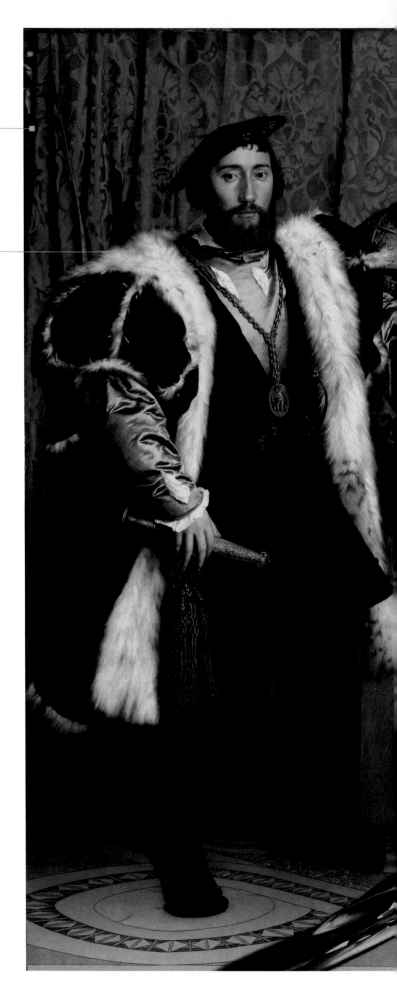

CRUCIFIX
In 16th-century Europe, people were very religious. They hung crucifixes on their walls to provide divine protection from diseases such as the plague.

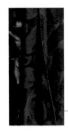

JEAN DE DINTEVILLE
The French ambassador to England, de Dinteville commissioned this painting. He wears an expensive sleeveless fur-lined coat.

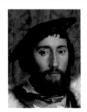

The Ambassadors

The Swiss-German painter and printmaker Hans Holbein worked at King Henry VIII's court in England for two long periods. One of the most accomplished portrait artists of the 16th century, Holbein painted *The Ambassadors* during his second stay in England. The painting depicts two rich Frenchmen at the English royal court.

HIDDEN MEANINGS

Holbein made this painting at a time of political rivalry between England and France. In addition, the French Church was divided. The objects surrounding the men symbolize different aspects of these political problems, and include an ingenious optical illusion.

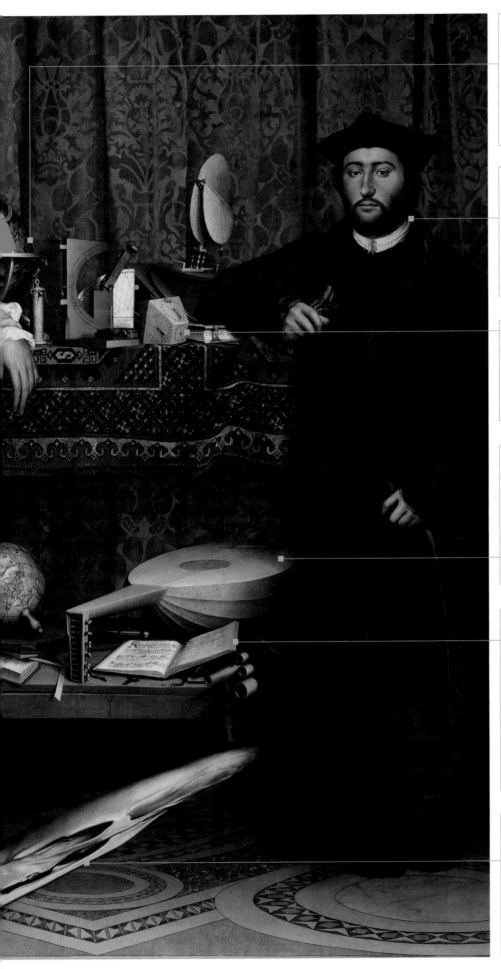

CELESTIAL SPHERE

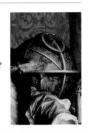

The objects on the upper shelf are concerned with the heavens. This celestial sphere shows the stars and planets, and suggest the quest for spiritual knowledge.

GEORGES DE SELVE

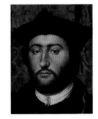

De Selve was the Bishop of Lavaur, and a friend of de Dinteville. On the book under his elbow is written his age: 25.

POLYHEDRAL SUNDIAL

An expensive instrument, this told the time by the shadows it cast. Only rich people owned polyhedral sundials.

LUTE

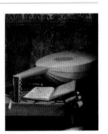

Objects on the lower shelf show the concerns of the world. This lute has a broken string, which suggests disagreements within the Church.

LUTHERAN PSALMBOOK

Open on pages that express aspects of Christianity upon which all factions agreed, this book may be a call for religious harmony.

SKULL

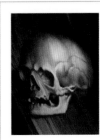

This strange shape is a distorted skull, warning of the inevitability of death. It can be seen in its correct proportions by standing to the right of the painting.

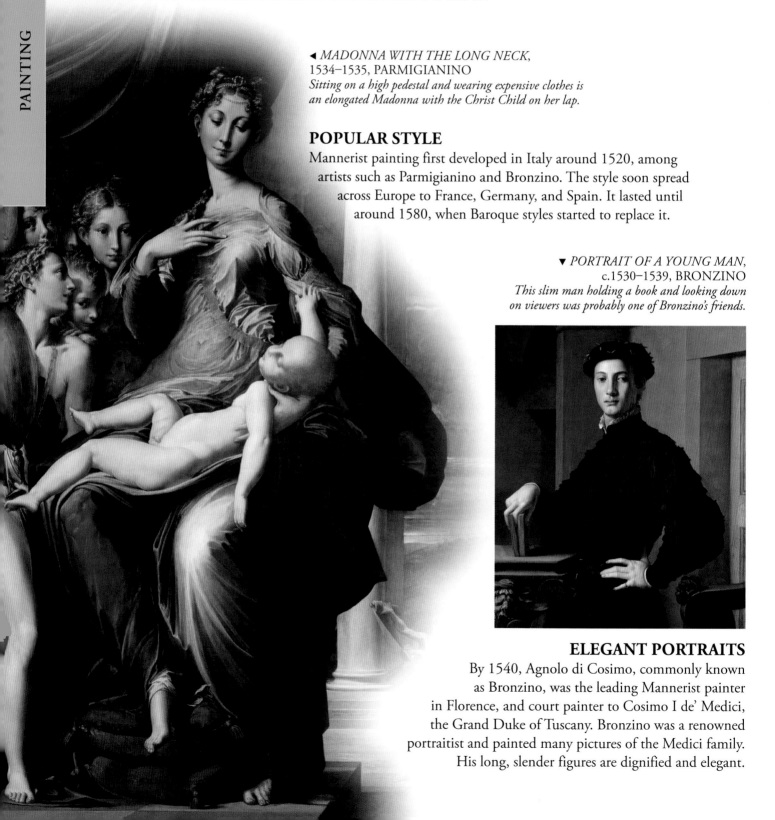

Mannerist styles

Mannerist artists deliberately stylized their paintings, elongating, distorting, or exaggerating figures for creative and emotional effects. The movement was named much later, so at the time, the artists who came to be called Mannerists did not have a label.

◀ *MADONNA WITH THE LONG NECK*,
1534–1535, PARMIGIANINO
Sitting on a high pedestal and wearing expensive clothes is an elongated Madonna with the Christ Child on her lap.

POPULAR STYLE

Mannerist painting first developed in Italy around 1520, among artists such as Parmigianino and Bronzino. The style soon spread across Europe to France, Germany, and Spain. It lasted until around 1580, when Baroque styles started to replace it.

▼ *PORTRAIT OF A YOUNG MAN*,
c.1530–1539, BRONZINO
This slim man holding a book and looking down on viewers was probably one of Bronzino's friends.

ELEGANT PORTRAITS

By 1540, Agnolo di Cosimo, commonly known as Bronzino, was the leading Mannerist painter in Florence, and court painter to Cosimo I de' Medici, the Grand Duke of Tuscany. Bronzino was a renowned portraitist and painted many pictures of the Medici family. His long, slender figures are dignified and elegant.

FRUITY COMPOSITIONS

As well as distorting things, Mannerists painted links between humans and the natural world. The Italian Mannerist Giuseppe Arcimboldo took this idea to an extreme by painting portraits made up entirely of items such as fruit, books, vegetables, or flowers. During the Renaissance, riddles and puzzles were very popular, and Arcimboldo's ingenious compositions were widely admired.

El Greco's extreme style made him unpopular in his lifetime. His work enjoyed fresh appreciation in the 20th century.

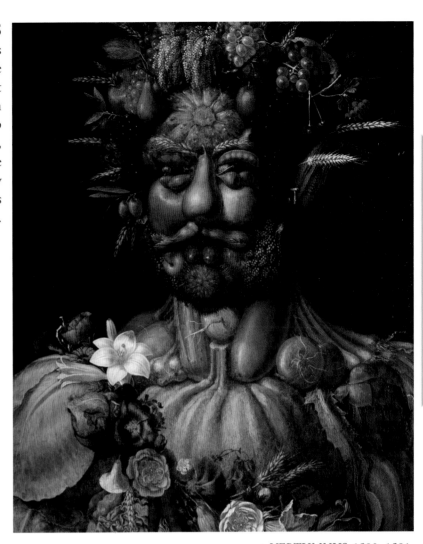

▲ *VERTUMNUS*, 1590–1591, GIUSEPPE ARCIMBOLDO
This portrait depicts the Holy Roman Emperor Rudolf II as Vertumnus, the Roman god of the seasons.

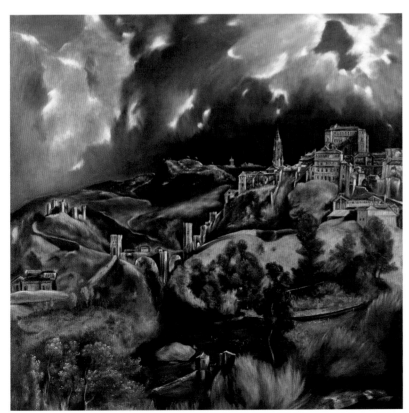

"THE GREEK"

Domenikos Theotokopoulos, commonly known by his nickname El Greco (Spanish for "The Greek"), was born in Crete, which was under Venetian rule at the time. He trained as an artist in Venice, where he developed his intense, distorted, and richly colored Mannerist style. By 1577, El Greco had moved to Spain, where he lived and worked for the rest of his life.

◄ *VIEW FROM TOLEDO*, 1596–1600, EL GRECO
Dramatic and atmospheric, this is the landscape from the city El Greco lived and worked in for most of his life.

Baroque and Rococo

From the 16th century, the Catholic Church fought back against the Protestant Reformation with a style of art designed to encourage people to stay with Catholicism. Full of emotion, action, and drama, the new style was called Baroque. By the beginning of the 18th century, in France this had evolved into a softer style called Rococo.

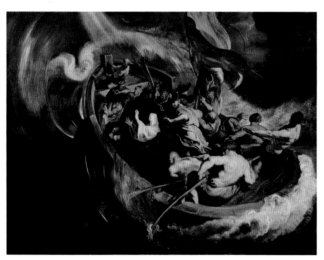

◄ *THE MIRACLE OF ST WALBURGA,* 1610, PETER PAUL RUBENS
Saint Walburga protects sailors against storms. This Flemish artist painted one of her miracles in a dynamic Baroque style.

TELLING TALES

Since most people in the 16th and 17th centuries could not read, the Church sought to tell its religious stories through art. Baroque paintings showed such tales, mainly taken from the Bible, in strong colors and tonal contrasts, and dramatic compositions.

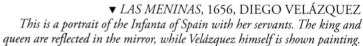

▼ *LAS MENINAS,* 1656, DIEGO VELÁZQUEZ
This is a portrait of the Infanta of Spain with her servants. The king and queen are reflected in the mirror, while Velázquez himself is shown painting.

Pablo Picasso made 58 paintings based on *Las Meninas*, playing with the composition by rearranging the figures in it.

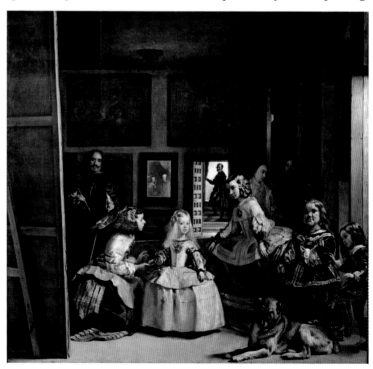

ARTISTS IN DEMAND

The Baroque style began in Italy, but soon spread across Europe. The greatest Baroque painters came from all parts of the continent, including Caravaggio in Italy, Rembrandt in the Netherlands, and Diego Velázquez in Spain. Their services were in high demand both from the Church and from royal patrons.

STONES AND SHELLS

The Rococo style began around 1715 in Paris. Contrasting with the dramatic Baroque styles, Rococo featured natural patterns, soft colors, and curving lines. The name comes from the French word *rocaille*, which means "stones and shells," due to the style's fondness for shell-like curves. Notable French Rococo artists include François Boucher, Jean-Antoine Watteau, and Jean-Honoré Fragonard.

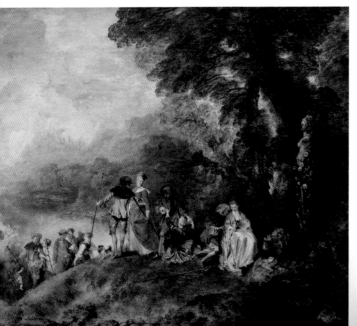

▲ *PILGRIMAGE TO THE ISLE OF CYTHERA,* 1717, JEAN-ANTOINE WATTEAU
This Rococo artist specialized in pictures of upper-class people enjoying outdoor parties and picnics—a type of painting he called "fêtes galantes."

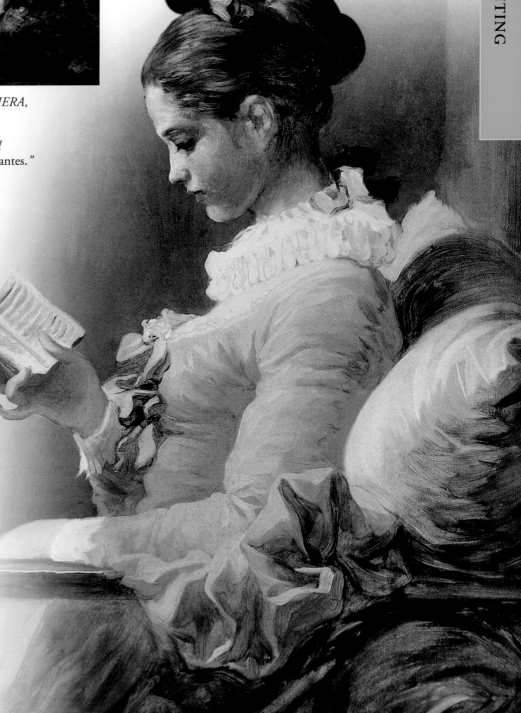

CHEERFUL BUT GRACEFUL

While Baroque paintings featured spectacular effects of light and shade, expressive brushwork, and thickly applied paint, Rococo paintings stressed soft, light colors, and gentle tonal contrasts. They were cheerful and graceful, often depicting wealthy people enjoying themselves or relaxing. Rococo subjects included imaginary landscapes, flattering portraits, or themes of love and romance.

▶ *A YOUNG GIRL READING,* 1776, JEAN-HONORÉ FRAGONARD
Rich and privileged, and dressed in expensive finery, this young lady relaxes, holding a book in her graceful hand.

Caravaggio

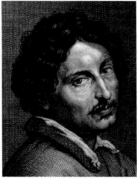

Orphaned from a young age, the Italian Caravaggio was the most revolutionary artist of his time. Abandoning traditional, accepted styles of art, he painted extremely realistically. He did not try to idealize (make perfect) his figures or religious events, but made them look as lifelike as he could, using a dramatic technique of intensely dark tones with vividly lit figures.

An etching of Caravaggio made after his death

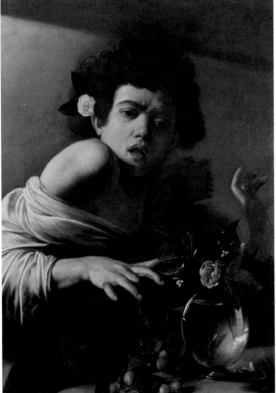

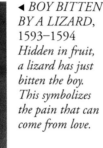

*◄ BOY BITTEN BY A LIZARD, 1593–1594
Hidden in fruit, a lizard has just bitten the boy. This symbolizes the pain that can come from love.*

HUMBLE MODELS

Caravaggio used poor people as his models and sometimes even himself, which upset many who thought that religious figures should be noble-looking and perfect. He also became known for his violent temper. In 1606, he accidentally killed a man and fled from Rome. He was later pardoned for the murder, but he was never forgiven for painting poor people as holy figures.

STRONG LIGHT

Caravaggio's dramatic painting technique used extremely dark shadows with small, brightly lit areas, usually coming from a single source of light. This is called tenebrism. He also used a similar, slightly less dramatic technique called chiaroscuro, with strong tonal contrast that makes his paintings appear very three-dimensional.

LIFE STORY

1571–1576	1577–1588	1592	1594–1596
Michelangelo Merisi da Caravaggio is born in Milan. In 1576, his family moves to the town of Caravaggio to escape the plague.	When Caravaggio is six, his father dies. Five years later, his mother dies. He is apprenticed to the artist Simone Peterzano in Milan for four years.	After a brawl, Caravaggio runs away from Milan. He reaches Rome with nothing, but soon earns money painting still lifes and figures.	Cardinal Francesco del M... hires Caravaggio, who sta... in the Cardinal's house, is paid a wage, and is given all his art supplies.

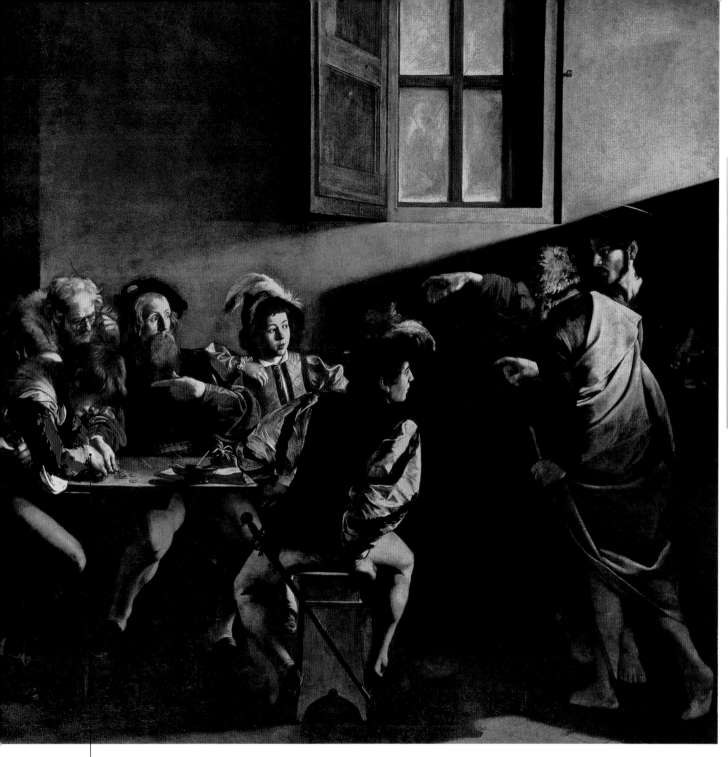

The figures are all dressed in regular clothing of the time. The models for the painting were ordinary people, and Caravaggio gives them subtle, lifelike features.

▲ *THE CALLING OF ST MATTHEW, 1599–1600*
This dramatically lit work made Caravaggio's career. Before he became an apostle, Matthew was a tax collector. As he counts his money, Jesus appears with Saint Peter and calls him.

1597–1601	1602–1607	1608–1609	1610
Caravaggio paints pictures about Saint Matthew for a church in Rome. They shock many, but also make him famous.	Caravaggio is imprisoned for fighting. After his release, he kills a man over a ball game. He flees to Naples, then Malta, and works for powerful patrons.	Despite great success, in 1608, Caravaggio is imprisoned after another fight, but he escapes to Sicily, then goes to Naples, where he is wounded in a fight in a tavern.	On hearing that he is to be pardoned, Caravaggio sails for Rome, but dies on the journey. Some believe that he was deliberately poisoned.

Baroque splendor

Blending the grandeur and realism of Renaissance art and the dynamic poses of Mannerism, Baroque paintings are dramatic, emotional, and energetic, made to impress people who saw them in churches or palaces. Baroque artists also painted grand-looking portraits for the upper and growing merchant classes.

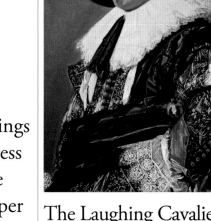

The Laughing Cavalier
A portrait to celebrate an engagement

- **Artist** Frans Hals
- **Date** 1624
- **Medium** Oil on canvas

In reality, neither laughing nor a cavalier, this 26-year-old man with a twinkle in his eye was Tieleman Roosterman, a cloth merchant. His embroidered silk doublet and lace collar and cuffs show that he was rich and fashionable. The embroidery on his doublet includes flaming torches, lover's knots, and bees, which were symbols of love and romance. These details suggest that this was probably an engagement portrait.

The Butcher's Shop
A gory religious allegory

- **Artist** Annibale Carracci
- **Date** Early 1580s
- **Medium** Oil on canvas

Although this painting appears to represent a scene from everyday life, it symbolizes the sin of temptation, which is a religious theme. As if on a stage, the figures and objects face the viewers, revealing the gory details of the slaughtered animals. This Italian artist painted using direct observation to heighten the realism of his work. His treatment of light and shadows enhances the sense that this is a real scene.

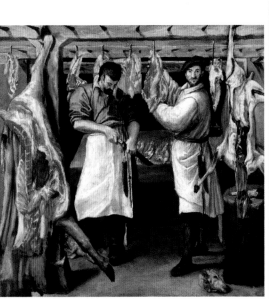
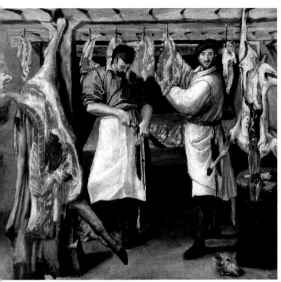

The Allegory of Painting
A work by an Italian in the English court

- **Artist** Artemisia Gentileschi
- **Date** c.1638–1639
- **Medium** Oil on canvas

In 1638, the Italian artist Artemisia visited London on the invitation of King Charles I. She probably painted this self-portrait while in England. She holds a brush in one hand and a palette in the other, and shows herself painting. As a working artist, Artemisia was unusual at a time when women rarely had jobs.

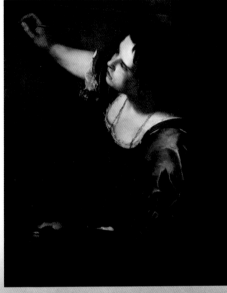

The Adoration of the Shepherds
Dramatic lighting in the manner of Caravaggio

- **Artist** Guido Reni
- **Date** 1640
- **Medium** Oil on canvas

In this brightly lit nativity scene, the source of all light is the baby Jesus himself, illuminating the face of every figure that is looking at him. The Italian artist Reni was in great demand during his lifetime for works depicting biblical or mythological scenes. His dramatic use of lighting shows the clear influence of Caravaggio.

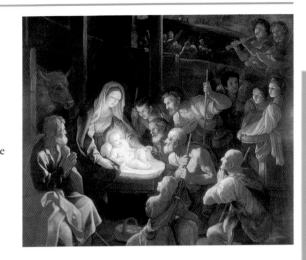

The Frozen Thames
An icy scene by a Dutch artist working in London

- **Artist** Abraham Hondius
- **Date** 1677
- **Medium** Oil on canvas

Hondius was a Dutch Golden Age painter whose dramatic works were influenced by the Baroque style. Born in Rotterdam, the Netherlands, Hondius moved to London in 1666, and stayed there for the rest of his life. During that period the Thames river froze over every winter and lively fairs were held on it.

▼ DANGEROUS FUN
On the edge of the Thames river in London, with the old London Bridge in the distance, people are skating, sliding, and even shooting on the ice.

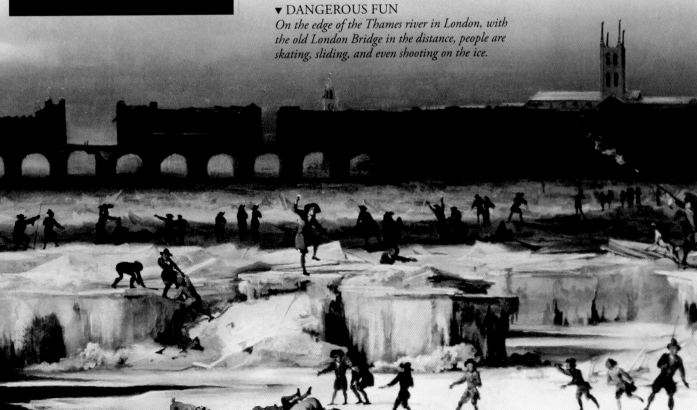

Las Hilanderas

Translated as "The Spinners," this work was painted between 1655 and 1660 by the Spanish artist Diego Velázquez. It tells a Greek myth about a weaving contest between a mortal, Arachne, and Athena, the goddess of wisdom, war, and crafts.

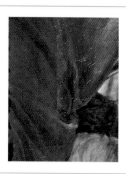

TEXTURES AND TECHNIQUES
To create extra vibrancy, Velázquez painted orange first and then applied the final colors on top. He first used thin paint, then covered this layer with thicker paint to create textures.

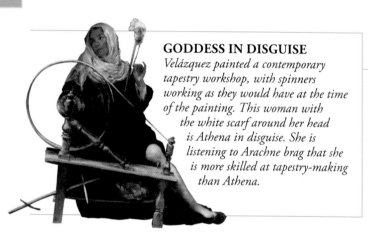

GODDESS IN DISGUISE
Velázquez painted a contemporary tapestry workshop, with spinners working as they would have at the time of the painting. This woman with the white scarf around her head is Athena in disguise. She is listening to Arachne brag that she is more skilled at tapestry-making than Athena.

THE CONTEST
The fable tells how Athena challenges Arachne to a contest to make the best tapestry, after which the loser will never weave again. Athena's tapestry shows what happens to those who defy the gods, while Arachne's tells stories about Zeus, the King of the Gods. Although beautifully made, Arachne's tapestry insults Zeus, and she loses the contest.

EARTHY TONES
Velázquez used a limited palette of earthy colors. For basic red, he used a pigment called burnt sienna, while yellow ochre pigment was his yellow. He also used an orange-red and French ultramarine, which is a bright, deep blue.

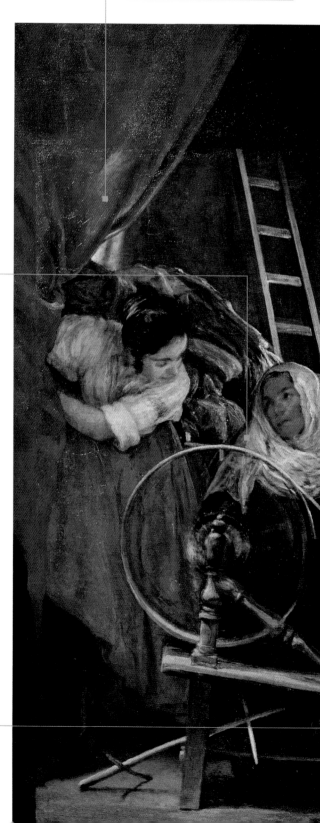

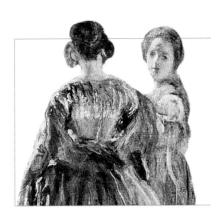

THE TAPESTRY
Velázquez painted another part of the myth in the background. The figures are dressed in contemporary 17th-century fashions. Athena wears her helmet of war as she argues with Arachne, whose tapestry angers her.

STICKY END
Arachne sits weaving. But after the contest, Athena rips her tapestry, destroys her loom, and slashes her face. Arachne kills herself, but Athena brings her back to life as a spider, and decrees that she and her descendants will weave forever.

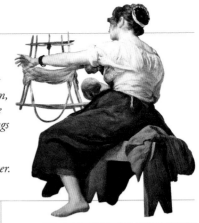

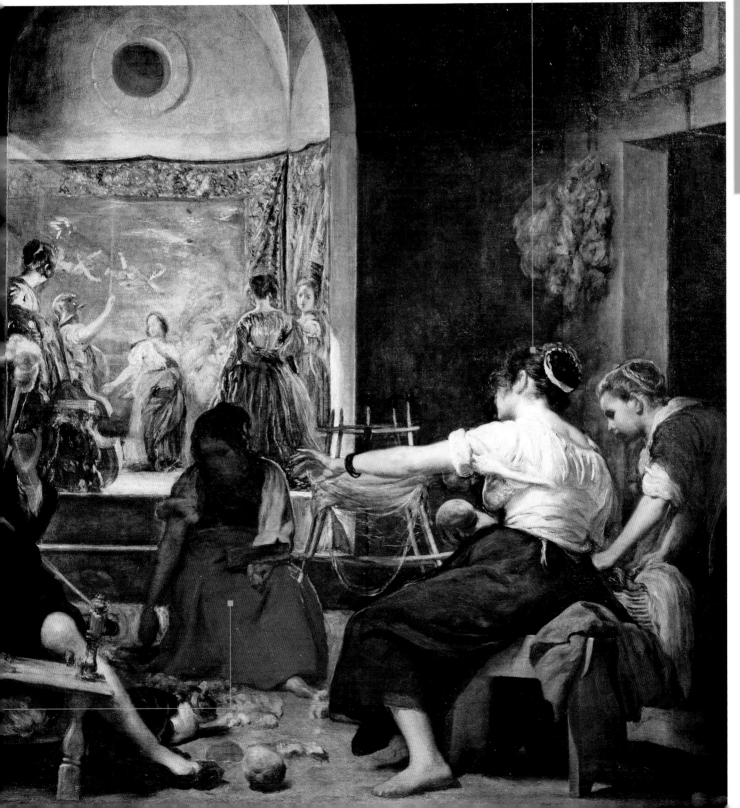

Rococo decoration

Moving away from the excessive Baroque designs that were typical of King Louis XIV's reign, the decorative Rococo style first flourished in France from the start of King Louis XV's reign in 1715. Rococo paintings were less serious and dramatic than Baroque ones, and usually significantly smaller.

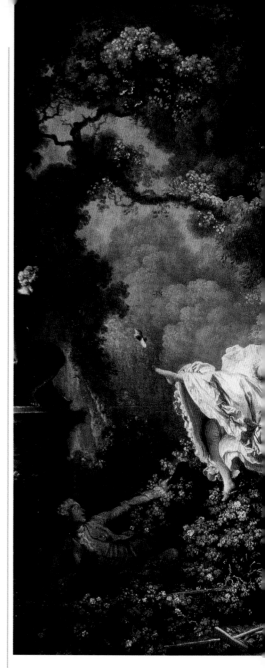

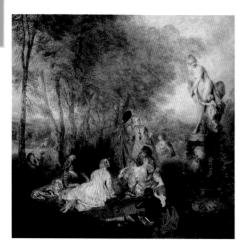

The Feast of Love
A painting of couples in a meadow

- **Artist** Jean-Antoine Watteau
- **Date** 1718–1719
- **Medium** Oil on canvas

This French artist invented a new Rococo style called *fêtes galantes*, or "elegant parties," which were softly colored scenes like this one of fashionably dressed people on country outings. Here, a group of wealthy young people have traveled to the woods in order to enjoy a romantic picnic.

Madame de Pompadour
The influential mistress of the king

- **Artist** François Boucher
- **Date** 1759
- **Medium** Oil on canvas

Intelligent and influential, Madame de Pompadour was the mistress of Louis XV and helped make Rococo style fashionable. She commissioned the greatest artists of the time to paint her portrait in order to show her strength and power. When she sat for this portrait, she was one of the king's main political advisors. She also commissioned Boucher to paint several other Rococo paintings.

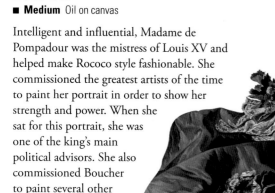

The Swing
A playful but controversial image

- **Artist** Jean-Honoré Fragonard
- **Date** 1767
- **Medium** Oil on canvas

Influenced by Watteau and Boucher, Fragonard was a prolific French Rococo painter. In his fluid, frothy style, he painted lively figures, often in gardens. This is his most famous painting, of a young lady on a swing. She is being pushed by the man standing behind her with his arms outstretched. Another man lies in front of her and admires her legs, a shocking image in those days, when women's legs were usually hidden under long skirts.

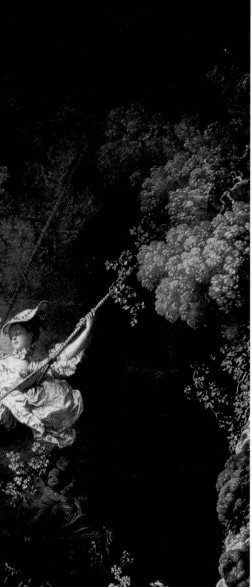

Lady Smith and her Children

A soft, curvy English Rococo style

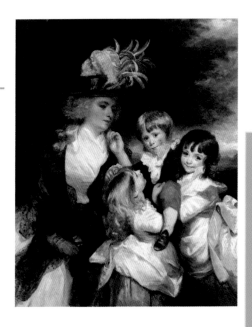

- **Artist** Sir Joshua Reynolds
- **Date** 1787
- **Medium** Oil on canvas

The Rococo style spread across Europe. In England, Joshua Reynolds, Thomas Gainsborough, and Élisabeth Vigée Le Brun all painted in delicate Rococo styles, including softly flattering portraits using loose brushmarks and curvy shapes, as seen here. Pictured is Charlotte, the wife of a member of Parliament, and their children, George Henry, Louisa, and Charlotte.

▶ MASKED THEATER

These two actors are dressed as Pulcinella, a popular character in Italian masked theater.

Pulcinella with Acrobats

A detail of a lively fantasy scene

- **Artist** Giovanni Domenico Tiepolo
- **Date** 1793
- **Medium** Fresco

This is a small detail from a fresco painted by the Italian artist Tiepolo that shows acrobats and actors entertaining a crowd. Tiepolo was known for his theatrical paintings, which often featured Pulcinella, a character who poked fun at those in power.

93

Dutch Golden Age

During the 17th century, great advances were made in the Netherlands in trade, science, and art. Dutch painters developed new techniques and styles, and increasingly painted ordinary people and everyday life rather than religious works. The period has become known as the Dutch Golden Age.

As foreign goods appeared in the Netherlands, a new form of still life developed, showing tables loaded with exotic food.

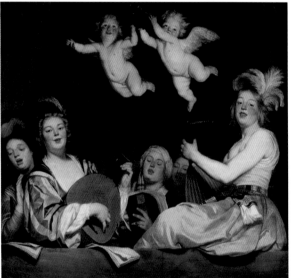

◄ *THE CONCERT*, 1623, GERRIT VAN HONTHORST
Noted for his use of light, this artist followed Caravaggio's ideas.

CITIES AND STYLES

Artists in different cities developed distinct styles, specialities, and subjects. With its huge wealth from trade, Amsterdam was the largest artistic center in the Netherlands, and portraits were in great demand there. In Utrecht, a group of artists painted using chiaroscuro, inspired by the Italian painter Caravaggio, while a new ornate style of still life developed in Antwerp.

TIME OF UNREST

In the 17th century, religious and political unrest divided the region into two nations. Flanders (now part of Belgium) remained Catholic, while the Netherlands became a Protestant republic. Aelbert Cuyp's painting below shows Dutch soldiers gathering to fight for independence from Spain.

▼ *THE MAAS AT DORDRECHT*, c.1650, AELBERT CUYP
In 1646, 30,000 Dutch soldiers gathered in a show of force to Spain in Cuyp's home town of Dordrecht.

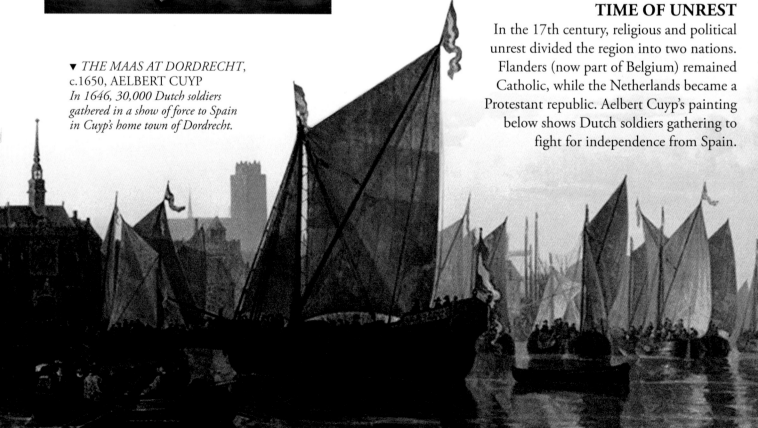

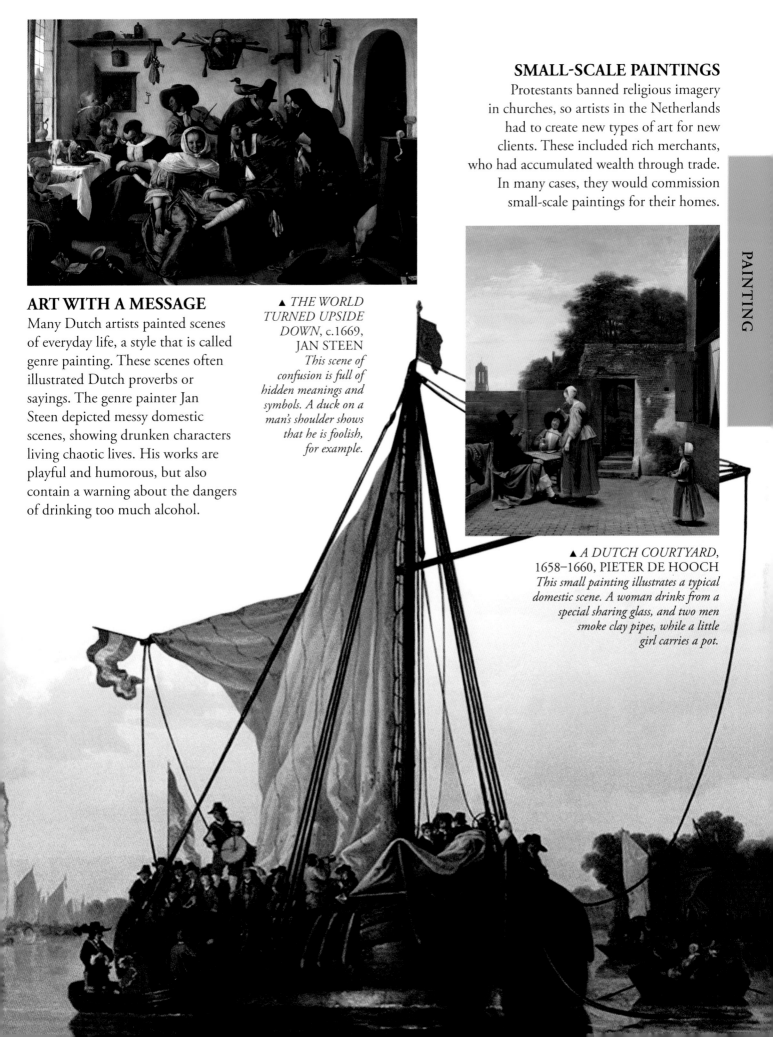

SMALL-SCALE PAINTINGS

Protestants banned religious imagery in churches, so artists in the Netherlands had to create new types of art for new clients. These included rich merchants, who had accumulated wealth through trade. In many cases, they would commission small-scale paintings for their homes.

ART WITH A MESSAGE

Many Dutch artists painted scenes of everyday life, a style that is called genre painting. These scenes often illustrated Dutch proverbs or sayings. The genre painter Jan Steen depicted messy domestic scenes, showing drunken characters living chaotic lives. His works are playful and humorous, but also contain a warning about the dangers of drinking too much alcohol.

▲ *THE WORLD TURNED UPSIDE DOWN*, c.1669, JAN STEEN
This scene of confusion is full of hidden meanings and symbols. A duck on a man's shoulder shows that he is foolish, for example.

▲ *A DUTCH COURTYARD*, 1658–1660, PIETER DE HOOCH
This small painting illustrates a typical domestic scene. A woman drinks from a special sharing glass, and two men smoke clay pipes, while a little girl carries a pot.

Johannes Vermeer

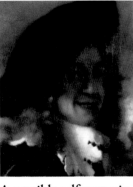

A possible self-portrait of Vermeer

There were many highly skilled painters during the Dutch Golden Age, but the two most famous are Rembrandt and Johannes, or Jan, Vermeer. Vermeer's works are incredibly lifelike, often portraying middle-class interiors in close detail, with clear, atmospheric light. He made most of his paintings in his own house.

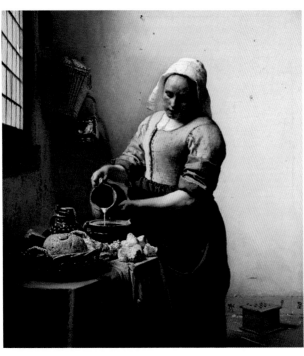

▲ *THE MILKMAID*, 1658
It is believed that Vermeer used an instrument called a camera obscura to study his subjects closely and produce the details seen here.

PERFECTIONIST

Vermeer spent his whole life in the town of Delft, working as both an artist and art dealer. Exceptionally skillful, he was also a perfectionist and worked extremely slowly. When he died aged 43, he left 11 children, and only 35 completed paintings. Highly respected by other artists, Vermeer's brushmarks are almost invisible, and he captured minute details in dim or bright light.

▶ *GIRL WITH A PEARL EARRING*, 1665
The focal point of this painting is a glinting pearl earring. Touches of white paint capture effects of light falling on different areas, such as the girl's headscarf.

A DETAILED VISION

Painting directly what he saw, Vermeer made painstakingly small brushstrokes to visually describe exact details. He used the Renaissance method of chiaroscuro to create contrasts between light and shade, and bought some of the most expensive pigments to create exactly the right effect.

LIFE STORY

1632	1650–1652	1653	1654–1658
Johannes Vermeer is born in Delft, the Netherlands. His father is an art dealer, but we know little else about his childhood.	It is not clear who trained Vermeer. He may have been taught by the Dutch artists Carel Fabritius or Abraham Bloemaert. Or he may have taught himself.	Vermeer manages to join the Guild of Saint Luke, an important association of painters. He marries Catharina Bolenes and becomes a Catholic.	The art dealer Pieter van Ruijven begins buying Vermeer's paintings. In 1657–1658, he produces two paintings, *The Little Street* and *The Milkmaid*.

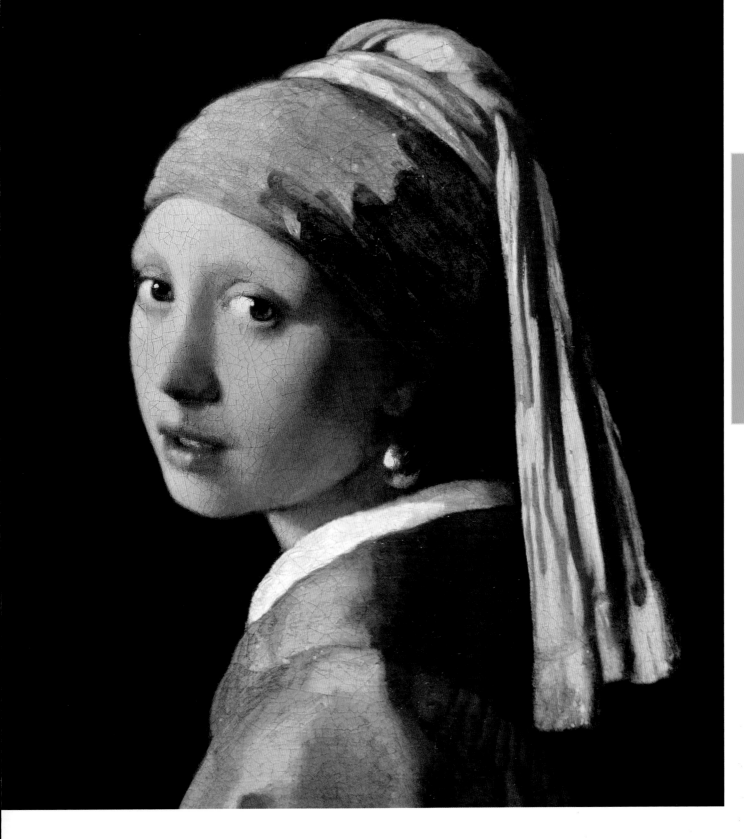

1659–1664	1665	1666–1672	1673–1675
Vermeer and his family live in the house of his mother-in-law, Maria Thins. In 1662, he is made chairman of the Guild of Saint Luke.	He paints *Girl with a Pearl Earring*. Van Ruijven and his wife leave him money in their will, suggesting their close friendship and respect for Vermeer.	Vermeer paints *The Art of Painting*, *The Astronomer*, and *The Geographer*. At war with France and England, the Netherlands suffers financially.	As a result of the economic crisis, Vermeer cannot sell his art and faces poverty. In December 1675, he dies after a short illness.

Scenes of everyday life

Dutch Golden Age artists used many of the same techniques as Baroque artists to create dramatic effects. However, while Baroque paintings were dramatic and grand, Dutch painters chose to portray scenes of everyday life, known as genre painting. It was also in this period that Dutch artists created the first landscape paintings in European art.

Ice Scene

Everyday scene in a winter landscape

- **Artist** Hendrick Avercamp
- **Date** 1610
- **Medium** Oil on wood panel

Amsterdam-born artist Hendrick Avercamp was one of the first 17th-century Dutch landscape painters. He specialized in painting winter scenes such as this one, with people having fun on a frozen river, skating, sledging, and playing games. Some people have fallen through the ice, and a man with a stick is playing a form of ice golf.

Serenade

A work by a rare female artist of the period

- **Artist** Judith Leyster
- **Date** 1629
- **Medium** Oil on wood panel

Leyster went against the conventions of her time and worked for her living, even after marriage. She painted genre works, portraits, and still lifes. This singing lute-player is painted in chiaroscuro, with a light source to the left of the painting, and is seen from below. Using small brushmarks, Leyster depicted the fine details in his colorful clothing.

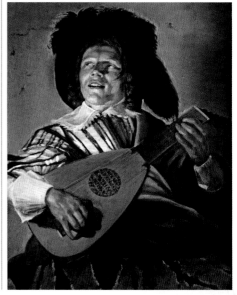

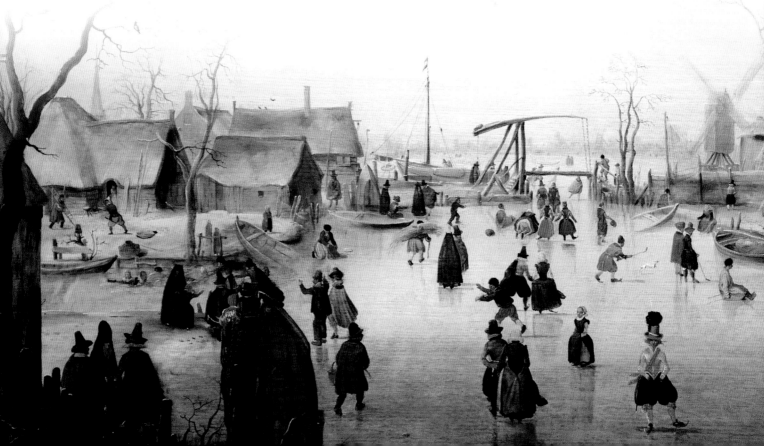

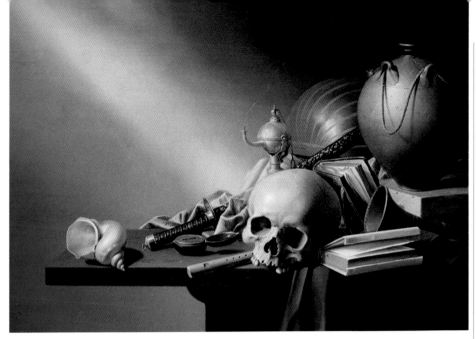

The Old Drinker
A small but detailed work

- **Artist** Gabriël Metsu
- **Date** c.1661–1663
- **Medium** Oil on wood panel

This painter from Leiden specialized in genre scenes. The number of drinks this old man has consumed are marked on the slate behind him. Like many Dutch Golden Age painters, Metsu used wooden panels rather than canvases, which allowed extra precision in small works—this one measures 9 x 8 in (22 x 20 cm).

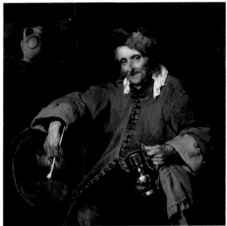

An Allegory of the Vanities of Human Life
Still life with a message

- **Artist** Harmen Steenwyck
- **Date** c.1640
- **Medium** Oil on oak panel

Steenwyck worked in Delft and became the leading painter of a subject called "vanitas," which emphasizes the shortness of life and the pointlessness of vanity. The books represent knowledge, musical instruments show worldly pleasures, and the shell symbolizes wealth, while the skull reminds the viewer of the inevitability of death.

▼ PAINTING
FROM SKETCHES
Avercamp painted this scene in his studio based on sketches he had made earlier.

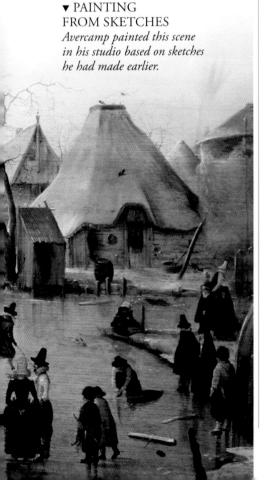

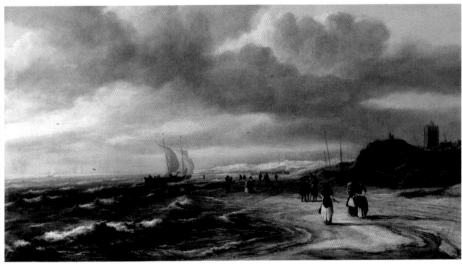

The Shore at Egmond-aan-Zee
A revolutionary style of landscape painting

- **Artist** Jacob van Ruisdael
- **Date** c.1675
- **Medium** Oil on canvas

Landscape was a new genre that began in the Netherlands and had a big influence on later art movements. Never before in European art had landscape been the main focus of a painting. This work, by one of the most celebrated landscape artists of the period, explores the forces of nature and themes of sea, sky, weather, and light.

Rembrandt

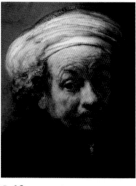

Considered by many to be the greatest Dutch painter of all time, Rembrandt van Rijn's works were innovative and expressive. Born in Leiden in the Netherlands, his paintings made him famous by the age of 19. His works depict a very wide range of subject matter, including self-portraits, biblical scenes, and landscapes.

Self-portrait
aged 55

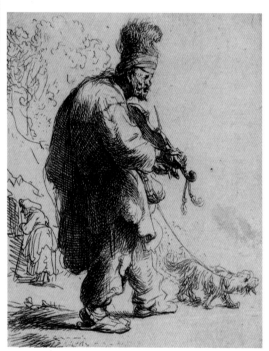

▲ *THE BLIND FIDDLER*, 1631
This is an etching, a form of print made by drawing on a copper plate with a needle.

PERSONALITY AND EMOTION

When he was 25, Rembrandt moved to Amsterdam and word of his talent quickly spread. He was soon taking commissions from aristocrats and royalty. Over his life, he also painted more than 40 self-portraits. In all his artworks, including his etchings, he used strong contrasts in shade, known as chiaroscuro, to enhance his subjects' personalities and emotions.

CHANGING FORTUNES

For more than 20 years, Rembrandt was the leading portrait painter of the richest families in Amsterdam, then the wealthiest city in Europe. In 1642, the year in which he finished his best-known work, *The Night Watch*, his young wife died. Grief-stricken and lonely, his paintings became darker and sketchier, with thicker paint and brushmarks, which make his later works look strikingly modern.

LIFE STORY

1606–1623	1624–1630	1631–1634	1635–1639
Rembrandt is born in Leiden, the Netherlands. At 13, he enrolls at Leiden University, but is soon apprenticed to a painter.	For six months, in 1624–1625, Rembrandt studies with artists in Amsterdam. At 19, he shares a studio with the artist Jan Lievens.	Rembrandt moves to Amsterdam where he is in great demand. In 1634, he marries Saskia van Uylenburgh.	Rembrandt pain and religious pic as portraits. Ma success, he and a big house in a

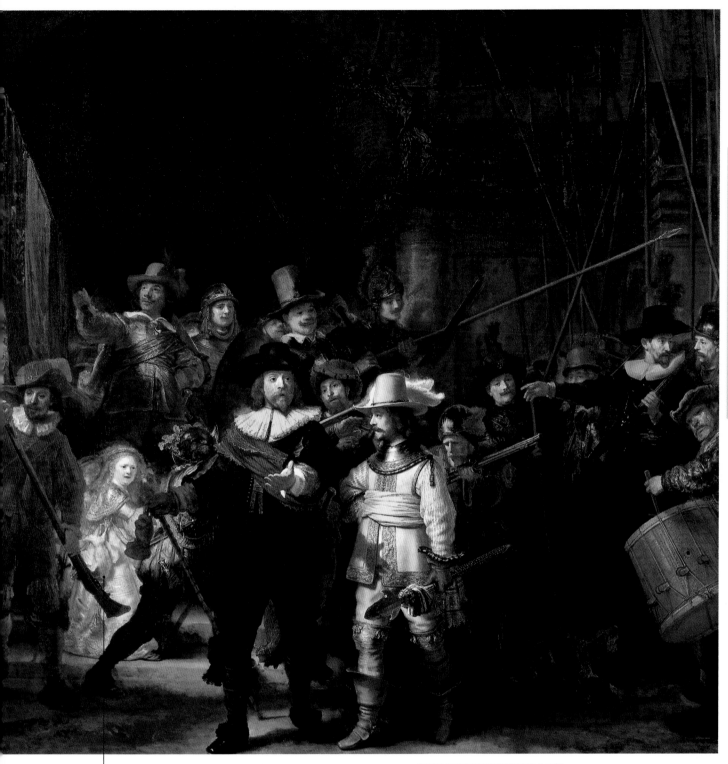

The girl in the gold dress is the mascot (a person who brings luck) of the guardsmen in the portrait.

▲ *THE NIGHT WATCH, 1642*
Two guardsmen lead their men in an informal group portrait that strongly conveys motion.

1642	1646–1655	1656	1658–1669
Saskia dies, leaving their baby son Titus and a will that says Rembrandt must not remarry. He paints the masterly *The Night Watch*.	Rembrandt employs Hendrickje Stoffels as a housekeeper. She becomes his mistress and model and poses for works such as *Bathsheba at her Bath* (1654).	As Rembrandt and Hendrickje are not married, they are shunned. His work falls out of favor. He spends unwisely, and is declared bankrupt.	Rembrandt's troubles continue and his house is sold. In 1663, Hendrickje dies. In 1669, Rembrandt dies at 63 and is buried in a poor man's grave.

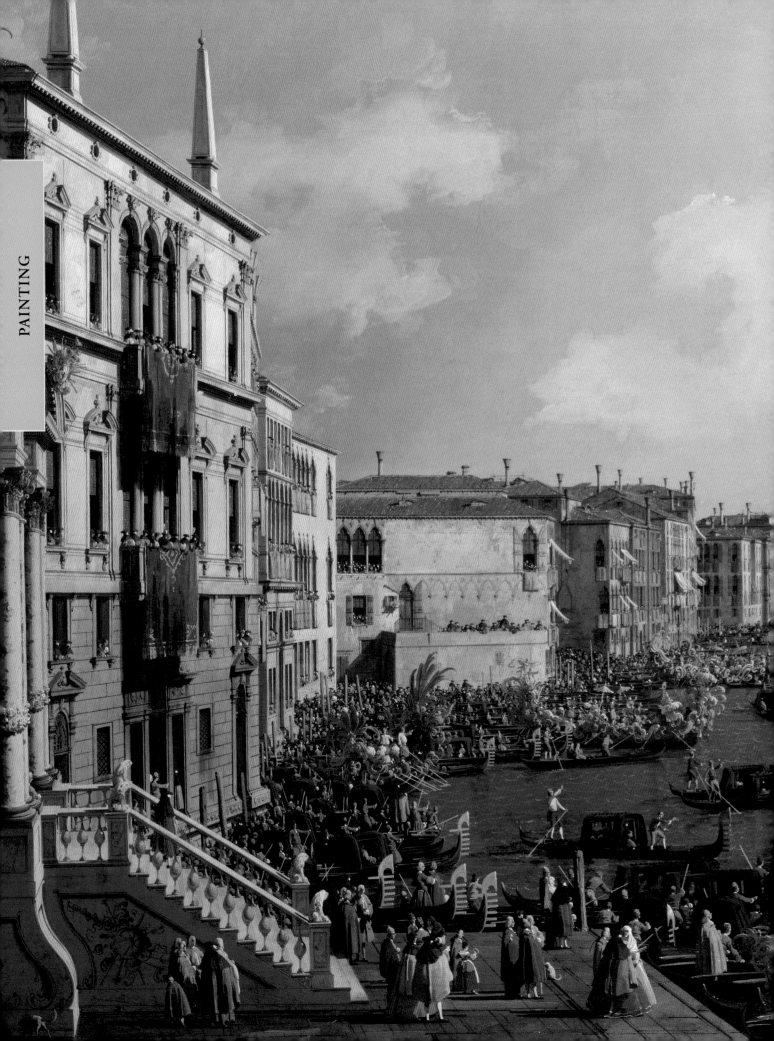

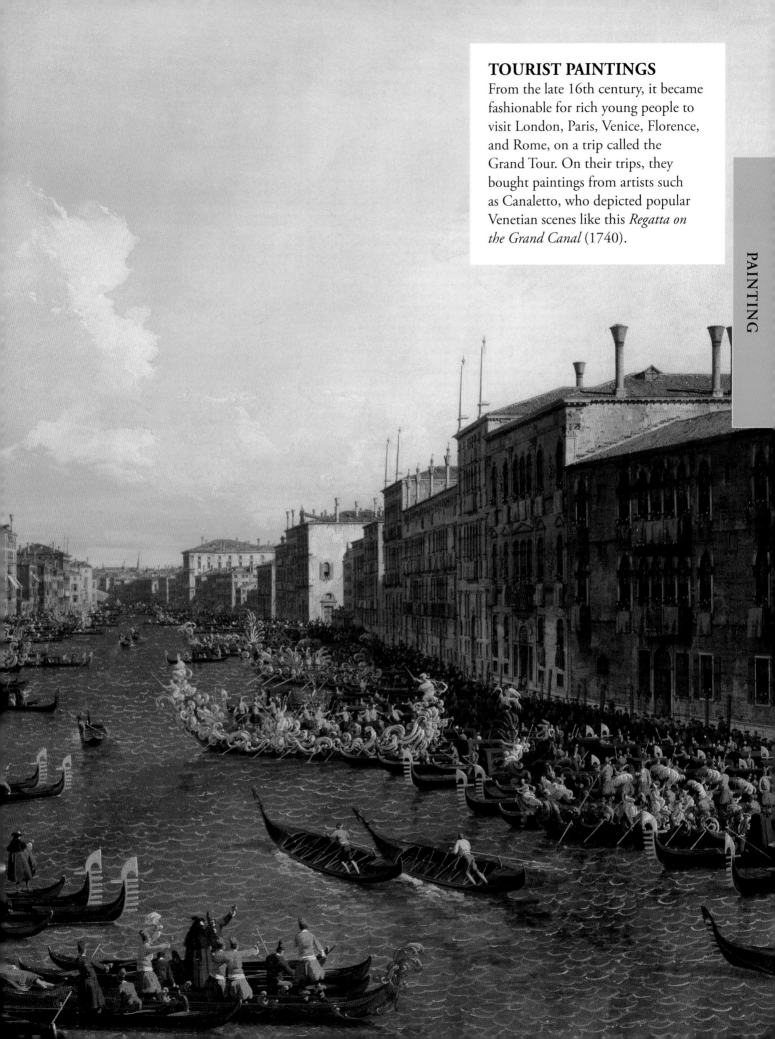

TOURIST PAINTINGS
From the late 16th century, it became fashionable for rich young people to visit London, Paris, Venice, Florence, and Rome, on a trip called the Grand Tour. On their trips, they bought paintings from artists such as Canaletto, who depicted popular Venetian scenes like this *Regatta on the Grand Canal* (1740).

Tales of bravery

In the late 18th century, an art movement developed in Europe that was inspired by ancient Roman and Greek forms, from paintings to buildings. Called Neoclassicism (New Classicism), its subject matter included tales of courage, heroism, and loyalty.

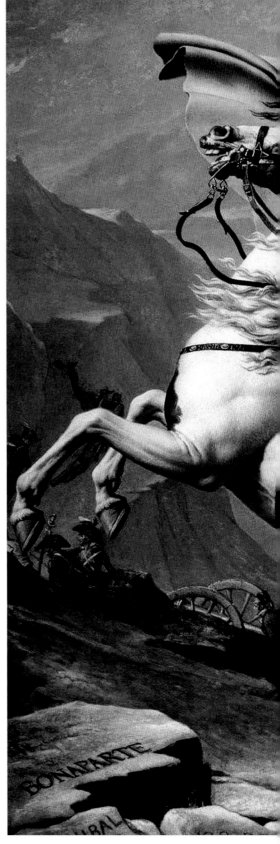

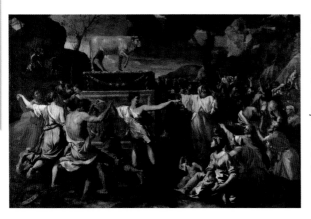

◄ *ADORATION OF THE GOLDEN CALF*, c.1634, NICOLAS POUSSIN
Here visualizing a moral tale about idol-worship from the Bible's Old Testament, Poussin was a major influence on Neoclassical painters more than 100 years later.

FINDING INSPIRATION

While Baroque art had expressed religious themes, Neoclassical painters depicted revolutionary stories. However, both movements sought to tell a moral tale. Whether it was the French Baroque artist Nicolas Poussin portraying scenes from the Bible, or Neoclassical art students looking to ancient Greece or Rome, artists from each movement looked to the past for inspiration.

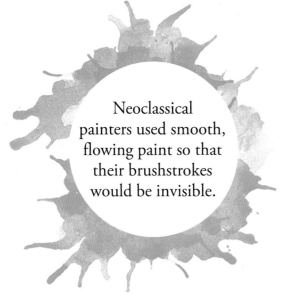

Neoclassical painters used smooth, flowing paint so that their brushstrokes would be invisible.

► *NAPOLEON CROSSING THE ALPS*, 1805, JACQUES-LOUIS DAVID
Napoleon is shown in a heroic pose on his rearing horse as he and his army enter Italy from France in 1800.

THE EMPIRE STYLE

The Neoclassical style was especially popular in France, where it captured the mood of the French Revolution (1789–1799). Later, it was promoted by Napoleon Bonaparte, who was Emperor of France between 1804 and 1814, and again in 1815. During his reign, art was used to tell heroic stories that celebrated French power; this became known as the Empire style.

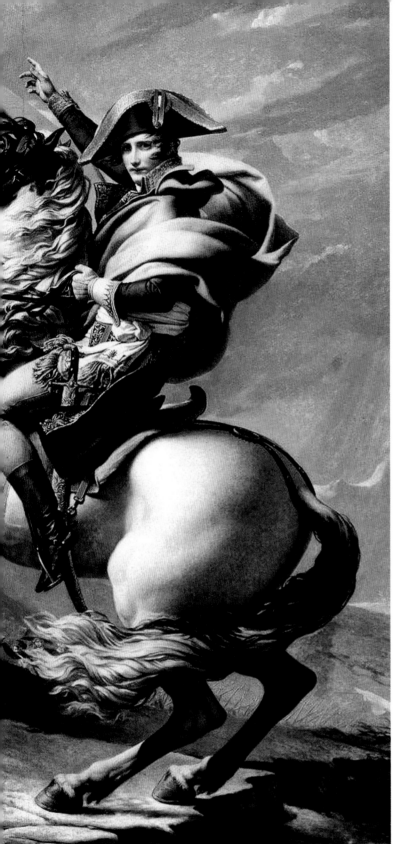

▼ *PARIS ABDUCTING HELEN,*
c.1784, GAVIN HAMILTON
Based on Homer's Greek epic The Iliad, *this painting shows the capture of Helen of Troy during the Trojan War, a favorite theme in ancient Greek and Roman art.*

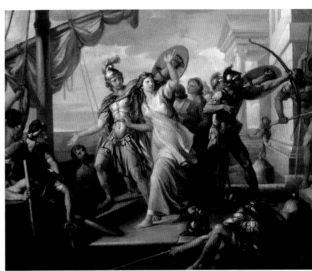

SEEKING NEW IDEALS

During the 18th century, an intellectual movement called the Enlightenment introduced a new way of thinking that promoted equality, liberty, and tolerance. These ideas inspired Neoclassical artists, such as Gavin Hamilton from Scotland, to recapture what they considered to be the simplicity and moral superiority of ancient Roman and Greek art.

▼ *OEDIPUS AND THE SPHINX,* 1806–1827, JEAN-AUGUSTE-DOMINIQUE INGRES
Oedipus, a tragic hero of ancient Greek mythology, is the subject of this French Neoclassical painting.

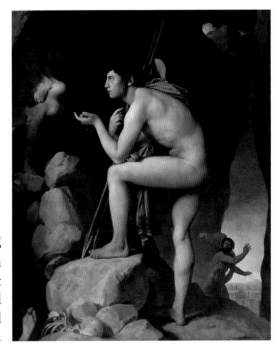

ROMAN STYLE

In 79 CE, the ancient Roman cities of Pompeii and Herculaneum were buried in lava following a huge volcanic eruption. In the first half of the 18th century, archaeologists excavated the cities and found artworks preserved under the volcanic ash. The scenes of mythical heroes painted by the Romans inspired many Neoclassical artists.

Roman inspiration

As artists sought inspiration from newly discovered ancient artworks in Italy, Rome became a popular destination for writers and artists in the 18th century. For French artists in particular, visiting Italy was seen as an important part of their artistic education. As the Neoclassical style developed, time spent studying at the prestigious Academy in Rome was highly prized.

Johann Joachim Winckelmann

Influential archaeologist and art historian

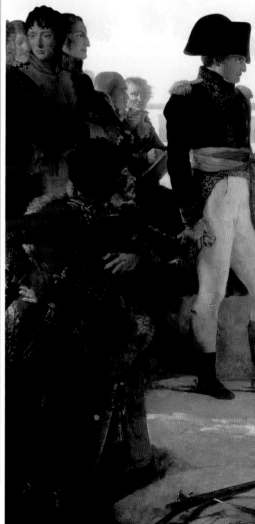

- **Artist** Anton von Maron
- **Date** 1768
- **Medium** Oil on canvas

German writer Johann Joachim Winckelmann was a huge influence on Neoclassical painters. His book *The History of Ancient Art*, published in 1764, explained in detail the differences between the periods of ancient Greek and Roman art. The Austrian portraitist von Maron painted this picture shortly before Winckelmann died.

Arcadian Shepherds

Life in an idealized landscape

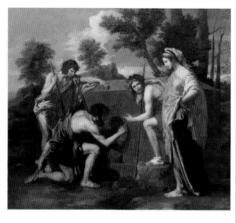

- **Artist** Nicolas Poussin
- **Date** 1639
- **Medium** Oil on canvas

This French Baroque painter spent most of his career in Rome, painting colorful and classically inspired subjects. Poussin's style and subject matter were highly influential on later French Neoclassical artists. Here, three shepherds and a statue-like woman stand around a large stone tomb. The natural setting and their ancient style of clothing show that they are in "arcadia"—a mythical Greek harmonious landscape.

▼ MERCIFUL LEADER
Napoleon is shown standing in front of rebels he has beaten in battle in Egypt. The image was intended to make the French people feel proud.

Ferdinand IV of Naples

Royal subject

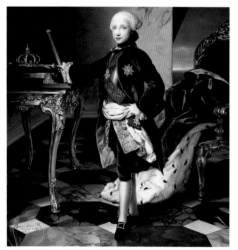

- **Artist** Anton Raphael Mengs
- **Date** 1760
- **Medium** Oil on canvas

German-born Mengs was one of the first Neoclassical painters. He was in demand across Europe, as many aristocrats wanted portraits painted in his noble Neoclassical style. Shown here is Ferdinand IV, the third son of King Charles III of Spain. He is pictured shortly after he was made King of Naples in 1759, at just nine years old.

Self-portrait with Daughter

A mix of Rococo and Neoclassical styles

- **Artist** Élisabeth Vigée Le Brun
- **Date** 1786
- **Medium** Oil on wood

Vigée Le Brun was a French painter who worked at the end of the Rococo period, but used Neoclassical styles. Her models (including herself in this painting) often wore ancient Roman-style clothes. Extremely successful, she became portrait painter to the French queen Marie-Antoinette.

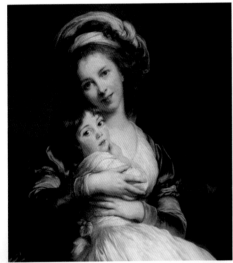

Princess Vittorina Spinola

Mixing potraiture with landscape painting

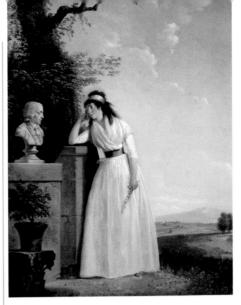

- **Artist** Jacques Sablet
- **Date** 1792
- **Medium** Oil on canvas

The Swiss-French artist Sablet started his career as a historical painter. However, he lacked the training of rival historical painters, such as Jacques-Louis David, and struggled to win commissions. Sablet switched instead to portraiture and landscapes, and his sympathetic style won admirers across Europe. Here, he has painted a Roman noblewoman standing next to a bust of the Austrian military commander Augustus d'Arenberg.

Napoleon Bonaparte Pardoning the Rebels at Cairo

An example of the French Empire style

- **Artist** Pierre-Narcisse Guérin
- **Date** 1808
- **Medium** Oil on canvas

The French painter Guérin created a slightly warmer, softer version of the Neoclassical style. He strongly influenced his pupils Théodore Géricault and Eugène Delacroix, who also found fame. This painting glorifies Napoleon, then the emperor of France, showing him magnanimously forgiving the defeated rebels of Cairo, Egypt.

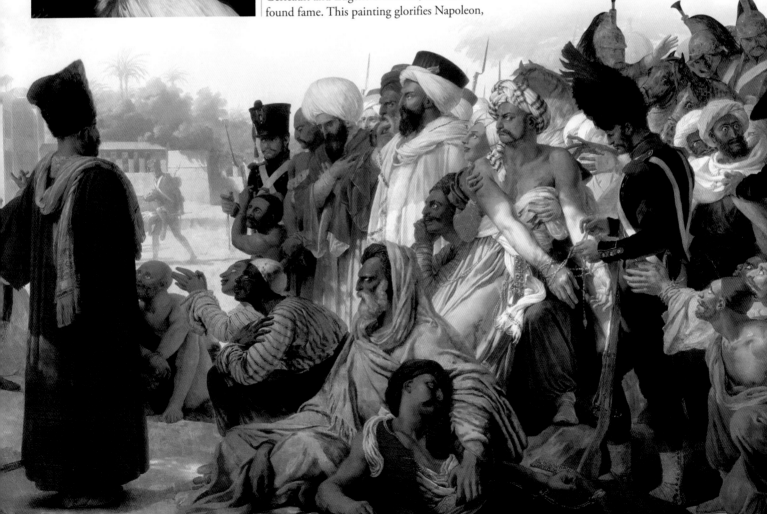

Oath of the Horatii

French artist Jacques-Louis David painted this work in 1784, five years before the French Revolution. After visiting the newly excavated ancient cities of Herculaneum and Pompeii, David became fascinated by ancient Rome. Here, he depicts an ancient Roman myth about a war between two cities, Rome and Alba Longa.

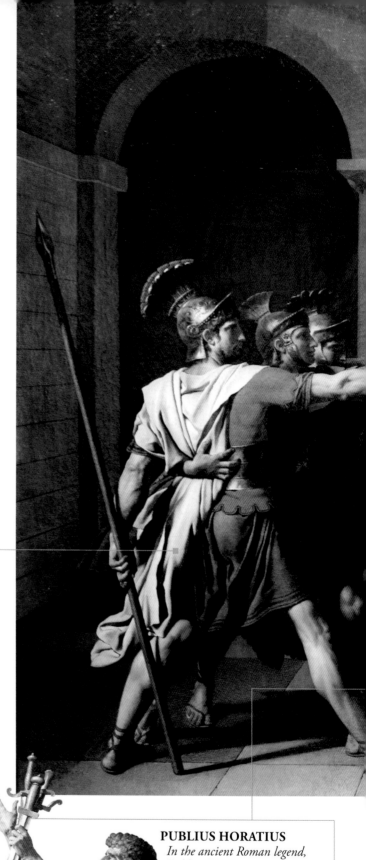

THE THREE BROTHERS
Stretching out their arms, with their Roman profiles and shining helmets, the three Horatii brothers declare that they will sacrifice their lives for Rome. In the end, only one brother survives.

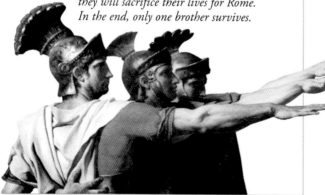

PRIZE-WINNING ARTIST
In 1774, David won the Prix de Rome, a competition whose prize was the chance to study in Rome. Inspired by the art and architecture of Italy, he stayed there for four years. When the French Revolution ended, he worked for the new government and later for Emperor Napoleon.

PUBLIUS HORATIUS
In the ancient Roman legend, Publius Horatius was an army officer. Here, he is sending his sons to fight the Curiatii brothers from Alba Longa. Standing proudly in his red cloak, he holds up three swords before giving one to each of his sons.

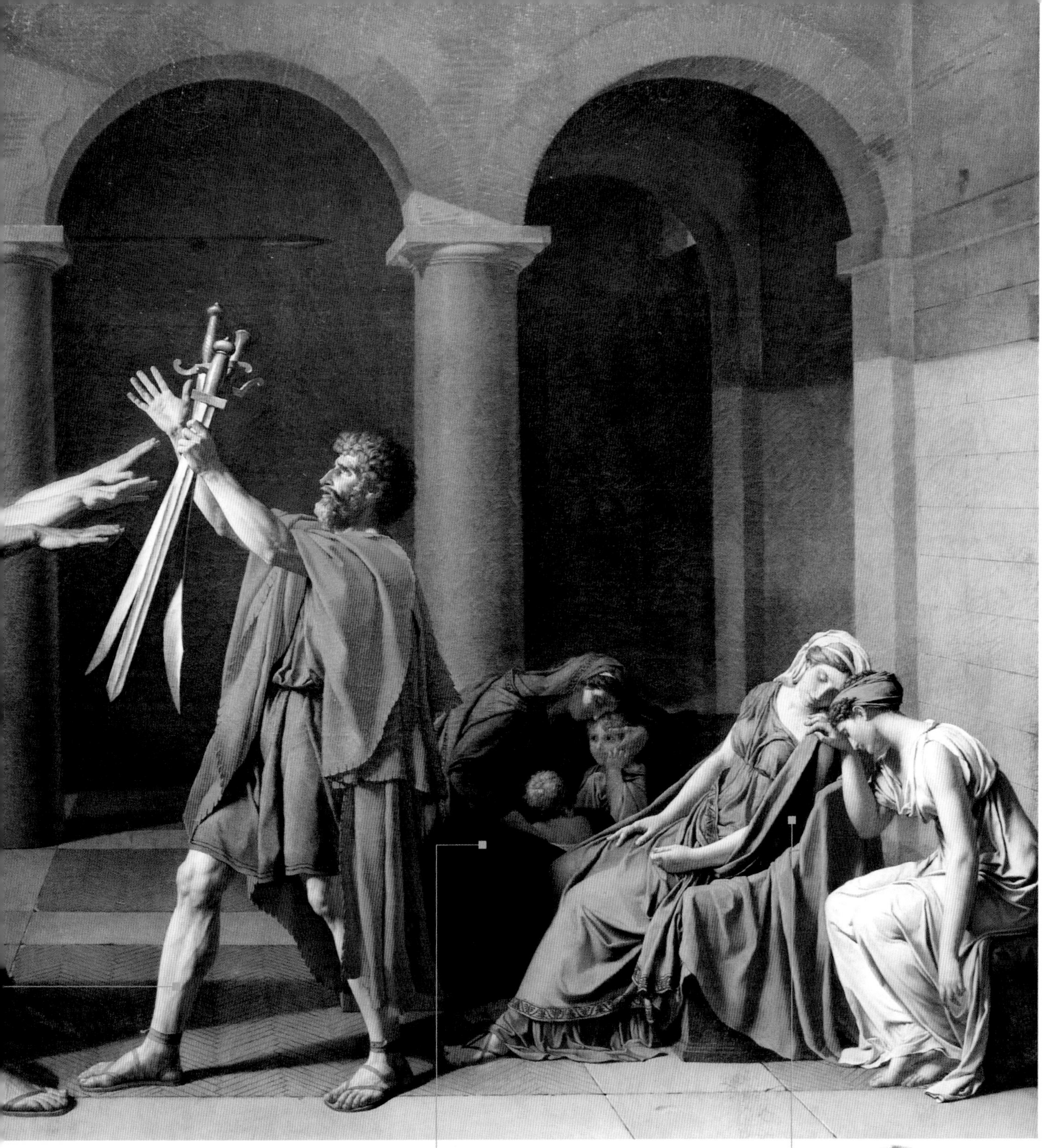

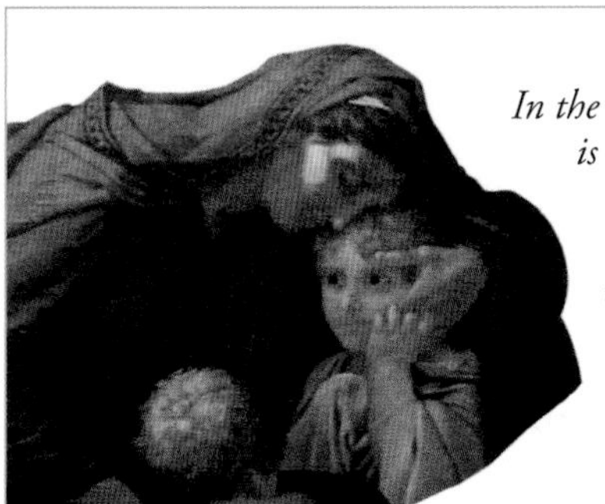

THE MOTHER
In the shadow of the men is the wife of Publius and mother of the brothers, huddling under a cloak with her grandsons. The older boy peeps out at the men in wonder.

SWOONING WOMEN
The woman in white with a blue turban is Sabina, a sister of the Curiatii brothers from Alba Longa, but married to one of the Horatii brothers. She leans on Camilla, a sister of the Horatii brothers but engaged to one of the Curiatii brothers.

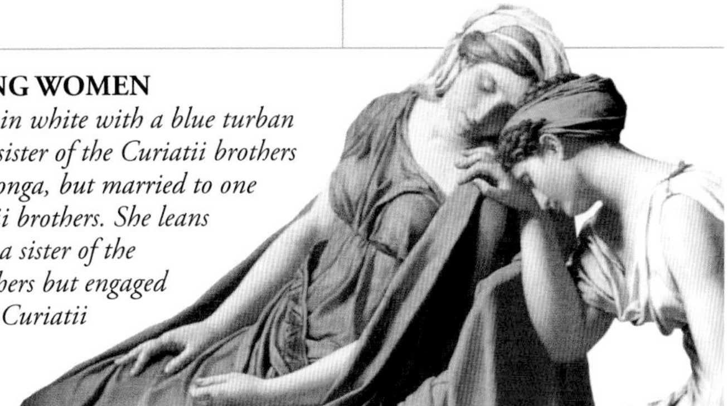

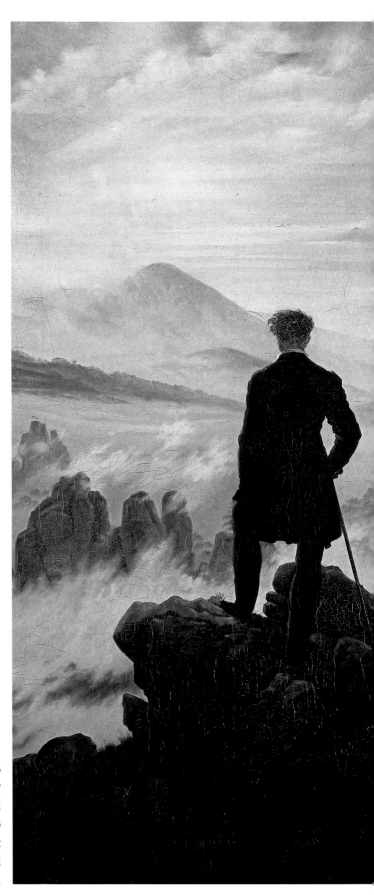

Romanticism

The Romantic movement developed at the start of the 19th century. Romantic painters were passionate, emotional, and nostalgic for the past. They were inspired by the power and beauty of nature, and also by chivalrous stories taken from the Middle Ages.

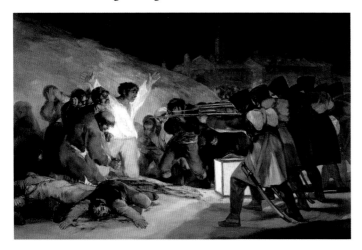

REACTING TO A CHANGING WORLD

Romanticism was in part a reaction against the Industrial Revolution, when new machine-run factories began mass-producing cheap goods. The Romanticists longed for a simpler time before these machines. Meanwhile, armed conflicts, such as the Spanish resistance to Napoleon's armies in the Peninsular War (as shown), also aroused strong feelings in Romantic artists.

▲ *THE THIRD OF MAY 1808,*
1814, FRANCISCO GOYA
This was a terrible, real event when Spanish rebels were rounded up and shot by the French invaders.

DRAMA AND ATMOSPHERE

Romantic artists expressed their individuality, but they also had some things in common. Many emphasized the use of color, rejecting the Neoclassical attention to form and outline. With sweeping brushstrokes that often seemed sketchy and unfinished, they created atmospheric pictures glowing with dramatic light.

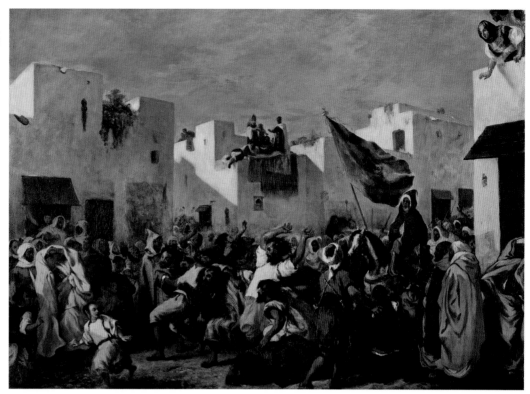

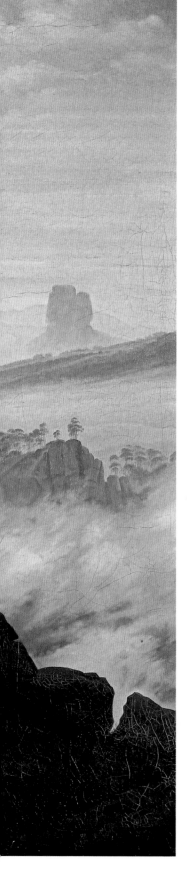

◀ *FANATICS OF TANGIER,*
1838, EUGÈNE DELACROIX
This is a dramatic painting of a real
event that the artist had witnessed in
Tangier, Morocco, in 1832, when
religious fanatics had filled the streets.

PAINTING SPECTACLES

Romantic artists embraced dramatic
tension. French painters Théodore
Géricault and Eugène Delacroix were
two of the most important Romantic
artists. They depicted theatrical scenes,
often filled with throngs of people,
and seen from striking viewpoints.

◀ *THE WANDERER ABOVE THE SEA OF*
FOG, 1818, CASPAR DAVID FRIEDRICH
The figure is shown from behind so that we share
the dramatic vista he is viewing. The scene
is based on the Elbe Sandstone Mountains in
Germany, but the work does not show a real view.

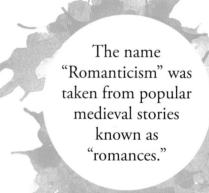

The name
"Romanticism" was
taken from popular
medieval stories
known as
"romances."

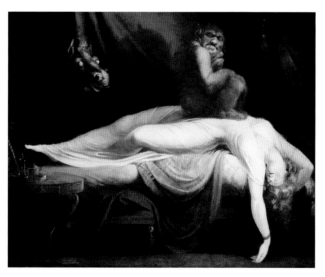

SCARY VISIONS

Some Romantic painters were
inspired by dreams and fantasies,
and often created nightmarish
pictures. The English painter
William Blake and London-based
Swiss painter Henry Fuseli
painted disturbing visions
taken from their imaginations.

◀ *THE NIGHTMARE,*
1781, HENRY FUSELI
While a woman sleeps, her arms thrown
back, a strange creature sits on her body.

Romantic scenes

Romantic artists produced paintings with a strong sense of movement, atmosphere, or emotion. In contrast to Neoclassical painters, Romantic painters often made heroes out of ordinary people rather than royalty or the nobility. Some artists used romantic novels or poetry as their subject matter.

Funeral of Atala

Passionate early Romanticist

- **Artist** Anne-Louis Girodet
- **Date** 1808
- **Medium** Oil on canvas

A pupil of Jacques-Louis David, Girodet helped to start the Romantic movement by painting scenes illuminated with glowing colors. Influenced by David, his technique is smooth, but his subjects are passionate. This picture depicts a Christian story told by a Romantic novelist. The eerie lighting imbues it with a powerful atmosphere.

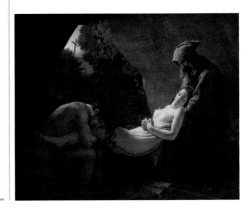

Clothed Maja

A painting for a prime minister

- **Artist** Francisco Goya
- **Date** 1800–1805
- **Medium** Oil on canvas

Goya painted this reclining lady for the Spanish prime minister, Manuel Godoy. It is a clothed version of an earlier work, which featured the same model in the same pose, but nude, which Godoy kept in a private collection. The *majas* were a group of lower-class Spanish women who were known for their extravagant lifestyles.

▼ DARING LOOK
The maja *looks straight back at the viewer. At this time, ladies were usually modest and would look down.*

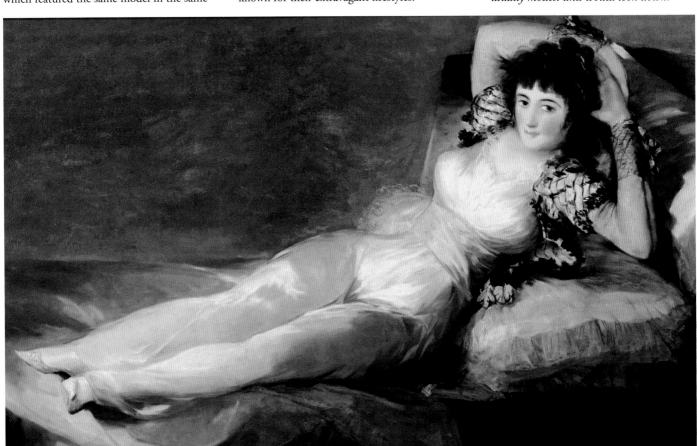

Slaves Stopping a Horse

A painting full of movement and anatomical detail

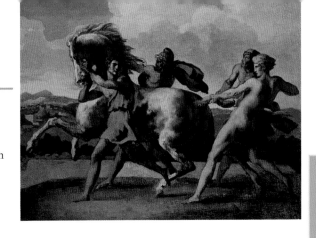

- **Artist** Théodore Géricault
- **Date** c.1817
- **Medium** Oil on canvas-backed paper

While staying in Rome in 1817, Géricault made sketches of a riderless horse race. This lively picture shows four men trying to hold on to a horse before it starts the race. Horses and men together were a common theme in Romantic art as they show action and power, nature and rhythm. Géricault studied anatomy and movement, and loved painting spectacular and dramatic scenes.

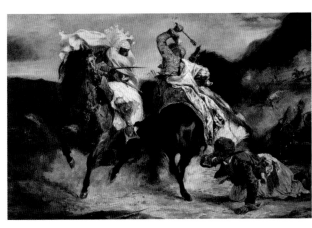

The Combat of the Giaour and Hassan

A dramatic fight scene based on a poem

- **Artist** Eugène Delacroix
- **Date** 1826
- **Medium** Oil on canvas

The French artist Delacroix based this painting on the poem *The Giaour*, a passionate tale of love and revenge by the English Romantic poet Lord Byron. Action and emotion are expressed in the painting through the use of bold colors, loose brushwork, and colored shadows. Romantic painters used energetic brushstrokes and bright colors in their imaginative paintings, and often did not strive for realism.

The Women of Algiers in their Apartment

An unusual subject matter for its time

- **Artist** Eugène Delacroix
- **Date** 1834
- **Medium** Oil on canvas

While traveling to North Africa, Delacroix was inspired by the light and surroundings. As a result of his travels, he painted subjects that seemed exotic to Europeans, including these women in their apartment. The intimate interior setting featuring ordinary people was unusual in art of the time. Delacroix particularly highlights the contrasting textures in the furniture and the glowing skin tones.

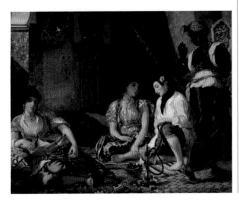

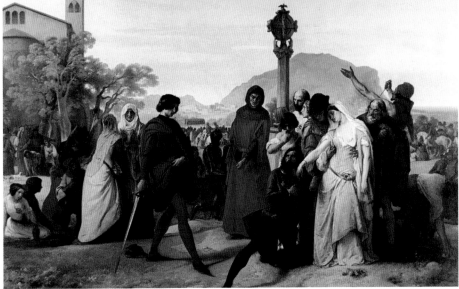

Sicilian Vespers

A portrayal of a historical rebellion

- **Artist** Francesco Hayez
- **Date** 1845–1846
- **Medium** Oil on canvas

Hayez was the leading Romantic artist in Milan, Italy. With twisting poses, rich colors, and chiaroscuro, this is his version of the story of the Sicilian Vespers—a bloody rebellion that took place in Sicily in 1282 against the rule of the French king Charles I. The rebellion started at a gathering for vespers, a prayer made at sunset.

Landscapes

Some 19th-century artists believed that the beauty and power of nature was a worthy subject for painting and could lift people's moods. They were inspired to paint just the landscape, with no added stories. This marked a move away from traditional themes, such as history painting, scenes of everyday life, still life, or portraits.

Unlike many of his contemporaries, Albert Bierstadt was primarily self-taught.

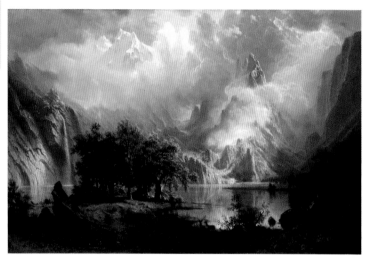

◄ *ROCKY MOUNTAIN LANDSCAPE,* 1870, ALBERT BIERSTADT
Bierstadt was born in Germany, but mainly painted dramatic mountain scenes in the United States.

THE POWER OF NATURE

Landscape painting became increasingly popular during the Romantic period (from about 1800 to 1850). Romantic artists—keen to convey strong emotions—would often show the land beneath moody, cloud-filled skies, which added to the atmosphere.

PAINTING THE WEATHER

English painter John Constable was celebrated for his "six footers"—huge 6-ft (1.8-m) canvases depicting scenes from near his home in Dedham Vale, England. He was interested in painting the changing effects of the weather, and applied small flecks of color to create a sense of liveliness in still scenes.

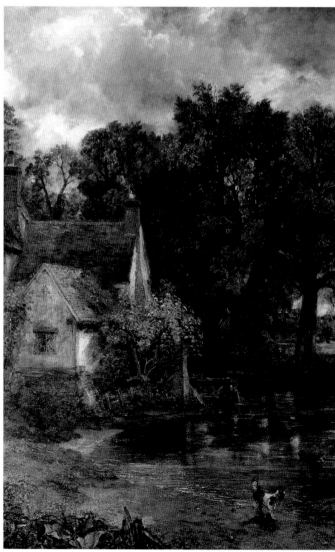

► *THE HAY WAIN,* 1821, JOHN CONSTABLE
This understated landscape painting also portrays working life. The hay wain of the title is the horsedrawn cart in the foreground. In the distance, haymakers work in the field.

GOD'S LIGHT

The German Romantic painter Caspar David Friedrich was especially interested in depicting the effects of light. He felt that his role as an artist was to express the power of God's creation, so there is a deep sense of spirituality in his landscapes. They are cool-looking and bleak, but full of strong emotion and atmosphere, and packed with religious symbolism.

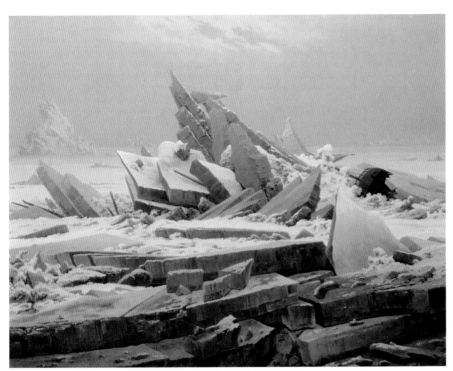

◀ *THE SEA OF ICE*, 1823–1824, CASPAR DAVID FRIEDRICH
This painting shows the power of nature over humans as a ship sinks into the ice. It conveys a sense of the fragility of life.

PORTABLE PAINTS

For centuries, artists mixed their own paints. They kept them in pigs' bladders, which had to be pierced with a pin to squeeze out the paint. These could not be resealed, and the leftover paint dried out. In 1840, the American painter John Goffe Rand invented the first collapsible tin tube to store ready-mixed paint. This kept the paint moist and made it easier for landscape painters to work outside.

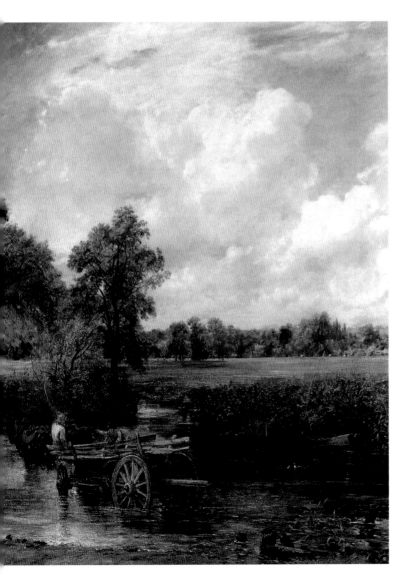

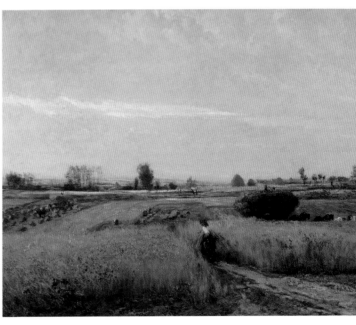

▲ *THE HARVEST*, 1851, CHARLES-FRANÇOIS DAUBIGNY
Daubigny painted scenes like this from his riverboat studio.

Glorious landscapes

The tradition of landscape painting has a long history in China, but landscapes were not a common subject in Western art before the 18th century. Inspired by Dutch Golden Age artists, 18th-century painters of panoramas, and the Romantic movement, new schools of landscape painting emerged in the United States and France during the 19th century.

The Harvesters

A scene of everyday life in the countryside

- **Artist** Pieter Bruegel the Elder
- **Date** 1565
- **Medium** Oil on wood

This was one of a series of six paintings showing different times of the year. In the months of July to August, during the harvest, a ripe field of wheat is being cut and stacked by workers. One group of peasants are having their picnic lunch under the shade of a pear tree. Others are still working. This Dutch painter was unusual at the time in depicting ordinary people in everyday situations.

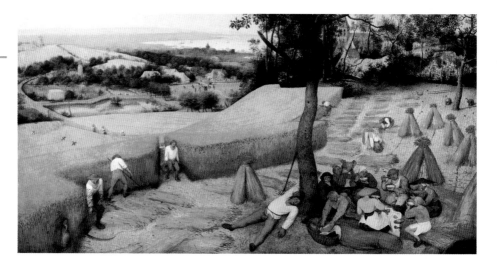

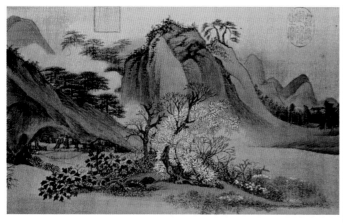

White Clouds and Green Mountains

An atmospheric Chinese landscape

- **Artist** Wu Li
- **Date** 1668
- **Medium** Ink and colors on silk

In China, landscape painting had long been an important art form. Wu Li painted these soft, misty clouds, green mountains, and gnarled trees to capture the silence and grandeur of the landscape. He was not attempting to create a lifelike scene, but rather the spiritual feeling of being in the mountains.

The Oxbow

By an American landscape painter influenced by the Romantic movement

- **Artist** Thomas Cole
- **Date** 1836
- **Medium** Oil on canvas

The American artist Thomas Cole studied landscape painting in Europe before turning his hand to American landscapes. Along with other artists, Cole formed the Hudson River School of landscape artists. Shown here is a view of a river named the Oxbow because of its curved shape. The sun is coming out after a thunderstorm.

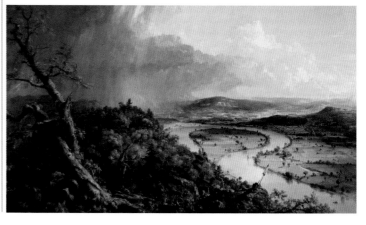

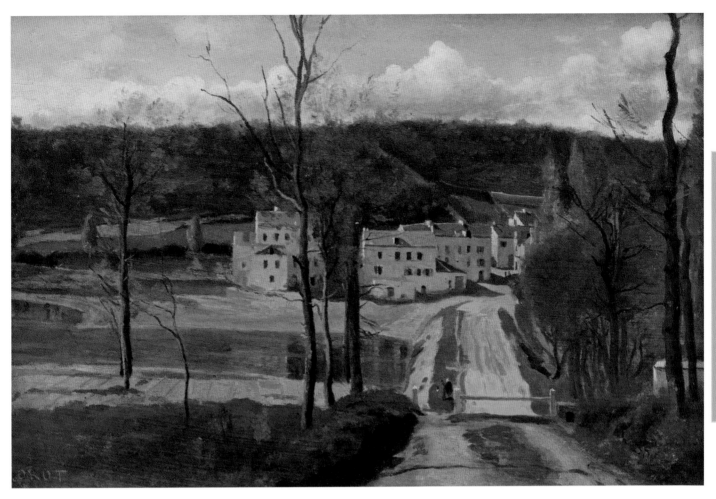

▲ SUNLIT SCENE
*Corot painted this scene near
his house outside Paris. He
concentrated on capturing the
dazzling effects of sunlight on
different parts of the landscape.*

Ville d'Avray, the Pond, and the Cabassud House
From the Barbizon School of French landscape painters

- **Artist** Jean-Baptiste-Camille Corot
- **Date** 1843–1850
- **Medium** Oil on paper mounted on canvas

In the 1840s, a number of artists, including Corot, began painting around the village of Barbizon near Paris, France. They used loose brushmarks and small patches of natural color to build up their scenes. They became known as the Barbizon School.

Hetch Hetchy Valley
An example of American luminism

- **Artist** Albert Bierstadt
- **Date** c.1890
- **Medium** Oil on canvas

One of the Hudson River School painters, the American artist Bierstadt captured the awe-inspiring atmosphere of this Californian landscape. His use of glowing color shows the influence of European Romantic landscape painting. The techniques Bierstadt used to create the effect of radiant light were part of a style known as luminism—an artistic style that was developed in the United States.

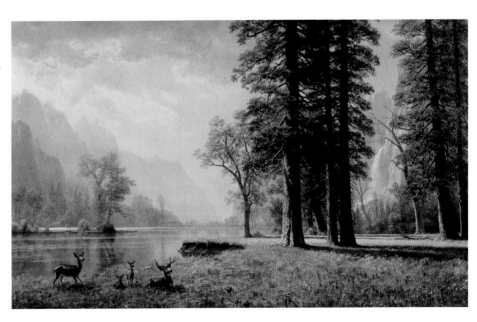

JMW Turner

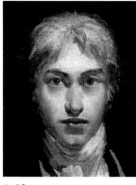

Self-portrait,
age 24

Joseph Mallord William Turner was an English Romantic painter who helped to raise the status of landscape painting. He began his artistic career in his early teens and became famous for dramatic scenes emphasizing atmosphere and the glowing effects of weather, color, and light.

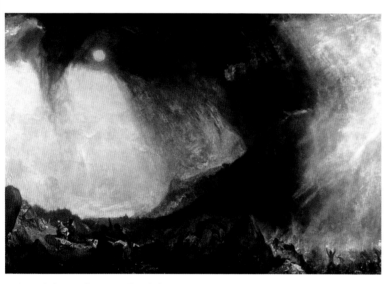

◀ *SNOWSTORM: HANNIBAL AND HIS ARMY CROSSING THE ALPS*, 1812
In this work, Turner uses overpowering, dramatic weather conditions to capture the perils of crossing the Alps.

PAINTER OF LIGHT

Over a career spanning 60 years, Turner became one of the most important landscape painters of the 19th century. He was nicknamed "the painter of light" due to his ability to paint luminous colors and create a powerful sense of atmosphere with oils or watercolors. His watercolors were first exhibited by the Royal Academy in London when he was just 15 years old. By the age of 27, he had became the youngest ever full member of the Academy.

▲ *THE FIGHTING TEMERAIRE*, 1839
The Temeraire *was an important ship at the Battle of Trafalgar, 30 years before this painting. Here it looks ghostly against the setting Sun.*

LIFE STORY

1775–1787	1788–1791	1796	1802–1811
Turner is born in London's Covent Garden in 1775. In 1787, his drawings are displayed and sold from his father's barber shop.	Turner works for architects and studies perspective with the artist Thomas Malton. At 15, he exhibits for the first time at the Royal Academy.	After several summers spent drawing and painting around England, Turner exhibits his first oil painting, *Fishermen at Sea*, which makes him famous.	In 1802, Turner visits Switzerland and France. In 1807, he becomes a professor of the Royal Academy.

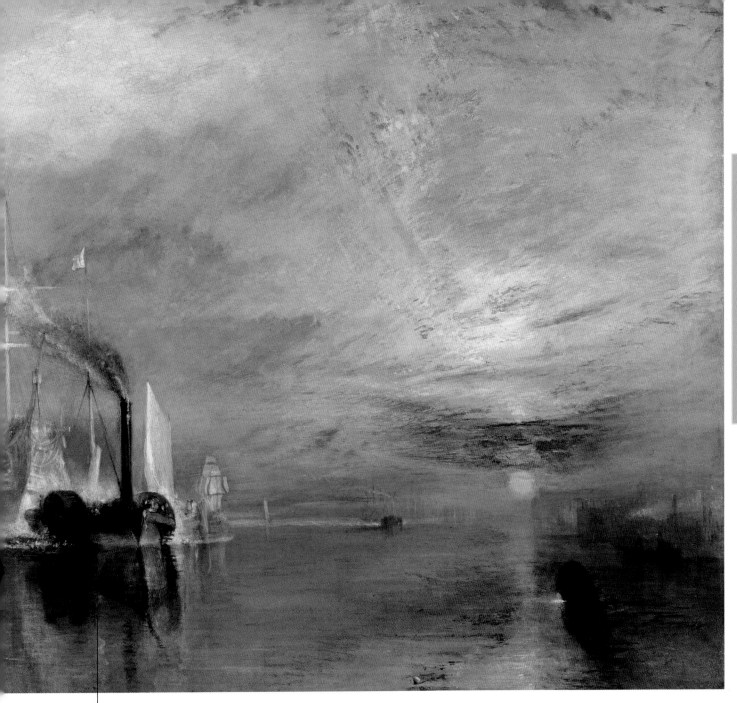

A small black tug leads the once great warship down the Thames river, London, to be broken up.

CHANGING STYLE

Inspired by Dutch Golden Age paintings, Turner made his name early in his career with a series of detailed landscapes, seascapes, and architectural works in oils, watercolors, and engravings. His style changed as he became older, and his later works are sweeping, expressive, almost abstract paintings. Today, these are the most famous of his works.

1812–1818	1816–1822	1823–1836	1851
Focusing on the effects of light, Turner's painting becomes more atmospheric, as he uses the power of nature to create drama.	As the Napoleonic wars end, peace in Europe allows Turner to travel abroad again. He visits Italy, including Rome, Naples, and Venice, as well as Scotland.	The British king asks Turner to paint the Battle of Trafalgar. He paints regularly at Petworth in Sussex, England, before setting off again on his European travels.	Turner dies in December 1851. His last words are "The Sun is God." He leaves more than 19,000 artworks to the British people in his will.

Realism

Beginning in France in the 19th century, Realism was a movement that sought to paint truthfully, and depict what real life was like for working people. Scientific progress in areas such as photography, combined with the invention of ready-mixed paint and portable easels, had made it easier for artists to move out into the world.

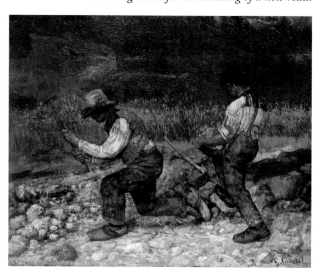

▼ *THE STONE BREAKERS*, 1849, GUSTAVE COURBET
Two poor laborers are shown breaking and removing stones for the building of a new road.

ORDINARY PEOPLE

The Realist movement began in the late 1840s, when a group of artist and writers began meeting at a café in Paris. There, they discussed politics and social issues as well as writing and art, and developed new ideas about authenticity. They decided to paint life directly as they found it, showing how ordinary people lived.

PAINTING THE MODERN WORLD

While artists since the Renaissance had painted realistically, their subject matter was often far removed from daily life. Realist artists chose to paint the results of the Industrial Revolution (c.1760–1840), depicting the building of bridges and trains, and the lives of those affected by these changes.

▼ *THE GLEANERS*, 1857, JEAN-FRANÇOIS MILLET
Known for his scenes of peasant life, Millet painted this on a large canvas of a kind normally used for important people.

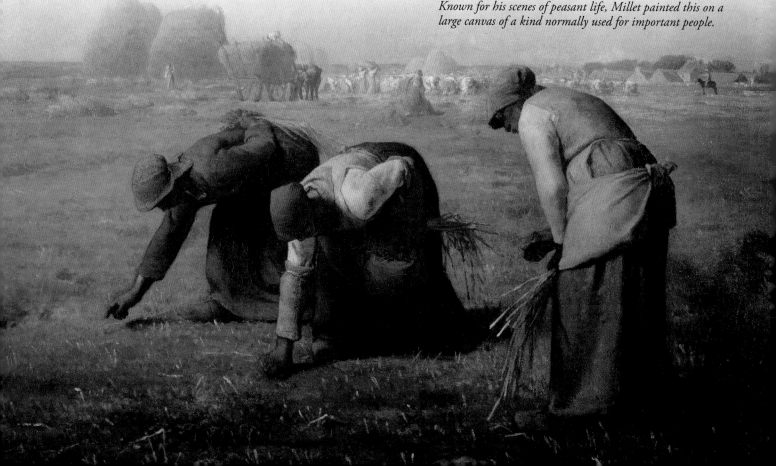

NATURAL PORTRAITS

Sumptuous surroundings, fancy ornaments, and stiff poses had no place in Realist portraits. Rather, Realist artists showed people wearing contemporary dress and in natural poses. This contrasted with the formal manner of traditional portraiture, for which the subjects would dress up in their finery.

▶ *THE WOMAN IN BLUE*, 1874, JEAN-BAPTISTE-CAMILLE COROT
Casually posed and fashionable, this woman was not portrayed in a traditional portrait style.

Today, many art historians consider the Realist movement as the beginning of modern art.

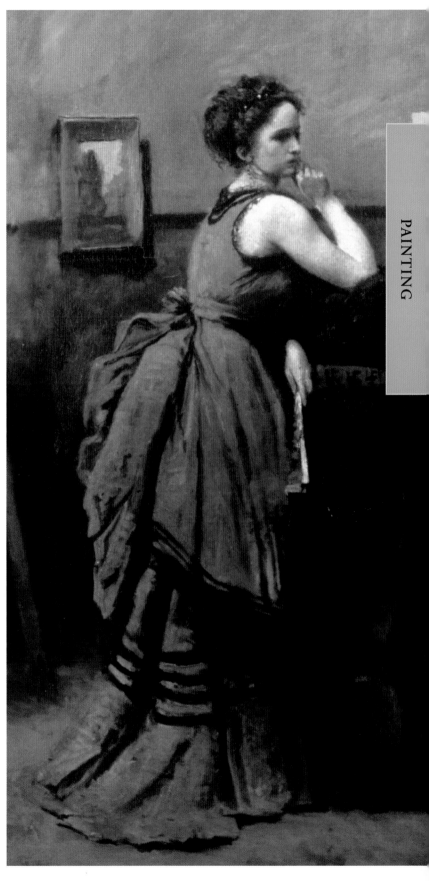

BOLD AND SKETCHY

The technology that had the greatest impact on Realism was photography. The first photographs were black and white, but they still provided a challenge to painting, as photos accurately reproduced moments in the real world. Realists tried new ways of painting, such as bold, sketchy brushstrokes, to capture a lively sense of immediacy that photographers could not achieve.

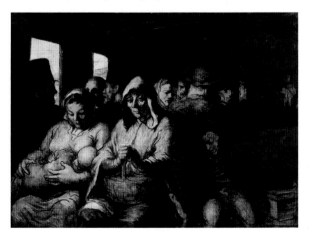

◀ *THIRD CLASS CARRIAGE*, 1864, HONORÉ DAUMIER
The poorest passengers on a train were the third-class travelers. With a sketchy Realist painting style, Daumier showed how they accepted their hard lives with dignity.

Painting modern life

By the late 19th century, the Industrial Revolution had been under way in Europe for about 100 years. In this time, towns and cities had grown enormously, radically changing how people lived. Realist artists set out to show these changes in their paintings, depicting the struggles of the poor as well as the leisure time of the newly formed middle classes.

A Fisherman Peers into the River

A painting by a pioneer of Russain Realism

- ■ **Artist** Vasily Perov
- ■ **Date** 1871
- ■ **Medium** Oil on canvas

Vasily Perov was one of the founders of the *Peredvizhniki* movement, often called "The Wanderers" in English. They were a group of Russian Realist painters in the second half of the 19th century. Perov was deeply influenced by his own wandering through Europe. Although he painted in a tighter style than the French Realists, Perov still aimed to capture the lives of ordinary people, not romanticizing or idealizing the truths he observed.

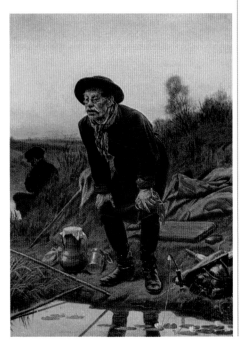

Barge Haulers on the Volga

An honest portrayal of the hardships of life

- ■ **Artist** Ilya Repin
- ■ **Date** 1873
- ■ **Medium** Oil on canvas

In this picture, 11 men drag a barge against the tide of the Volga river in Russia. The men look exhausted, but like other Realists, Repin portrays their dignity as they work, showing how difficult working people's lives can be. This is one of the most famous paintings of the *Peredvizhniki* movement. Although their work took ordinary things as its subject matter, to many Russians of the time, it was revolutionary because it went against the established artistic conventions.

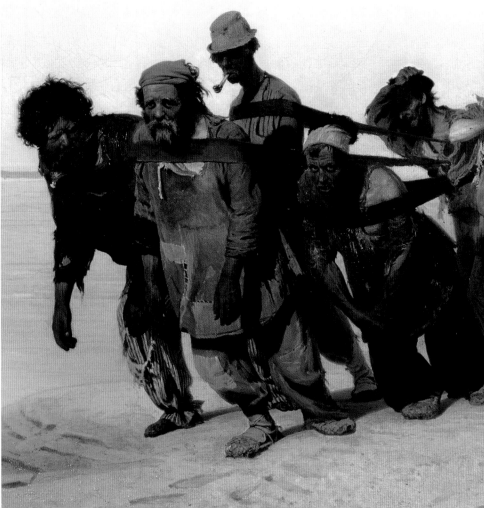

In the Orchard

An everyday subject on a large canvas

- **Artist** James Guthrie
- **Date** 1885–1886
- **Medium** Oil on canvas

Scottish artist James Guthrie produced this big painting, measuring 60 x 70 in (152 x 178 cm), while he was staying in a small village near the Berwickshire coast. It shows a boy and girl collecting apples that have fallen from the trees in a sunlit orchard, with a gaggle of geese looking on. Until then, Guthrie had been known mainly as a portraitist, but this work made him famous as a Realist painter.

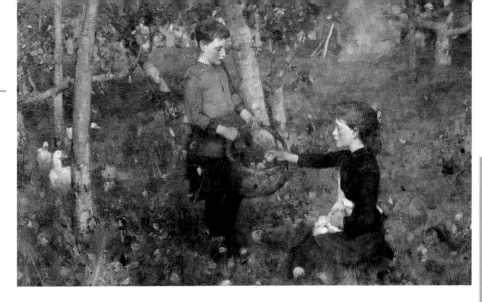

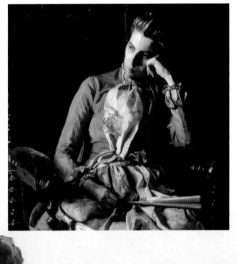

Miss Amelia van Buren

A naturally posed portrait by an American Realist

- **Artist** Thomas Eakins
- **Date** c.1891
- **Medium** Oil on canvas

This American painter was inspired by French Realism after studying in Paris. Back in the United States, Eakins painted portraits, figures in landscapes, wrestling matches, and surgeons at work. The subject of this painting, who was a student of Eakins, twists her head and arms away from viewers as if she is thinking about something else.

▼ **HARD LABOR**
Repin shows the intense effort made by each of the men as they put their whole body weight into their labor.

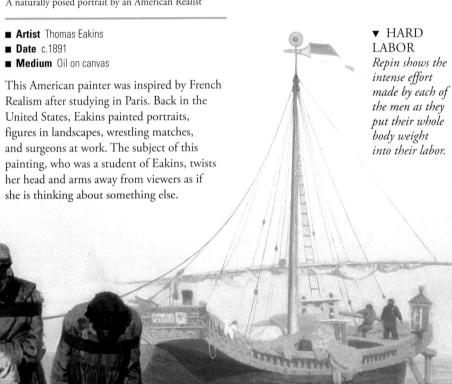

PAINTING

Burial at Ornans

The French Realist painter Gustave Courbet painted this scene of ordinary life in a size usually reserved for more "noble" subjects. The huge canvas, measuring 22 x 10 ft (6.6 x 3.1 m), depicts a true event—the funeral of the artist's great-uncle in 1848.

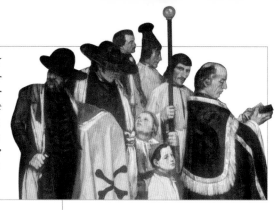

INNER DIGNITY
These figures appear reserved, suggesting their inner dignity. They represent a cross-section of society, including a priest, a mayor, farmers, laborers, and some of Courbet's family.

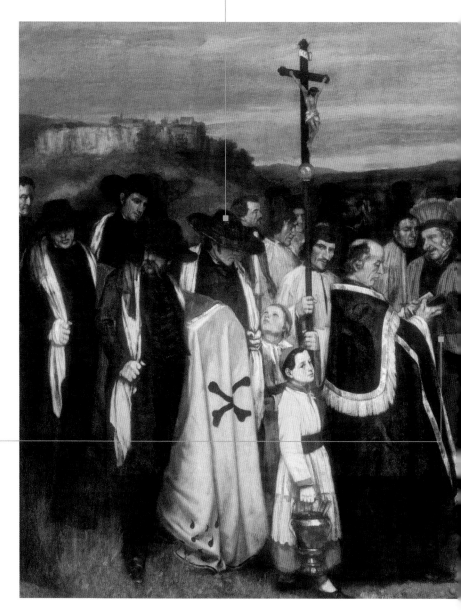

DRUNKEN BEADLES
Beadles were church officials who helped at religious functions. The red noses and cheeks show that they are drunk. Generally, churchmen were depicted more respectfully in paintings of this time.

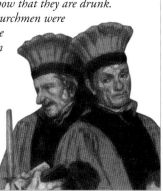

THE BURIAL OF ROMANTICISM

Courbet called this work *Painting of Human Figures, the History of a Burial at Ornans.* He exhibited it in 1851 at the Paris Salon—the official annual French exhibition—describing it as "the burial of Romanticism." Such a huge canvas would usually have shown a grand scene from history, not a peasant's funeral. It shocked many viewers.

LINE OF MOURNERS

The long line of larger-than-life figures resembles a fresco on a building from classical antiquity. The mourners' obvious grief makes the work seem more real, while its large size makes viewers feel as if they are part of the story.

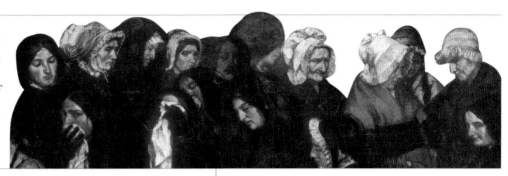

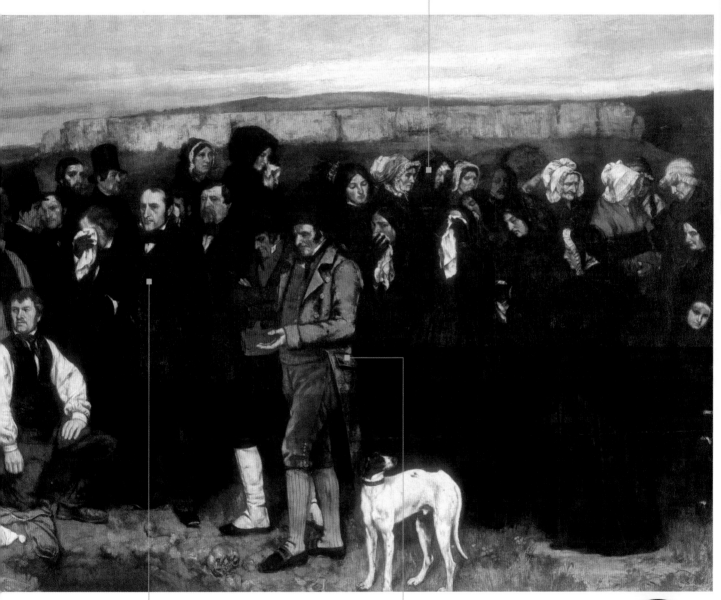

ORDINARY AND UGLY

French critics complained about the ugliness of the painting. It shows an ordinary person's funeral, with dull, unattractive mourners, such as these men. Traditionally, paintings of funerals were reserved for heroes or religious figures.

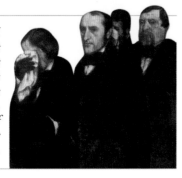

WAR VETERAN

The figure in green in the front by the empty grave is a veteran of the French Revolution. At the time, the French middle and upper classes often ignored the fact that peasants and the working class had fought alongside them during the Revolution.

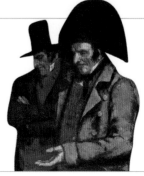

125

The Pre-Raphaelites

In 1848, the same year that the Realists formed in Paris, a group of English painters and poets began a new secret society. They felt nostalgic about the past, and thought that industrialization was damaging society. The group looked back to a time before the Italian painter Raphael, calling themselves the Pre-Raphaelite Brotherhood.

▼ *A CONVERTED BRITISH FAMILY SHELTERING A CHRISTIAN MISSIONARY FROM THE PERSECUTION OF THE DRUIDS,* 1850, WILLIAM HOLMAN HUNT
Typical of the style, Hunt's painting is full of detail.

BEFORE RAPHAEL

The Pre-Raphaelites believed that art had moved in the wrong direction since the time of Raphael at the start of the 16th century. They thought Raphael's emphasis on old Classical forms had made art artificial, and objected to the way that he was celebrated as a great master. Instead, they aimed to follow the styles of early Renaissance artists such as Botticelli, whose work emphasized color and detail.

▼ *OPHELIA*, 1852, JOHN EVERETT MILLAIS
This drowning woman is from Shakespeare's play Hamlet. *The Pre-Raphaelites often chose tragic subjects.*

BRIGHT AND BEAUTIFUL

The Pre-Raphaelites objected to the influence of Sir Joshua Reynolds, the founder of the English Royal Academy of Arts. They called him "Sir Sloshua," because they thought his paintings were sloshy and messy. By contrast, the Pre-Raphaelites were meticulous, and their paintings appear bright. They achieved this by coating canvases with white before painting.

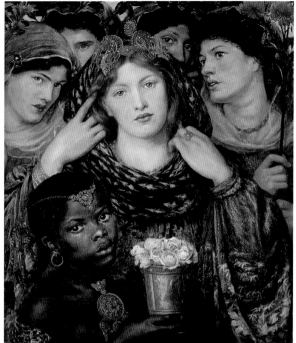

◄ *THE BELOVED*, 1866, DANTE GABRIEL ROSSETTI
The subject of this painting is the power of a woman's beauty, which is brought out by the vivid colors.

The Pre-Raphaelites believed that art should imitate nature as closely and honestly as possible.

▶ *THE BEGUILING OF MERLIN*, 1877, EDWARD BURNE-JONES
This painting shows a story from a legend about the magician Merlin's love for the mysterious Lady of the Lake.

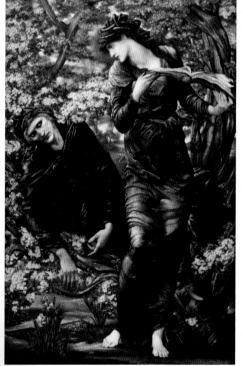

PAINTING TRUTHFULLY

The artists thought that Raphael's emphasis on Classical art had damaged the way art was taught, making it unimaginative and artificial. The Pre-Raphaelites signed their paintings PRB—for "Pre-Raphaelite Brotherhood"—and although criticized by many, they were admired by the art critic John Ruskin, especially for their belief that the purpose of art was to imitate nature as closely and honestly as possible.

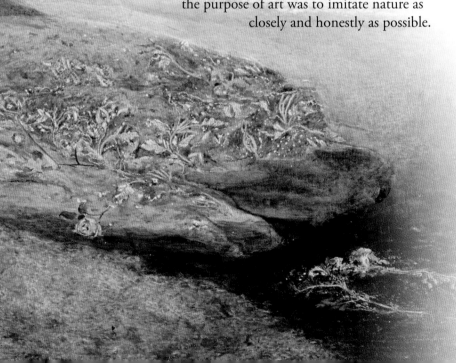

CONTINUED INFLUENCE

By 1853, the original Pre-Raphaelite Brotherhood had broken up. However, Dante Gabriel Rossetti continued to be described as a Pre-Raphaelite, and the term was also used for later artists who worked in similar ways, such as Edward Burne-Jones. Initially widely hated, they ended up becoming highly influential on art movements such as Symbolism.

PAINTING LIFE

Although Ford Madox Brown was never a member of the Pre-Raphaelite Brotherhood, *Work*, painted between 1852 and 1865, is considered an important Pre-Raphaelite piece. This detailed, colorful painting features rich, middle-class, and poor people to show how life is for each class.

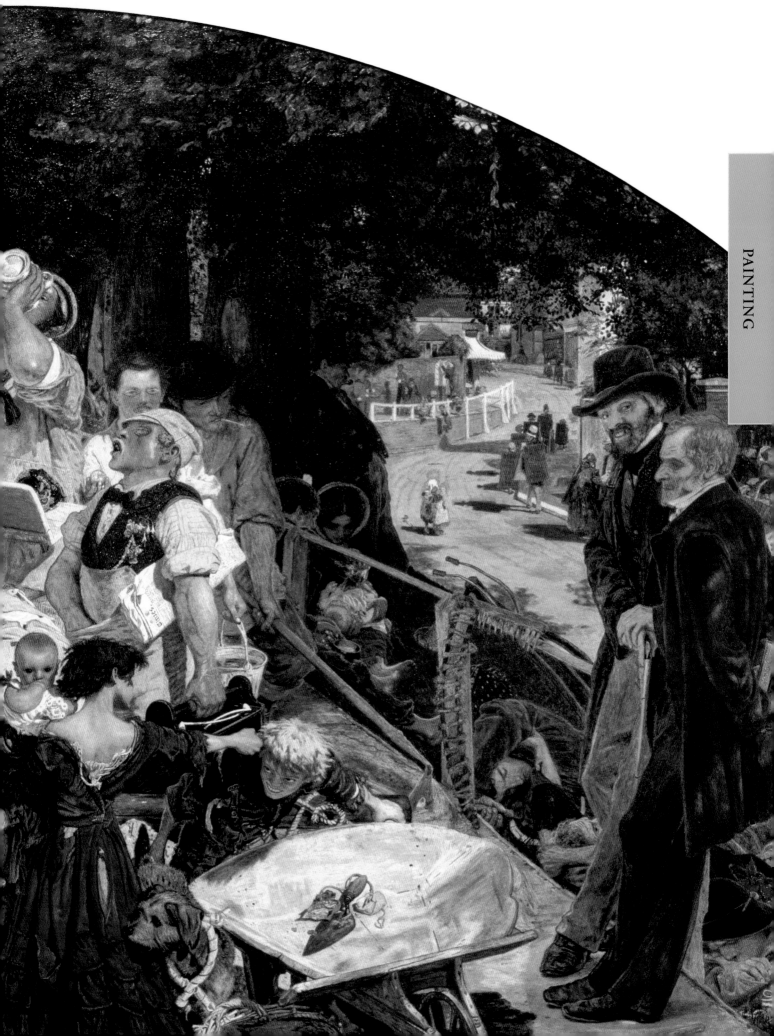

Non-European modern art

While Western modern art movements were developing and changing quickly, in many other parts of the world, change was much slower, and artists often followed ancient traditions. Many modern European artists, searching for new styles and meanings, found inspiration in non-Western art.

AFRICAN INSPIRATION

During the 19th century, some Europeans believed that the art of non-Western societies was "pure" because they were not as concerned with material wealth as Europeans. African masks, for instance, used basic shapes to capture the essence of human features rather than detailed likenesses. This became known in the West as "primitive art."

▲ KUBA MASK, DATE UNKNOWN
This mask dates from the time of the Kuba Kingdom in Central Africa, which flourished between the 17th and 19th centuries.

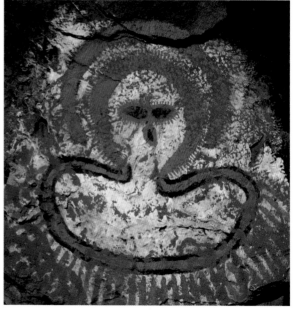

► WANDJINA SPIRIT, DATE UNKNOWN, CAVE PAINTING
With large eyes and no mouth, Wandjinas are symbols of fertility and rain. They are found only in Kimberley, Western Australia.

DREAMTIME PAINTINGS

Aboriginal paintings depicting spiritual beliefs known as Dreamtime have been produced in Australia since prehistoric times. The paintings depict ancestral beings who maintain a constant spiritual presence. Although Dreamtime artists have individual styles, they all use certain shapes and lines as symbols, such as footprints representing hunters.

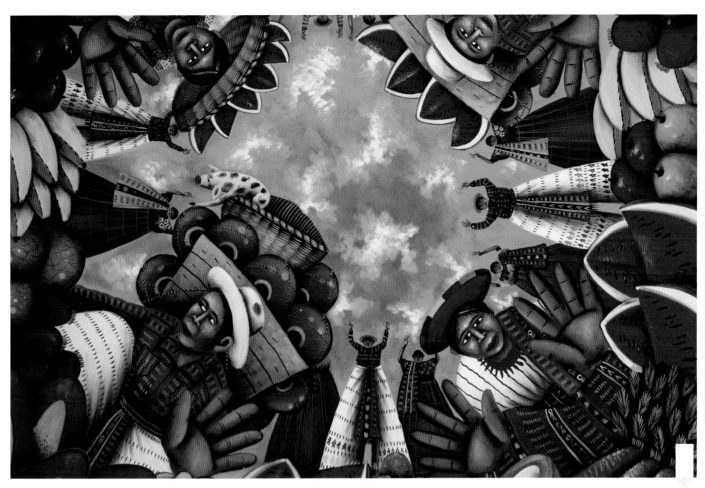

▲ *BIRD'S EYE*, c.2000, ANTONIO COCHÉ
*This colorful picture (in fact a worm's-eye view)
is a naive-style painting from Guatemala.*

NAIVE ART

Naive art is deliberately simplistic in style. It was developed by artists in different parts of the world as a movement away from what they saw as the dishonesty of Western art. Naive artists were mainly inspired by early art from cultures far from Europe that some considered primitive, which is why naive artists are sometimes called "modern primitives."

In the early 20th century, Pablo Picasso changed his art style after seeing African masks in a Paris museum.

▶ *PLUM BLOSSOM*, 1950, QI BAISHI
Qi Baishi used simple brushmarks in the flowing xieyi *style for this painting.*

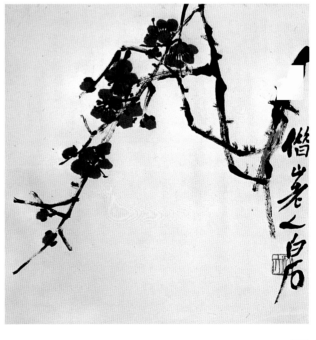

TRADITIONAL SKILLS

Traditional Chinese painting is known as *guóhuà*, meaning "native painting." Artists hold their brushes vertically, and make marks that look like calligraphy. They usually paint on paper or silk, which is then mounted on scrolls. There are two main painting techniques: *gongbi*, meaning "meticulous," and *xieyi*, meaning "freehand style."

Japanese printmaking

From 1615 to 1868, a feudal military government called the Tokugawa Shogunate ruled Japan and kept it isolated from the world. During this time, a distinctive style appeared called *ukiyo-e*, which means "pictures from the floating world." It appeared first in painting, then in woodblock prints.

A Winter Party

A flowing, elegant social scene

- **Artist** Utagawa Toyoharu
- **Date** c.1780s
- **Medium** Color and gold on silk

Influenced by classical Chinese painting, *ukiyo-e* artists created shapes using flat colors and bold, flowing, well-defined lines. Here, Utagawa Toyoharu has depicted a man with four female companions drinking hot tea and listening to music in front of a wintry garden.

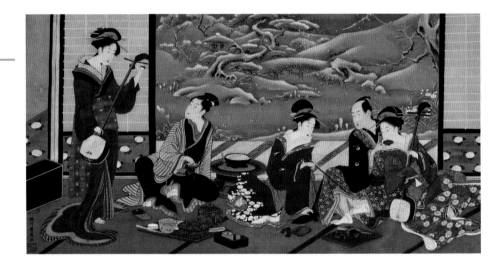

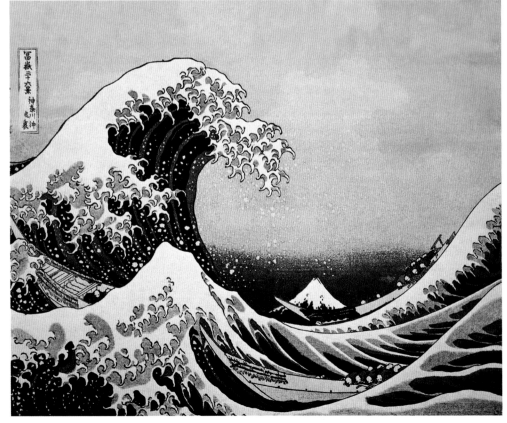

The Great Wave of Kanagawa

A print that has gained worldwide fame

- **Artist** Katsushika Hokusai
- **Date** 1832
- **Medium** Color woodblock

Today, Katsushika Hokusai is the most well-known *ukiyo-e* artist, and this print is probably his most famous work. The dramatic, asymmetrical composition uses only a few colors and lots of grasping and curving lines. It is part of a series of prints called "The Thirty-Six Views," all of which feature Mount Fuji. These became famous across the world from 1868 on, when Japan began trading with other countries once again.

◄ BALANCED IMAGE
This work shows Hokusai's understanding of balance. The huge wave dramatically frames Mount Fuji in the distance.

Diptych of a sword fight

A dynamic image in two parts

- **Artist** Ando Hiroshige
- **Date** 1830s
- **Medium** Color woodblock

This print is a diptych, which means that it is made of two parts. It shows two men engaged in a sword fight. The diagonal composition, lack of background, and detailed costumes mean that the viewer's eye is drawn straight to the action. *Ukiyo-e* painters like Hiroshige made bright colors from pigments derived from natural substances, such as safflower or crushed shells. Later, when Japan began to trade with the rest of the world, Japanese artists also used synthetic dyes imported from the West.

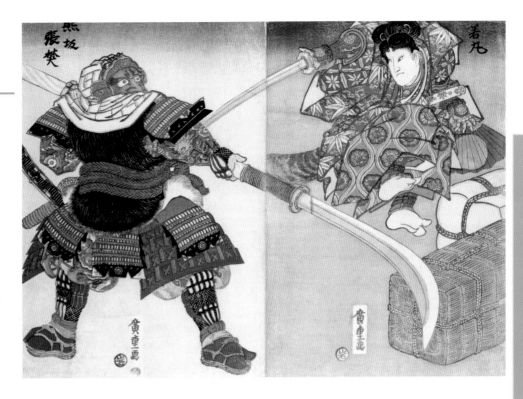

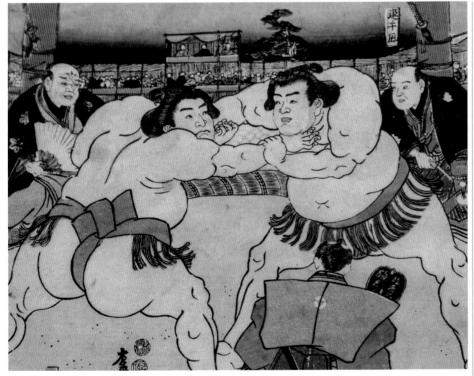

Sumo wrestlers

A popular subject for Japanese art lovers

- **Artist** Utagawa Kunisada
- **Date** c.1850
- **Medium** Color woodblock

Prints of Sumo wrestlers were especially popular in Japan from around 1775 to 1850. From 1825, Kunisada and his pupils made most of them. During his life, he became rich and famous for works such as this one. All elements of the print are outlined in black sumi ink, the same type of ink that was used for calligraphy.

Yoshida station

A typical scene that sparked a craze in Europe

- **Artist** Utagawa Hiroshige
- **Date** 1861
- **Medium** Color woodblock

Toward the end of the 19th century, as Japan opened up its borders, prints such as this one were used as wrapping paper for Japanese ornaments and furniture sold in Europe. The prints started a craze for Japanese art that became known as *Japonisme*. Here, a bridge and sailing boats cross a river at Yoshida station in the city of Toyohashi, Japan.

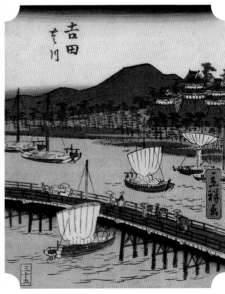

133

Édouard Manet

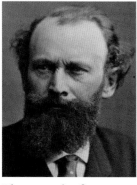

The French painter Édouard Manet was trained in the traditional way, by studying earlier artists and painting large historical, biblical, or mythical scenes. However, he broke away from this training to follow Realist ideas, painting life around him in cafés, theaters, parks, and train stations. He also developed a new, freer style.

Photograph of
Manet, age 42

RAPID AND SKETCHY

When he broke from convention to paint images of ordinary urban life, Manet was ridiculed. Traditional painting was precise, with small, careful brushmarks, and everything looking as lifelike as possible, but Manet painted with rapid, loose brushstrokes and sketchy patches of color. He reduced details and used few tones, so his pictures look almost flat.

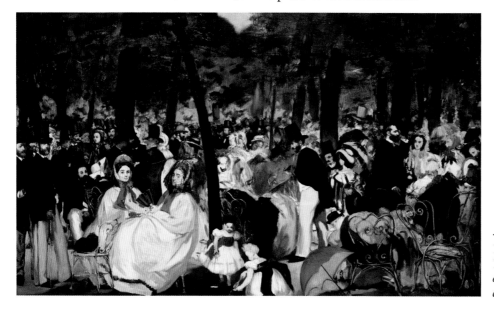

◄ MUSIC IN THE
TUILERIES GARDENS, 1862
This was Manet's first major painting
of modern city life. In it, a fashionable
crowd listens to a band in a popular park.

LIFE STORY

1832	1848	1850–1856	1857–1862
Édouard Manet is born in Paris to a wealthy family. His father hopes he will study law, but he wants to be an artist.	To please his father, Manet trains for the Navy. However, he fails the exams, and his father agrees to let him become an artist.	Manet trains with artist Thomas Couture. From 1853 to 1856, he visits and studies art in the Netherlands, Italy, and Germany.	Back in Paris, Manet begins to paint in a Realist style with a sketchier approach. He exhibits *Music in the Tuileries Gardens*, but critics laugh at it.

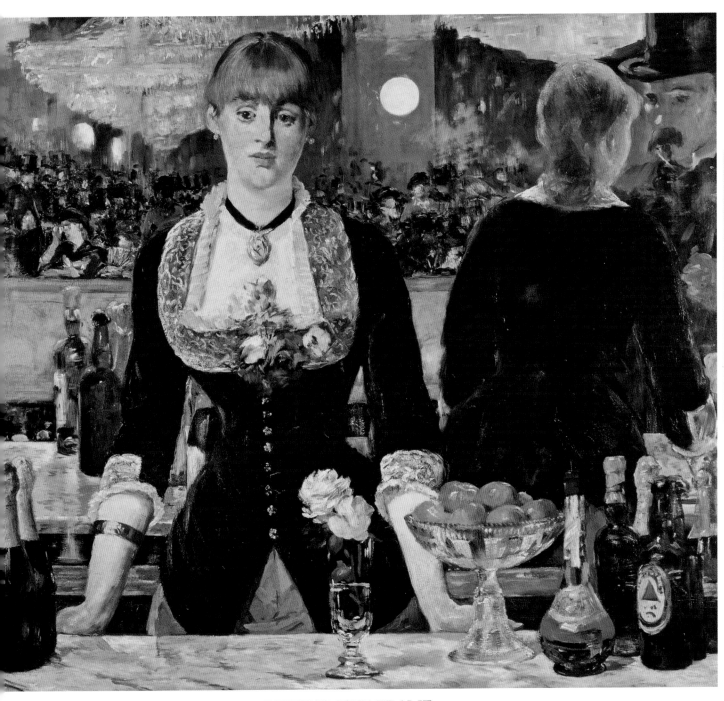

▲ A BAR AT THE
FOLIES BERGÈRE, 1882
In a busy music hall, Suzon
the barmaid serves a customer.
The hall is reflected in the
mirror behind her, including a
trapeze artist's feet (top left).

BEYOND THE FRAME

Rather than applying careful, thin layers of paint, Manet placed color where
he saw it, building up his pictures spontaneously. In this way, he captured
the effect of light and atmosphere we see during an instant glance. He also
made use of photographic techniques by "cutting off" objects at the edges
of his compositions to create a sense that they continue beyond the frame.

1863–1865	1873	1874	1875–1883
Manet scandalizes critics by including a naked figure in his *The Luncheon on the Grass*. The Paris Salon rejects it for exhibition.	Manet becomes friends with fellow French artist Claude Monet, who invites Manet to exhibit at the first Impressionist exhibition. He refuses.	Manet's paintings inspire the Impressionists. One of them, the French painter Berthe Morisot, convinces him to paint *en plein air* (in the open air).	Manet makes lithographs for *The Raven*, by American poet Edgar Allan Poe. In 1881, he is honored by the French state. He dies in 1883.

Impressionism

In the 1860s, a group of French painters started to work in a radical new way. They painted quickly in the open air, rather than working in a studio from sketches. Using bold marks and bright colors, they sought to capture everyday life without trying to produce a precise likenesses. This group would later come to be known as the Impressionists.

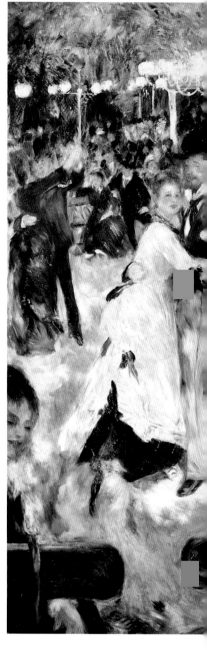

▼ *IMPRESSION, SUNRISE,*
1872, CLAUDE MONET
With its free, sketchy brushmarks, this painting gave the Impressionist movement its name.

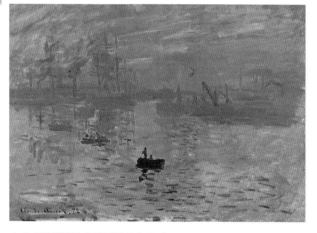

FLEETING MOMENTS

The artists worked in Paris and met regularly. The ideas they discussed included new color theories, photography, landscape painters, and the Realists, especially Manet. Abandoning traditional art styles and subjects, they painted life around them, capturing passing moments, such as the fleeting effects of sunlight. *Dance at the Moulin de la Galette* by Renoir is a stunning example of the genre.

A MOVEMENT IS BORN

During the 19th century in France, artists hoping to sell their work sent it to a jury who decided whether to show it at the Paris Salon, a large annual exhibition. After many rejections by the jury, in April 1874, one group of artists opened their own exhibition. A painting by Claude Monet called *Impression, Sunrise,* was described insultingly by an art critic as being unfinished and not real art, merely "impressions." The name stuck, and from then on, the movement was called Impressionism.

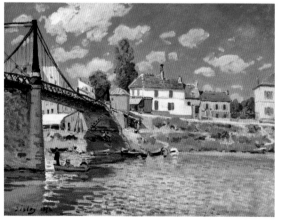

▲ *BRIDGE AT VILLENEUVE-LA-GARENNE,*
1872, ALFRED SISLEY
Sisley painted this modern bridge with bright colors and flat marks.

SLOW ACCEPTANCE

Between 1874 and 1886, the Impressionists held eight exhibitions in Paris. Most of the works were painted from unusual viewpoints and used colors (rather than black) in shadows. The bright colors and short brushstrokes contrasted with the styles expected by the official art world, and it took until the 1880s before this new style was admired.

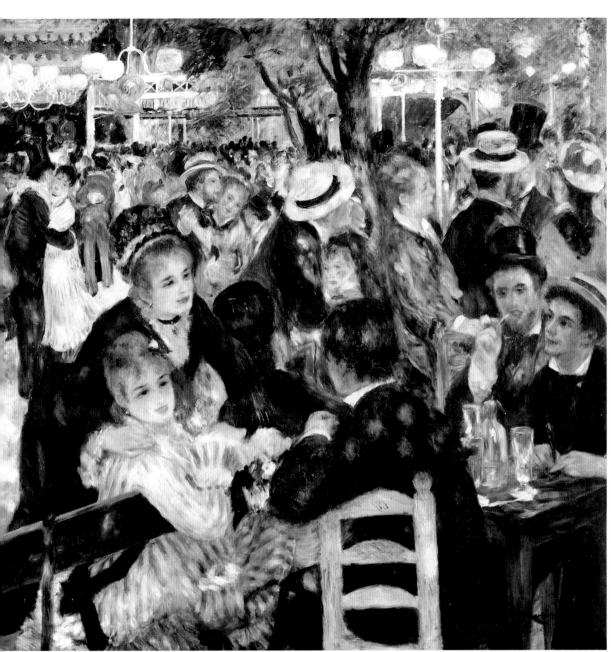

◄ *DANCE AT THE MOULIN DE LA GALETTE,* 1876, AUGUSTE RENOIR
Patchy colors of light fall on the people in this sunlit scene. Renoir has depicted working-class Parisians dressed in their best for a dance in Monmartre, Paris.

▼ *THE ARTIST'S GARDEN AT VÉTHEUIL,* 1881, CLAUDE MONET
Monet painted many scenes in his garden featuring family members.

The Impressionists captured the momentary effects of sunlight by painting *en plein air* (in the open air).

THE EFFECTS OF LIGHT

The Impressionists were interested in the effects of light and changing weather, and this was reflected in their paintings of landscapes and scenes of everyday life. Using new, synthetic, brightly colored paints ready-mixed in tubes, they were able to work outside and in front of their subjects rather than in their studios.

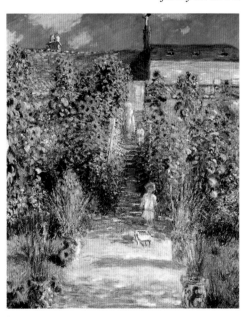

Capturing a moment

The Impressionists were influenced by Realist painters in their choice of subject matter, painting landscapes and scenes from modern life, as well as ordinary people absorbed in everyday activities. But they aimed to capture moments of time as most people see things: glimpses of life with bright colors but few details.

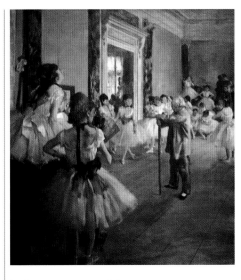

The Dance Class
A painting inspired by photographic techniques

- ■ **Artist** Edgar Degas
- ■ **Date** 1871–1874
- ■ **Medium** Oil on canvas

Degas exhibited with the Impressionists, but his work was a little different as he preferred working in his studio to outdoors. This work depicts the end of a ballet class with the famous choreographer Jules Perrot. With its diagonal composition, it was influenced by Japanese prints. The picture looks like a snapshot, showing Degas' understanding of photography. From the 1870s, Degas drew and painted dancers obsessively.

Barges on the Seine at Bougival
A strikingly modern-looking scene

- ■ **Artist** Camille Pissarro
- ■ **Date** 1871
- ■ **Medium** Oil on canvas

The oldest member of the Impressionist group, Pissarro was a huge influence on his younger colleagues. Although they followed the Realists with their scenes of towns and countryside, their techniques of quick brushstrokes and dabs of bright colors were new. Pissarro's painting of barges looks modern, dynamic, and expressive.

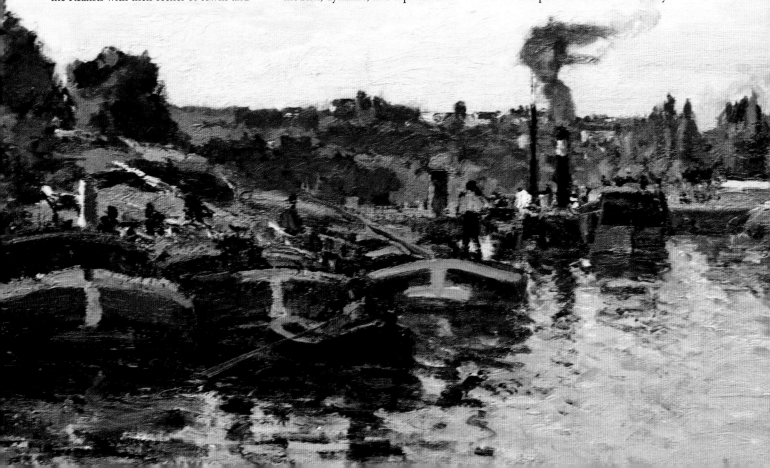

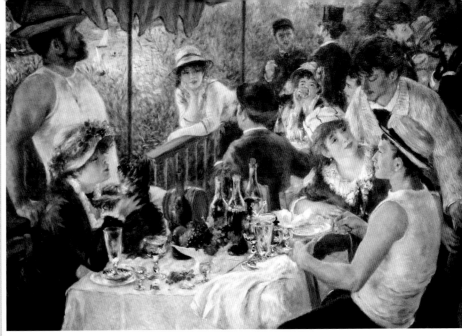

The Tea

A composition inspired by Japanese prints

- **Artist** Mary Cassatt
- **Date** c.1880
- **Medium** Oil on canvas

Between striped wallpaper and a silver tea service, two friends drink tea and chat. Meeting regularly, the Impressionists influenced one another's work. This asymmetrical composition with cropped edges shows the influence of Cassatt's friendship with Degas and their shared admiration of Japanese prints. Her soft, bright colors and emphasis on light reveal the influence of Pissarro.

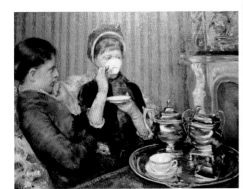

Luncheon of the Boating Party

Experiments with new color theories

- **Artist** Pierre-Auguste Renoir
- **Date** 1880–1881
- **Medium** Oil on canvas

The Impressionists experimented with new ideas about color. One of these was to create shadows by the reflected light of surrounding and sometimes unseen objects. In this work, depicting a group of Renoir's friends on a balcony, the light source is the river to the left. The white tablecloth and men's singlets reflect the light and illuminate the scene.

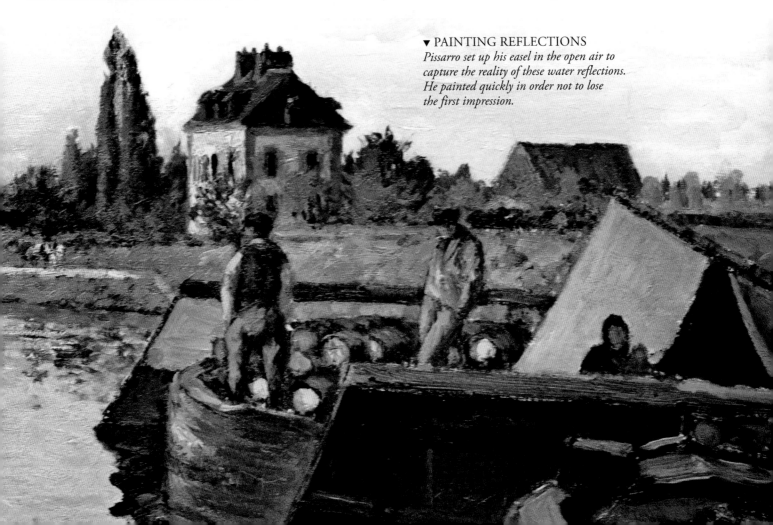

▼ PAINTING REFLECTIONS
Pissarro set up his easel in the open air to capture the reality of these water reflections. He painted quickly in order not to lose the first impression.

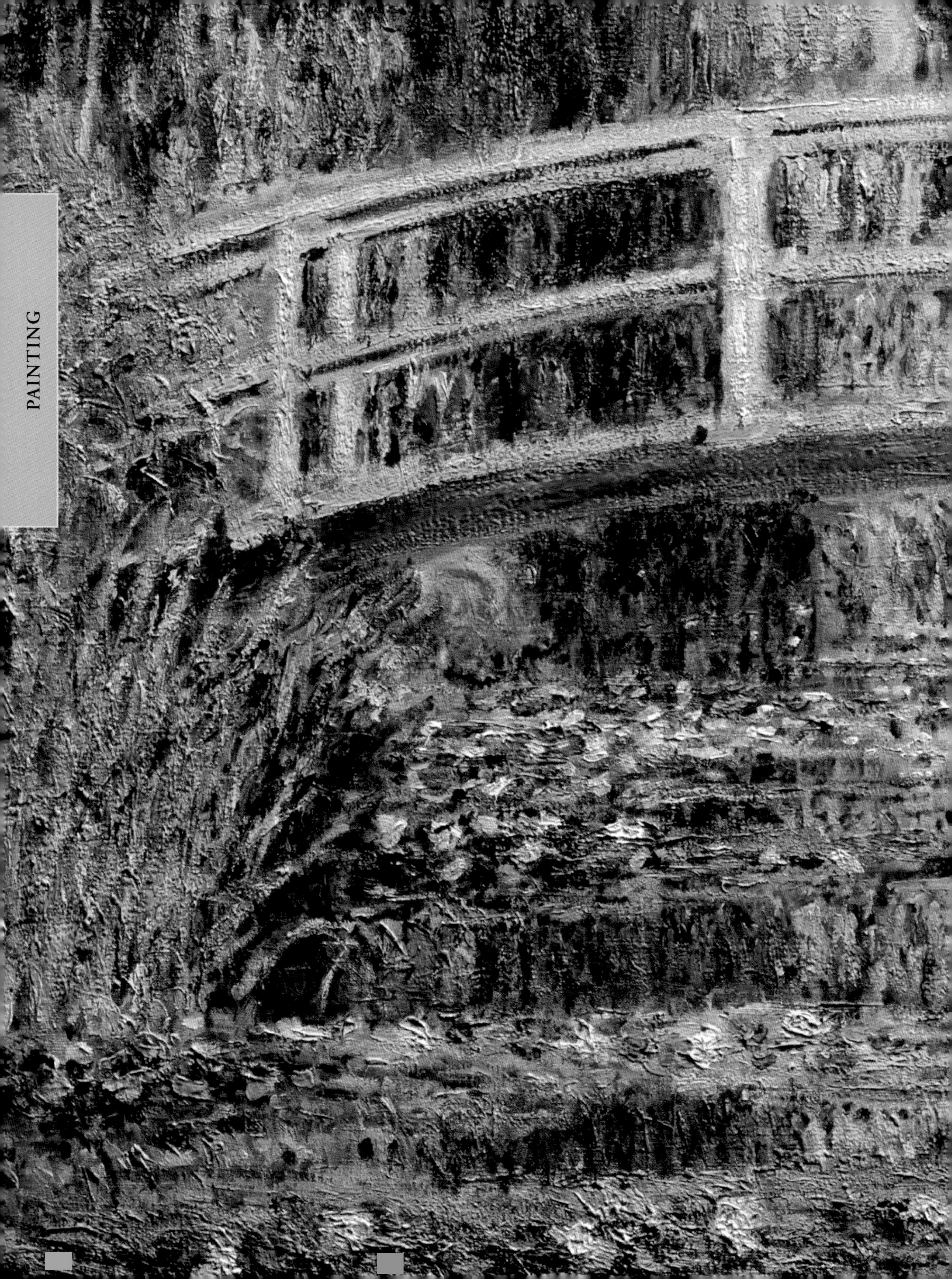

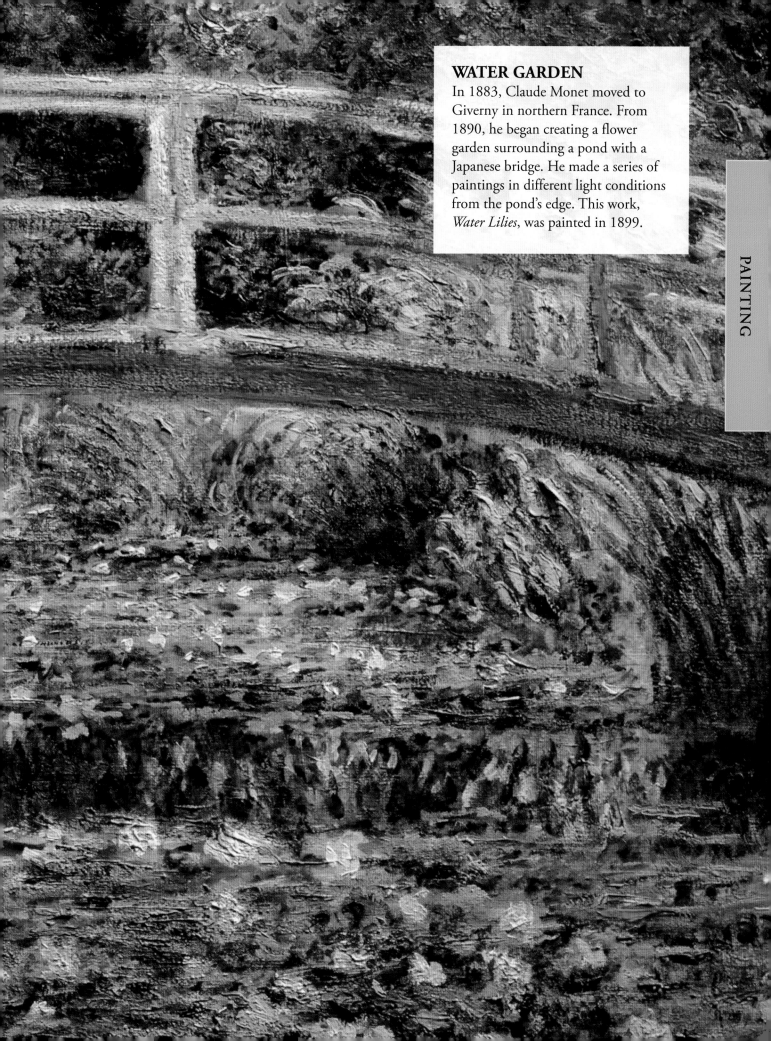

WATER GARDEN
In 1883, Claude Monet moved to Giverny in northern France. From 1890, he began creating a flower garden surrounding a pond with a Japanese bridge. He made a series of paintings in different light conditions from the pond's edge. This work, *Water Lilies*, was painted in 1899.

Post-Impressionism

After Impressionism came Post-Impressionism, a period of great artistic innovation. Artists experimented with color, shapes, and brushstrokes to express their ideas in very different ways. Most Post-Impressionist artists were not understood in their lifetime, but many would prove highly influential after their deaths.

Toulouse-Lautrec was not only a great painter, he is also famous for the posters he designed for Paris nightclubs.

COLOR AND SHAPE

The most influential of the Post-Impressionist artists was the French painter Paul Cézanne. He explored the same same subjects again and again, mostly landscapes and still lifes. Working very slowly, he sought to simplify the shape and structure of objects, using color to give them depth. His work was hugely influential on Cubist painters such as Picasso, and paved the way for abstract art.

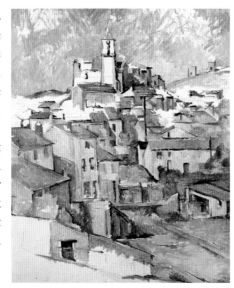

◄ GARDANNE, 1885–1886, PAUL CÉZANNE
Geometric shapes make up this hilltop town in the south of France, an area Cézanne loved for its bright light and strong colors.

SYMBOLISM

Some artists moved away from Impressionism's exploration of the natural world. Instead, they wanted their art to have inner meaning, or to convey a sense of mystery or fantasy. This style of art became known as Symbolism because it featured symbols that people were familiar with, for example, from the Bible or mythology. The French artist Paul Gauguin painted in a style that added to the sense of the unreal, using strong lines, and areas of bold, flat, unnatural color.

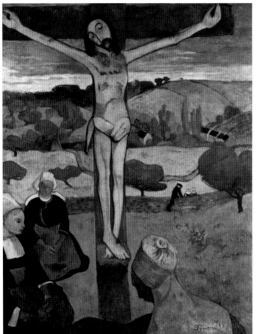

◄ YELLOW CHRIST, 1889, PAUL GAUGUIN
Placing Christ on the cross in the landscape of northern France, Gauguin conveys the strong, simple faith of the local women praying at his feet.

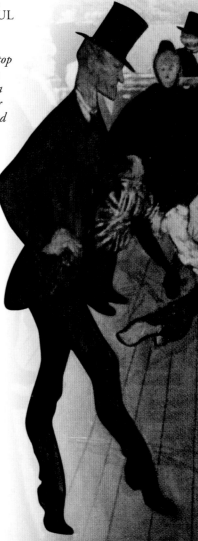

TINY DOTS OF PAINT

Some Post-Impressionists, such as the French artist Georges Seurat, experimented with optical effects. Seurat developed a technique called pointillism, in which he placed tiny dots of color next to one another. From a distance, the dots blended together to make colors that appear to almost glow.

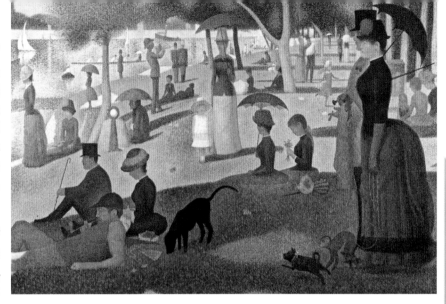

▶ *SUNDAY AFTERNOON ON THE ISLAND OF LA GRANDE JATTE*, 1884–1886, GEORGES SEURAT
This Paris scene feels almost frozen in time, yet also busy with people and detail, such as the monkey on the right.

INDIVIDUAL CHARACTER

The important French Post-Impressionist artist Henri de Toulouse-Lautrec was inspired by the Impressionist painter Degas, and his scenes of life backstage at the ballet. Toulouse-Lautrec's style was very different, however, and his world was Paris nightlife. Influenced by Japanese art, he used long, curving lines to create striking, silhouettes that made every character unique.

▼ *AT THE MOULIN ROUGE*, 1892–1895, HENRI DE TOULOUSE-LAUTREC
This composition places the viewer right in and among the crowd of this Parisian nightclub.

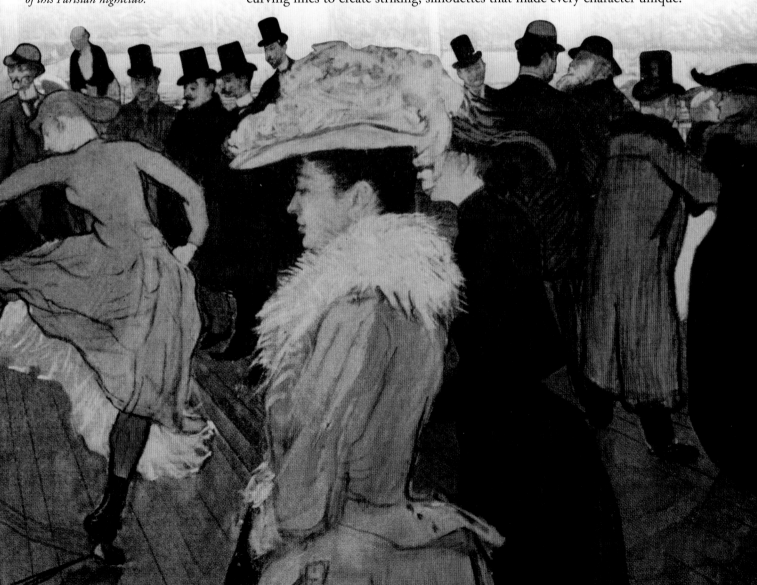

The Starry Night

Today, the works of the Dutch Post-Impressionist artist Vincent van Gogh are famous throughout the world. However, he received little acclaim in his day, and led a troubled life. In 1889, he painted *The Starry Night* while he was a patient in an asylum.

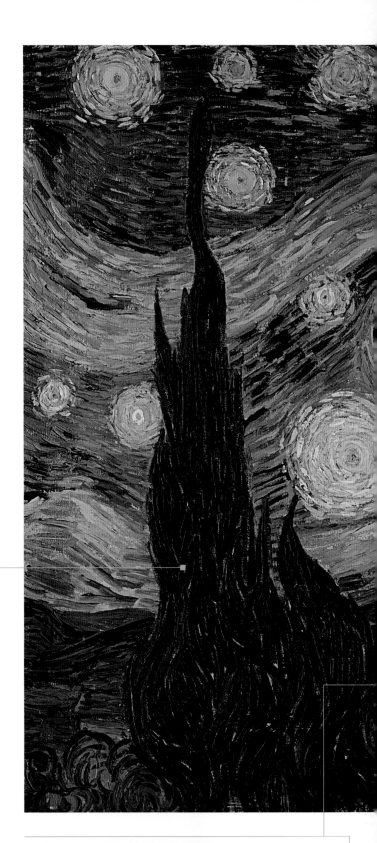

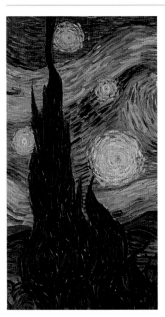

SYMBOLISM
Art historians have tried to interpret the painting. One theory is that the sky represents God, the village represents the world, and the cypress trees van Gogh himself. The composition suggests a biblical story, of Joseph describing a dream to his 11 brothers: "The Sun, the Moon, and the eleven stars bowed down to me."

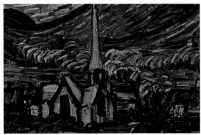

DUTCH CHURCH
The steeple of the village church is of a kind typical of the Netherlands, and was probably based on a church van Gogh remembered from his home.

TORTURED ARTIST

In 1888, van Gogh moved to Arles in the South of France, where his works became brighter, with bold brushstrokes. He was joined there by the French artist Paul Gauguin. Following a row with Gauguin, van Gogh cut off his own ear, after which he was admitted to the asylum at Saint-Paul-de-Mausole, France.

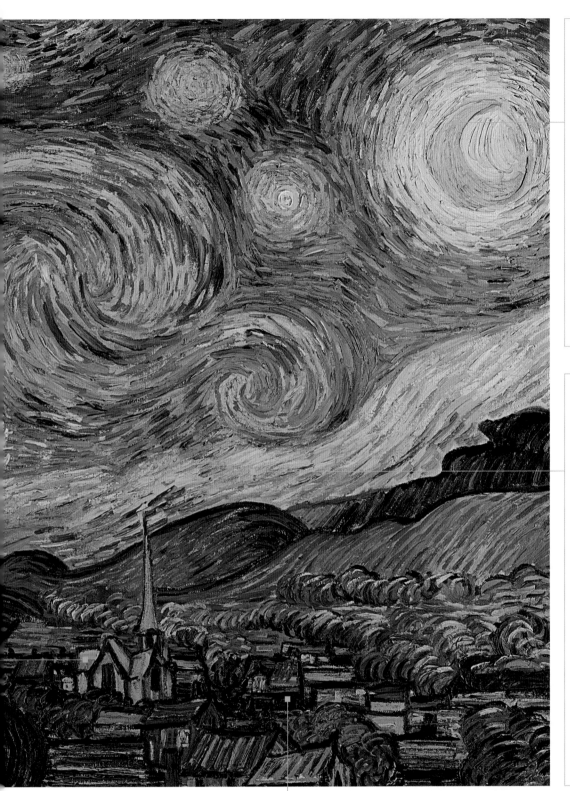

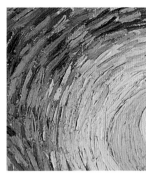

COMPLEMENTARY COLORS

The swirling Moon- and star-filled sky takes up most of the composition. Orange and blue are complementary colors—placed next to each other, both appear brighter.

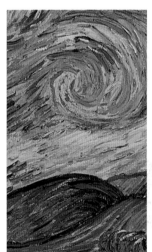

IMPASTO PAINT

Using short brushstrokes and the application of thick paint (a style known as impasto), van Gogh gives the sky an impression of movement and misty radiance.

THE VILLAGE

Van Gogh painted The Starry Night *from his window at the asylum of Saint-Paul-de-Mausole. However, the village itself is not visible from the window. Like the swirls of stars, the village shown here is imaginary.*

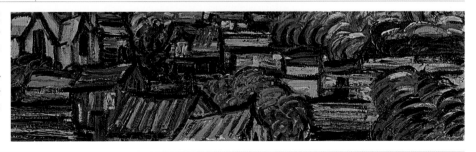

145

Imaginative art

At the end of the 19th century, two new art and design styles developed. As a reaction against Realism, both styles were highly imaginative. The Symbolists created mysterious pictures, often based on ancient mythology, while Art Nouveau painters made highly stylized images.

Orpheus

A typically mysterious Symbolist work

- **Artist** Gustav Moreau
- **Date** 1865
- **Medium** Oil on wood

This French Symbolist was influenced by Renaissance master Leonardo da Vinci and Romanticist Eugène Delacroix, and painted highly imaginative pictures based on ancient Greek and Roman mythology. Orpheus was a legendary Greek musician. Here, an unnamed girl mourns over his head, placed on his lyre.

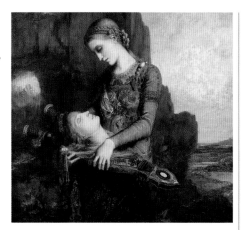

Island of the Dead

An image described by the artist as "a dream picture"

- **Artist** Arnold Böcklin
- **Date** 1883
- **Medium** Oil on wood

The Swiss Symbolist Böcklin was inspired by Romanticism. He painted five different versions of this eerie work, experimenting with different light and color; this is the third version. A man rows a boat to an island. Next to him is a shrouded figure standing next to a draped coffin. Tall, dark cypress trees and a strange light add to the unsettling atmosphere.

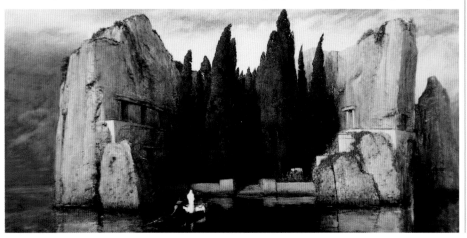

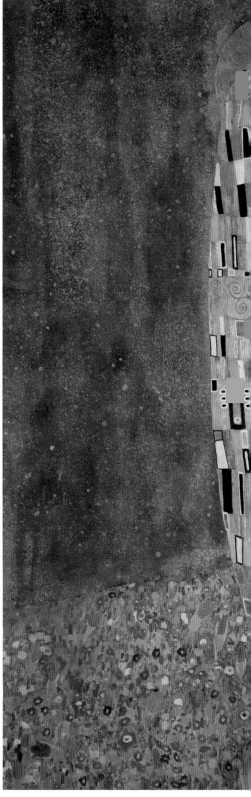

▲ MIX OF STYLES
This Art Nouveau painting is also Symbolist. The patterns on the man's clothing symbolize masculinity, while those on the woman's clothing symbolize femininity.

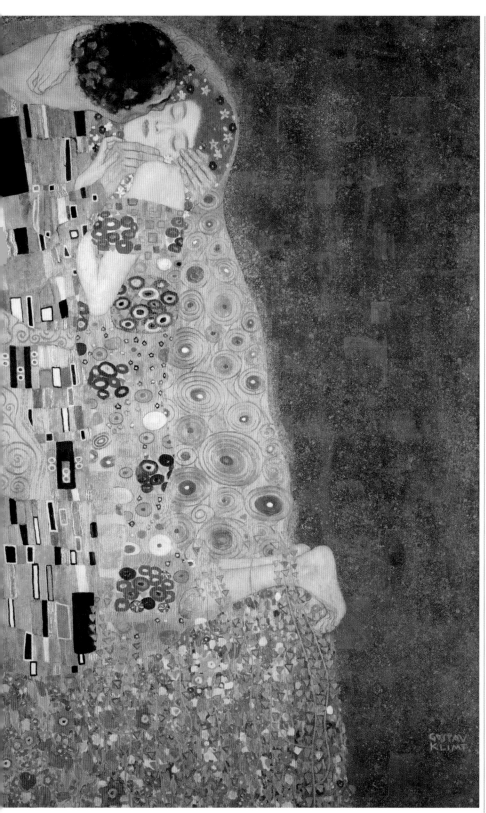

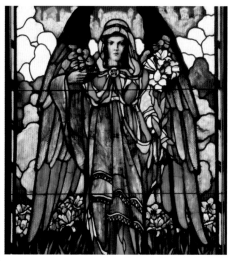

Hollywood Angel
A stained glass window in Chicago

- **Artist** Tiffany Studio
- **Date** c.1910
- **Medium** Stained glass

Among other things, American artist and designer Louis Comfort Tiffany produced innovative colored glass designs, having invented a new method of making stained glass. Based on curving, natural forms and flowing lines, Art Nouveau works such as this had numerous influences, including Celtic and Islamic art and design, Rococo and Symbolist art, and Japanese design.

Return from the Washroom
An illustration that forms a social commentary

- **Artist** Théophile Alexandre Steinlen
- **Date** 1912
- **Medium** Color soft ground etching

This Swiss-born French painter made expressive Art Nouveau illustrations in a simplified, elongated style that influenced many others, including Pablo Picasso. Steinlen produced hundreds of illustrations, which often made visual comments about problems in society. This work depicts poor women in Paris.

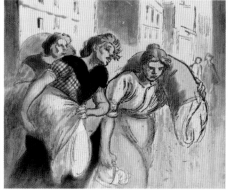

The Kiss
A radical, stylized Art Nouveau work

- **Artist** Gustav Klimt
- **Date** 1908
- **Medium** Oil and silver and gold leaf on canvas

In 1897, in Vienna, Austria, some artists and architects broke away from what they saw as the old-fashioned Vienna establishment to create Art Nouveau (meaning "new art").

Klimt was the most influential artist of the group. This is one of his most famous paintings—an embellished, stylized image of a man kissing a woman's cheek.

Painting emotions

Expressionism is an artistic style that started in Germany at the start of the 20th century. This movement included artists who showed strong emotions in their paintings, often using distorted shapes. Fauvism was another movement of the time that used strong colors and simplified forms to bring out an immediate emotional reaction from viewers.

DISTORTED IMAGES

Expressionist art attempted to depict the anger, anxiety, and fear caused by the upheavals taking place in German society at the time. Feelings became the most important element of the art, not the representation of reality. Individual Expressionists had their own ways of presenting their feelings in their paintings, but they all distorted or exaggerated objects, people, and colors.

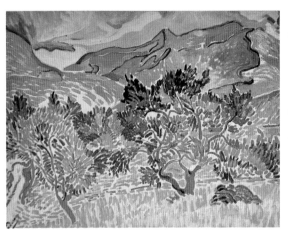

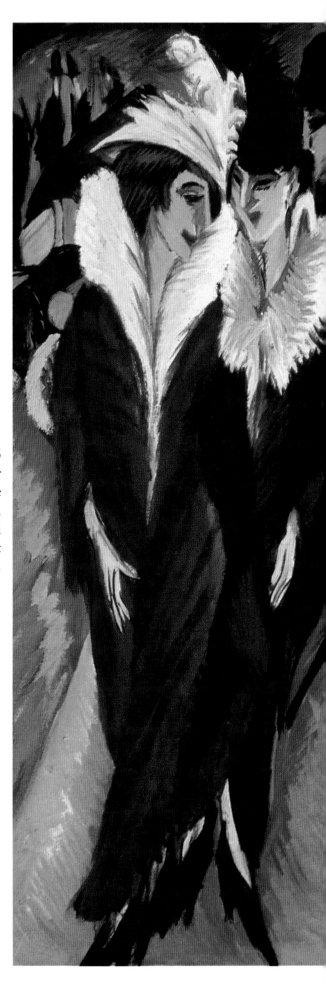

◀ *MOUNTAINS AT COLLIOURE*, 1905, ANDRÉ DERAIN
Produced while Derain was on a painting holiday with Henri Matisse, the colors and shapes in this work express his optimism at the time.

SHOCKING AUDIENCES

In 1903 in Paris, the first Salon d'Automne (Autumn Salon) was set up by the artists Henri Matisse, Maurice de Vlaminck, Albert Marquet, André Derain, and Georges Rouault. They intended it to be a new exhibition for modern art. In 1905, when these artists exhibited at the Salon d'Automne, their wildly colored and seemingly messy works unsettled audiences.

WILD BEASTS

The paintings at the Salon d'Automne were condemned by art critics. Building on the work of the Post-Impressionists, the artists used unnatural, bright colors and short, lively marks, ignoring perspective and simplifying details. A critic insultingly said that the paintings looked like wild beasts (*fauves* in French), and the new art movement became known as Fauvism.

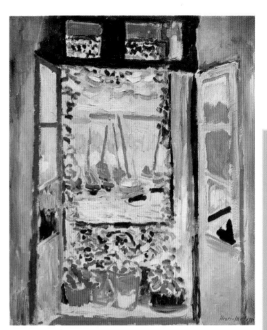

▲ *THE OPEN WINDOW, COLLIOURE,* 1905, HENRI MATISSE
Looking out onto a small fishing port, the unnatural colors of this Fauvist painting suggest happiness.

To make their colors as bold as possible, Fauvists would sometimes apply paint to the canvas directly from the tube.

◄ *STREET, BERLIN,* 1913–1915, ERNST LUDWIG KIRCHNER
Clashing colors and strange angles create a sense of discomfort in this Expressionist work.

SIMPLE SHAPES, VIVID COLORS

The simplified shapes and vibrant colors of the Fauvists' work reflected each artist's connection to nature, which, unlike Expressionism, was usually happy or joyful. However, Fauvism did not last long, and three years after the 1905 exhibition, most of the Fauvists were painting in different ways.

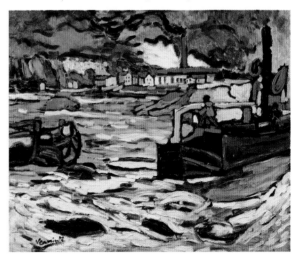

► *BARGES ON THE SEINE,* 1905–1906, MAURICE DE VLAMINCK
Using thick paint in bold, strong colors applied in slabs, this Fauvist work conveys a sense of activity and motion.

Edvard Munch

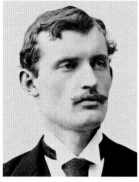

Photograph of
Munch, age 26

The Norwegian painter and printmaker
Edvard Munch made disturbing images
that grew out of his interest in Symbolism
and reflected his own psychological problems.
His mother died when he was five and his
sister died when he was 14, and Munch
constantly worried about death and his health.

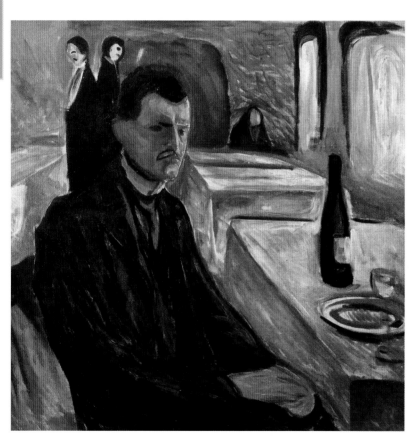

SELF-PORTRAITS

Recording his changing age
and emotions, Munch painted
self-portraits from the age of
18 until he was 80. Like his
other works, many of his
self-portraits feature intense
color and a sense of mystery.
His art combined images of
the world around him with his
own emotional and spiritual
vision, in a similar way to the
works of Vincent van Gogh.

◄ *SELF-PORTRAIT WITH
A BOTTLE OF WINE*, 1906
*One of only a few people in a
restaurant, a somber-looking
42-year-old Munch is sitting
by himself.*

LIFE STORY

1863	1868–1877	1879–1884	1885–1890
Munch is born in Ådalsbruk, Norway. His father is an army doctor. In 1864, the Munch family moves to Kristiania (now Oslo).	In 1868, Munch's mother dies of tuberculosis. When he is 13, he leaves school due to illness. When he is 15, his sister Sophie also dies of tuberculosis.	Munch studies engineering, then painting. In 1883, he trains with painter Frits Thaulow and shows a painting at the Autumn Exhibition in Kristiania.	Munch exhibits in the Norwegian section of the Paris World's Fair and stays to study art in Paris. In 1889, he holds his first one-man exhibition.

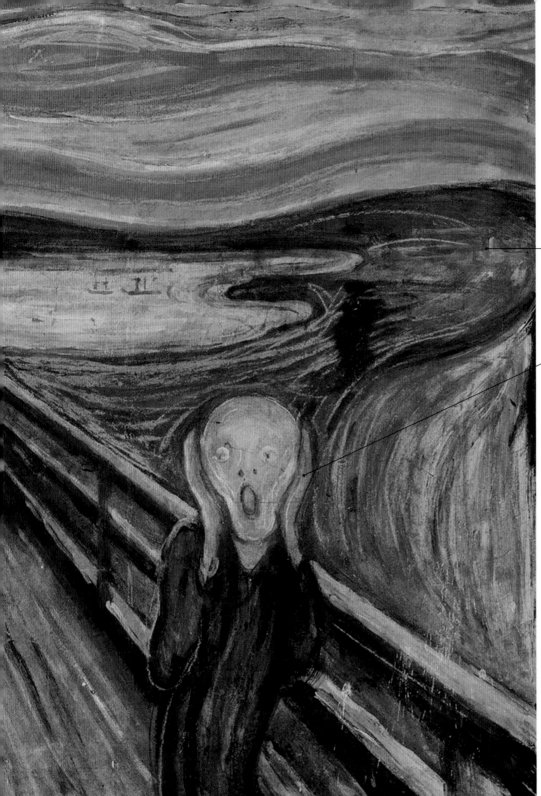

◀ *THE SCREAM,*
1893 VERSION
This is one of the most
recognizable paintings in
the world. It is one of four
versions of the picture that
Munch originally called
The Scream of Nature.

Flowing, swirling
lines represent the
Kristianiafjord
in Norway.

Holding his skull-like
face in his thin
hands, the figure
screams directly at
the viewer.

IN HIS OWN WORDS

In *The Scream,* Munch was painting his own inner, tortured feelings. He described what inspired him to paint it: "I was walking along the road with two friends—the sun was setting—suddenly the sky turned blood red—I paused, feeling exhausted, and leaned on the fence—there was blood and tongues of fire above the blue-black fjord and the city—my friends walked on, and I stood there trembling with anxiety—and I sensed an infinite scream passing through nature."

1889–1894	1895–1899	1900–1932	1944
He travels around France, Belgium, Denmark, and Germany. In 1894, he produces his first prints.	Over several years, Munch's works are shown in Denmark, Norway, Germany, and France. In 1896, he creates his first color lithographs and woodcuts.	Munch travels widely across Western Europe. Continually worried about his health, he spends some time at German health spas.	On his death in 1944, Munch leaves more than 20,000 works of art to the city of Oslo, Norway, many of which are now on display at the Munch Museum.

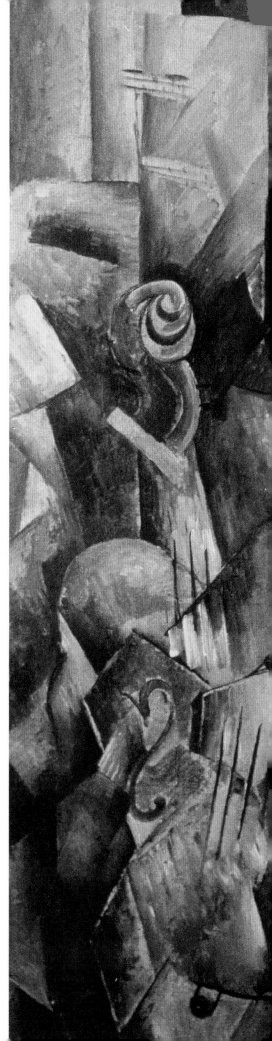

Cubism and Futurism

One of the most influential art movements of the 20th century, Cubism involved artists abandoning perspective and realism to paint a subject from several different angles at once. It was inspired by the work of French painter Paul Cézanne. Another important modern movement was Futurism, which depicted technology, speed, and movement.

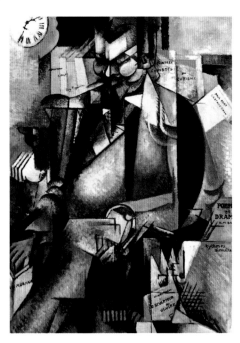

GEOMETRIC FORMS

In 1907, the Spanish artist Pablo Picasso and French artist Georges Braque visited an exhibition of Cézanne's work in Paris, France. They were inspired by what they saw to start making paintings made of broken shapes. Like Cézanne, the artists tried to capture the simple geometric forms, such as oblongs and triangles, found in nature.

◄ *L'EDITEUR*, 1913,
ALBERT GLEIZES
In this portrait of publisher Eugéne Figuière, the subject is broken up and merges with the background.

DIFFERENT POINTS OF VIEW

Cubists painted their subjects from several different angles in the same picture, often including clues about what their paintings were about or which way up they should be. In 1911, the French journalist Louis Vauxcelles described the paintings as looking like "little cubes," and the name Cubism stuck.

▶ *VIOLIN AND PALETTE*, 1909, GEORGES BRAQUE
The fractured representation of the violin in this painting was typical of Cubist works.

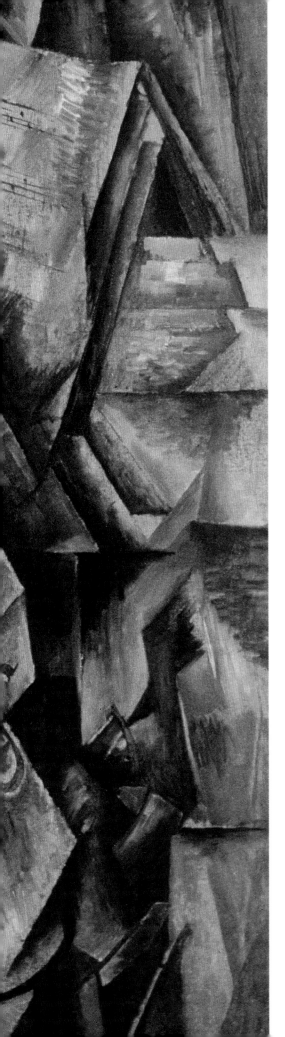

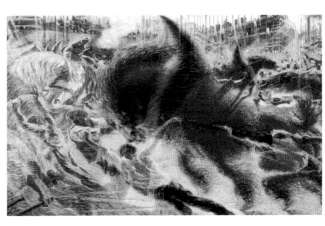

▶ *THE CITY RISES*, 1910, UMBERTO BOCCIONI
This Italian painter is celebrating the building of a city. Figures are blurred to give the impression that they are moving.

FORWARD THINKING

Futurist artists first exhibited in Milan, Italy, in 1911. Futurist painters, sculptors, writers, architects, and designers were interested in exploring modern technology. Among other things, they declared that old art should be destroyed to make way for new art for the modern world.

In 1909, the Italian poet Filippo Tommaso Marinetti launched the Futurist movement on a newspaper's front page.

SPLINTERED SHAPES

With splintered shapes and bright colors, Futurist painters emphasized the speed of new machines, such as cars. Their works captured the bustle of the modern city, rejecting more traditional ideas of the beauty and harmony of the natural world.

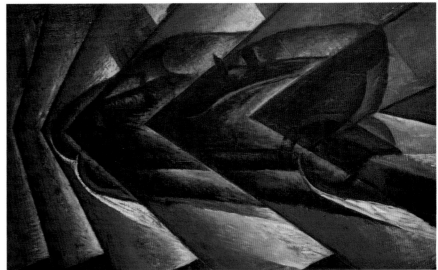

▲ *AUTOMOBILE IN CORSICA*, 1912, LUIGI RUSSOLO
Italian Russolo painted a car bursting through sound waves to convey the idea of speed.

Pablo Picasso

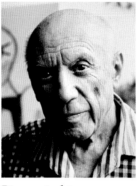

Picasso in his
studio, age 90

Celebrated for starting and shaping several different art
styles and movements, Spanish-born Pablo Picasso was
one of the most influential artists of the 20th century.
He abandoned a realistic style at an early age and went
on to change the face of modern art. During his long
life, Picasso produced more than 20,000 artworks,
including drawings, paintings, and sculptures.

THE HORRORS OF WAR

In 1937, during the Spanish Civil
War, the Spanish government asked
Picasso to paint a picture for a big
exhibition being held in Paris, France.
He produced a huge painting showing
the horrific effects of the bombing
of a Spanish town called Guernica.

MULTI-TALENTED ARTIST

Picasso found inspiration all around him—in African
masks, children's toys, and Impressionist paintings. He
was particularly inspired by the works of the French
artist Paul Cézanne. Picasso created art of many kinds,
including costumes and scenery for ballets, ceramics,
and sculpture, in addition to thousands of paintings.

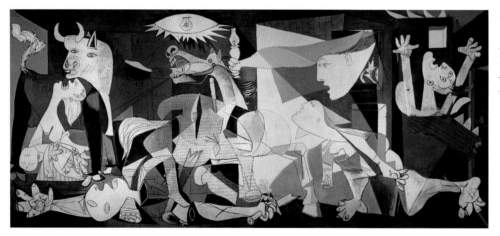

◄ *GUERNICA,*
1937
Picasso's distorted
images express the
suffering of the
Spanish Civil War.

LIFE STORY

1881–1895	1896–1904	1905–1906	1907
Pablo Picasso is born in Málaga, Spain. In 1895, his father takes a job at an art school in Barcelona, and Picasso goes there to study.	Picasso studies art in Madrid. In 1900, he and a friend travel to Paris. When his friend dies, Picasso paints sad blue pictures. This is his Blue Period.	From 1905, Picasso paints circus and carnival characters, mainly in pink. This is known as his Rose Period. In 1906, he meets French artist Henri Matisse.	Picasso is inspired by African sculpture and Cézanne's paintings. He paints *Les Demoiselles d'Avignon* and meets Georges Braque.

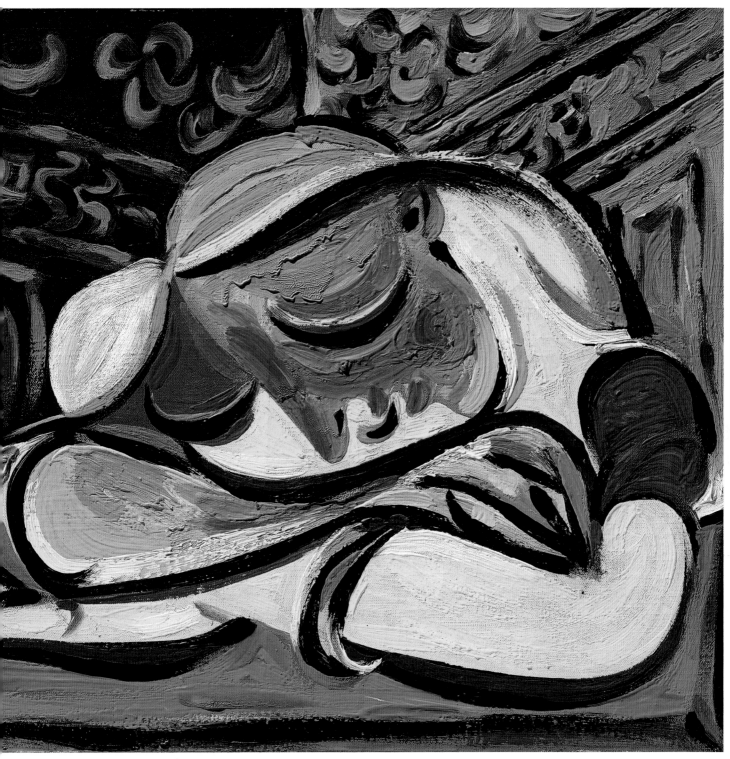

▲ *YOUNG GIRL SLEEPING*, 1935
Picasso invented many expressive styles, using bold and unexpected colors. The sleeping figure is his muse Marie-Thérèse Walter.

1908–1923	1924–1938	1939–1947	1948–1973
Picasso and Braque invent Cubism. From 1914, as World War I rages, Picasso makes paintings in a Neoclassical style.	The Surrealist movement begins. In 1936, the Spanish Civil War starts. The town of Guernica is bombed, and Picasso paints a huge work about the atrocity.	World War II begins, ending in 1945. In 1941, Picasso writes a play, and in 1945, he makes lithographic prints. In 1947, he moves to the south of France.	In 1958, Picasso buys a castle in France. He continues painting, printing, and making sculpture and pottery until his death at the age of 91.

New abstract styles

In the early 20th century, artists across Europe became interested in developing new styles of abstract art. Suprematist paintings used only straight lines or geometric shapes, while Neoplastic artists went even further, reducing everything to straight vertical or horizontal black lines and rectangular blocks of color.

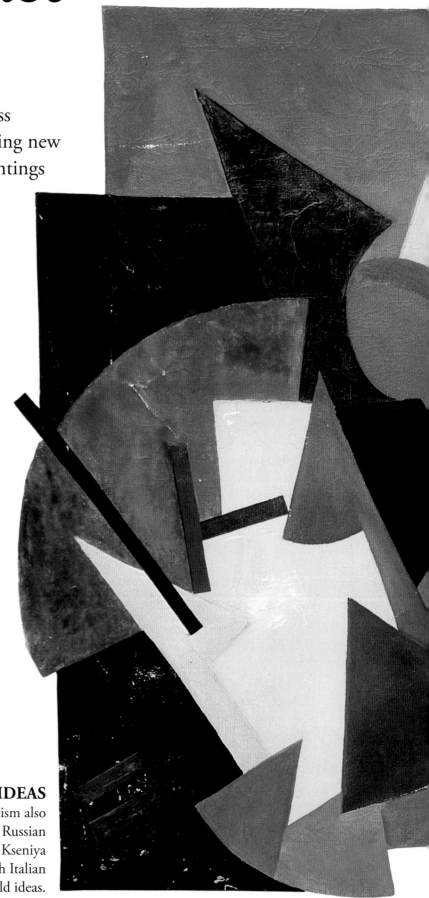

◄ *BLACK SQUARE*, 1915, KAZIMIR MALEVICH *Malevich believed this painting was "pure" art.*

SUPREME SIMPLICITY

Influenced by Cubism and Futurism, the Russian artist Kazimir Malevich attempted to reduce his paintings to just the barest essentials, using simple shapes and colors. Malevich believed that his new style would be superior to art of the past, and called it Suprematism.

A WORLD OF NEW IDEAS

Primarily a Russian movement, Suprematism also influenced abstract art all over the world. Russian Suprematist artists, such as Malevich and Kseniya Boguslavskaya, were closely associated with Italian Futurists. Both groups sought to overthrow old ideas.

"THE STYLE"

In 1917, the Dutch painter, designer, writer, and critic Theo van Doesburg published an exciting new magazine called *De Stijl* (*The Style*), which contained the new ideas of some artists and architects. The painter Piet Mondrian, also from the Netherlands, wrote for the magazine about his ideas for a "pure" form of art.

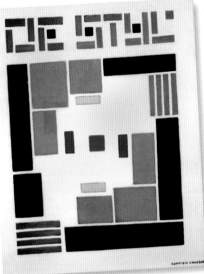

▲ *DE STYL*, 1950,
VILMOS HUSZÁR
Hungarian Huszár designed the cover for the first issue of De Stijl *in 1917. This painting was inspired by his original cover design.*

◄ *FLIGHT OF AN AEROPLANE*, 1916,
OLGA ROZANOVA
This Russian Suprematist created a sense of upward movement with bright colors and jagged edges.

Mondrian believed that his highly simplified paintings revealed what he called the "basic forms of beauty."

BLOCK PAINTINGS

Influenced by Cubism, Suprematism, and Van Doesburg, Piet Mondrian's painting style became called *De Stijl* after the magazine (see above), although he called it Neoplasticism. Mondrian reduced everything that he painted to straight black vertical and horizontal lines on smooth, white-painted canvases, shading in areas with primary colors or grey.

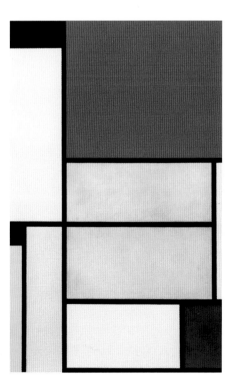

► *TABLEAU 1*, 1921,
PIET MONDRIAN
This painting represents a rejection of traditional, representative art.

Dada and Surrealism

When World War I broke out, one group of artists was angered by the pointless loss of life, so they began an "anti-art" movement, which they called Dada. After the war, a new artistic movement called Surrealism emerged, inspired by Dada. Surrealists depicted the world of dreams.

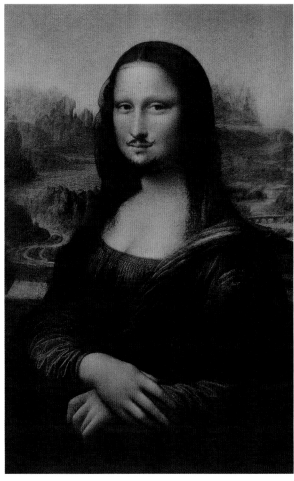

▲ *L.H.O.O.Q.*, 1919, MARCEL DUCHAMP
French artist Duchamp painted a moustache on a cheap copy of Mona Lisa, an act of typical Dadaist mischief.

PROTEST ART

Dada was a protest against the horrors of war and the people who had allowed it to happen. Dadaists staged concerts and other performances, wrote essays and poems, and created art that was absurd or rude. It was their intention to shock and offend their audiences.

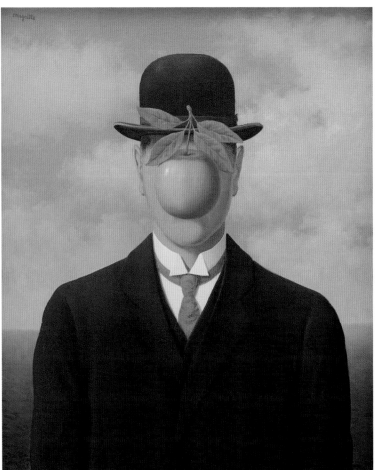

EXPLORING THE DREAM WORLD

Surrealism is a literary and artistic movement that began in 1924 in Paris, France. Surrealist artists were influenced by Dada and the work of the Austrian doctor and psychoanalyst Sigmund Freud, who studied unconscious thoughts and the meaning of dreams.

◄ *THE SON OF MAN*,
1964, RENÉ MAGRITTE
Using a realistic painting style, Magritte depicted objects in odd sizes and unexpected places. In this work, he hides the man's identity with a floating apple.

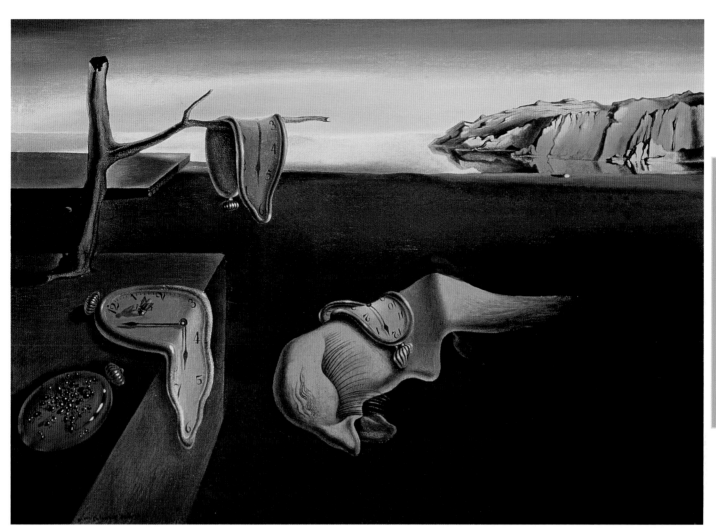

REALISTIC BUT STRANGE

One group of Surrealists painted realistic-looking, familiar objects in strange dreamlike situations. Spaniard Salvador Dalí, Belgian René Magritte, and Frenchman Yves Tanguy all worked in this way, demonstrating considerable artistic skill to create this unique style.

▲ *THE PERSISTENCE OF MEMORY*, 1931, SALVADOR DALÍ
Dalí described his weird but lifelike Surrealist images as "hand-painted dream photographs." Here, clocks melt in a barren landscape.

Marcel Duchamp first used the term "anti-art" in 1913. He wanted to change ideas of what could be considered art.

▶ *HARLEQUIN'S CARNIVAL*, 1925, JOAN MIRÓ
This Surrealist artist painted colorful, imaginary images from his unconscious mind, creating playful-looking scenes.

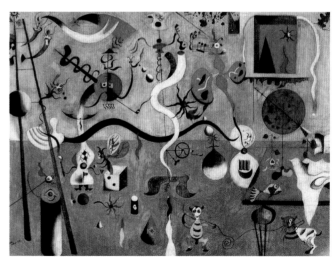

AUTOMATIC PAINTING

Another style of Surrealism was intended to allow the unconscious mind to take over. This was called Automatism. Spanish artist Joan Miró and Swiss artist Paul Klee often worked in this way. Miró claimed he did not eat and painted in a trance-like state because he was so hungry.

Georgia O'Keeffe

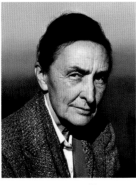

Born on a farm in Wisconsin, the American painter Georgia O'Keeffe was influenced by many artists, including Auguste Rodin and Henri Matisse, and also by the Art Nouveau style. Over her long career, she produced more than 2,000 works, usually of objects found in nature, and was a pioneer of modern art.

Georgia O'Keeffe in 1956

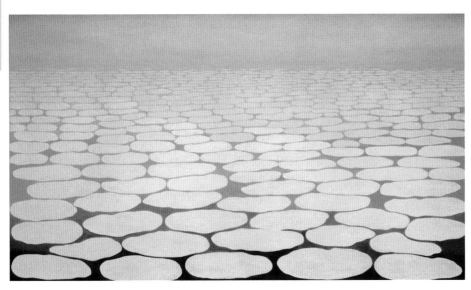

◄ *SKY ABOVE THE CLOUDS III, 1965 Painted when O'Keeffe was 77, this is her abstract view of the sky as seen from an airplane window.*

EXPERIMENTS IN ABSTRACTION

Influenced by the American painter Arthur Wesley Dow's ideas about the use of lines and color to portray the natural world, in 1915 O'Keeffe experimented with abstract compositions. Ten years later, she had become famous for her images of the American landscape.

LARGE-SCALE FLOWERS

In 1924, the year she married, O'Keeffe began painting large, brightly colored flowers in detailed close-up. She said: "I decided that if I could paint that flower in a huge scale, you could not ignore its beauty." She experimented with abstract art, but based her images on natural objects such as shells and bones. From 1929, she began painting more often in New Mexico. Fascinated by the desert landscape, she painted subjects she found and observed there, such as animal bones and cloud formations.

LIFE STORY

1887–1902	1905–1911	1912–1915	1916–1928
Georgia O'Keeffe is born, the second of seven children. When she is 18, the family moves to Williamsburg in Virginia.	O'Keeffe studies art in Chicago. In 1907, she moves to the Art Students' League in New York City, where she is taught by painter William Merritt Chase.	In his New York gallery, the photographer and art dealer Alfred Stieglitz shows O'Keeffe drawings inspired by the American painter Arthur Wesley Dow.	Stieglitz puts on O'Keeffe's first solo exhibition. She visits New Mexico for the first time. In 1924, O'Keeffe and Stieglitz marry. She starts painting flower canvases.

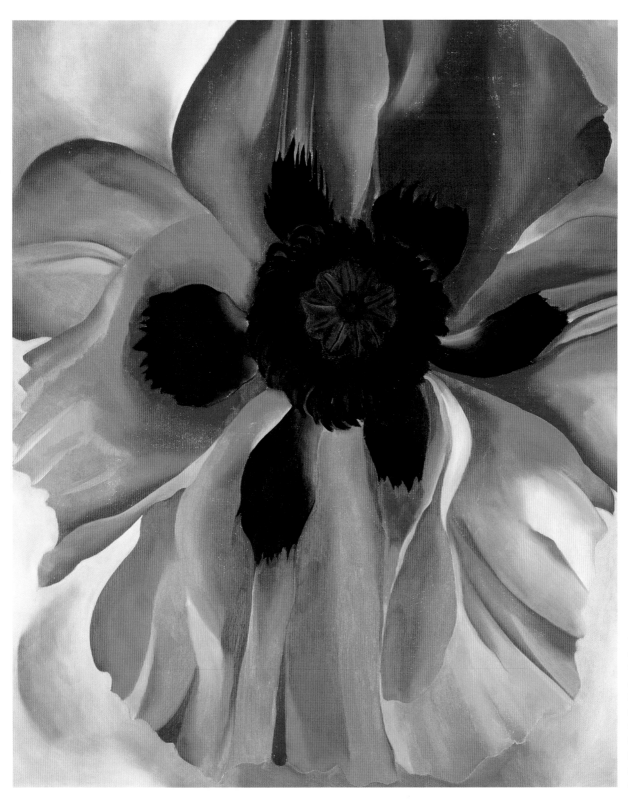

◄ *RED POPPY NO. VI*, 1928 *O'Keeffe filled a 3-ft-tall (meter-tall) canvas with this bright red poppy, revealing details that might be missed in a real, small flower.*

1929–1937	1938–1939	1940–1950	1951–1986
The couple live in New York. O'Keeffe travels to Bermuda and New Mexico. She paints flowers for a cosmetics company.	O'Keeffe is awarded an honorary degree—the first of many—and travels to Hawaii to paint pineapples for the advertising agency N.W. Ayer and Son.	Stieglitz dies in 1946. In 1949, O'Keeffe moves to Abiquiu, near Santa Fe in New Mexico. Her new paintings are inspired by the desert landscape around her.	O'Keeffe continues painting, but in 1971, her eyesight begins to fail. She takes up pottery. At the age of 98, she dies at her home in Santa Fe.

Abstract Expressionism

Originally called the New York School, Abstract Expressionism was the first major art movement to begin in the United States. It started in New York in the 1940s. Abstract Expressionists believed that artistic ideas should come from the unconscious mind.

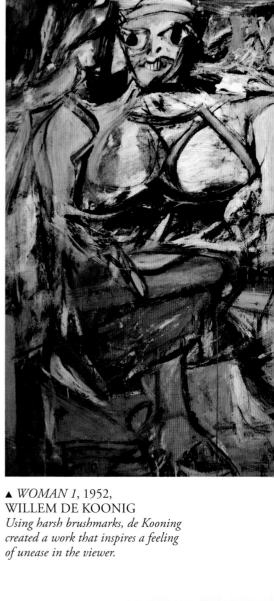

▲ *WOMAN 1*, 1952, WILLEM DE KOONIG
Using harsh brushmarks, de Kooning created a work that inspires a feeling of unease in the viewer.

COLOR FIELD

One technique used by Abstract Expressionists was called Color Field. Paintings made using this technique were created on huge canvases, with large areas painted in one, two, or three colors, which either blended into each other or were placed in separate areas.

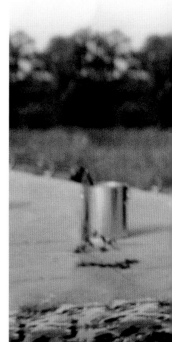

◄ *UNTITLED*, 1964, MARK ROTHKO
Rothko used softly painted rich colors to inspire viewers' feelings in this large work, which measures 81 in x 76 in (205 cm x 193 cm).

PAINTING

INNER FEELINGS

Often anxious about the modern world, Abstract Expressionists painted in a way that expressed their own feelings and aimed to inspire viewers' emotions. In a 1948 essay about the movement, artist Barnett Newman, who created Color Field paintings, wrote that "instead of making cathedrals out of Christ, man, or 'life,' we are making it [art] out of ourselves, out of our own feelings."

Many Abstract Expressionists used the Surrealist method of automatism, or painting instinctively.

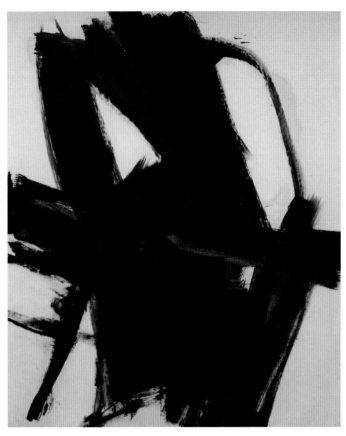

▼ *MERCE C*, 1961, FRANZ KLINE
In Kline's tribute to the choreographer Merce Cunningham, the strokes of dense black paint suggest the movement of dancers and music with a strong beat.

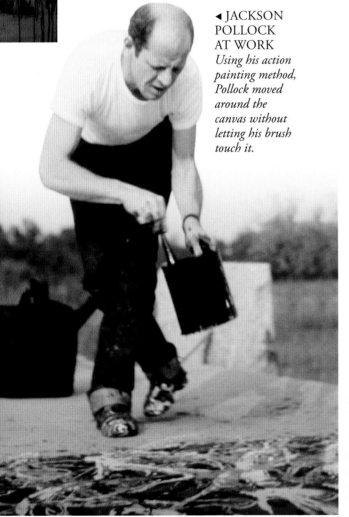

◄ JACKSON POLLOCK AT WORK
Using his action painting method, Pollock moved around the canvas without letting his brush touch it.

COMMON CHARACTERISTICS

Although each artist worked differently, Abstract Expressionist paintings had several things in common. Most of them were painted on huge canvases and painted very quickly. They had no focal—or main—point to attract viewers' eyes. They also used lots of paint, emphasizing the flat surfaces.

ACTION PAINTING

The artist Jackson Pollock invented a completely new, energetic technique for his paintings. He poured, splashed, and dribbled household paint from large cans onto huge canvases on the floor, using sticks, trowels, knives, and his hands. This dynamic method became known as "action painting."

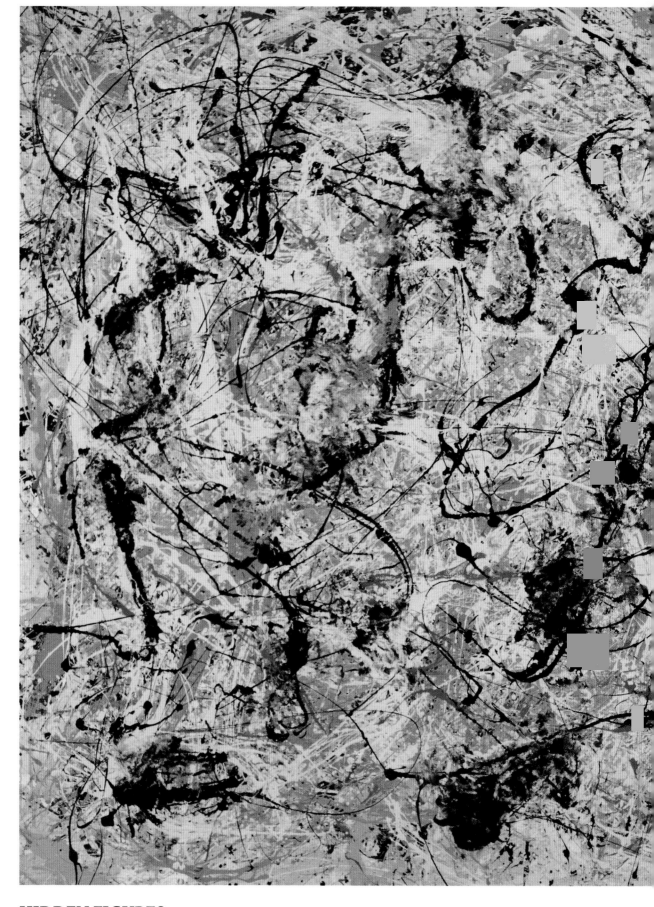

HIDDEN FIGURES

In 1950, the American Abstract Expressionist Jackson Pollock made this painting—called *Number 28*—by flicking and splattering paint all over the canvas. He started the work by drawing figures, which he eventually obscured until they were unrecognizable.

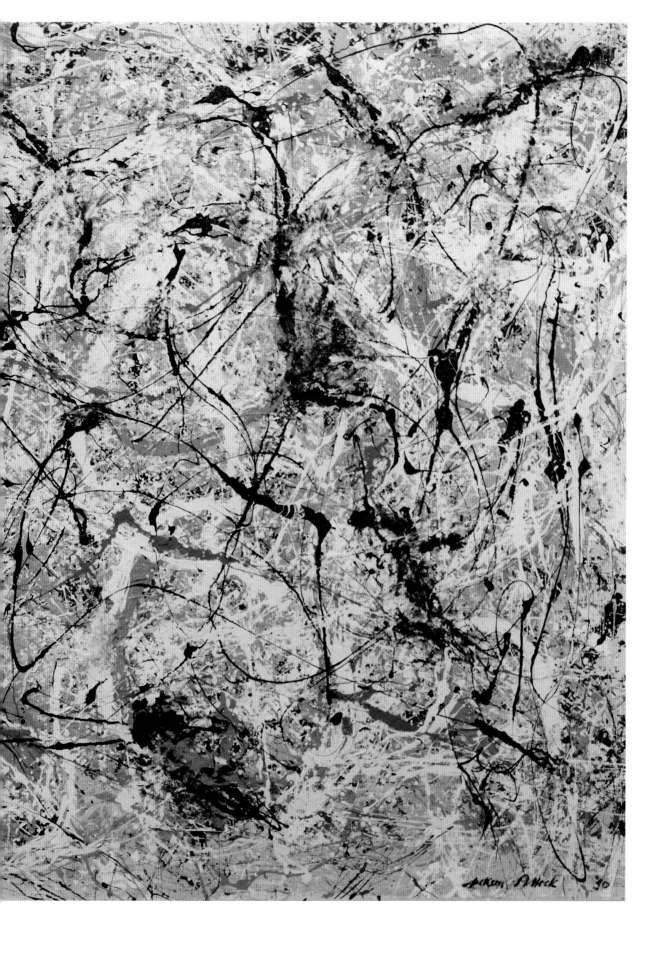

Pop and Op Art

Pop Art developed in the 1950s, first in London and then in New York. It was playful and unconventional, and borrowed imagery from advertising, television, and comic books. Op Art, short for "Optical Art," is an abstract, geometric style that emerged in the 1960s. Artists used optical illusions to trick the eye.

▼ *GREEN MARILYN*, 1962, ANDY WARHOL
This American artist's work is strongly influenced by the celebrity culture and mass media of the 1960s. Here, the film star Marilyn Monroe gets a garish green treatment.

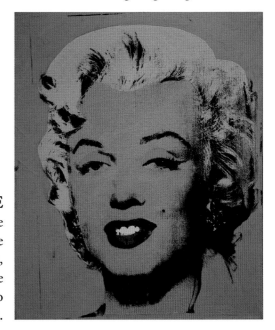

POPULAR CULTURE

In much of the Western world during the 1950s and 1960s, people began buying more mass-produced goods. New forms of music, films, and goods became known as "popular culture." The bold paintings of Pop artists were intended to express visually this new popular culture.

Pop artists used fun imagery from pop culture. Their work was not intended to convey the artist's feelings.

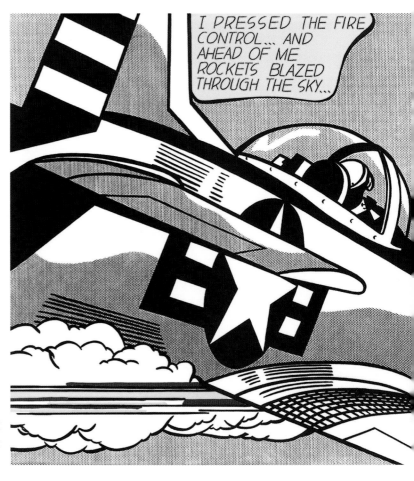

CONSUMER CULTURE

Some artists began making art that reflected the modern world. They featured objects (such as food packaging), people (such as film stars), and production methods from popular culture (such as magazine printing techniques). This was intended to be art that everyone could relate to and enjoy.

PLAYING TRICKS

Optical illusions are images that play tricks on the eye, making the viewer believe that they are seeing something that is not there. Op artists painted lines, shapes, and patterns on flat canvases. The effect on the observer could sometimes be disorienting.

◄ *BLAZE 4,* 1964, BRIDGET RILEY
This British artist used white lines in repeating patterns to trick our brains into seeing movement.

PSYCHOLOGICAL EFFECTS

Although Op Art images are painted on flat canvases, they are created to make us think we are seeing movement, or believe that the image we are looking at is bulging toward or away from us. Op artists used techniques from scientific fields such as psychology to create these effects.

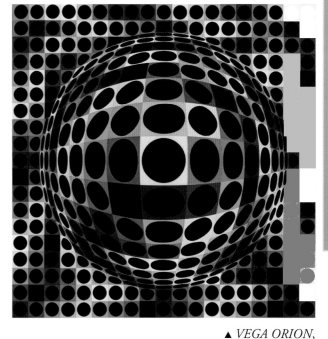

▲ *VEGA ORION,* 1971, VICTOR VASARELY
This Hungarian Op artist has used brightly colored shapes that appear to bulge out of the center, creating the illusion of a sphere.

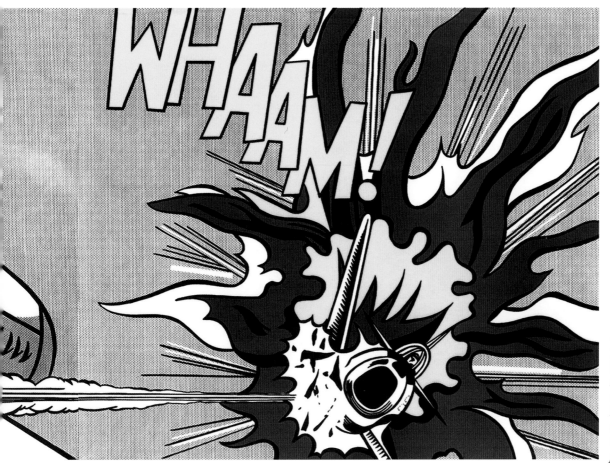

◄ *WHAAM!,* 1963, ROY LICHTENSTEIN
Fun and dramatic, this American Pop artist's huge, comiclike paintings reflected 1960s popular culture.

Contemporary art

Since the end of the 20th century, the idea of what art is has become very broad. Today, artistic trends change rapidly, perhaps reflecting political movements or the invention of new media. Artists may use movies, the Internet, or collage in their works. They have even turned discarded rubbish into works of art.

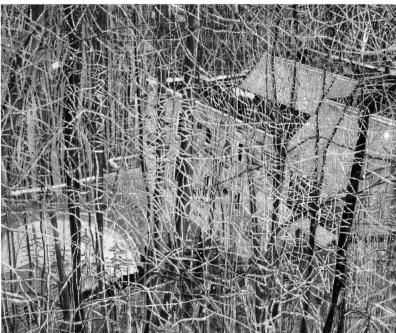

NEW WAYS OF SEEING

Painters today continue to explore subjects in new ways. The British artist Lucian Freud took portraits to a new level by spending thousands of hours examining his subjects, seeking a deeper truth about the person not obvious to the casual observer. The Scottish landscape painter Peter Doig often finds inspiration in movies, photographs, and discarded postcards.

◄ *THE ARCHITECT'S HOME IN THE RAVINE*, 1991, PETER DOIG
There are potentially two subjects in this painting: the trees in the foreground and the house in the background.

DARING TO BE DIFFERENT

Mainstream movements in the 20th century such as Dada and Pop Art made use of "non-art" materials, from clothing to newspaper clippings. This freedom to experiment with new materials inspires many of today's artists to try all sorts of media. Some painters continue to embrace traditional techniques, such as oil painting on canvas or calligraphy, while also learning and practising new methods in computer technology, especially in digital imaging.

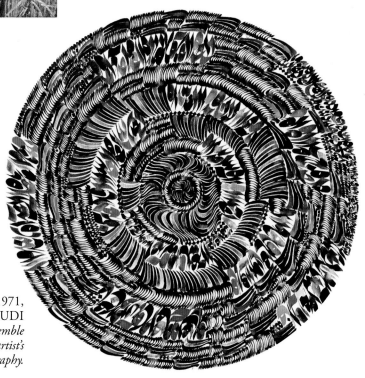

► *MIUZ SKFE*, 1971, CHARLES HOSSEIN ZENDEROUDI
Colored marks that resemble writing reflect this Iranian artist's experimentation with calligraphy.

REAL AND ABSTRACT

Some modern artists paint either realistic or abstract works, while others combine the two styles in one painting. For example, some aboriginal Australian artists today use centuries-old abstract painting methods to link their art with that of their ancestors.

Installation artists may turn a whole room into a work of art, to change the way people perceive space.

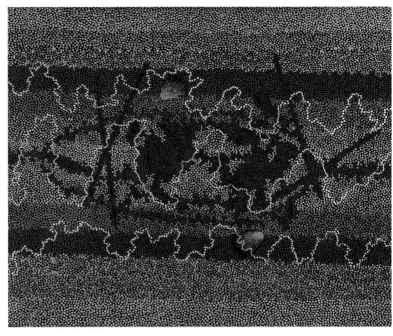

▲ *BUSH FIRE DREAMING*, 1982, CLIFFORD POSSUM TJAPALTJARRI
By the 1980s Tjapaltjarri replaced a brush with a chewed-off end off a stick to apply precise dots to these paintings.

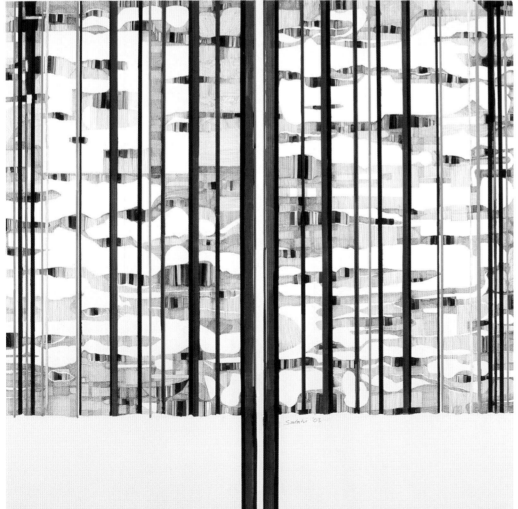

PERSONAL JOURNEYS

Some artists create works to reflect historical events or their personal experiences. The German artist Gerhard Richter, for example, uses paint and photography to explore his childhood during World War II. The Sudanese artist Ibrahim El-Salahi is influenced by the many places he has lived or worked in. As a result, he often combines African, Western, and Arabic styles to paint about the journeys he has been forced to take due to political strife in his homeland.

◄ *THE TREE*, 2003, IBRAHIM EL-SALAHI
Highlighting this artist's influences, the subject of this painting is the English countryside, yet the vertical lines represent the haraza trees that grow along the River Nile in Sudan.

SCULPTURE PARK
Many sculptures are displayed outside. This piece, called *Mirror*, by the Spanish sculptor Jaume Plensa, is seen here at the Yorkshire Sculpture Park in England.

SCULPTURE

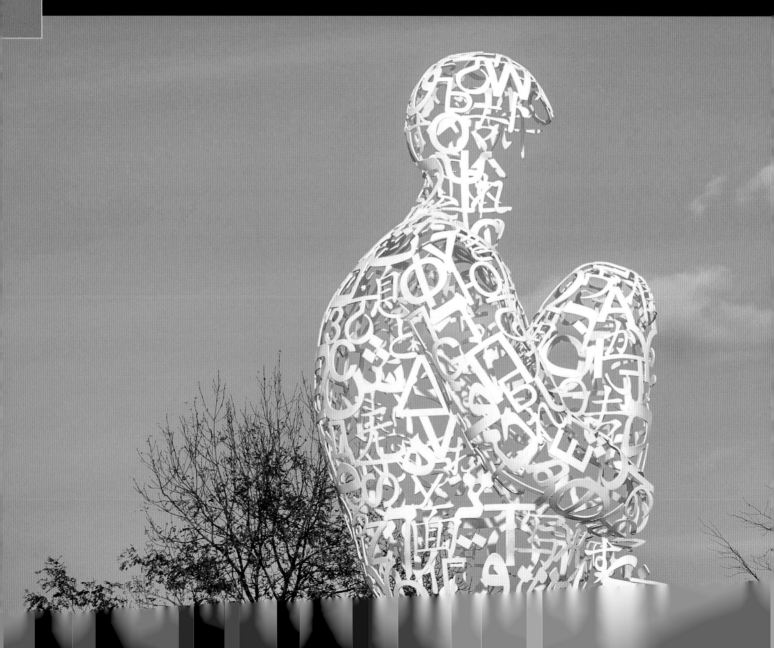

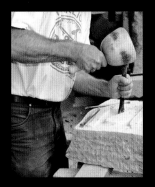
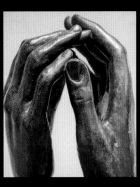
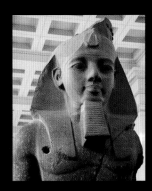

Sculptures are three-dimensional works of art. Often depicting the human form, they may be carved from stone or wood, cast from metal or plaster, or shaped from other materials.

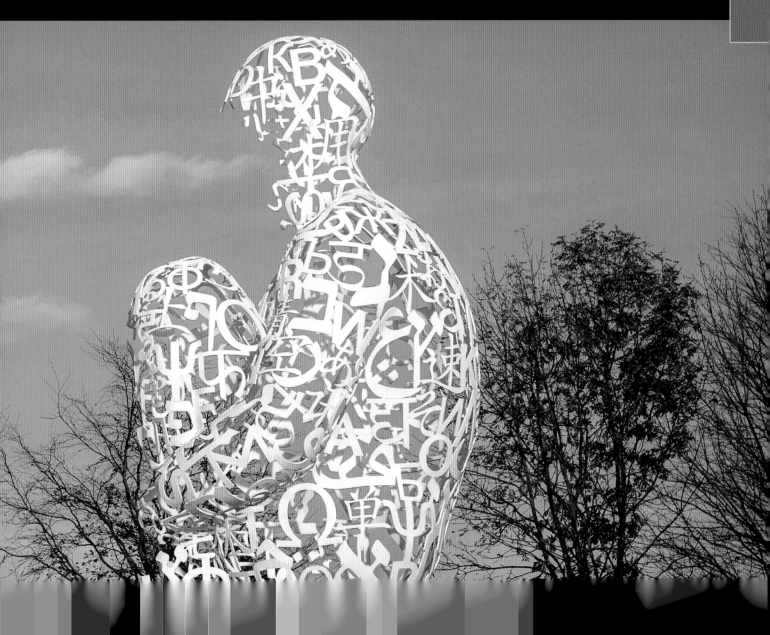

Ancient sculpture

Some of the oldest works of art made by prehistoric people are objects carved into, or from, stone. These pieces are thought to have had religious significance. As the first cities flourished around the world, the first monumental sculptures were built. Some of them, such as the Great Sphinx in Egypt, still stand today.

Egyptians believed that large sculptures in tombs and temples had spiritual energy.

LUCKY CHARMS

Some of the earliest works of sculpture ever found are tiny, plump female figures made between 30,000 and 10,000 years ago in central Europe. They have no hands, feet, or faces. Small enough to be held in one hand, they were possibly made as lucky charms to help women bear children.

◀ *VENUS OF WILLENDORF*, c.25,000 BCE
This is a copy of a limestone sculpture. It measures only 4.5 in (11 cm) high, and is named after the Austrian village where it was discovered.

The Sphinx is carved from a single piece of limestone

SYMBOLIC STATUES

Ancient Egyptian art was linked to gods and the afterlife. Inside temples and burial chambers were huge statues of Egyptian pharaohs, nobles, and gods, and small clay or wood statuettes. Like their paintings, Egyptian sculptures followed set rules. Men were larger than women and figures were all highly stylized. If standing, they have one foot forward; sitting, their hands are on their laps.

▲ THE GREAT SPHINX AT GIZA, c.2500 BCE
The Sphinx has a lion's body and a human head. Its face is thought to represent that of the Egyptian pharaoh Khafra, whose pyramid stands behind.

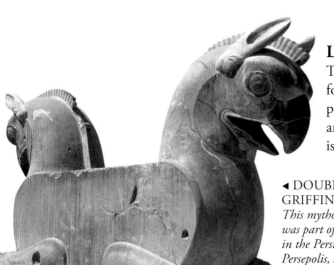

LEADING THE WAY

The ancient Persians, from the region of modern-day Iran, founded one of the first civilizations in the world. They produced sophisticated architecture, painting, sculpture, and metalwork. Most Persian sculpture that has survived is in the form of reliefs on palace walls and cliff faces.

◄ DOUBLE-HEADED GRIFFIN, c.500 BCE
This mythological creature was part of a grand building in the Persian city of Persepolis, and demonstrates the artists' refined skills.

MESOAMERICAN CULTURE

Between 1500 BCE and 1200 CE, several civilizations lived in parts of Central America, a region culturally known as Mesoamerica. As one Mesoamerican civilization disappeared, another emerged. Later civilizations took ideas from earlier ones, adding their own traditions. The first Mesoamerican civilization was the Olmec culture, which made colossal stone statues.

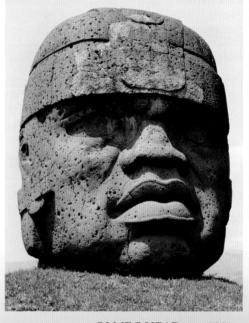

▲ OLMEC HEAD, pre-900 CE
Living in what is today south-central Mexico, the Olmecs made colossal stone heads, some 9 ft (3 m) tall.

Greek and Roman sculpture

In ancient Greece and Rome, statues were made to honor the most important figures in society. These were often displayed in public places. Statues were also made depicting noble warriors, athletes, or mythical figures. Sculptors prided themselves on producing perfectly proportioned figures.

The female figure wears a soft cap and pointed shoes, typical clothing of the Etruscans.

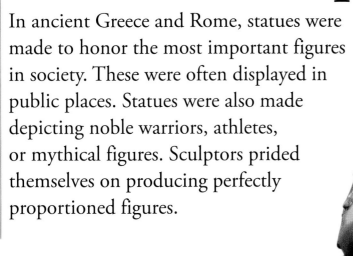

Sarcophagus of the Spouses

From an Italian civilization that predates the Roman Empire

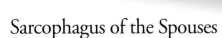

- **Date** c.520 BCE
- **Material** Terra-cotta

This terra-cotta sculpture is Etruscan, from a town near Rome, Italy. It held cremated human remains, so it was a sarcophagus (a stone coffin). Once painted in bright colors, it was shaped to show a married couple enjoying a banquet, indicating to the gods how they should live in the afterlife.

▲ DINING TOGETEHR
In Etruscan society, women and men ate together at banquets. This sculpture makes clear the husband's affection for his wife.

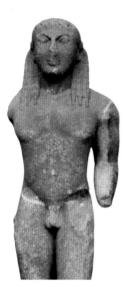

Kouroi and korai
Egyptian-inspired Greek statues

- **Date** c.580 BCE
- **Material** Marble

From about 800 BCE, the earliest Greek sculpture was inspired by the Egyptians. By about 615 BCE, two particular kinds of Egyptian-style statues were made. *Kouroi* (pictured) were huge, free-standing nude male figures with their hands to their sides and one leg forward. The female equivalents were called *korai*, but they were clothed.

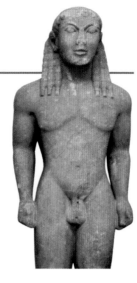

Discobolus
Much-admired Greek classic figure

- **Date** 2nd century CE
- **Material** Marble

This life-size marble statue is a Roman copy of a lost Greek bronze sculpture. The original had been made in about 460–450 BCE by the famous Greek sculptor Myron. It was much admired and copies were made both in bronze and in marble, which was cheaper. Successful Greek artists signed their sculptures, and they greatly influenced many later sculptors in both Greece and Rome.

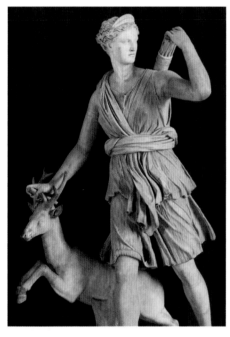

Artemis the Huntress
Figure with perfect proportions

- **Date** c.2nd century CE
- **Material** Marble

Greek sculptors aimed to create flawless figures. From the start of the Classical to the end of the Hellenistic period (about 480–431 BCE), artists sculpted lifelike figures. They worked out perfect proportions, gave faces expressions, and created the appearance of movement, with one leg placed slightly in front of the other. This is a later Roman copy of a Greek sculpture from this period.

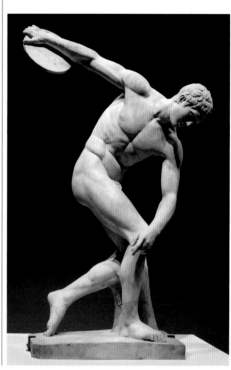

The Dying Gaul
Statue with added Roman realism

- **Date** 3rd century CE
- **Material** Marble

Roman sculpture sought the perfection of Greek art, but the Roman sculptors added even greater realism. For their finest sculptures, Roman artists used bronze and marble. This is a copy of an original sculpture from the 1st or 2nd century CE. It is thought to depict a warrior who has just been fatally wounded. His agony can be felt from the pain in his face and his twisted pose.

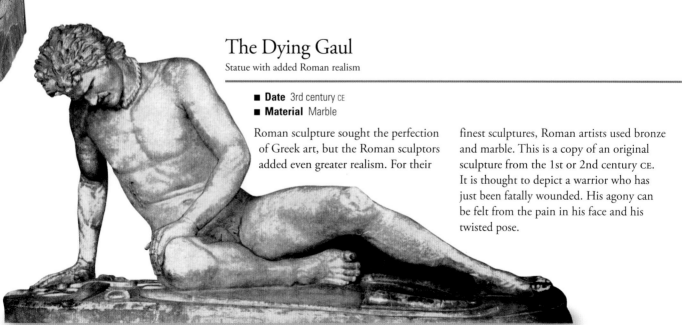

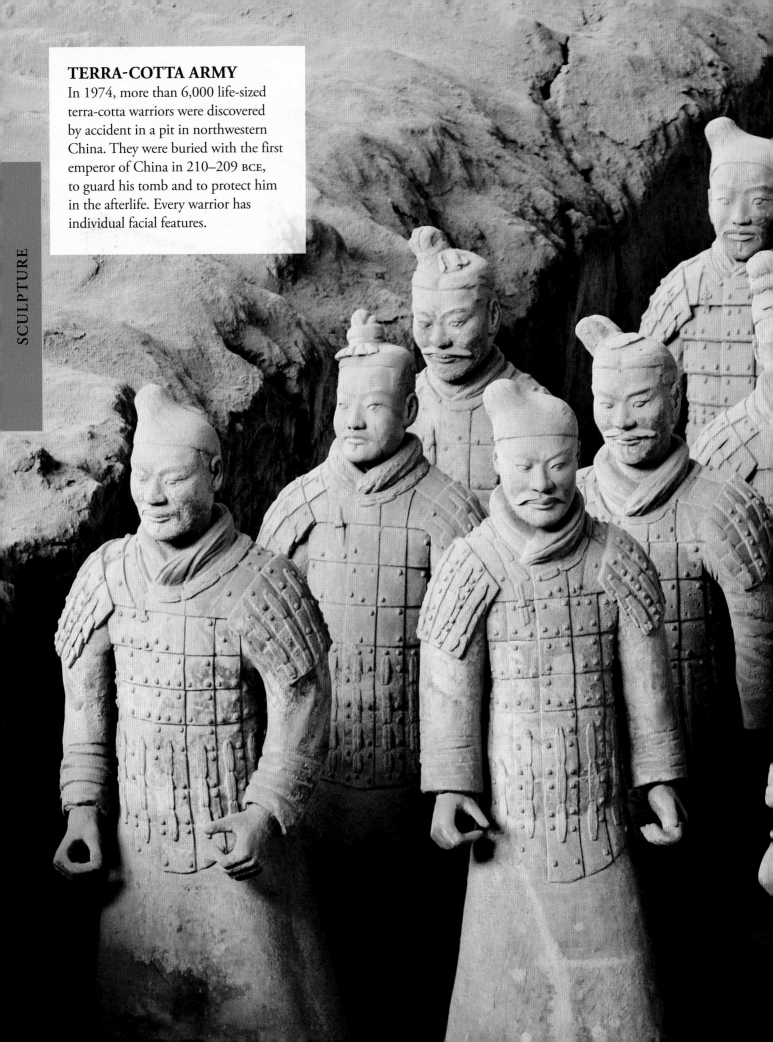

TERRA-COTTA ARMY

In 1974, more than 6,000 life-sized terra-cotta warriors were discovered by accident in a pit in northwestern China. They were buried with the first emperor of China in 210–209 BCE, to guard his tomb and to protect him in the afterlife. Every warrior has individual facial features.

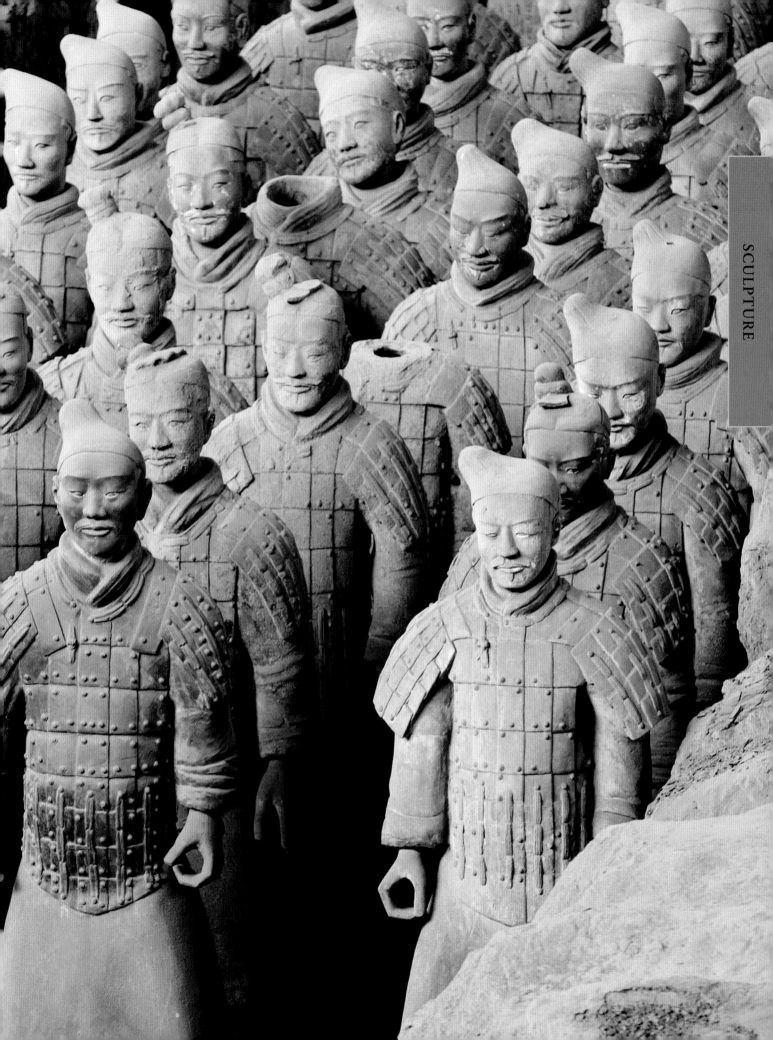

Renaissance sculpture

In the 15th century in Italy, the remains of ancient Greek and Roman sculpture began to be uncovered. This inspired Italian sculptors to revive a classical approach to art, making everything appear exceptionally lifelike. They created statues of saints, biblical and mythological figures, and the rich and powerful people of the time.

Michelangelo carved *Pietà* from a single slab of Carrara marble, a favorite material in ancient Rome.

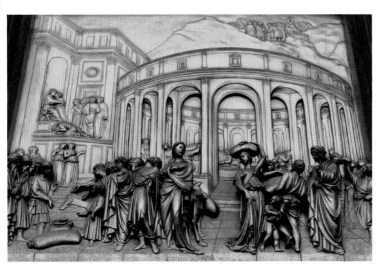

◄ *THE GATES OF PARADISE, 1425–1452, LORENZO GHIBERTI*
Made in bronze, these scenes from the Old Testament are lifelike and detailed.

THE GATES OF PARADISE

In 1425, the goldsmith Lorenzo Ghiberti was commissioned to design a pair of huge doors for the Florence Baptistery. Featuring panels showing biblical scenes in relief, the doors are marvels of craftsmanship. The Renaissance master Michelangelo admired them so much he nicknamed them "The Gates of Paradise."

NATURAL BEAUTY

Michelangelo is widely considered the greatest sculptor of the High Renaissance. From 1498 to 1499, he created a statue of the *Pietà*—the body of Jesus on his mother Mary's lap after the Crucifixion—in Rome, blending beauty with naturalism. Five years later, he completed another huge marble statue in Florence, of the biblical hero David.

ELONGATED FIGURES

Some sculptors who followed Michelangelo developed a more decorative style, creating elongated figures in twisted poses that paved the way for the Mannerist artistic style. The leading Mannerist sculptor was Flemish-Italian Giambologna, who created statues in positions that made them appear to be moving.

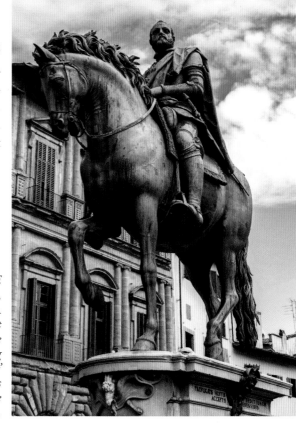

◄ *PIETÀ*, 1499, MICHELANGELO
Expressive and lifelike, a young-looking Mary holds her dead son Jesus.

► *COSIMO DE MEDICI*, 1594, GIAMBOLOGNA
Imitating ancient Roman statues, the horse has one leg raised. Cosimo de' Medici was a powerful figure in Florence.

This is the only work that Michelangelo signed

► *DAVID*, 1624, GIAN LORENZO BERNINI
The twisting David is about to throw a stone at Goliath.

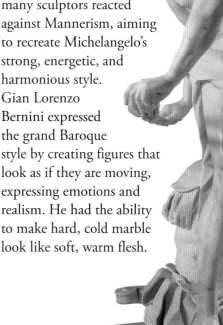

BAROQUE STYLE

In the 17th century, many sculptors reacted against Mannerism, aiming to recreate Michelangelo's strong, energetic, and harmonious style. Gian Lorenzo Bernini expressed the grand Baroque style by creating figures that look as if they are moving, expressing emotions and realism. He had the ability to make hard, cold marble look like soft, warm flesh.

179

Neoclassical and beyond

Fueled by discoveries made in the buried ancient Roman cities of Pompeii and Herculaneum during the 18th century, Neoclassical sculpture reflected a fresh interest in the art of ancient Greece and Rome. This style continued until the end of the 19th century, when sculptors began searching for more expressive forms.

Napoleon as Mars
A modern figure in an ancient pose

- **Artist** Antonio Canova
- **Date** 1802–1806
- **Medium** White marble, gilded bronze

This Italian artist is considered by many to be the greatest of the Neoclassical sculptors. He was renowned for his serene marble figures, often commissioned by European royalty.

This huge statue is of Napoleon I of France posing as the Roman god Mars. It was intentionally made to look like an ancient statue.

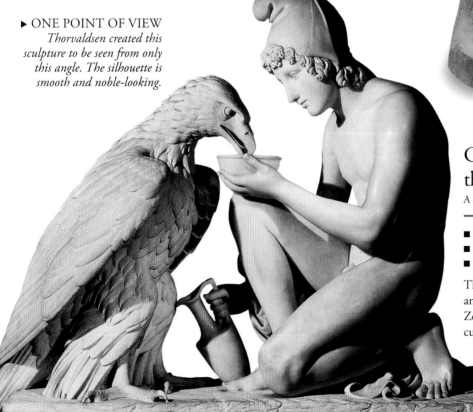

▶ ONE POINT OF VIEW
Thorvaldsen created this sculpture to be seen from only this angle. The silhouette is smooth and noble-looking.

Ganymede with the Eagle of Zeus
A scene from an ancient Greek myth

- **Artist** Bertel Thorvaldsen
- **Date** 1817
- **Medium** Marble

This is a sculpture of Ganymede, a hero from ancient Greek myths. He is kneeling to allow Zeus, in the shape of an eagle, to drink from a cup. In the ancient myth, Ganymede was chosen by the gods to be the cupbearer of Zeus, the King of the Gods. In this work, the Danish Neoclassical sculptor Thorvalsen demonstrates his skill in creating pure, classical lines.

Triumph of the Republic

A patriotic and symbolic work

- **Artist** Jules Dalou
- **Date** 1879–1899
- **Medium** Bronze

This French sculptor created works that were both symbolic and realistic. This sculpture is more flowing and exuberant than the cool, clean lines of Neoclassicism. The huge work took him 20 years to make. The female figure balancing on the globe represents the French Republic, and the figures below, being led by lions, represent Liberty, Labor, and Justice.

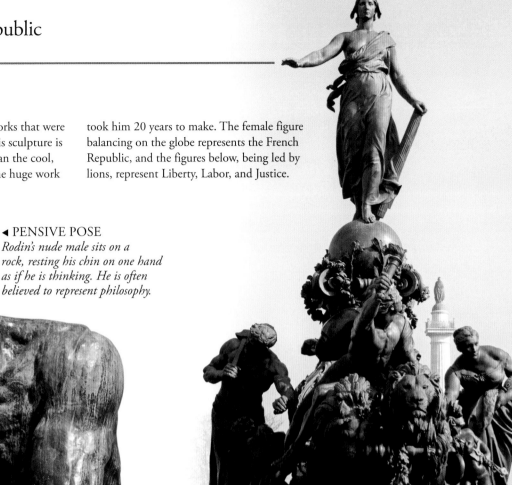

◄ PENSIVE POSE
Rodin's nude male sits on a rock, resting his chin on one hand as if he is thinking. He is often believed to represent philosophy.

The Thinker

A hugely influential work

- **Artist** Auguste Rodin
- **Date** 1903
- **Medium** Bronze

As the 19th century continued, many sculptors rebelled against Neoclassicism and began creating art that expressed greater emotion. From the 1860s, Rodin blended classical styles and traditional methods with a more natural feel. This French sculptor's original, expressive works were extraordinarily lifelike. At first, his work was criticized for looking too real, but by 1900, he was the most famous sculptor in the world.

Modern sculpture

By the late 19th century, some European sculptors had begun to abandon the classical Greek forms of sculpture. After centuries of attempting to create work that looked as lifelike as possible, sculptors began to experiment, searching for new ways to portray the human form, or making abstract shapes.

MOVING FORMS

In the early 20th century, sculptors made forms that suggested motion. The Swiss sculptor Alberto Giacometti made thin, striding figures. Umberto Boccioni, an Italian Futurist inspired by the noise and speed of the modern world, made distorted figures that appeared to move.

◄ *WALKING MAN 1*, 1960, ALBERTO GIACOMETTI
This 6-ft (1.8-m) spindly figure made of bronze has a look of grim determination on his face.

CHALLENGING TRADITION

During the Dada period (see page 158), the French artist Marcel Duchamp tried to exhibit *Fountain*, which was simply a urinal. By presenting it as a work of art, Duchamp introduced the idea of "readymades," or "found objects." For him, ideas were more important than skill. This ethos is now known as "conceptual art."

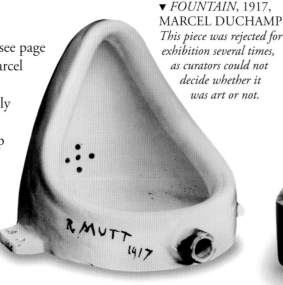

▼ *FOUNTAIN*, 1917, MARCEL DUCHAMP
This piece was rejected for exhibition several times, as curators could not decide whether it was art or not.

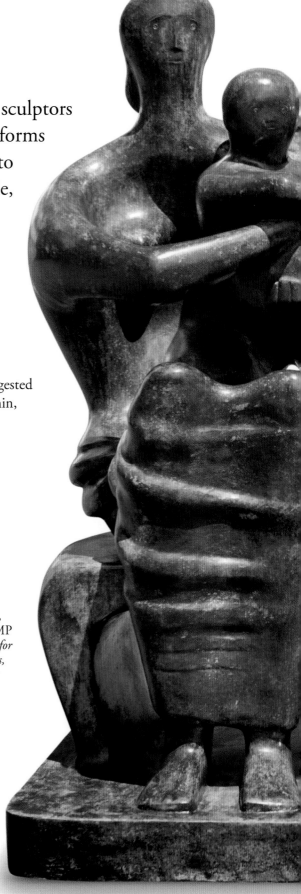

▼ *FAMILY GROUP*, 1949, HENRY MOORE
Although not lifelike, it is clear that these smooth shapes represent a mother, a father, and a child.

Moore compared the human body to the landscape

LOUISE BOURGEOIS

The French sculptor Louise Bourgeois was heavily influenced by her childhood family life. Much of her art was highly personal and explored themes such as fidelity and domesticity. She often featured elements from the natural world, such as insect eggs, plants, or entrails to symbolize femininity, beauty, and pain.

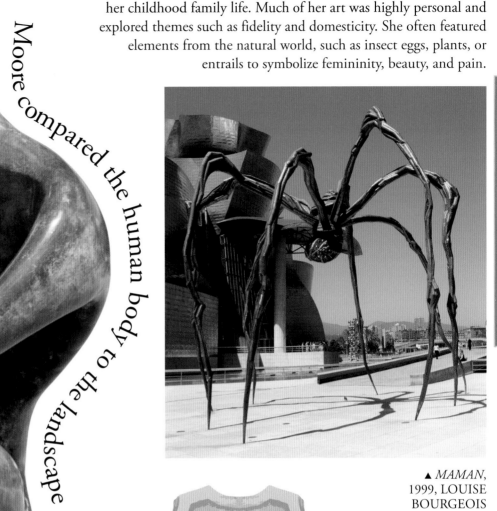

▲ *MAMAN*, 1999, LOUISE BOURGEOIS
Bourgeois sculpted this immense stainless steel spider to symbolize her mother's strength as a homemaker and a weaver.

In 1991, British artist Damien Hirst pushed the limits of sculpture by displaying the body of a dead shark in a tank.

HENRY MOORE

Using traditional materials including wood, bronze, and stone, the British artist Henry Moore created sculptures that represented recognizable objects, but in a simplified form. For Moore, the presentation of the materials used to make a work was as important as its subject. He also believed that the space around a sculpture was important, so many of his works are exhibited in large outdoor venues.

Barbara Hepworth

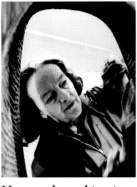

Hepworth working in her studio in 1964

This British artist achieved incredible success in the art world at a time when it was unusual for women to work as sculptors. Her early work was based on human figures or animals, but she became celebrated worldwide for her later, more abstract works that simplified natural forms. She was an expert in "direct carving"—carving her sculpture directly without making initial models.

FAMILY MATTERS

Many of Hepworth's early works were based on the theme of mother and child, reflecting her own experiences with her four children. Some sculptures depict relationships between families, and symbolize warmth, love, and protection. Hepworth said she wanted to release the "life" of the materials she was using and emphasize their qualities of shape, color, and surface.

▲ *MOTHER AND CHILD, 1934*
This work was created as two separate and connecting pieces. The larger piece is the "mother" and the smaller part in front is the "child".

INSPIRED BY NATURE

From an early age, Hepworth was fascinated by the forms found in nature, and she decided to become a sculptor when just a teenager. She carved all sorts of stone, such as marble, and also worked with bronze and brass. She was inspired by the landscape, particularly by ancient stones, and the contours and textures of plants, rocks, and hills.

LIFE STORY

1903–1920	1921–1925	1926–1932	1933–1936
Born in Yorkshire, England, in 1903, Hepworth later attends Leeds School of Art, where she meets the sculptor Henry Moore.	Hepworth studies sculpture at the Royal College of Art (RCA), London, and then in Florence, Italy, where she learns how to carve marble.	Hepworth and her first husband, British sculptor John Skeaping, set up a studio in London. She meets British abstract painter Ben Nicholson, whom she later marries.	Hepworth, Nicholson, and artist Paul Nash start the Unit One art movement. During this period, Hepworth's work becomes more abstract.

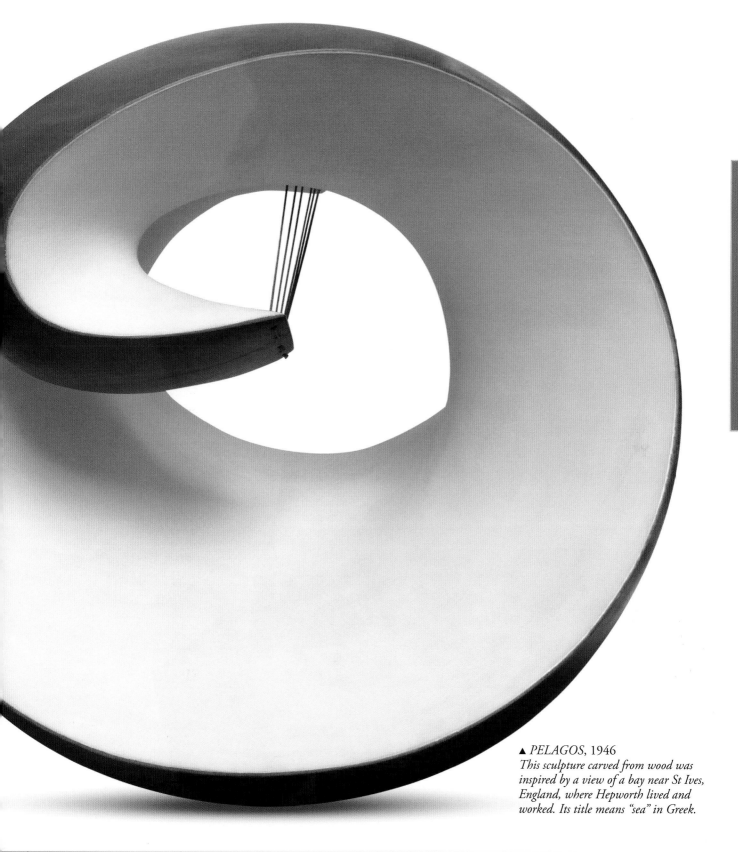

▲ *PELAGOS*, 1946
This sculpture carved from wood was inspired by a view of a bay near St Ives, England, where Hepworth lived and worked. Its title means "sea" in Greek.

1937–1938	1939–1949	1950–1959	1960–1975
Hepworth designs a book about Constructivist artists, who believed that art and design should serve the social good.	Hepworth moves to Cornwall in southwest England with her family. In 1949, she and Nicholson start the Penwith Society of Arts.	As well as stone, Hepworth works with bronze. She creates a sculpture for the Festival of Britain: two stone figures, placed on London's South Bank.	Hepworth buys a huge building near her studio in St Ives, and works there on large-scale sculptures. She dies in May 1975.

PHOTOGRAPHY

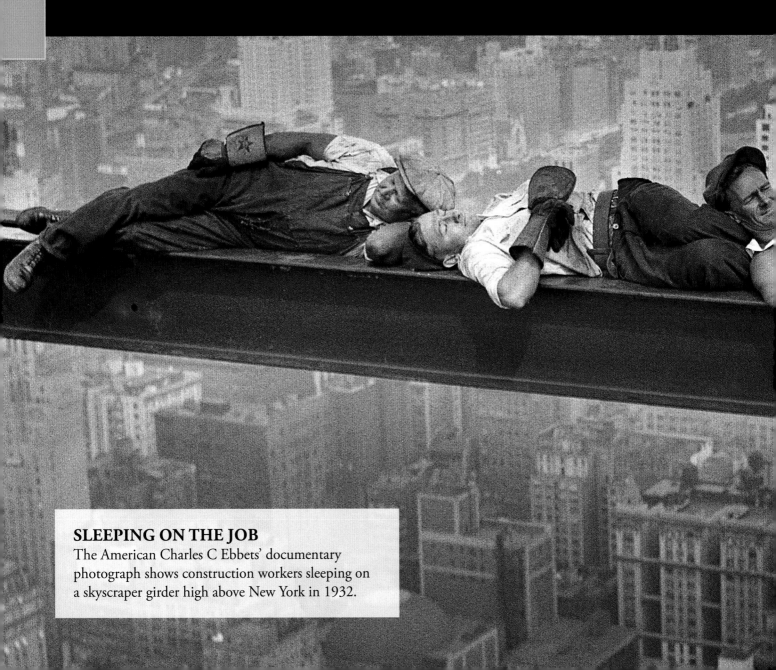

SLEEPING ON THE JOB
The American Charles C Ebbets' documentary photograph shows construction workers sleeping on a skyscraper girder high above New York in 1932.

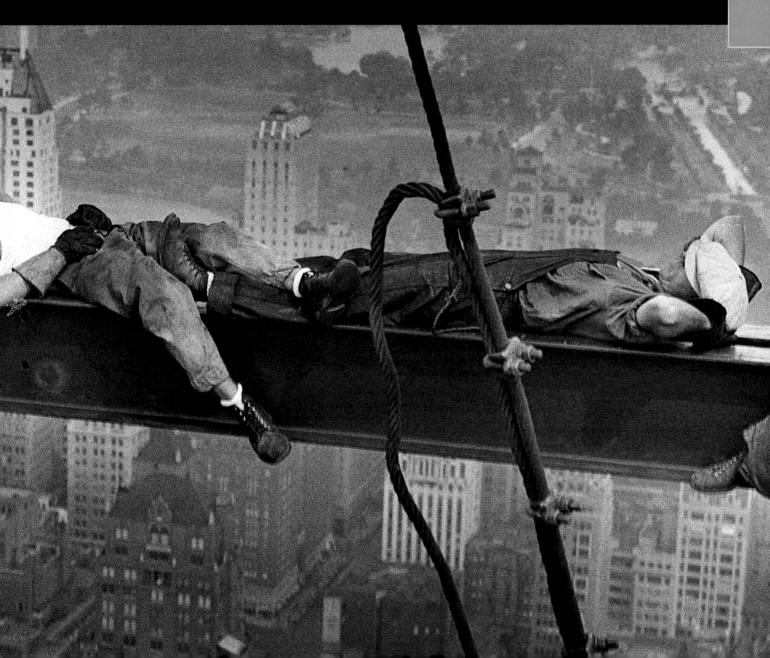

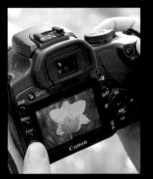
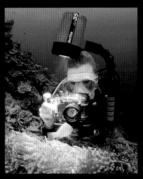
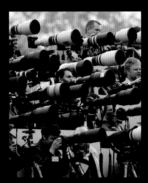

Photography is the process of recording a permanent image by focusing light on a light-sensitive surface. Invented in the 1820s, it has since developed into an important art form.

Early photography

As far back as the 4th century BCE, a "camera obscura" produced an image on a wall by passing light into a dark room through a tiny hole. Over time this device became smaller, and it was portable by the mid-17th century. By 1819, cameras used light-sensitive chemicals to "fix" an image on a plate of metal of glass. This was the start of photography.

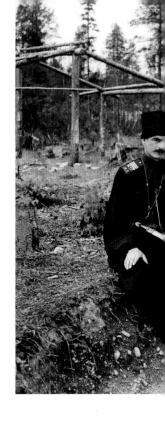

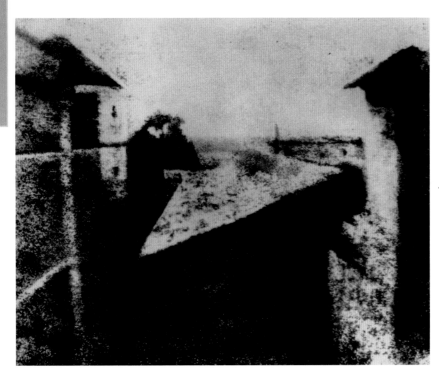

◀ *VIEW FROM THE WINDOW AT LE GRAS,* 1826, JOSEPH NICÉPHORE NIÉPCE
This French inventor created the earliest known fixed photograph. The exposure lasted eight hours.

THE FIRST PHOTOGRAPHS

To create the first photographs, the light-sensitive chemicals needed to be exposed to the light for hours. The length of time they were left exposed, called exposure, meant that only static subjects such as houses could be photographed. Any movement created a blur.

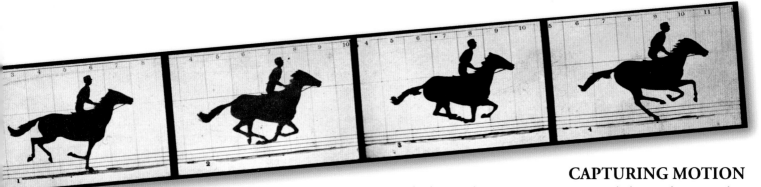

▲ *HORSE IN MOTION,* 1879, EADWEARD MUYBRIDGE
Muybridge's experiments with photographing movement eventually led to the invention of cinema.

CAPTURING MOTION

By the late 19th century, new, improved chemicals meant that cameras required much shorter exposure times. This allowed fast-moving subjects to be recorded without blur. English photographer Eadweard Muybridge used a series of cameras lined up in a row to show how a horse's legs move as it gallops.

EARLY COLOR PHOTOGRAPHY

The first cameras could only make images in black and white. In 1904, French brothers Auguste and Louis Lumière invented the first commercially successful way to make color photographs. Called Autochrome, this process made colors by mixing different proportions of the three primary colors —red, green, and blue.

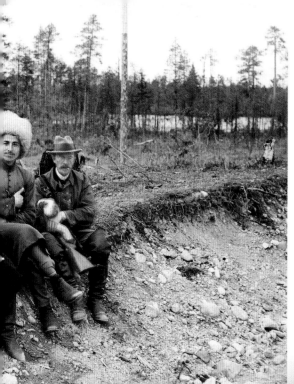

▲ *PHOTOGRAPHER AND COSSACKS*, 1916, SERGEY PROKUDIN-GORSKY
This Russian chemist and photographer (right in image) made thousands of color photographs documenting life in his native land.

CAPTURING LIFE

Since the early 20th century, documentary photographers have used the power of the image to show audiences—often via newspapers and online—a visual record. From highlighting the tragic fallout of war to documenting a mass protest, this photographic style can reveal the truth behind an event and shape public opinion.

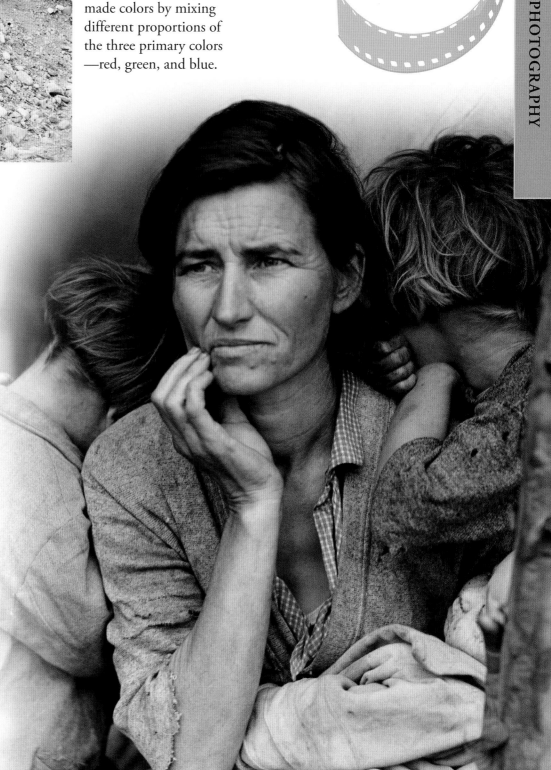

▶ *MIGRANT MOTHER*, 1936, DOROTHEA LANGE
This American photographer documented the poverty caused by the Great Depression in the 1930s. By patiently observing her subject, she captured the despair of a mother wondering how she is going to feed her children.

Tetons— Snake River

Ansel Adams was an American landscape photographer who specialized in photographing the American wilderness. He mainly worked in black and white using large-format cameras. This photograph, called *Tetons—Snake River*, was taken by Adams in the Grand Teton National Park, Wyoming, in 1942.

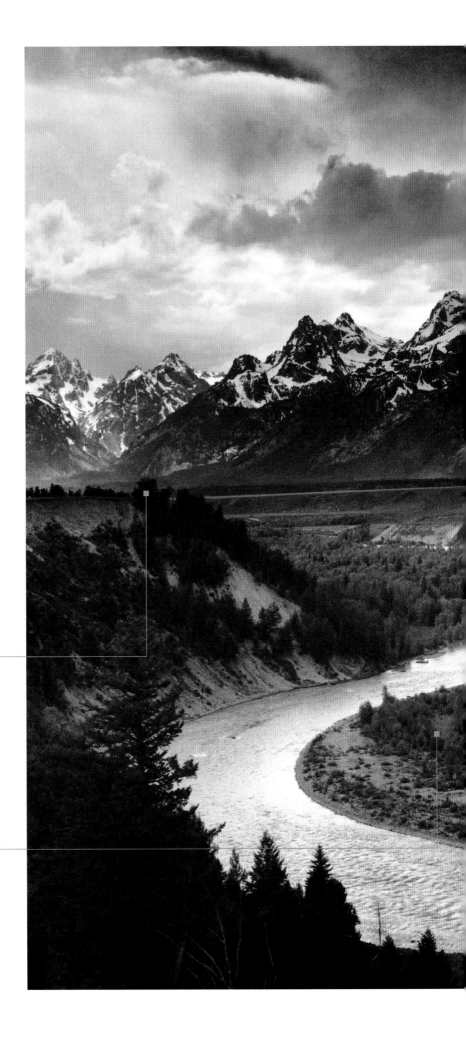

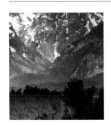

CONTRAST
The difference in brightness between the shadows and the highlights is called contrast, and can create a sense of drama.

COMPOSITION
As it curves through the photograph, the shape of the Snake River leads the eye to the mountain range in the background.

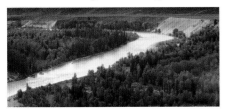

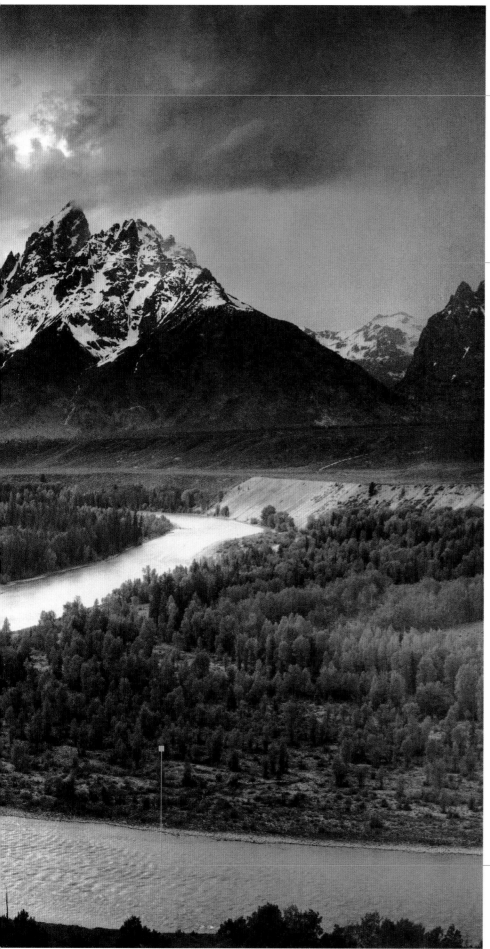

STORMY WEATHER

Unsettled, stormy weather produces spectacular light effects. Adams waited for these conditions to capture moments such as this one.

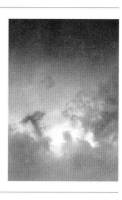

BACKGROUND DETAIL

The Teton mountain range forms part of the Rocky Mountain Ranges. The tallest peak, Grand Teton, is 13,775 ft (4,199 m) high.

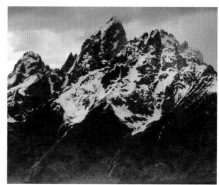

NATIONAL PARKS

Adams campaigned to expand the National Park system of the United States. His photography illustrated what would be lost if the nation's wilderness areas were not protected. Due to his efforts, both as a photographer and as a tireless campaigner, several new National Parks were created during his lifetime.

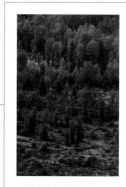

FOREGROUND DETAIL

The small size of the pine trees in the foreground shows the gigantic scale of the Tetons landscape.

191

Evolution of the camera

Cameras have evolved from the simple wooden boxes of the 19th century to today's sophisticated devices capable of instantly sending images worldwide. The biggest change in the past two decades has been the shift from the use of light-sensitive film to cameras with built-in digital sensors.

Plate camera

Using chemicals to capture images on glass

- **First produced** 19th century
- **Country of origin** UK
- **Material used** Glass plate

Early photographs were produced on plates of glass coated with a thin layer of light-sensitive chemicals. The chemicals were expensive and dangerous to handle, and early photographers needed to be skilled chemists. Light entered the camera through a lens in the front, and created an image on the plate in the back. The rear of the camera could slide back and forth to bring the image into focus.

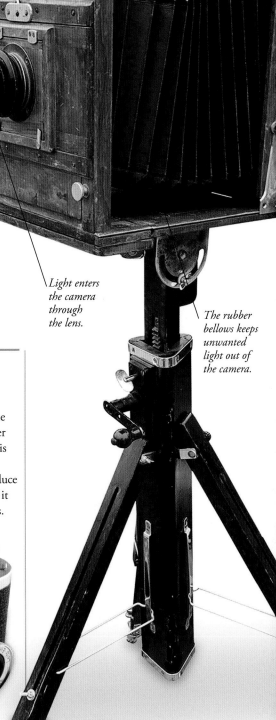

Light enters the camera through the lens.

The rubber bellows keeps unwanted light out of the camera.

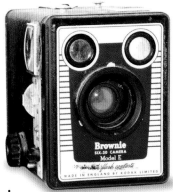

Box Brownie

The first roll film camera

- **First produced** 1900
- **Country of origin** USA
- **Material used** Roll film

Unlike bulky plate cameras, George Eastman's relatively affordable Kodak Brownie could be carried around, creating the idea of a "snapshot." His camera used a roll of film, and when the film was finished, it was sent to a laboratory where the photographs were developed. This point-and-shoot camera brought photography to the masses. In fact, the famous Kodak slogan was: "You press the button, we do the rest."

Leica Rangefinder

Small and easy to carry

- **First produced** 1924
- **Country of origin** Germany
- **Material used** Roll film

The development of smaller film rolls in the early 20th century allowed for much smaller cameras, such as the Leica Rangefinder. This camera featured a mechanism that allowed photographers to measure distance and produce sharply focused images. Its small size made it instantly popular with street photographers.

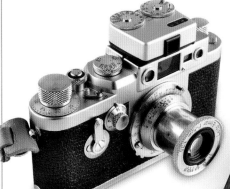

Single Lens Reflex

The professional photographer's camera of choice

- **First produced** 1930s
- **Country of origin** Japan
- **Material used** Roll film

The Single Lens Reflex (SLR) camera uses precise engineering to give the photographer the best view possible through the viewfinder. Instead of looking through a separate viewfinder to the side like other cameras, the photographer looks directly through the camera's lens to see exactly what will be recorded when the photograph is made. The light from the lens is reflected up to the viewfinder by a mirror. At the moment of taking the photo, the mirror swings out of the way to allow the film to be exposed.

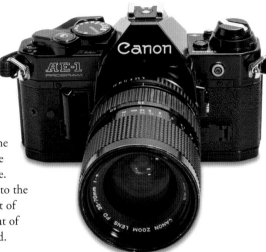

Digital camera

Photography turns digital

- **First produced** 1975
- **Country of origin** USA
- **Material used** Memory card

Digital cameras use a sensor to create photographs electronically, storing them as digital files on a memory card in the camera. The photographs can then be copied to a personal computer (PC) or tablet to be shared via the Internet. The images can also be printed using relatively affordable home printers.

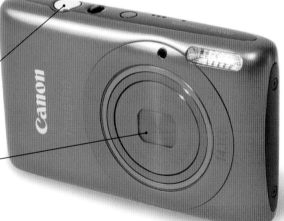

The user presses the shutter button to take a photograph.

The lens is shielded by an built-in electronic lens cover when the camera is not in use.

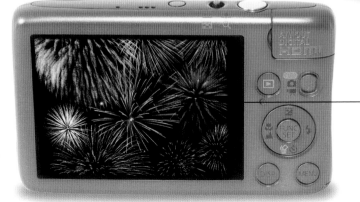

A color screen shows exactly what the photograph will look like.

Polaroid

Photographs in an instant

- **First produced** 1948
- **Country of origin** USA
- **Material used** Film pack

A glass plate or roll of film needs to be developed in a special chemical bath to produce a visible image. The Polaroid Instant camera, developed by American inventor Edwin Land, used a self-developing film pack to make a finished photographic print within minutes of exposure. The image slowly appeared as you held the film in your hand.

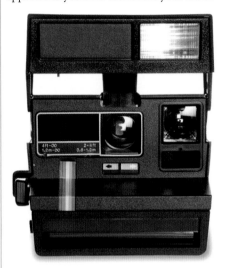

Camera phone

Photographs in an instant

- **First produced** 2000
- **Country of origin** Japan
- **Material used** Memory card

The first camera phone in Japan did not make a big impression, but by 2002, the Finnish company Nokia had created one that was popular worldwide. Today, many mobile phones have high-quality built-in cameras, and users can share digital photographs—via online social media sites—in an instant.

A "selfie stick" grips a camera phone for a steady shot.

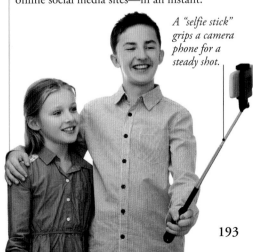

► TWIGGY
Fashion photographers such as David Bailey made British model Twiggy (Lesley Lawson) a household name in the 1960s.

Photography types

Professional photographers normally specialize in one particular type of photography. Photojournalists need to be intrepid, taking lots of photos in rapid succession, often in dangerous situations. Landscape or wildlife photographers, on the other hand, need patience, and may wait for days or weeks to capture the perfect shot.

Fashion photography made Twiggy a cultural icon

PORTRAITURE

Portrait photography is the art of capturing an individual or small group of people in a way that brings out their personality. Portrait photographs are normally taken in a studio so that the photographer has control over the lighting, making it easier to create a particular effect or mood.

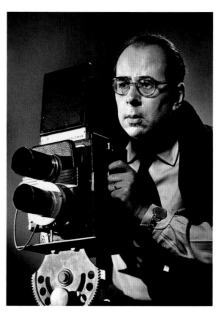

▲ PHILIPPE HALSMAN
This American photographer is pictured here in the moody, shadowed style he used to capture the famous figures of 1940s and 1950s.

FASHION SHOOTS

Fashion photography shows off the latest clothing by designers or fashion houses. Fashion photography began in the 19th century. Over time, it has developed a distinct style, relying on striking models or exotic locations to enhance the glamour of clothes. A session of fashion photography is called a shoot. Some fashion photographers, such as American photographer Richard Avedon, have become as famous as their models.

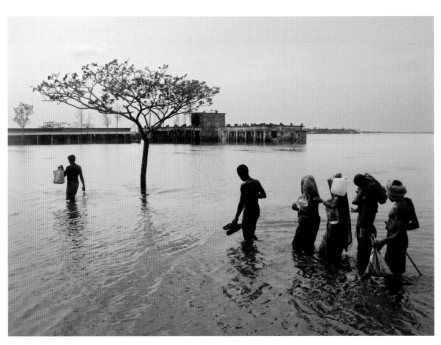

PHOTOJOURNALISM

Photojournalists make images that illustrate news stories. They work closely with news editors and print journalists to ensure that they are in the right place at the right time. Photojournalists take risks to travel to dangerous places in order to tell their stories. Often the pictures they take can convey far more than a written article.

◄ PADMAPUKUR, BANGLADESH, 2009, JONAS BENDIKSEN
Photography is able to convey the human cost of natural disasters, such as this flooding in Bangladesh in 2009.

THE NATURAL WORLD

Landscape photography captures the beauty of planet Earth, from rugged mountain ranges to scorching deserts. People who specialize in this style consider visual elements of foreground and background, the focal point, and the quality of the light, in order to produce the best photographs.

▼ NORTHERN LIGHTS, NORWAY, 2012, ARILD HEITMANN
Skilled landscape photographers are able to capture fleeting and rare natural phenomena such as the northern lights.

George S. Cook took the first photographs under fire in battle during the American Civil War (1861–1865).

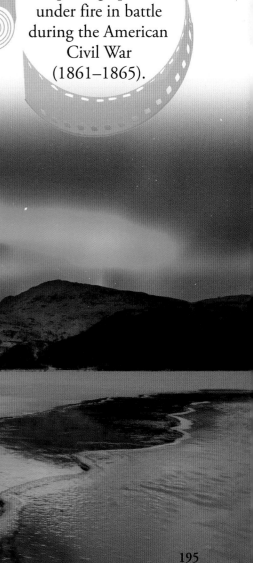

Julia Margaret Cameron

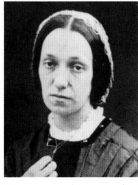

Cameron, photographed in 1862

British pioneer of photography Julia Margaret Cameron produced portraits of family, friends, and servants that still influence photographers today. Her portraits were often deliberately soft and technically flawed. This approach helped her to bring out the personality of her subject more effectively than a conventional portrait. Cameron photographed many famous people of her time, creating a valuable record for historians.

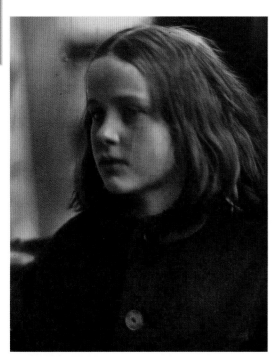

▲ ANNIE, 1864
This portrait took several minutes to expose, meaning that the photograph is slightly blurred and soft, a style that Cameron used for the rest of her career.

FIRST SUCCESS

In January 1864, Cameron created a portrait photograph of eight-year-old Annie Philpot. After completing the portrait, Cameron wrote to Annie's father, telling him of "My first perfect success in the complete Photograph owing greatly to the docility and sweetness of my best and fairest little sitter." Annie had been asked to sit still for several minutes.

▶ SIR JOHN HERSCHEL, 1867
This famous astronomer was a longtime friend of Cameron. Before sitting for this portrait, Herschel was asked to wash his white hair in order to create a halo effect around his face.

FAMOUS FIGURES

Cameron met many notable figures of mid-Victorian Britain through her well-connected younger sister, Sarah. The famous people she photographed include the scientists Charles Darwin and John Herschel, the art critic John Ruskin, and the poet Alfred, Lord Tennyson. Tennyson was a frequent, if sometimes reluctant, subject as he and Cameron lived near one another on the Isle of Wight in the 1860s.

LIFE STORY

1815	1815–1835	1835–1838	1838–1848
Julia Margaret Pattle is born in India on June 11, 1815. She is the fourth of 10 children born to James and Adeline Pattle.	Julia spends most of her childhood in France with her sisters and grandmother. Her education is more extensive than usual for a girl at the time.	In 1835, Julia is sent to southern Africa to recover after illness. There she meets the scientist John Herschel, a pioneer of early photography.	In 1838, Julia marries Charles Hay Cameron in Calcutta. The couple have six children, the youngest of whom, Henry, later becomes a photographer.

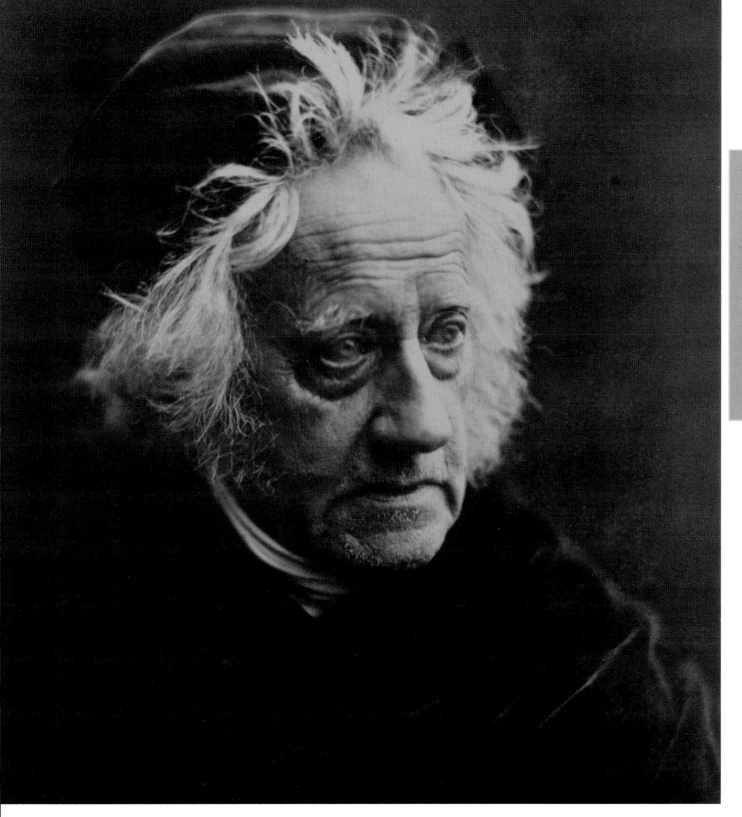

1848–1860	1860–1875	1875	1879
Julia and Charles live in a number of homes in southern England. Julia meets many influential artists and scientists.	Julia and Charles settle on the Isle of Wight. In 1863, she sets up a studio after receiving photographic equipment from her daughter.	The Camerons emigrate to Ceylon (now Sri Lanka). Julia Cameron's photographic career is effectively ended by the move.	Julia Cameron dies on January 26, 1879 in Sri Lanka. Her last word, describing the view from her bedroom window, is "Beautiful."

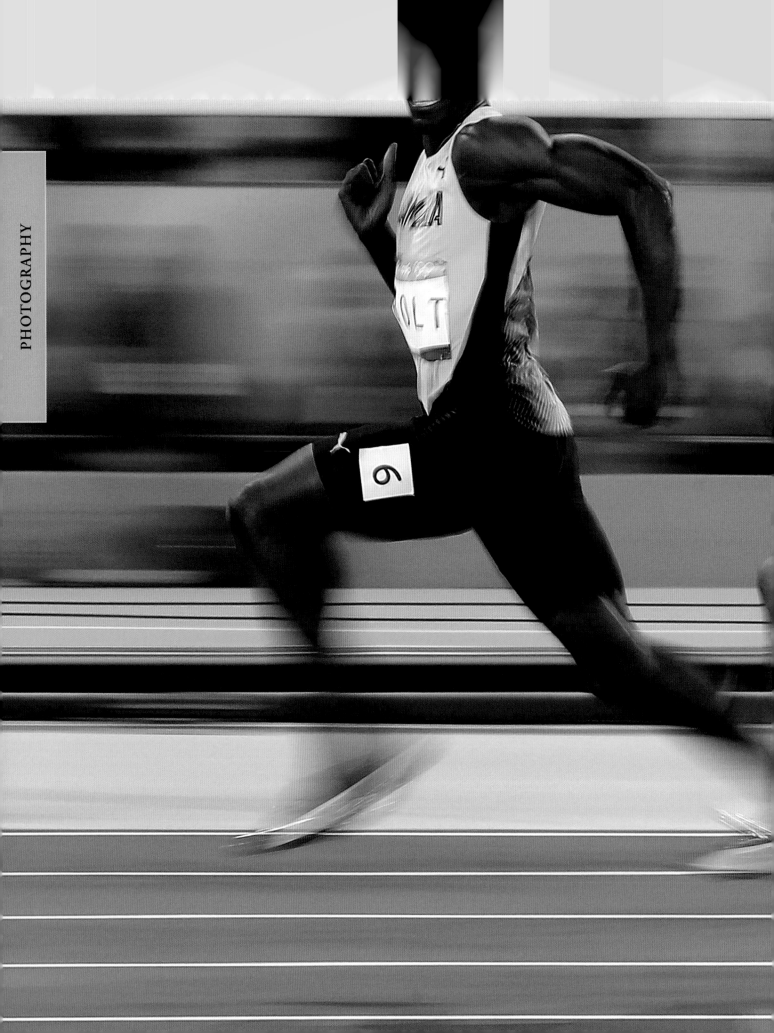

PHOTOGRAPHY

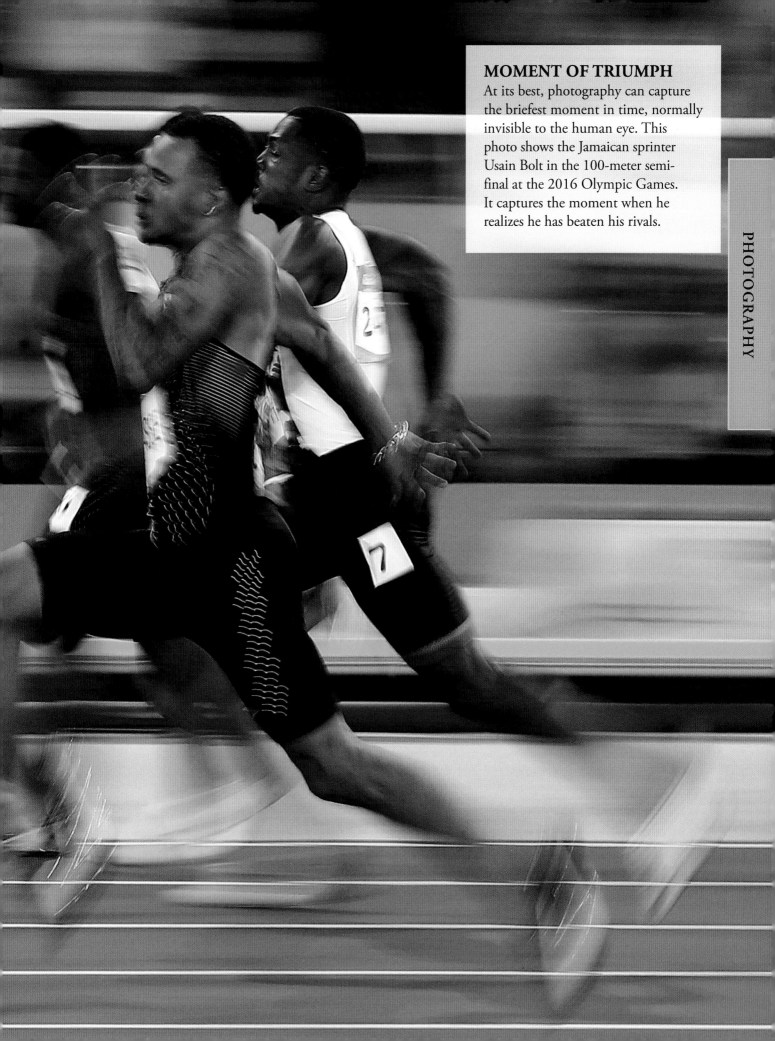

MOMENT OF TRIUMPH
At its best, photography can capture the briefest moment in time, normally invisible to the human eye. This photo shows the Jamaican sprinter Usain Bolt in the 100-meter semi-final at the 2016 Olympic Games. It captures the moment when he realizes he has beaten his rivals.

CULTURAL FUSION
Mariachi is a Mexican style of music that combines the rhythms of indigenous American peoples with instruments introduced from Europe.

MUSIC

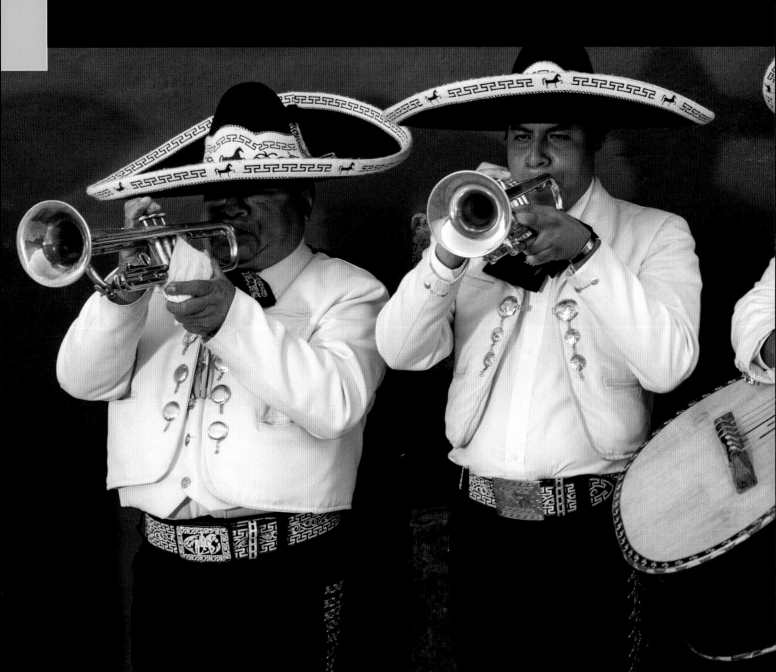

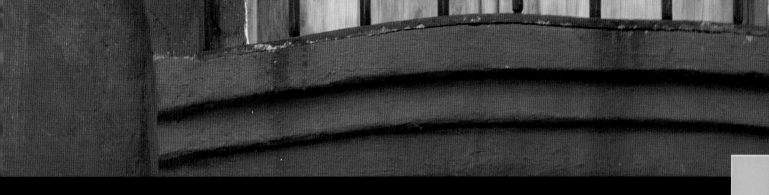

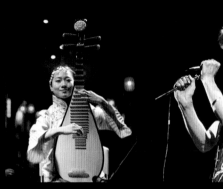

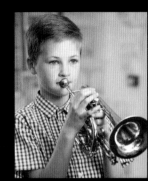

People have made music for thousands of years—it is the oldest form of artistic expression. From religious rituals to modern-day pop, music can be gentle or loud, calming or energetic.

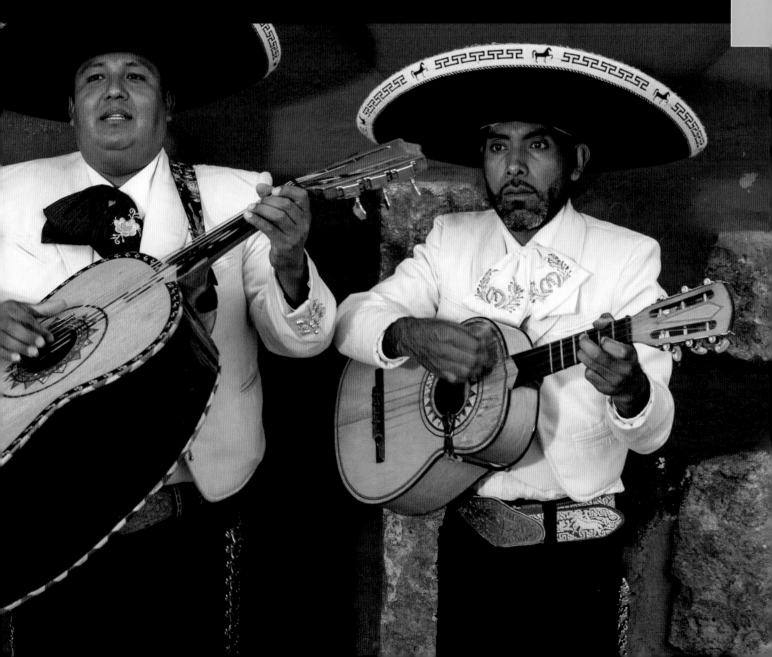

Ancient music

Music is one of the oldest art forms of all. Even Stone Age hunter-gatherers are believed to have made simple instruments from logs and animal bones. However, it was in the period known as antiquity, when the first civilizations were founded, that music began to take on many of its modern forms.

The oldest instruments discovered are simple flutes carved from mammoth tusks and bird bones.

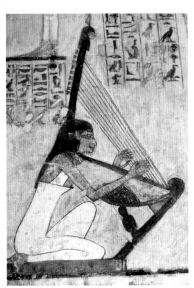

ANCIENT EGYPT
Music had an important social purpose in ancient Egypt, where it was used both in religious rituals and to accompany celebrations. Early Egyptian music was mainly sung or chanted, but by the time the civilization reached its peak, in around 1500 BCE, numerous instruments were being played, including bronze trumpets, wooden lyres, and flutes made from reeds.

◀ TOMB MUSIC
An Egyptian tomb painting from around 1425 BCE shows a woman playing a harp.

THE FIRST WRITTEN MUSIC

Most ancient music was not written down. However, scholars in the ancient Middle Eastern city of Ugarit, Syria, invented a basic form of musical notation using marks pressed into wet clay. Dating to 1400 BCE, the oldest surviving piece of music contains the words and music of a hymn to the goddess Nikkal.

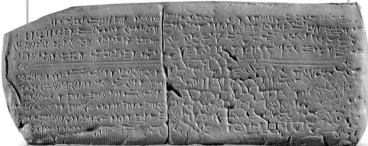

The hymn to Nikkal was written on a clay tablet.

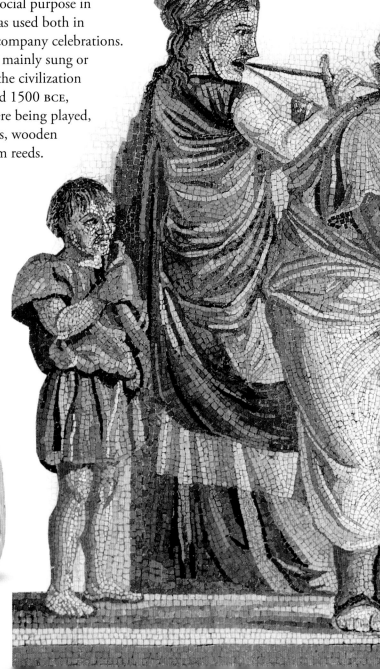

MUSIC OF LEGENDS

China can trace its musical history back more than 3,000 years. According to Chinese legends, music was invented as a way of bringing order to the natural world. The first musician is said to have been a man named Ling Lun, who created a set of bamboo pipes to imitate the sound of a bird's song. Early instruments included tuned metal bells, flutes, and the guzheng, or Chinese zither.

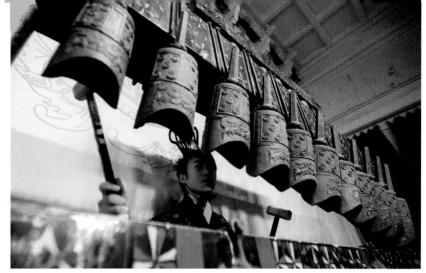

▲ KEEPING UP TRADITIONS
The bianzhong is an ancient Chinese instrument consisting of a set of bronze bells that are hit with a mallet.

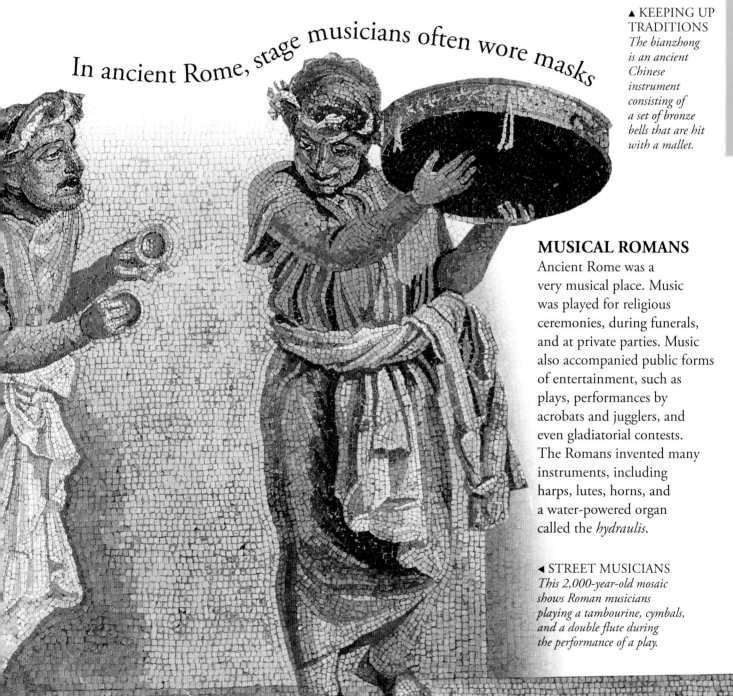

In ancient Rome, stage musicians often wore masks

MUSICAL ROMANS

Ancient Rome was a very musical place. Music was played for religious ceremonies, during funerals, and at private parties. Music also accompanied public forms of entertainment, such as plays, performances by acrobats and jugglers, and even gladiatorial contests. The Romans invented many instruments, including harps, lutes, horns, and a water-powered organ called the *hydraulis*.

◄ STREET MUSICIANS
This 2,000-year-old mosaic shows Roman musicians playing a tambourine, cymbals, and a double flute during the performance of a play.

Medieval and Renaissance music

Music in Europe underwent a huge change in the medieval period (c.500–1400 CE). New instruments and musical styles were developed and a system of musical notation began to be commonly used. This was followed by the Renaissance (c.1400–1600), when many of the rules and traditions of what would later be called classical music were established.

▼ THE STAVE
This piece of written music from 13th-century Italy uses a four-line stave rather than a modern five-line one.

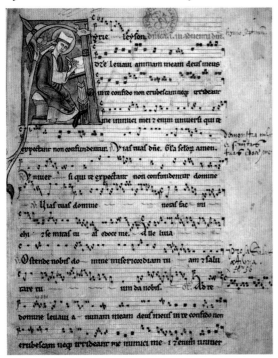

WRITING MUSIC DOWN

Modern musical notation can trace its origins to the medieval period. At first, simple symbols called neums were used. These were written above the words of a song to show roughly where the music went up and down. A more complex system was devised in the 11th century using a stave— a set of horizontal lines on which symbols could be written to show the pitch and length of notes.

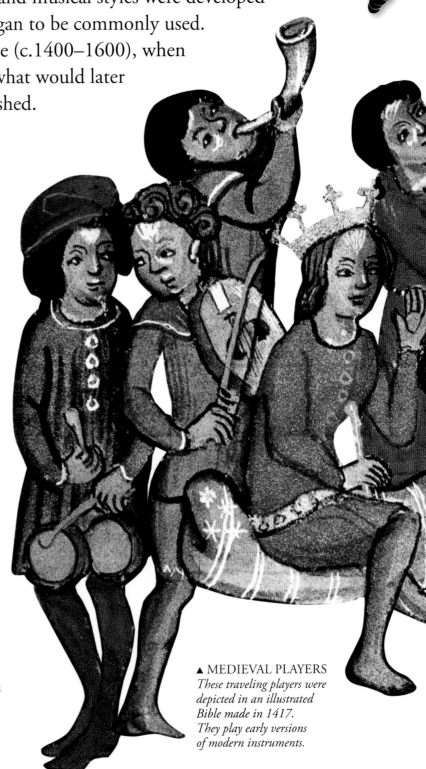

▲ MEDIEVAL PLAYERS
These traveling players were depicted in an illustrated Bible made in 1417. They play early versions of modern instruments.

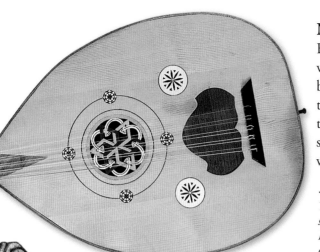

NEW INSTRUMENTS

Before the Renaissance, most music was sung, with or without instruments. However, in the 1500s, musicians began composing instrumental music, which helped to spur the creation of new instruments. These included the ancestors to many modern instruments, such as the shawm, which evolved into the oboe, and the sackbut, which became the trombone.

◀ LUTE
The lute was the main stringed instrument during the Renaissance, and the precursor of the modern guitar.

TRAVELING PLAYERS

Many medieval and Renaissance musicians made a living by traveling around, putting on concerts in villages and in royal and aristocratic homes. They sang songs about local legends, historic events, chivalry, and love, and could also recite poetry, juggle, or perform tricks. These musicians were called by various names across Europe, including minstrels in England, troubadours in France, and minnesingers in Germany.

Modern musical notation based on the stave was invented in the 11th century by Italian monk Guido of Arezzo.

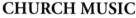

CHURCH MUSIC

Music played an important role in Christian worship. Early on, this music took the form of simple songs made up of a single melody performed without musical accompaniment. This is known as plainchant, or Gregorian chant. Later music featured interweaving melodic parts—a style called polyphony.

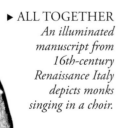

▶ ALL TOGETHER
An illuminated manuscript from 16th-century Renaissance Italy depicts monks singing in a choir.

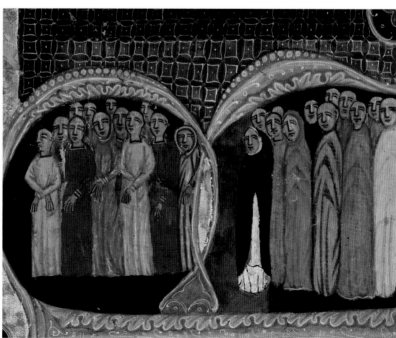

Baroque music

In the Baroque period (1660–1750), musical pieces became more elaborate. Composers created complex melodies and made increasing use of harmony—playing different notes at the same time to produce chords. Several new musical forms emerged, including dramatic operas and the concerto, in which a soloist is accompanied by an orchestra.

Baroque means "misshapen pearl" in Portuguese. It was first used as an insult for the elaborate arts of the time.

MUSICAL PLAYS

In 16th-century Italy, a group of composers began creating long dramatic works in which all the parts were sung to musical accompaniment. Known as operas, these musical plays were originally put on in the homes of rich families. As their popularity spread across Europe, operas began to be staged for the paying public. The first opera houses were constructed in the mid-1600s.

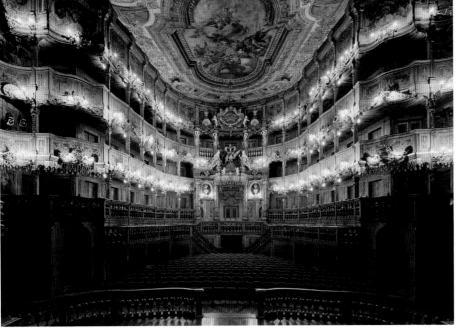

◄ GRAND OPERA HOUSE
The ornate Margravial Opera House was built in Bayreuth, Germany, in the 1740s.

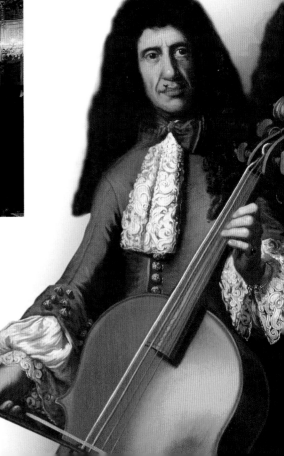

ORCHESTRAS AND CHAMBER MUSIC

The 1600s saw the creation of the first orchestras. These could be large productions, with violins, violas, cellos, bassoons, oboes, horns, trumpets, and a harpsichord, although there were no fixed rules regarding the type or number of instruments. Small orchestras were also popular and became known as chamber orchestras because they could fit inside a large palace room, or chamber.

KEYBOARD INSTRUMENT

With its distinctive twanging sound, the harpsichord was the most important keyboard instrument of the Baroque age. Although it had been around since the Middle Ages, the instrument only began to be widely used following technical improvements in the late 16th century that made it louder. It helped to popularize the use of chords and harmonies in music.

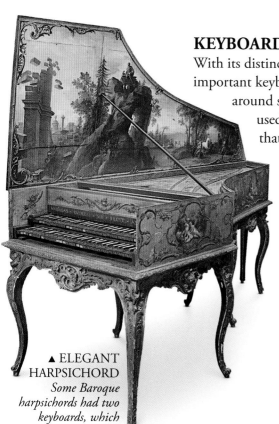

▲ ELEGANT HARPSICHORD
Some Baroque harpsichords had two keyboards, which extended their range.

J.S. BACH

The German Johann Sebastian Bach is one of the most celebrated of all Baroque composers. His dense, complicated music brought him great success. However, by the end of his life, his music was regarded as old-fashioned compared to the new "classical" sounds. His work then enjoyed a revival during the 19th century, and is still popular today.

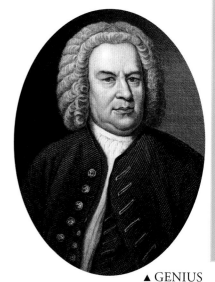

▲ GENIUS
Bach was also a highly skilled organist.

▼ COURT MUSICIANS
A chamber orchestra plays at the court of the Grand Duke of Tuscany in Florence, c.1685.

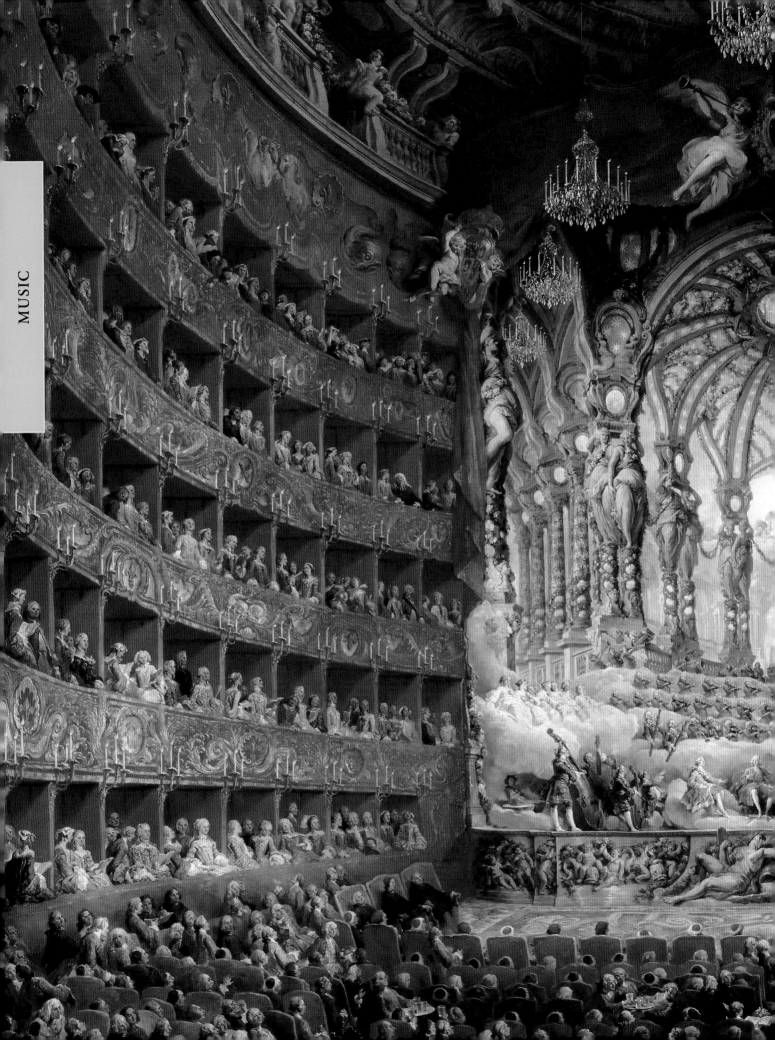

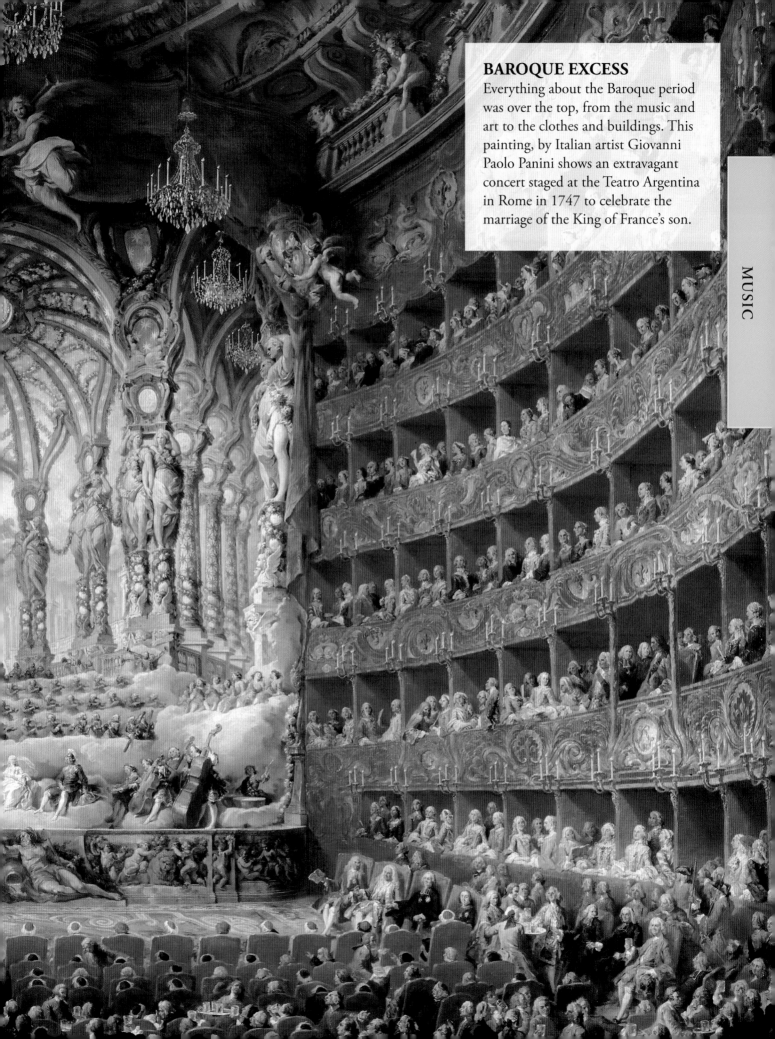

BAROQUE EXCESS
Everything about the Baroque period was over the top, from the music and art to the clothes and buildings. This painting, by Italian artist Giovanni Paolo Panini shows an extravagant concert staged at the Teatro Argentina in Rome in 1747 to celebrate the marriage of the King of France's son.

The Classical period

The term "classical music" has two meanings. It can refer generally to all orchestral music, and also specifically to the music of the Classical period (1750–1820). At this time, orchestras became larger and pieces grew longer. The music was simpler than the complex style of the Baroque period, with more emphasis on melody.

The symphony, a long musical piece played by a large orchestra, was invented during the Classical Period.

CELEBRITY COMPOSER

The Austrian composer Joseph Haydn was one of the first celebrity musicians, staging concerts across Europe to large audiences. He was an astonishingly prolific composer, writing more than 100 symphonies and hundreds of other works. He is also remembered for popularizing a new instrumental grouping—the string quartet, which consists of two violins, a viola, and a cello. Both Mozart and Beethoven were students of Haydn.

▶ STRING QUARTET
Haydn (far right) performs with a string quartet in 1780. The composer wrote 83 pieces for the string quartet.

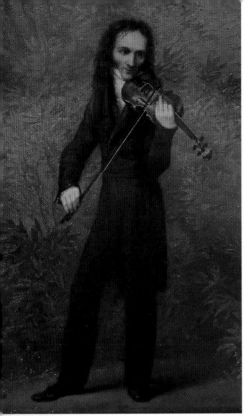

CATCHY TUNES

In the Classical period, musicians moved from creating complex compositions with interweaving musical themes to writing more expressive and melodic pieces. The most popular composers, such as Mozart, Haydn, and Paganini, were the ones who wrote the catchiest, most hummable tunes.

◀ VIOLIN VIRTUOSO
The most celebrated violinist of the Classical age, the Italian Niccolò Paganini was also a skilled composer.

THE PIANO PERIOD

The main keyboard instrument in the Classical period, a piano's strings are hit with small hammers. This means that it can be played loudly or softly, depending on how hard the keys are pressed. The name is short for *pianoforte*, meaning "soft-loud" in Italian.

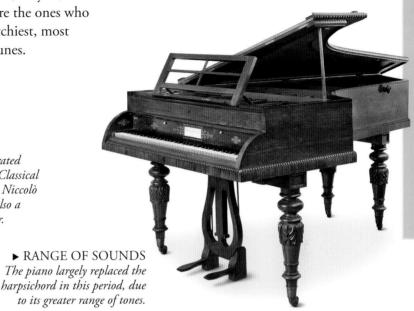

▶ RANGE OF SOUNDS
The piano largely replaced the harpsichord in this period, due to its greater range of tones.

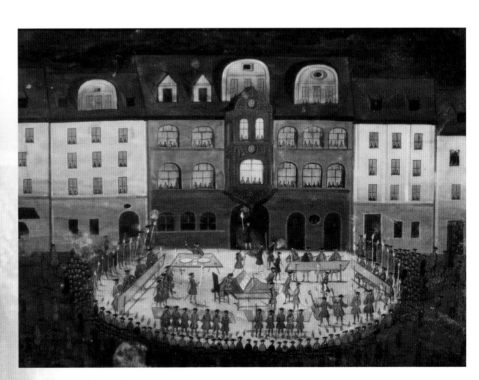

MORE INSTRUMENTS

In the 17th-century Baroque period, a typical orchestra was made up mainly of strings, with a few woodwind instruments and a harpsichord. However, during the Classical period, large woodwind and brass sections were added.

▲ OUTDOOR CONCERT
A large orchestra performs outdoors in Germany in the mid-18th century.

Wolfgang Amadeus Mozart

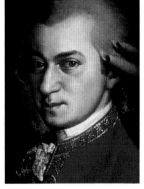

Portrait of Mozart
age about 24

The Austrian composer Wolfgang Amadeus Mozart is generally regarded as one of the finest composers of all time. Almost all his symphonies and operas are still regularly performed today. However, despite his great success as a composer, he was a poor businessman, and died in poverty at just 35 years old.

EXTRAORDINARY LIFE

Mozart spent his life performing and writing music. By the age of four he could already play several instruments, including the violin and keyboard. At five, he composed his first piece of music, and he wrote his first opera at just 11. Mozart spent his early years traveling around Europe with his father, showing off his incredible musical abilities at royal courts. In total, he wrote 41 symphonies and 22 operas. His final opera, *The Magic Flute*, was completed just three months before his death.

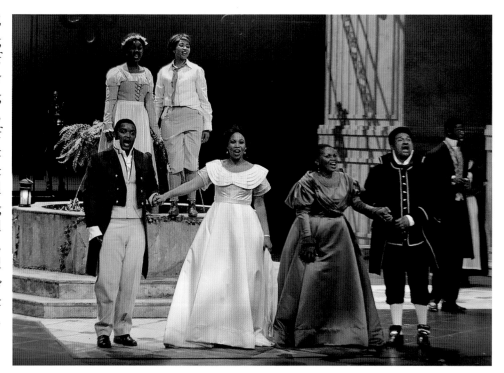

▲ ENDURING POPULARITY
Mozart's music is still hugely popular all across the world. This is a performance of his 1786 opera, The Marriage of Figaro, *in South Africa in 2014.*

LIFE STORY

1756–1763	1764–1767	1782	1791
Born in Salzburg, Austria, in 1756, Mozart is taught music by his ambitious father, who soon has his son touring Europe.	The gifted young musician writes his first sonata at the age of eight. He will complete an opera, *Apollo et Hyancinthus*, three years later.	Now a successful composer, Mozart moves to Vienna, Europe's Classical capital, and marries Constanze Weber.	Following months of ill health, Mozart dies. His final musical piece, *Requiem Mass in D Minor*, is unfinished, but is still performed today.

Ludwig van Beethoven

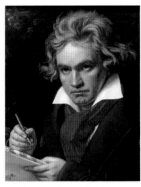

**Portrait of Beethoven
in 1818, aged 48**

This great German composer's music marks the transition from Classicism to Romanticism. Beethoven began his career writing in the Classical style of composers such as Mozart and Haydn. However, over time, he developed his own distinctive emotional style. His works were long, loud, and passionate—features that would become the hallmarks of the Romantic movement.

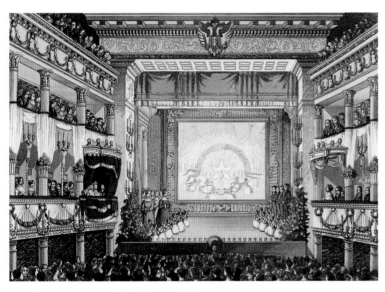

◄ OPENING NIGHT
This is a painting of the first performance of Beethoven's only opera, Fidelio, *in Vienna, in 1805. It was not a success, which led him to make major changes.*

SLOW PERFECTIONIST

Beethoven was a perfectionist, and continued to rewrite pieces until he was totally happy with them, rather than moving on to something new. In total, he completed just nine symphonies and only one opera, *Fidelio*, which took him 10 years to complete. He rewrote one of the opera's arias (solos) 18 times before he was satisfied.

SILENT MUSIC

Beethoven began losing his hearing in his early 20s and, by 1814, he was completely deaf. He had to get his friends to write down what they wanted to say to him in notebooks. But his feeling for music was so great that he was able to continue composing. Indeed, he wrote some of his best-loved work, including his *Ninth Symphony*, when he could no longer hear.

► HEARING AID
Beethoven used this ear trumpet to help him listen to conversations before he went completely deaf.

LIFE STORY

1770–1783	1792–1802	1808	1827
Born in Bonn, Germany, the gifted young Beethoven has his first piece of music published when he was just 13.	Beethoven moves to Vienna, Austria, to study under Joseph Haydn. Within the decade, Beethoven has started to lose his hearing.	He premieres his most famous work, the *Fifth Symphony*—its dramatic opening has since become one of the most famous musical refrains of all time.	Having suffered from a mystery illness for several years, Beethoven dies at 56 years old. Huge crowds attend his funeral in Vienna, Austria.

Romantic composers

In the Romantic period (1820–1910), compositions became longer and more ambitious, orchestras grew larger, and composers tried to express more powerful emotions. Romanticism rejected the modern industrialized world. Instead, music embraced literary and philosophical themes derived from myth, tragedy, and the beauty of nature.

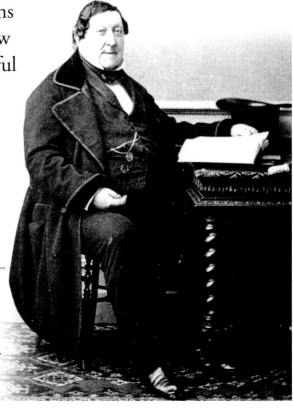

Gioachino Rossini

Composer of some of 19th-century opera's most memorable tunes

- **Lived** 1792–1868
- **From** Italy
- **Notable works** *The Barber of Seville, William Tell*

In the early 19th century, the premiere of a Rossini opera was a huge event. His works were enormously popular and were staged at opera houses across Europe. However, at the height of his fame, at just 37 years old, the Italian composer stopped writing operas and entered semi-retirement. He spent the rest of his life writing chamber music and religious pieces for solo voice.

Franz Liszt

A piano virtuoso and skilled composer

- **Lived** 1811–1886
- **From** Hungary
- **Notable work** *Hungarian Rhapsody No. 2*

In his lifetime, many people believed that Franz Liszt was the greatest pianist in the world. He wrote music mainly for the piano, coming up with elaborate, difficult pieces that showcased his technical skills. Audiences flocked to his concerts. Later in life, Liszt turned his hand to writing orchestral pieces and also worked as a conductor and music teacher.

Richard Wagner

Driven, egotistical composer of epic operas

- **Lived** 1813–1883
- **From** Germany
- **Notable works** *Tristan and Isolde, Parsifal, The Ring of the Nibelung*

Wagner composed music for operas, which he believed were the highest art form, combining orchestration, singing, acting, and set design. His most famous composition, a cycle of four operas based on German and Norse mythology called *The Ring of the Nibelung*, takes 18 hours to perform—and took him 25 years to write.

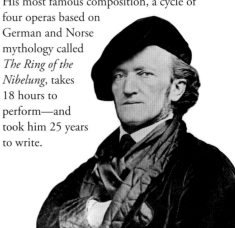

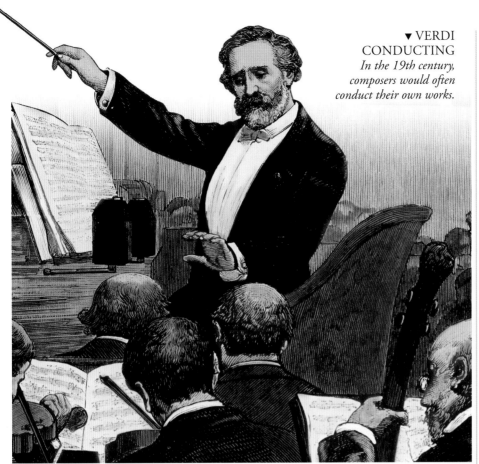

▼ VERDI
CONDUCTING
*In the 19th century,
composers would often
conduct their own works.*

Johannes Brahms

Perfectionist who spent 22 years on his first symphony

- **Lived** 1833–1897
- **From** Germany
- **Notable works** *Academic Festival Overture, German Requiem*

Though born in Germany, Brahms spent much of his career in Vienna, Austria, one of the 19th century's leading centers of classical music. His works were strongly influenced by the classical composers, especially Beethoven, and are noted for their highly structured, romantic style, which gave him a reputation as both a traditionalist and an innovator.

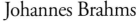

MUSIC

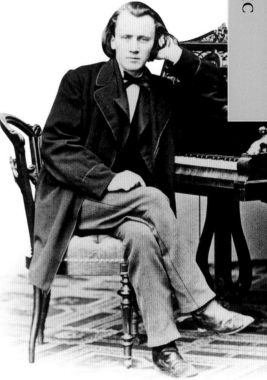

Giuseppe Verdi

Innovative composer who put drama into opera

- **Lived** 1813–1901
- **From** Italy
- **Notable works** *Aïda, Rigoletto, La Traviata*

Now regarded as Italy's greatest opera composer, Verdi's career did not start well. As a teenager, he failed the entrance exam to a prestigious music school, and his wife and two young children died while he was writing his second opera, which turned out to be a flop. However, his career recovered, and he produced many celebrated works. When he died of a stroke at 87, there was a day of national mourning across Italy.

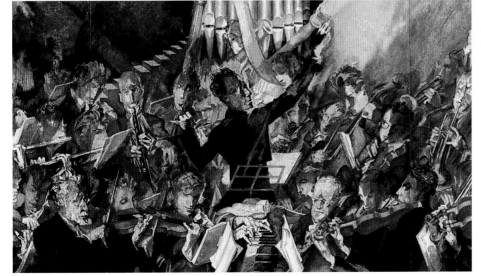

Gustav Mahler

A bridge between Romanticism and Modernism

- **Lived** 1860–1911
- **From** Austria
- **Notable works** *Fifth Symphony*

Nineteenth-century critics were divided in their opinion of Mahler. Some found his complex symphonies exhilarating, but others found them depressing. In his lifetime, he was famed mainly as a conductor of other people's work. His own compositions became popular only after his death. One critic of the time wrote that the audience is "always pleased to see him with baton in hand, just as long as he's not conducting one of his own works."

Symphony orchestra

A modern symphony orchestra is usually split into four sections: strings, woodwind, brass, and percussion. Many orchestras have more than 100 members, but there is no set number—it all depends on which musical pieces are being played. A conductor stands in front of the musicians, guiding their performance.

PERCUSSION

The number and type of orchestral percussion instruments is more varied than for other sections. The timpani, xylophone, cymbals, bass drum, and snare drum are some of the most commonly used. In much orchestral music, percussion is used to add drama rather than to keep a beat.

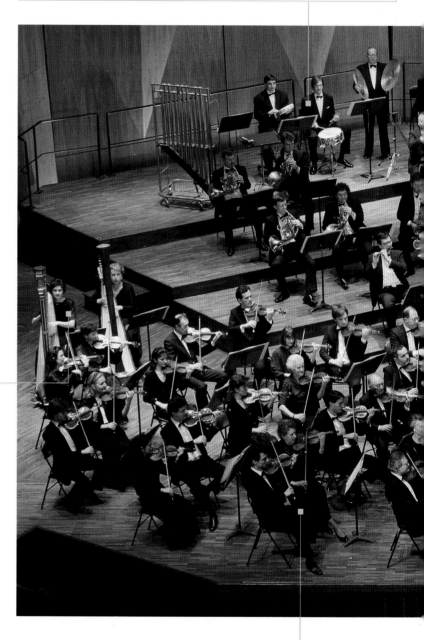

HARPS

Harps and pianos are not considered official parts of the orchestra and do not have their own section. If used, they are usually placed to the orchestra's side, next to the strings.

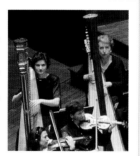

QUIET TO LOUD

The instruments in an orchestra are arranged in a semi-circular pattern around the conductor. To achieve a well-balanced sound, the instruments are organized by volume. The quietest instruments, the strings, are in the front, with the woodwind instruments behind them. The brass instruments are behind the woodwind, while the loudest instruments, the percussion, are at the rear.

VIOLINS

There are usually 10 first violins, which play the main melody, and 10 second violins, which play supporting harmonies. The principal violinist leads the tuning of the orchestra before a performance.

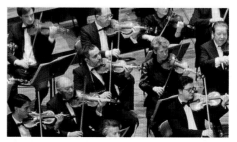

WOODWIND

The woodwind instruments in a standard orchestra are the piccolo (one), flutes (two to four), oboes (two to four), clarinets (four), and bassoons (two to four).

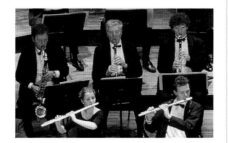

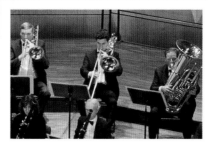

BRASS

A standard orchestra has four brass instruments. These are, from highest pitched to lowest pitched: trumpets (between two and four), trombones (three), French horns (four), and a tuba (one).

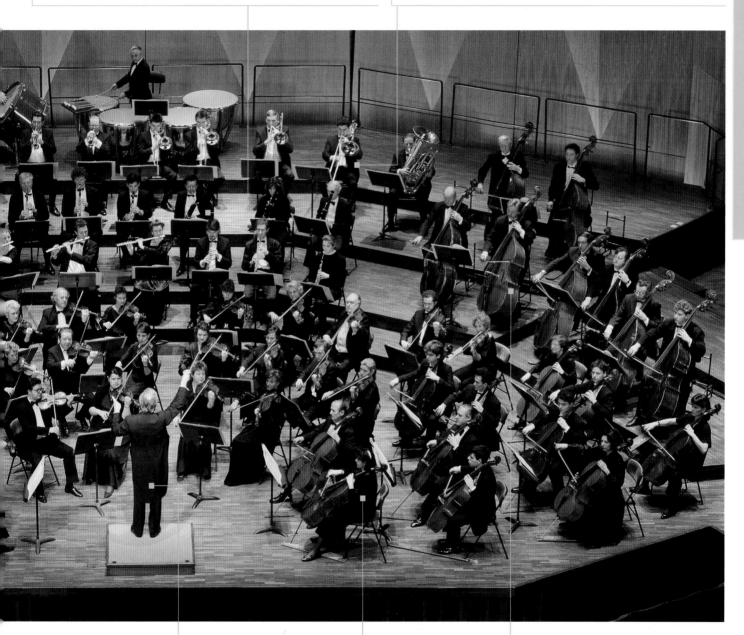

CONDUCTOR

The conductor has several roles: to make sure the musicians start and finish together, to keep time, to cue in musicians, and to get them to play louder or softer in certain passages.

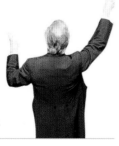

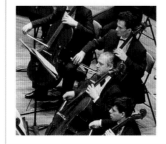

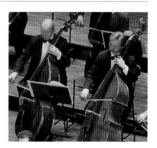

STRINGS

The string section comprises four instruments: the violins (20 in total) play the high notes, while the violas (eight) play the middle range. The cellos (10) and double basses (six) play low-pitched parts.

String instruments

All string instruments produce sound in the same way—by the vibration of their strings. This sound is then amplified (made louder)—either acoustically, usually by the hollow body of the instrument, or electrically, by an amplifier. All string instruments are played in one of three main ways: by plucking, strumming, or bowing.

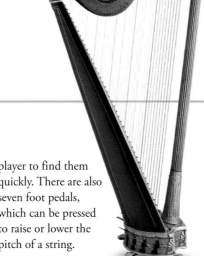

Harp
Shimmering textures and delicate melodies

- **Invented** c.3500 BCE
- **From** Unknown
- **Number of strings** 4–47

Hand-held harps have been around for thousands of years. The modern concert harp is much larger and heavier, and has to be rested on the ground while being played. It has so many strings that the C strings are colored red and the F strings are black to allow the player to find them quickly. There are also seven foot pedals, which can be pressed to raise or lower the pitch of a string.

Lute
One of the oldest stringed instruments

- **Invented** c.3000 BCE
- **From** Middle East
- **Number of strings** 11–13

The lute has been around a long time, possibly for more than 5,000 years. It was the most popular plucked string instrument throughout the Medieval, Renaissance, and Baroque periods before eventually giving way to the guitar. In the Middle East, the oud, or Middle Eastern lute, is still widely used in the traditional music of the region.

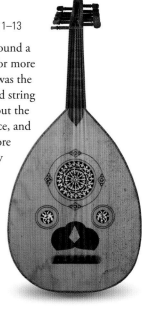

Pipa
Plucked with the fingernails

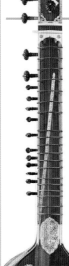

- **Invented** c.2nd century CE
- **From** China
- **Number of strings** 11–13

Resembling a thin lute, the pipa has been played in China for around 2,000 years. It has a short neck and frets that run across the body of the instrument, marking out the position of notes. Unlike a guitar, the pipa is held upright while being played, and the strings are plucked rather than strummed. A closely related and similar-looking instrument called a biwa is played in Japan.

Sitar
The richly textured sound of India

- **Invented** c.14th century
- **From** India
- **Number of strings** 18–20

One of the main instruments of Indian classical music, the sitar has around 20 strings. Six strings are used to play the main melody, which is largely improvised, while another 12 vibrate without being plucked, "filling out" the sound. Two further strings play a drone—a single note that continues throughout a piece of music.

Violin
A smooth, bright sound

- **Invented** 16th century
- **From** Italy
- **Number of strings** 4

One of the main orchestral instruments, the violin's design has remained virtually unchanged since the 18th century. Held under the chin, it is played either by being plucked or by drawing a bow fitted with horsehair across the strings. The instrument also features in many modern styles of music, including jazz and country.

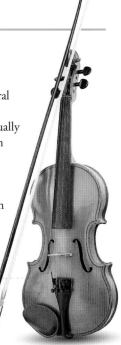

Double bass

A deep, bouncing sound that underpins the orchestra or jazz band

- **Invented** 16th century
- **From** Italy
- **Number of strings** 4

This is the largest and lowest-sounding member of the string family. Held upright on the ground when played—which is why it's also known as an upright bass—its sounds can be produced either with a bow or, more typically in jazz and rock 'n' roll, by plucking the strings.

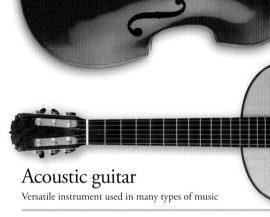

Acoustic guitar

Versatile instrument used in many types of music

- **Invented** 1850
- **From** Spain
- **Number of strings** 6

The modern acoustic guitar was developed by the Spanish instrument maker Antonio de Torres. It is the descendant of the lute, one of the oldest of all string instruments. The term "cithara," from which the English word "guitar" derives, was first used to describe lutelike instruments in the 12th century. The guitar's flat neck enables a player to tackle several notes at once, making the instrument well suited to playing chords.

Ukulele

A light, fun sound

- **Invented** 19th century
- **From** Hawaii
- **Number of strings** 4

Resembling a small guitar, the ukulele's name translates as "jumping flea:" this refers to the fast strumming style used to play it. Sometimes regarded as a "joke" instrument because of its high-pitched, twangy sound, the ukulele has grown in popularity in recent years—partly because it is relatively easy to learn.

Electric guitar

Crashing chords and wailing solos

- **Invented** 1930s
- **From** USA
- **Number of strings** 6

The electric guitar works by turning its strings' vibrations into electrical signals that can be made louder using an amplifier. It was invented to allow the guitar to be heard over the loud brass sections of big bands. The solid-body electric guitar dominated popular music between the 1950s and the 1970s.

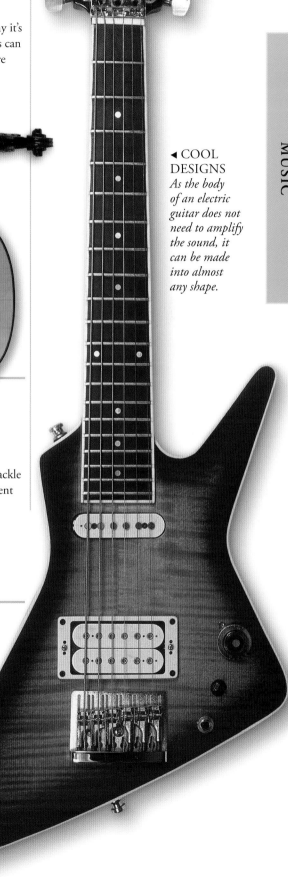

◀ COOL DESIGNS
As the body of an electric guitar does not need to amplify the sound, it can be made into almost any shape.

Frédéric Chopin

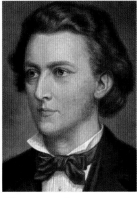

Chopin in Paris,
in his early 20s

Frédéric Chopin was one of the earliest Romantic composers. He was a gifted child musician, performing his first piano concert aged just eight. At 21, he moved from his home in Poland to Paris, France, where he composed and taught piano. Devoted to the music of Bach, he encouraged his pupils to play the Baroque composer's works every day to strengthen their fingers.

PIANO VIRTUOSO

As a teenager, Chopin was hailed as one of the greatest virtuoso pianists in the world. All the pieces he composed had a piano part, which was often extremely technically challenging. Although his playing received rave reviews, he suffered frequently from ill health, and in later life he rarely performed in public, preferring to concentrate on composition.

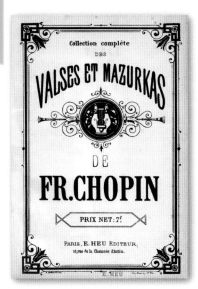

▲ DANCE MUSIC
Chopin wrote the music for numerous dances, including 18 waltzes and several traditional Polish dances called mazurkas.

PROLIFIC COMPOSER

Chopin composed about 230 works for the piano. He wrote beautiful and sophisticated nocturnes (music evocative of the night) that was performed in private salons. He also developed the concept of the concert *étude*—dazzlingly difficult and thrilling pieces for concert performance.

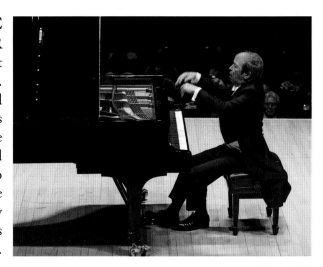

▲ STILL POPULAR
American concert pianist Murray Perahia performs some of Chopin's works at Carnegie Hall, New York, in 2015.

LIFE STORY

1810	1831	1837	1839–1849
Chopin is born in Zelazowa Wola in central Poland. By the age of seven, he has published his first piece of music.	Chopin moves to Paris, France, were he starts a relationship with the French novelist, Amantine Dupin, better known by her pen name, George Sand.	Chopin composes one of his most famous pieces, the third movement of his *Sonata No. 2*, later known as the *Funeral March*.	Chopin's relationship with Sand ends. In 1847, his health deteriorates, and he dies a little over two years later, on October 17, 1849.

Piotr Ilyich Tchaikovsky

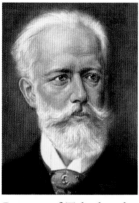

Although the Russian composer Tchaikovsky showed musical talent as a child, his first job was as a civil servant. After four years he began a career in music. His early pieces proved successful and he soon became renowned as a highly original composer. Despite suffering bouts of depression, he continued to compose, writing some of the best-known symphonies and ballets.

Portrait of Tchaikovsky made after his death

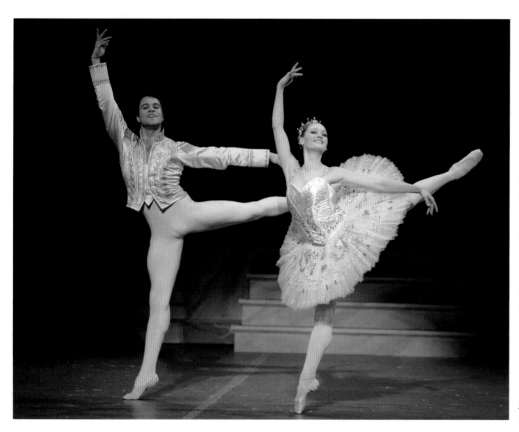

GOING OUT WITH A BANG

Today, Tchaikovsky is best known for his ballets, including *Swan Lake, The Nutcracker,* and *Sleeping Beauty,* all of which are still regularly performed. Many of his pieces are extremely ambitious. The *1812 Overture,* for instance, which was written to commemorate Russia's defeat of the French emperor Napoleon, is supposed to feature real cannon blasts at its climax. Today, fireworks are often used instead.

◄ *THE NUTCRACKER Dancers at the Boston Ballet perform one of Tchaikovsky's best-loved works.*

LIFE STORY

1840	1861–1868	1876–1882	1893
Born in the small town of Votkinsk, Russia, Tchaikovsky composes his first song when he was just four years old.	He enters the St Petersburg Conservatory to study composition, and premieres his first major work, the *First Symphony*, in Moscow.	Following the success of the ballet *Swan Lake* (1876) , Tchaikovsky premieres the *1812 Overture* to great popular acclaim.	Tchaikovsky dies of cholera at the age of 53, nine days after conducting a performance of his *Sixth Symphony* in St Petersburg.

Modern classical music

In the 20th century, many of the old rules of composition were turned on their head as composers experimented with every aspect of music, from key signatures to instrumentation. This approach, which became known as Modernism, mirrored similar movements taking place in other art forms, including painting and literature.

In 1952, the American composer John Cage premiered his piece *4' 33"*: 4 minutes, 33 seconds of total silence.

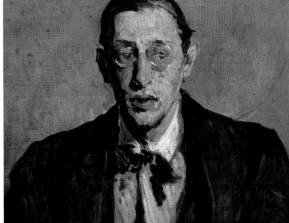

RUSSIAN INNOVATION

In the early 20th century, many of the most innovative composers were Russians, such as Dmitri Shostakovich and Sergei Prokofiev. The most influential Russian composer was Igor Stravinsky. His orchestral ballet score, the *Rite of Spring*, has been described as the "music that changed everything." Its spiky sounds seemed so alien to the audience at its premiere in Paris, France, that it nearly caused a riot.

▲ *STUDY FOR A PORTRAIT OF IGOR STRAVINSKY*, 1913, JACQUES-EMILE BLANCHE
This portrait of Stravinsiky was made the same year that his Rite of Spring *was first performed.*

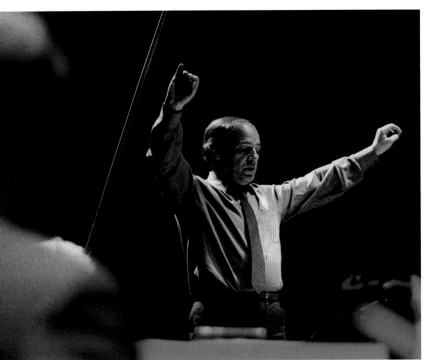

EXPERIMENTAL SOUNDS

In the 20th century, experiments in music gave rise to several new genres. These included Minimalism, which saw composers rejecting large orchestral pieces in favor of small, hypnotic works involving just a few notes and a handful of instruments. Meanwhile, composers of Serialism, such as the Austrian Arnold Schoenberg, wrote music using mathematical formulas, while the creators of Aleatory music aimed to leave parts of the performance up to chance (Aleatory means "random").

◄ MUSIC OF CHANCE
The French composer Pierre Boulez, seen here in 1972, was one the founders of Aleatory music in the 1950s.

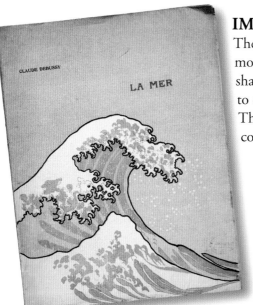

IMPRESSIONIST MOODS

The music of the Impressionist period (1890–1920) was gentler and more reflective than Modernist music. As with the painting style that shares its name, this music prioritized atmosphere over drama, seeking to convey moods rather than describing everything in great detail. The main composers associated with the movement were the French composers Claude Debussy and Maurice Ravel.

▲ MUSIC OF THE SEA
In 1905, Debussy published his most famous work, La Mer, *made up of three symphonic "sketches" about the sea.*

▶ STRANGE NEW INSTRUMENTS
Stockhausen conducts an orchestra in the performance of one of his own works, Inori, *in 1973, which features cooking pots as instruments.*

PUSHING THE BOUNDARIES

The German composer Karlheinz Stockhausen spent his life testing the limits of music. He wrote both Serial and Aleatory compositions, and was an early pioneer of electronic synthesizer music. Stockhausen also took instrumentation to radical extremes in his search for new sounds. One of his operas featured a string quartet playing in helicopters above the concert hall. The sounds of both were broadcast to the audience.

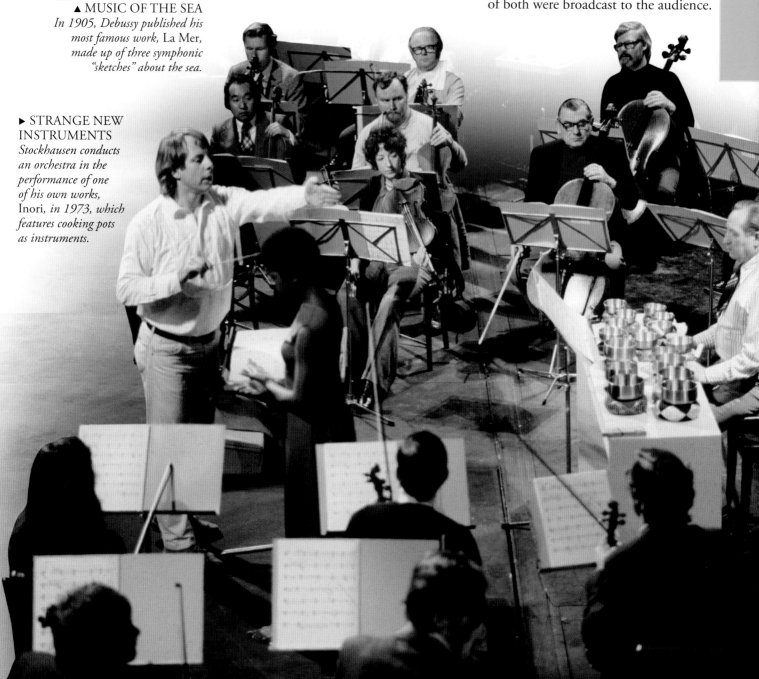

Woodwind instruments

The sound of woodwind instruments is made by moving air. This usually requires the musician to blow into the instrument. However, some instruments in this family, such as the bagpipes, use bellows (an air bag that can be squeezed) to move the air. Today, the wood of many woodwind instruments has been replaced by metal or plastic.

Bagpipes

Produce a constant, wavering sound

- **Invented** c.1000 BCE
- **From** Origin uncertain
- **Material** Wood and animal skin

The bagpipes' distinctive wailing sound is produced when air stored in a bag is squeezed out through a set of pipes. Traditional Scottish Great Highland bagpipes consist of a blowpipe (through which air is blown into the bag), a chanter (on which the melody is played), a bag (which is squeezed by the arm to release the air), and several drone pipes (which play a single note to accompany the melody). Many countries have a form of bagpipes, but they are most traditionally associated with Scotland.

Bansuri

The longer the flute, the richer the tone

- **Invented** c.200 BCE
- **From** India
- **Material** Bamboo

Believed to be thousands of years old, the bansuri is a simple flute used in traditional Indian music. It has just six tone holes for changing notes and is played in the transverse, or side-blown, style. This means the player holds it horizontally and blows into a hole on the top of the instrument.

Oboe

A bright, nasal tone that sounds almost like the human voice

- **Invented** Mid-17th century
- **From** France
- **Material** Wood, nickel silver

The oboe looks similar to a clarinet, but is smaller. It also has a double reed—two thin pieces of wood fixed to each other that vibrate together to produce the sound when the oboe player blows on them. The instrument's name comes from the French term *haut bois*, which means "high wood," a reference to the oboe's high-pitched sound.

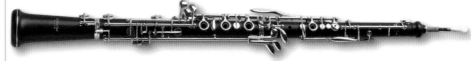

Shawm

A bright, wavery voice

- **Invented** 12th century
- **From** Germany
- **Material** Wood

This wooden instrument was hugely popular in Europe in Medieval and Renaissance times. With just seven finger holes and a thumb hole, it has a limited range, but can produce a high, piercing tone that carries a long way, making it well-suited for outdoor playing. From about 1700 onward, it was gradually replaced by the oboe, which is played in the same way but has a greater range.

Clarinet

A hugely versatile instrument with a wide range

- **Invented** 17th century
- **From** Germany
- **Material** Wood

Most orchestras have four clarinets in a range of keys—an e flat, two b flats and a bass—which play both melodies and harmonies. Yet they are played in the same way. The clarinettist blows over a single wooden reed attached to the mouthpiece. This vibrates, creating the sound that travels through the instrument and out of the bell. In the 20th century, the clarinet became a popular jazz instrument.

The mouthpiece uses a single reed made from a type of grass.

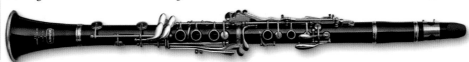

The reed is held in place on the mouthpiece by a metal device called a ligature.

▶ SAX FAMILY
There are nine different sizes of saxophone. The tenor saxophone, shown here, is the most popular.

Saxophone
Ideal for fast-paced, note-packed jazz solos

- **Invented** 1840
- **From** Belgium
- **Material** Brass

Played using a reed mouthpiece and with similar fingering to a clarinet, the saxophone is classed as a woodwind instrument. However, its Belgian inventor, Adolphe Sax (who named it after himself), wanted it to have some of the characteristics of brass instruments. So, he made it out of metal and gave it a wide bell, like a trumpet, to make it louder. Although the saxophone does not often feature in classical music, in the 20th century it has become one of the major jazz and pop solo instruments.

Bassoon
Raspy bass sounds

- **Invented** c.1846
- **From** France
- **Material** Wood

The bassoon is the lowest-sounding woodwind instrument in a standard classical orchestra. Its relative, the contra-bassoon, is the lowest-sounding instrument in the whole orchestra, but is less commonly played. It is held vertically or diagonally in front of the player, who will usually wear a neck strap to support the instrument's heavy weight. The modern bassoon is a descendant of a simpler Renaissance instrument called the dulcian.

Flute
A bright, happy lilt

- **Invented** (Modern style) 1847
- **From** Germany
- **Material** Silver or nickel

Basic flutes, consisting of a hollow tube with holes that can be covered by the fingers to change notes, have been around for thousands of years. Forty-thousand-year-old versions made of mammoth tusk have been found, making them perhaps the oldest melodic instruments. The modern concert flute (as shown), which uses a sophisticated system of rods, keys, and pads to cover the holes, was invented by the German instrument maker Theobald Boehm. It has a soft, bright sound.

Piccolo
A high, trilling tone

- **Invented** (Modern style) around 1862
- **From** Germany
- **Material** Silver or nickel

Resembling a miniature flute, the piccolo is the highest-sounding instrument in a standard orchestra. As with the flute, the piccolo is side-blown, which means the player blows over a hole in the side known as an embouchure.

As piccolo parts are less common than flute parts, few orchestras employ specialist piccolo players. Instead, one of the flute players will usually take on the piccolo parts when needed.

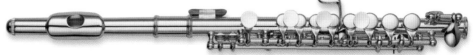

Stage and screen

In the late 19th and early 20th centuries, plays featuring catchy songs, known as musicals, were hugely popular in theaters. Many of these musicals were later adapted for movies. The development of cinema, and later of television, spurred the creation of new musical forms, such as theme tunes and incidental music.

FROM STAGE TO SCREEN

It was once thought that cinema might kill off live theater, but stage musicals continue to be popular. Some composers, such as Irving Berlin and Cole Porter, had careers writing for both. Many musicals have made the transition from stage to screen with huge success. In recent years, films such as *The Lion King* and *Billy Elliot* have made the opposite journey, moving successfully to the stage.

▼ LONG-RUNNING
Having first opened in 1985, the London production of the stage musical Les Misérables *is still going strong.*

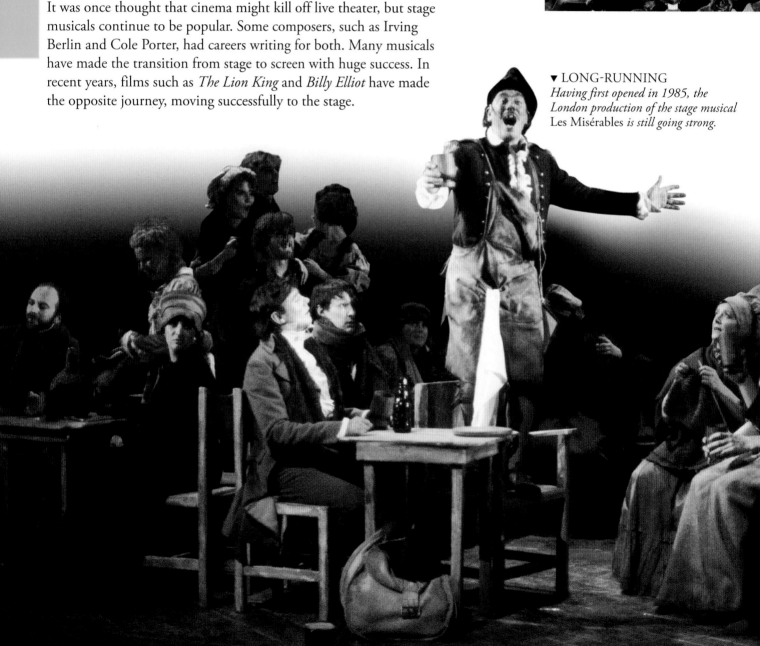

THE SILENT ERA

Early films did not have recorded sound, but they were not shown in complete silence. Instead, the action on screen was accompanied by a pianist or an organist. The musicians would try to match what they played to the mood of the film, playing quickly during chase sequences, or slow, romantic passages during love scenes.

◄ PLAYING ALONG
A pianist accompanies the action during a screening of a film in New York in around 1925.

The first feature-length movie to have recorded sound was a musical called *The Jazz Singer*, released in 1927.

▶ JOHN WILLIAMS
This American composer has written the music for films such as Jaws, Star Wars, ET, *and the* Harry Potter *movies.*

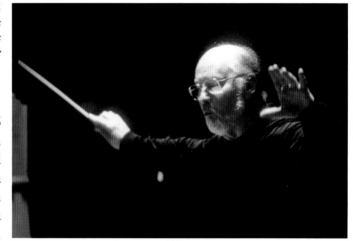

FILM SCORES

Once sound for film had been invented, composers began to write music specifically for films. This usually involved writing a catchy piece of music for the start, known as a theme tune. Most films also feature incidental music, which plays during scenes to create a mood, such as suspense in a horror movie or excitement in an action movie.

BOLLYWOOD

India has one of the world's most successful film industries, which is commonly known as "Bollywood." Most Bollywood films are musicals featuring elaborate song and dance routines. The songs are usually recorded by professional musicians, with the actors then lip-syncing the words on screen.

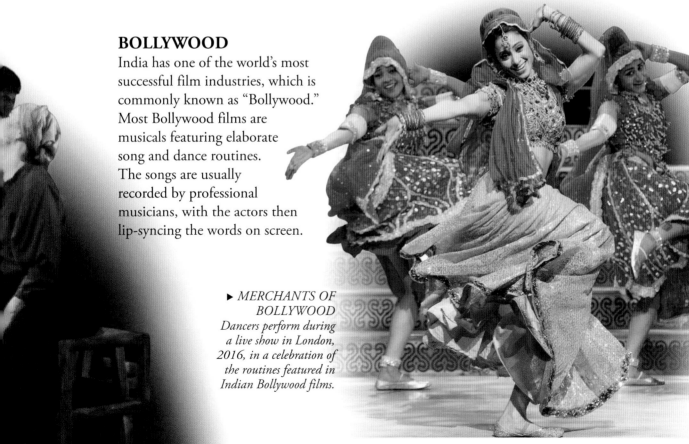

▶ *MERCHANTS OF BOLLYWOOD*
Dancers perform during a live show in London, 2016, in a celebration of the routines featured in Indian Bollywood films.

Jazz music

At the start of the 20th century, a new style of music emerged in the southern city of New Orleans. Jazz was a mixture of European harmonies and African-American rhythms and playing styles. Jazz performances typically feature a lot of improvisation, with individual musicians taking turns to perform instrumental solos.

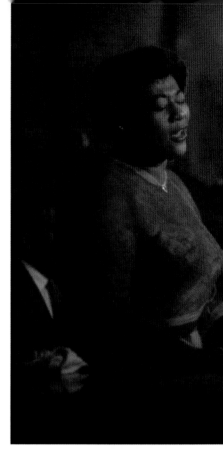

▲ ELLA FITZGERALD
A versatile jazz singer, Fitzgerald was famed for the clarity of her tone and her ability to improvise.

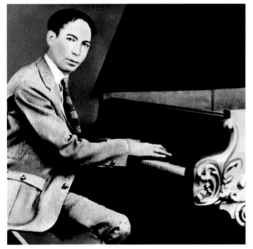

▲ JELLY ROLL MORTON
This New Orleans ragtime pianist and composer became one of the first jazz stars in the early 20th century

EARLY INFLUENCES

One of the main influences on early jazz was a style of music known as ragtime, which was popular in the late 19th century. Played on a piano and with an up-tempo, danceable beat, it took its name from its jerky, "ragged" rhythm, an effect called syncopation. The American pianist Scott Joplin scored major ragtime hits with his songs *Maple Leaf Rag* and *The Entertainer*.

BIG BANDS, BIGGER SOUND

Like ragtime, jazz had a syncopated sound, but it involved more musicians. A typical jazz band of the 1910s contained a rhythm section of guitar (or banjo), double bass (or tuba), and piano and drums. There was also a front-line melody section of trumpet, trombone, and clarinet. The bands grew larger over time and by the 1930s could contain up to 25 musicians. These "big bands" played a dance-oriented music known as "swing" because it seemed to swing along.

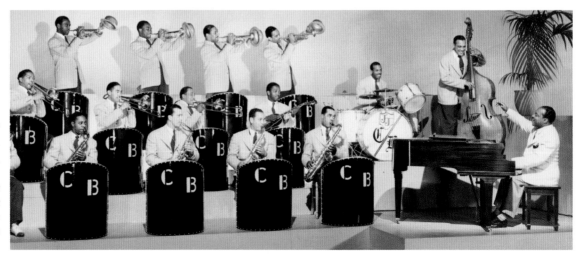

▶ COUNT BASIE AND HIS ORCHESTRA
Big band leaders, such as Count Basie (pictured at the piano), became big stars in the 1930s.

COMPLEX BEBOP

After World War II, a complicated type of jazz emerged that people preferred to listen to and appreciate, rather than dance to. Played by highly skilled musicians, such as the saxophonist Charlie Parker, the new jazz featured complex rhythms and fast solos that often involved unusual melodies and harmonies. Named after the honking "bebop" sound of the saxophone, it wasn't universally popular. Many jazz musicians and fans preferred the traditional, or "trad," jazz of the pre-war era.

The first jazz recording, a song called *Livery Stable Blues*, was made by the Original Dixieland Jazz Band in 1917.

▼ MILES DAVIS
Popular around the world, this influential trumpeter collaborated with musicians in a wide variety of styles, including funk and pop.

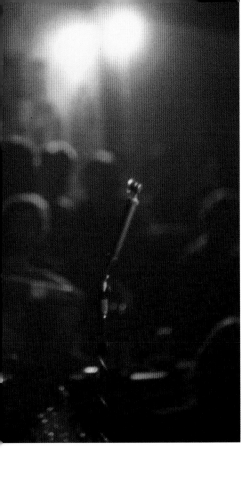

MODERN TRENDS

A style called "cool jazz" emerged in the 1950s as a slower, more relaxed counterpart to bebop. It was popularized by the trumpeter Miles Davis, who also experimented with jazz-funk fusion in the 1970s. Other notable new styles include "free jazz," in which the musicians all improvise at the same time, creating unusual clashes of sounds and rhythms. The saxophonist Ornette Coleman was one of the major figures of free jazz.

Brass instruments

Musicologists (people who study music) classify instruments by how they are played, rather than what they are made of. If the sound is made by the player vibrating, or buzzing, their lips against the mouthpiece, then it is a brass instrument. This means that a didgeridoo is a brass instrument, even though it's made of wood.

Didgeridoo
The low, rumbling sound of Australia

- **Invented** c.500 CE
- **From** Australia
- **Material** Wood

The didgeridoo is one of the main instruments of Australia's Aboriginal people. Traditionally made from branches of eucalyptus that have been hollowed out by termites, it makes a low, pulsing sound. Skilled didgeridoo players achieve this through a technique called circular breathing. This involves storing air in their cheeks while taking in air in through their nose in order to keep blowing and producing a continuous sound.

Serpent
Looks like a snake, sounds like a tuba

- **Invented** 17th century
- **From** France
- **Material** Wood

This strange-looking instrument is an early ancestor of the tuba. With just six tone holes, it had a narrow range but was widely used in the 18th century—Mozart featured it in several of his compositions. From the early 19th century onward, it was replaced by the modern valved tuba.

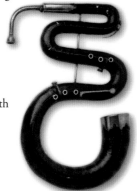

Trombone
Sliding from high-pitched to low-pitched

- **Invented** 15th century
- **From** Europe
- **Material** Brass

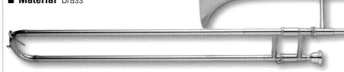

A trombone player changes notes using a metal slide, which moves up and down the length of the instrument. Rapid changes to the slide's position produce the instrument's distinctive swooping sound. The trombone is the descendant of an earlier Renaissance instrument called the sackbut (which means "pull push" in French). The name "trombone" comes from the Italian word for "big trumpet."

French Horn
Perfect for long, sustained notes

- **Invented** 1818
- **From** Germany
- **Material** Brass

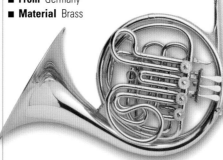

In the early 19th century, brass horns with valves to change notes were introduced. This made the instrument easier to play and also gave it a wider range. The French horn's large bell makes it one of the orchestra's loudest instruments, although the player can muffle the sound by placing their hand inside the bell. Despite its name, it was actually invented in Germany.

Trumpet
Bright melodies and powerful fanfares

- **Invented** 1818 (modern trumpet)
- **From** Germany
- **Material** Brass

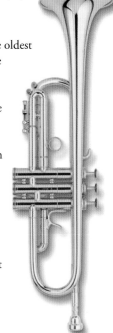

The trumpet is one of the oldest wind instruments. Simple versions made of shells, tusks, and animal horns have been found that date back thousands of years. The modern trumpet is made of curved brass with a flared bell at one end for projecting the sound, and three valves, which the musician can press in various combinations to change notes. In the 20th century, the trumpet became one of the main solo jazz instruments.

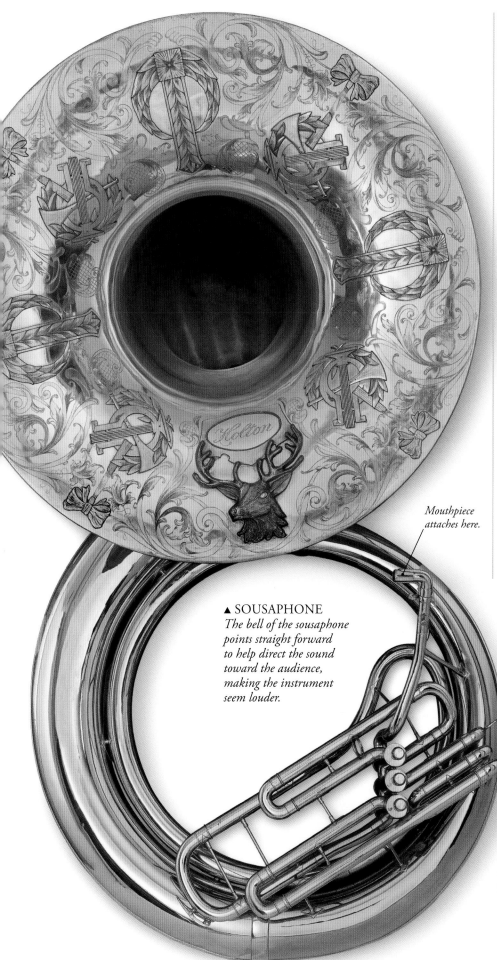

Tuba

Heavy instrument with rich bass sounds

- **Invented** 1835
- **From** Germany
- **Material** Brass

The largest and lowest-sounding member of the orchestra's brass section, the tuba is made from over 16 ft (5 m) of metal tubing, bent around and coiled in on itself. It is very heavy, so is usually played sitting down. The tuba was a regular feature in early jazz bands, but was later replaced by the double or electric bass.

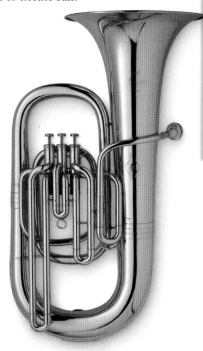

Mouthpiece attaches here.

▲ SOUSAPHONE
The bell of the sousaphone points straight forward to help direct the sound toward the audience, making the instrument seem louder.

Sousaphone

A tuba on the march

- **Invented** 1893
- **From** USA
- **Material** Brass

The size and weight of the tuba make it impractical for marching bands. In 1893, the American composer and bandleader John Philip Sousa asked an instrument maker to design a new, lighter type of tuba that could be worn around the body, supported by the shoulder. This became the sousaphone. Like the tuba, it has three valves for changing notes. It weighs around 11 kg (24 lb), so is still quite heavy, but crucially, it is much easier to carry than a tuba.

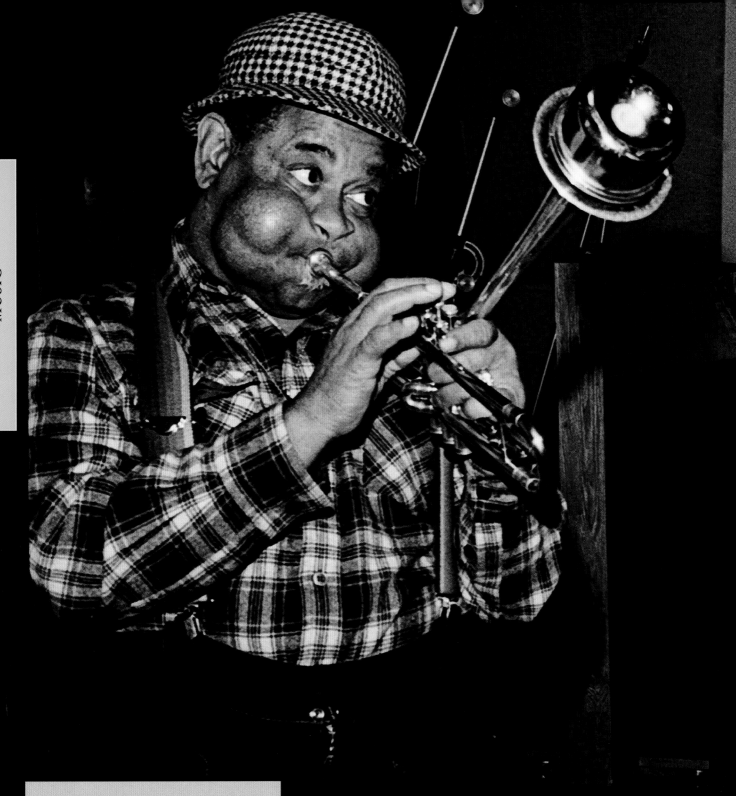

JAZZ PIONEER
With his distinctive bulging cheeks, Dizzy Gillespie made his name as a virtuoso jazz trumpeter during the bebop era. He is shown here in 1981 in a New York City studio, playing with the soul and disco singer Chaka Khan during a recording of his song *A Night in Tunisia*.

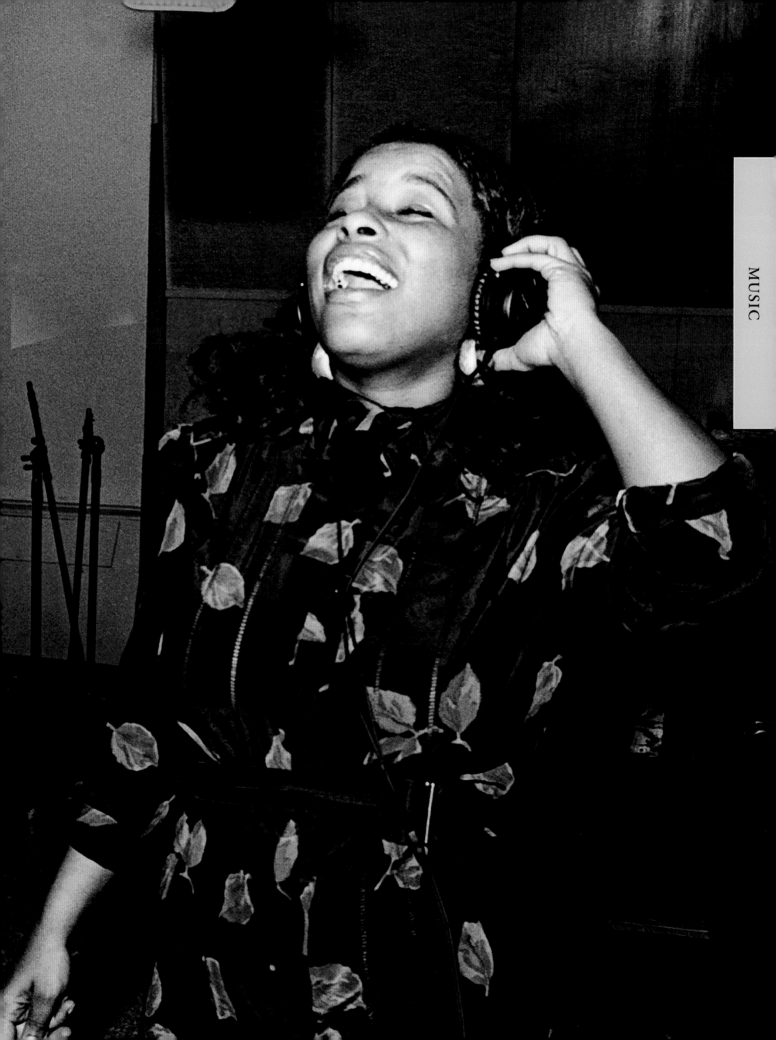

Rock and roll

In the early 1950s, a new form of music appeared in the United States, and it soon became popular all over the world. Known as "rock and roll," its success was fueled by the development of vinyl records, which sold millions of copies worldwide. Radio, television, and film helped to spread the fame of its new stars.

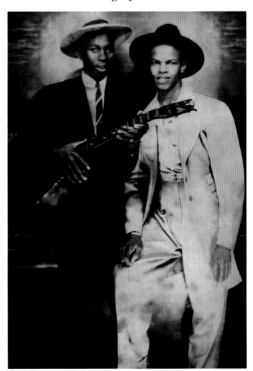

▼ EARLY INFLUENCE
The blues songs of Robert Johnson (shown here on the left in 1935) had a big influence on rock and roll.

ROCK AND ROLL ORIGINS

The scales and chord progressions of rock and roll were influenced by the blues—a slow, mournful music that originated in African-American communities of the American south in the early 20th century. This developed into an up-tempo, dance-oriented style called R&B (short for "rhythm and blues"). R&B was combined with country, and rock and roll was born.

◄ THE BEATLES
Selling more than 250 million records, The Beatles are officially the best-selling band in history.

THE FAB FOUR

In 1964, a four-piece rock and roll act from Liverpool, England, became the best-known band in the world. They had a string of number one hits and were followed wherever they went by hordes of screaming fans—a phenomenon known as "Beatlemania." The Beatles were one of a number of British rock and roll bands to have success in the United States in the 1960s.

MUSIC FOR THE YOUNG

To audiences in the 1950s, rock and roll was new and exciting. Some people considered the fast-paced music a dangerous influence on society—which only increased its appeal for many other people. Where a swing band of the previous decade may have had up to 25 members, a rock and roll band could have just four: a drummer, a bass player, a guitarist or pianist, and a singer. Largely performed by young, good-looking musicians, the music was aimed at young people.

NEW ROCKIN' SOUNDS

Rock and roll developed into many new styles. One of the earliest was called rockabilly, as performed by artists such as Buddy Holly, Carl Perkins, and early-career Elvis Presley. Rockabilly had a stripped-back sound characterized by twanging electric guitars, echoed vocals, and a distinctive bass style known as "slap back" in which the strings were snapped rhythmically by the fingers.

The Beatles' first appearance on US television in 1964 drew an audience of 73 million people, a record for the time.

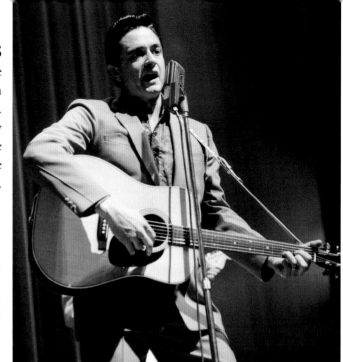

► JOHNNY CASH
This American singer-songwriter became a big star in the 1950s performing both country and rockabilly songs.

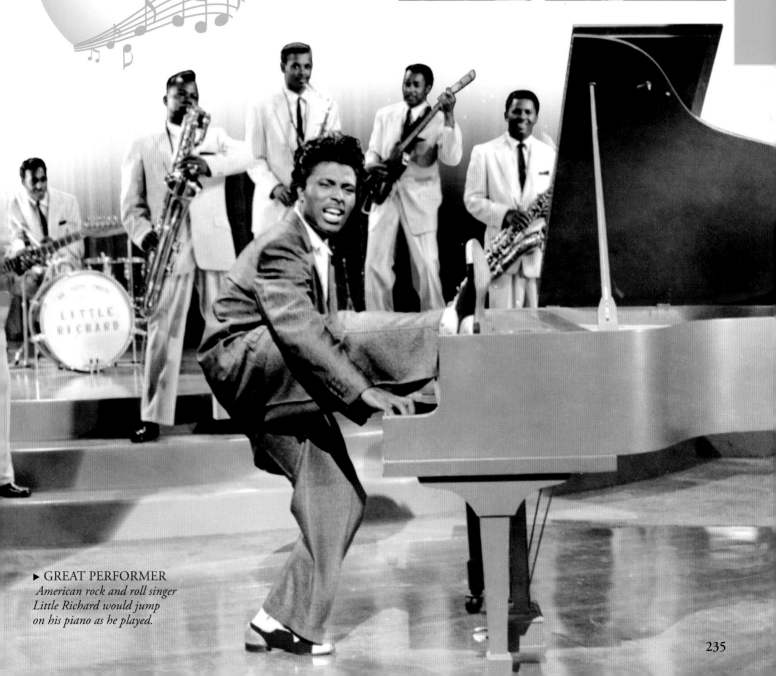

► GREAT PERFORMER
American rock and roll singer Little Richard would jump on his piano as he played.

235

Keyboard instruments

Keyboard instruments produce their sounds in many different ways. The sound of the piano is the result of vibrating strings, while a pipe organ's enormous volume is caused by air pumped through its pipes. Many modern instruments, such as synthesizers, rely on electronic components to create their sounds.

MUSIC

Pipe organ
The biggest, loudest keyboard sound of all

- **Invented** c.13th century
- **From** Central Europe
- **Number of keys** Up to 427

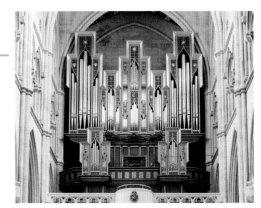

The pipe organ is one of the most difficult instruments to play. An organist usually has to manage several keyboards (known as manuals), as well as various pedals and stops (pull knobs). The stops release the air that rushes into the organ's pipes, causing them to make a sound. Different pipe lengths produce different pitches. Organs are among the biggest instruments of all. The largest ever constructed, in 1932, in Atlantic City, USA, has 33,112 pipes.

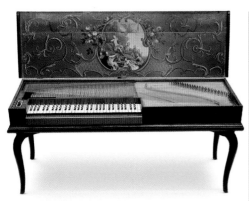

Clavichord
A small keyboard for delicate Renaissance melodies

- **Invented** c.14th century
- **From** Central Europe
- **Number of keys** 45

The earliest of the stringed keyboard instruments, the clavichord is the ancestor of both the harpsichord and the piano. The sounds are made when small metal blades, called tangents, strike brass or iron strings inside the instrument. It produces a delicate, buzzy sound that is far too quiet for anything other than private practice or small-scale public performances. Many Renaissance clavichords were ornately decorated.

Harpsichord
Black and white keys the opposite way round to a piano

- **Invented** Early 16th century
- **From** Italy
- **Number of keys** 61

Invented during the Renaissance, the harpsichord became popular in the Baroque period, when a second keyboard was added to many instruments, increasing their range. Instead of being struck, the strings in a harpsichord are plucked with quills. This produces a loud, ringing sound that enabled the harpsichord to become one of the main orchestral instruments of the age. By the late 18th century, it had been largely replaced by the piano.

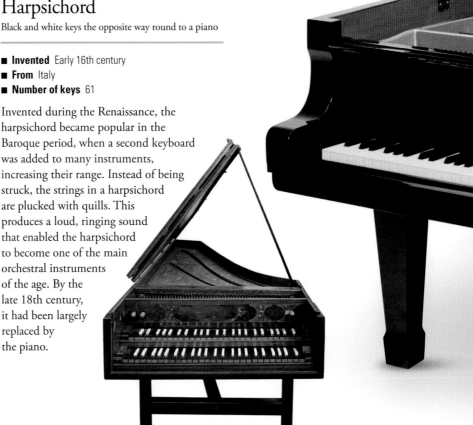

Piano

The most versatile of the traditional keyboard instruments

- **Invented** 1700
- **From** Italy
- **Number of keys** 88

The piano is the most widely used keyboard instrument, featuring in everything from classical music and jazz to pop and soul. When a key is pressed, it causes a small, felt-lined hammer to strike a string inside the instrument, sounding the correct pitch. Classical music is nearly always played on large grand pianos, which have their strings arranged horizontally. The smaller upright piano, in which the strings are vertical, was invented in Austria in the late 18th century.

▲ GRAND PIANO
A grand piano has three pedals, which are pressed to soften or sustain notes.

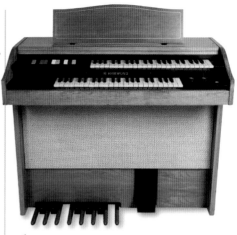

Electric organ

Soft, mellow soul sounds and raucous funk riffs

- **Invented** 1920s
- **From** USA
- **Number of keys** 61 (Hammond organ)

The first electric keyboards were made in the 1920s, but they did not become widely popular until the 1930s. The Hammond organ, invented by American engineer Laurens Hammond in 1935, was one of the most successful makes. It used spinning electrical components called tone wheels to create a distinctive, organ-like sound. It was initially marketed to churches as a cheap alternative to pipe organs. However, it soon became popular with jazz musicians and would later feature in many soul and funk bands.

Synthesizer

A universe of sounds at your fingertips

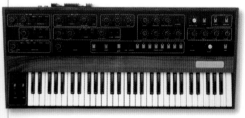

- **Invented** 1960s
- **From** USA
- **Number of keys** 25–88

The most adaptable of all keyboard instruments, synthesizers produce their sounds purely electronically. Synthesizers can be used to replicate real instruments, such as pianos or violins, or to create new electronic sounds that no other instrument can make. Many of the biggest-selling popular songs of the past 40 years have been created using synthesizers. Their range of automatic features means that they're much easier to play than a traditional keyboard instrument.

Elvis Presley

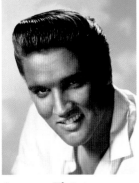

Known as the "King," Elvis Presley was the biggest star of the rock and roll era. With his good looks, hip-shaking dance moves, and soulful voice, he helped to turn the music into a global phenomenon in the 1950s. In the 1960s, he starred in a string of hit movies, and he was a popular live performer during the 1970s.

A young Elvis in a publicity shot

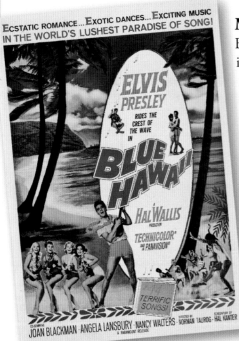

ECSTATIC ROMANCE...EXOTIC DANCES...EXCITING MUSIC
IN THE WORLD'S LUSHEST PARADISE OF SONG!

▲ BLUE HAWAII
This is a poster for a 1961 Elvis movie.
It was a light, cheery musical that was
typical of the star's film career.

MOVIE STAR

Beginning in 1956 with *Love me Tender*, Elvis starred in 31 movies. They were usually based around a simple, romantic plot and featured lots of songs. The movies were popular, but Presley grew increasingly unhappy with his film career. He had wanted to become a serious actor, not star in lighthearted musicals. He retired from films in 1969 to concentrate on live performances.

RECORD BREAKER

Although the exact numbers aren't known, most experts believe Elvis to be the best-selling solo artist of all time. He has sold more than 200 million albums across the world, second only to the Beatles, and more than 600 million records in total. He also had 18 number one singles in the United States, again, second only to the Beatles.

▶ LIVE IN LAS VEGAS
In 1970, a film crew followed Elvis on
his first tour in 13 years. Here Elvis is in
rehearsal for one of his Las Vegas shows.

LIFE STORY

1935	1946–1948	1953	1956
Elvis Aaron Presley is born in Tupelo, Mississippi. His twin brother dies at birth. Elvis grows up as an only child.	Elvis's mother buys him his first guitar for his 11th birthday. He and his family move to Memphis, Tennessee, when he is 13.	Elvis pays to record two songs at Sun Studios in Memphis, supposedly as a gift for his mother. Sun later releases his first records.	Having signed to RCA, a major record company, Elvis releases the single *Heartbreak Hotel*, which sells over a million copies.

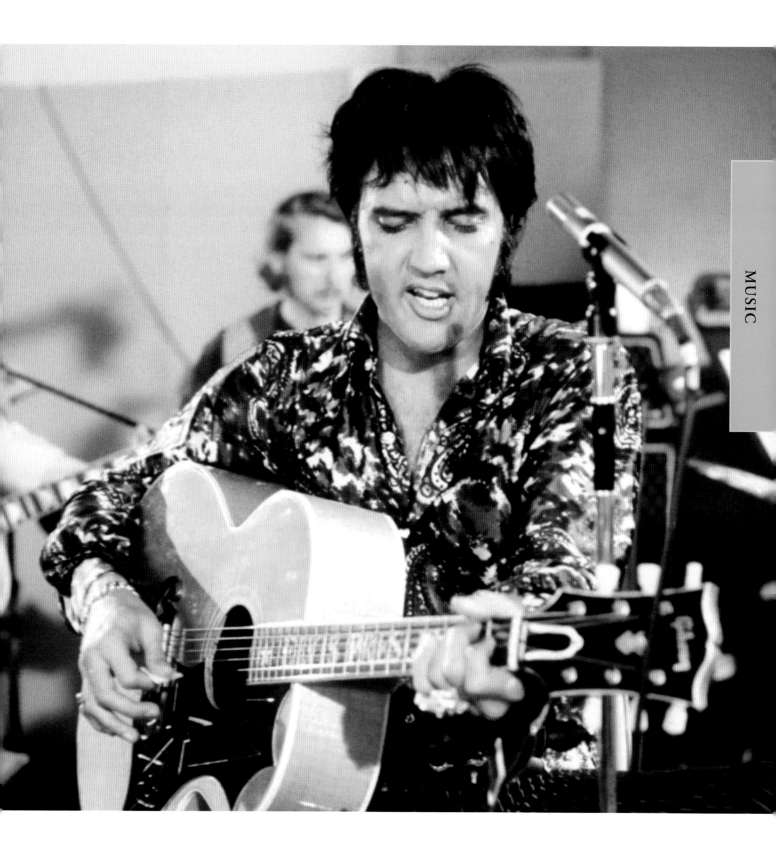

1957	1958–1960	1970-1977	1977
Constantly followed by fans, Elvis buys a private mansion, Graceland, on the edge of Memphis, where he lives for the rest of his life.	Elvis is drafted into the US Army, serving for two years. He does not see combat and leaves the army as big a star as he had been before.	Following the success of his TV special, Elvis returns to live performance, continuing to tour the United States throughout the 1970s.	After years of unhealthy living, a now very overweight Elvis dies of a heart attack in the bathroom of Graceland at just 42 years old.

Percussion instruments

Percussion instruments can be divided into three main categories based on how they are played: those that are hit, those that are scraped, and those that are shaken. Most percussion instruments are used to keep a rhythm. However, there are also tuned percussion instruments that can play a melody or chords.

Maracas

Also known as shic-shacs or rumba shakers

- **Invented** c.500 BCE
- **From** South America
- **Made of** Dried gourds, wood, or plastic filled with beans, beads, or stones

These rattles are used in many styles of Latin American music. They are played by being shaken backward and forward in time with the music, which produces the instrument's distinctive "shic-shac" sound.

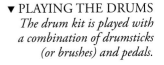

Chau gong

Used as an alarm to clear the streets in ancient times

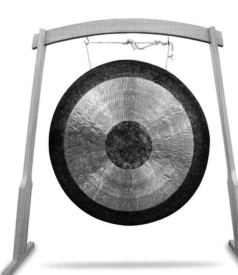

- **Invented** c.2000 BCE
- **From** China
- **Made of** Metal (usually brass or bronze)

Also known as the tam tam, the chau gong dates back at least 4,000 years. It was originally used in religious ceremonies. Played with a mallet, it produces a shimmering, rolling sound when struck lightly. When struck hard, it makes a loud metallic splash that seems to reverberate forever.

Xylophone

Its name translates as "wooden sound"

- **Invented** c.9th century CE
- **From** Southeast Asia
- **Made of** Wood or plastic keys, metal resonators

Consisting of a series of tuned wooden blocks, the xylophone is played with mallets. Hard mallets are used for a loud, bright sound; soft ones for quieter, gentler tones. Metal bars beneath the blocks, called resonators, amplify the sound. Large orchestral xylophones have their bars laid out like the keyboard of a piano.

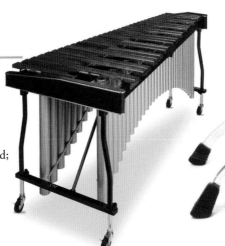

▼ PLAYING THE DRUMS
The drum kit is played with a combination of drumsticks (or brushes) and pedals.

The ride cymbal is used for keeping a high-pitched rhythm.

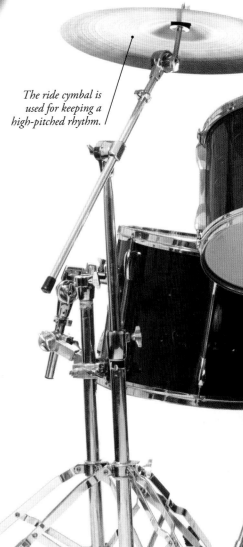

Timpani

Adds low, rumbling menace to symphonic sounds

- **Invented** c.15th century
- **From** Turkey
- **Made of** Copper body, animal-skin (or plastic) head

Also known as a kettle drum, the timpani produce loud, booming beats. They have been used since Baroque times to add drama and color to orchestral pieces. Unlike most other types of drum, the timpani can be tuned to specific pitches using a pedal at the base to tighten or loosen the drum skin. They are played with mallets.

Congas

For complex, hand-played rhythms

- **Invented** 19th century
- **From** South America
- **Made of** Wooden body, animal-skin (or plastic) head

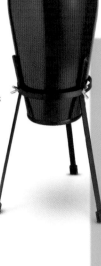

Congas are long, thin drums that are usually played in pairs. Drummers beat out the rhythm using their fingers and the palms of their hands. The instrument features prominently in Latin American musical styles that need syncopated beats, such as rumba and salsa.

Claves

The click-clack rhythm of Cuban dance

- **Invented** 19th century
- **From** Cuba
- **Made of** Wood

One of the simplest percussion instruments, claves consist of just two short pieces of wood. These can be struck together to produce a bright, clicking rhythm, which is also known as a clave. Clave beats form the basis of many Cuban musical styles, including rumba, son, and conga.

Drum kit

The percussive sound that dominates popular music

- **Invented** 1920s
- **From** USA
- **Made of** Metal, wood, and plastic

A combination of several different percussion instruments, the drum kit was invented as a way of saving both space and manpower. It allows a single drummer to tackle a variety of rhythm instruments, usually including the snare drum, hi-hat, tom-toms, cymbals, and bass drum, using their hands and feet. Drum kits feature heavily in popular music and jazz, but single percussion instruments still tend to be used in classical orchestras.

The bass drum is played with the foot using a pedal.

241

Popular music

In the 1960s, rock and roll evolved into several different styles, including pop, rock, and funk, all known as "popular music." Since then, even more styles have emerged, such as disco and rap. These have often been aided by the introduction of new technology, such as synthesizers and samplers.

Michael Jackson's *Thriller* is the best-selling album of all time, with more than 30 million sales.

ALBUM ROCK

Rock and roll had been based on short songs, but rock songs tended to be longer, and placed greater emphasis on the ability to play instruments well. During the rock era, the long-playing (LP) album came to be seen as a work of art in itself rather than just as a collection of songs.

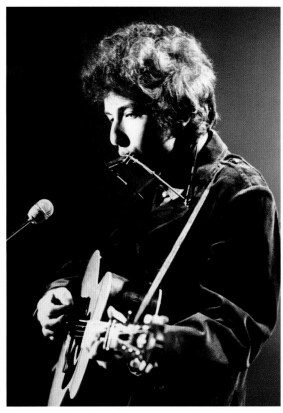

▶ BOB DYLAN
Seen here playing guitar and harmonica, this singer-songwriter helped to create a style of music called folk-rock in the 1960s.

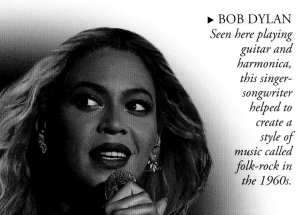

POPULAR APPEAL

Pop is a form of popular music based on short, catchy songs designed to have maximum appeal. Pop is one of the most changeable types of music, as it has no set style or instruments. Rather, it aims to reflect whatever is most popular at the time it is made. Pop songs are usually very simple, with a catchy hook or chorus that stays in the listener's head.

◀ BEYONCÉ KNOWLES
After starting in a band singing a form of R&B, Beyoncé has become one of the biggest pop stars in the world.

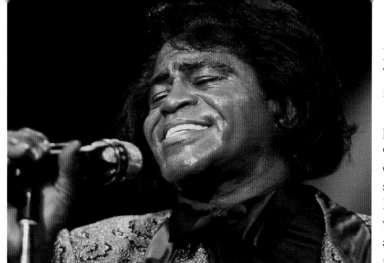

▶ JAMES BROWN
Known as the "Godfather of Soul," James Brown was an early pioneer of funk music.

FUNK AND DISCO

The rhythm is all-important in these musical styles, which emerged in the 1960s and 1970s. Designed to get people dancing, funk uses a range of instruments, including drums, electric guitar, and brass "horn" sections, to make danceable grooves. Disco is more heavily song-based, with prominent use of strings, but also has an insistent, danceable rhythm called four on the floor.

RAP MUSIC

Many pop genres are adaptations of existing forms of music, but rap took this to a whole new level. It emerged in New York in the 1970s when people began rapping (speaking rhyming verses) over instrumental records. Improvements in technology allowed performers to sample pieces of old records and stitch them together to create new ones. Rap became a huge cultural force in the 1980s, when many rap songs had political messages.

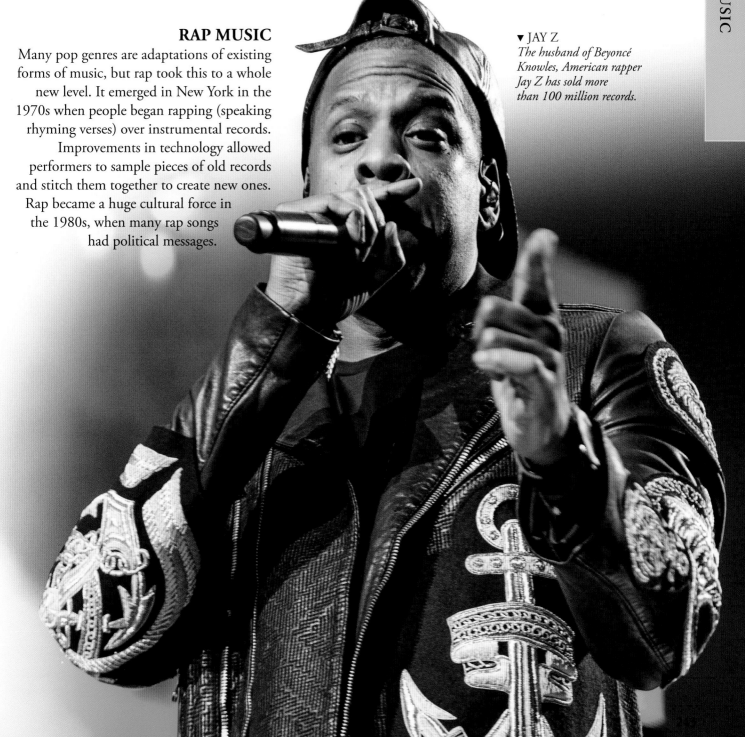

▼ JAY Z
The husband of Beyoncé Knowles, American rapper Jay Z has sold more than 100 million records.

World instruments

The world is full of music. Every country and culture has its own style and way of making music, and, of course, its own instruments. Many instruments date back hundreds—and sometimes thousands—of years, and the music they create often forms an important part of a country's national identity.

Gamelan

A mix of shimmering percussion sounds that gently build and fade

- **Invented** c.200 CE
- **From** Indonesia
- **Type** Percussion

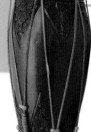
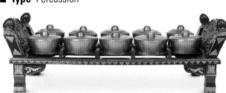
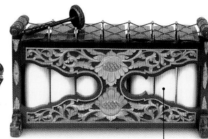

In an Indonesian gamelan orchestra, musicians perform pieces using a range of percussion instruments, including two-headed drums called kendang, kettle-shaped gongs called bonang, and slenthem—tuned metallophones (metal bars) that are hit with mallets. The music is often performed to accompany religious and cultural ceremonies, particularly on the islands of Bali and Java.

From left to right: kendang, bonang, and slenthem.

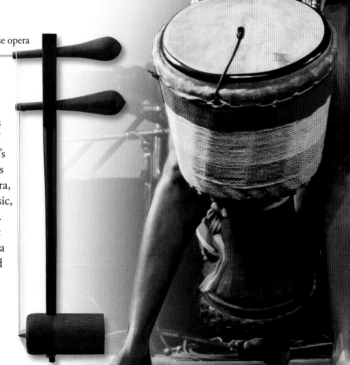

Rebab

Wailing, voice-like tones

- **Invented** c.700 CE
- **From** Iran
- **Type** Strings

Many different styles of music are played across the Middle East and North Africa. One of the most commonly used instruments is the rebab, a stringed instrument played with a bow. It is also known as a "spike fiddle" because it has a metal spike on the bottom that allows it to be rested on the ground.

Jinghu

High-pitched sound of Chinese opera

- **Invented** c.1000
- **From** China
- **Type** Strings

China's musical traditions stretch back thousands of years. One of the country's best-known musical forms is Beijing (or Peking) opera, which is a mixture of music, dance, theater, and mime. The opera's main melodic instrument is the jinghu, a two-stringed fiddle played with a bow.

Djembe

Bare hands create fast, loud rhythms

- **Invented** c.1200
- **From** West Africa
- **Type** Percussion

In West Africa, much of the music is based on drumming. Musicians play different rhythmic patterns on drums and other percussion instruments at the same time to create a dynamic effect. One of the most commonly used drums is the djembe, which is made from a hardwood shell covered in goatskin. Drummers use their fingers and palms to create the drum's three basic sounds, known as bass (low-pitched), tone (medium-pitched), and slap (high-pitched).

Koto

The national instrument of Japan

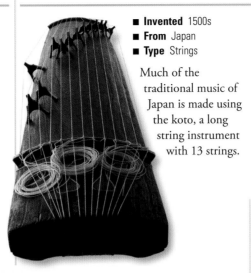

- **Invented** 1500s
- **From** Japan
- **Type** Strings

Much of the traditional music of Japan is made using the koto, a long string instrument with 13 strings.

It is played by plucking the strings with one hand using finger picks, while pressing down the strings with the other hand. Each string also has a bridge (a thin wooden slat that supports the strings) that can be moved up and down to change its pitch.

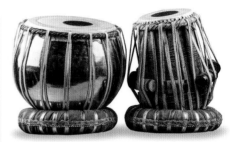

Tabla

Fast-paced, finger-tapped beats

- **Invented** 1700s
- **From** India
- **Type** Percussion

Indian classical music is largely improvised, using forms that have been handed down through the generations. Rhythms called talas are created using tabla drums, which are played using the fingers and palms of the hand. Stringed instruments, such as the sitar, then improvise over the top of the rhythm.

Steel drum

The cheerful metallic melodies of carnival

- **Invented** 1930s
- **From** Trinidad and Tobago
- **Type** Percussion

Steel drums were invented on the islands of Trinidad and Tobado, after traditional African wooden drums had been banned by the authorities. They are made by carefully beating the base of an empty steel oil drum to form dents of different sizes that correspond to different pitches.

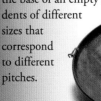

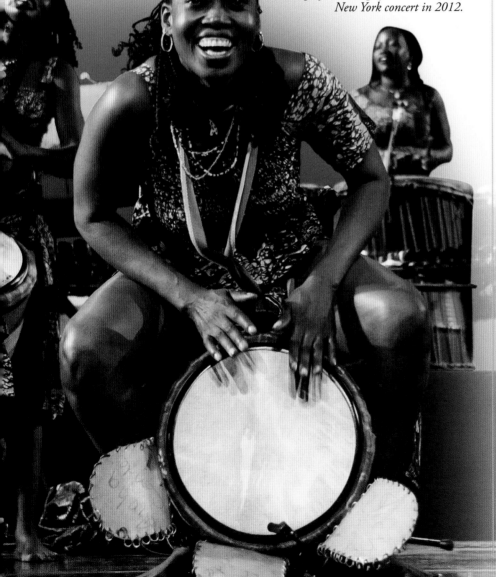

▼ DRUMMING BAND
Members of Nimbaya!—the Women's Drum and Dance Company of Guinea —perform using djembe drums at a New York concert in 2012.

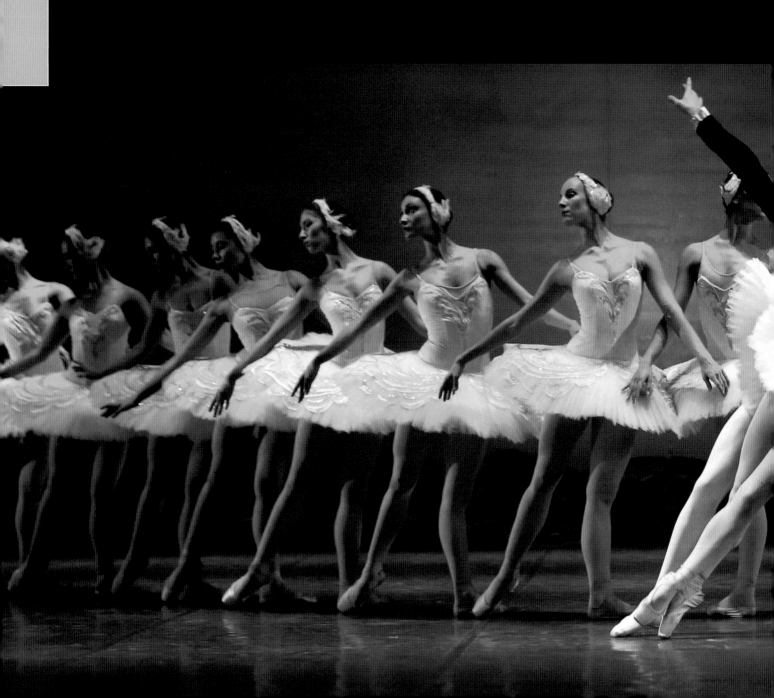

GRACEFUL MOVEMENTS
Dancers require years of training to learn the difficult, precise moves of classical ballet. Here, the Russian State Ballet performs the popular work *Swan Lake*.

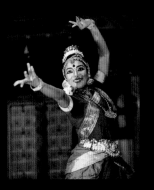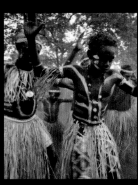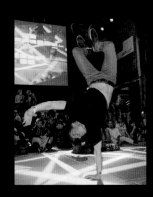

People everywhere share the urge to move their bodies in dance. Although many ancient dances were ceremonial, most dance today is viewed as a form of entertainment.

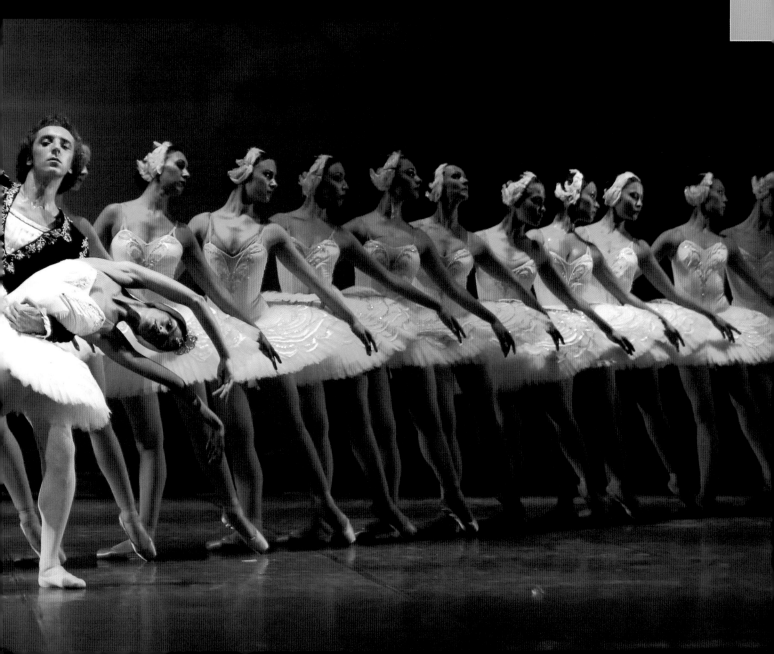

Ceremonial dances

Dancing has always played an important role in human life. Around the world, all societies hold dances for festivals, such as those held for coming-of-age ceremonies or to honor the dead. In the past, dances were also held before hunting or going to war. Many of these dances are still performed, but just for entertainment.

Communal dancing is often used as a way of uniting and uplifting a community.

BEFORE THE HUNT

Dances were often performed to bring about a successful hunt. At the beginning of every hunting season, the Native American Mandan people held a Buffalo Dance. Men wearing buffalo skins would dance together, imitating the movements of these animals. They believed that this attracted buffalo to the Mandan hunting grounds.

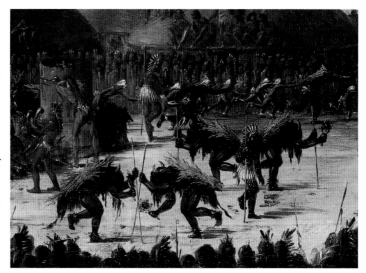

◄ *MANDAN DANCE OF THE BUFFALO*, 1832, GEORGE CATLIN
In the 1830s, Catlin toured Native American lands to paint scenes of everyday life.

HONORING THE DEAD

Many tribal peoples hold festivals that include dancing in honor of the dead. One of the biggest is the Kuarup festival, held every August by several tribes living beside Brazil's Xingu River. In a festival lasting for many days, the tribes gather to honor their dead with song, dance, and wrestling matches.

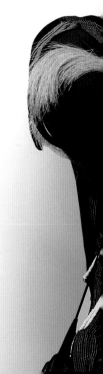

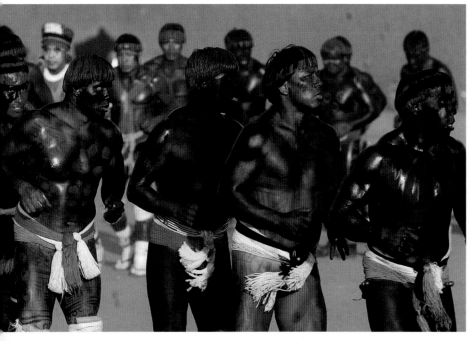

◄ KUARUP CEREMONY
Xingu dancers decorate their bodies with bright red paint and dance together in lines.

WAR DANCING

Historically, before going to war, South African Zulu men would perform the Indlamu, a stamping dance, in which they raised their legs high in the air and then stamped them on the ground in unison. This was a display of strength and aggression, and a way of motivating men to go into battle.

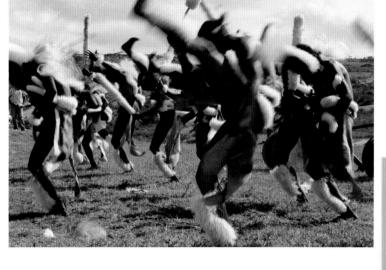

▶ ZULU WAR DANCE
Today, this dance is only performed at celebrations.

COURTSHIP DANCE

Every September, the nomadic Wodaabe people of West Africa gather to celebrate Guérewol, a courtship festival. At the festival, young Wodaabe men dance, while flashing their teeth and rolling their eyes. The men perform for the women, who act as judges. Each man will spend hours putting on his make-up before the dance.

▼ FRIENDLY COMPETITION
These young men are competing against one another to attract a woman.

The Wodaabe dance is a male beauty contest

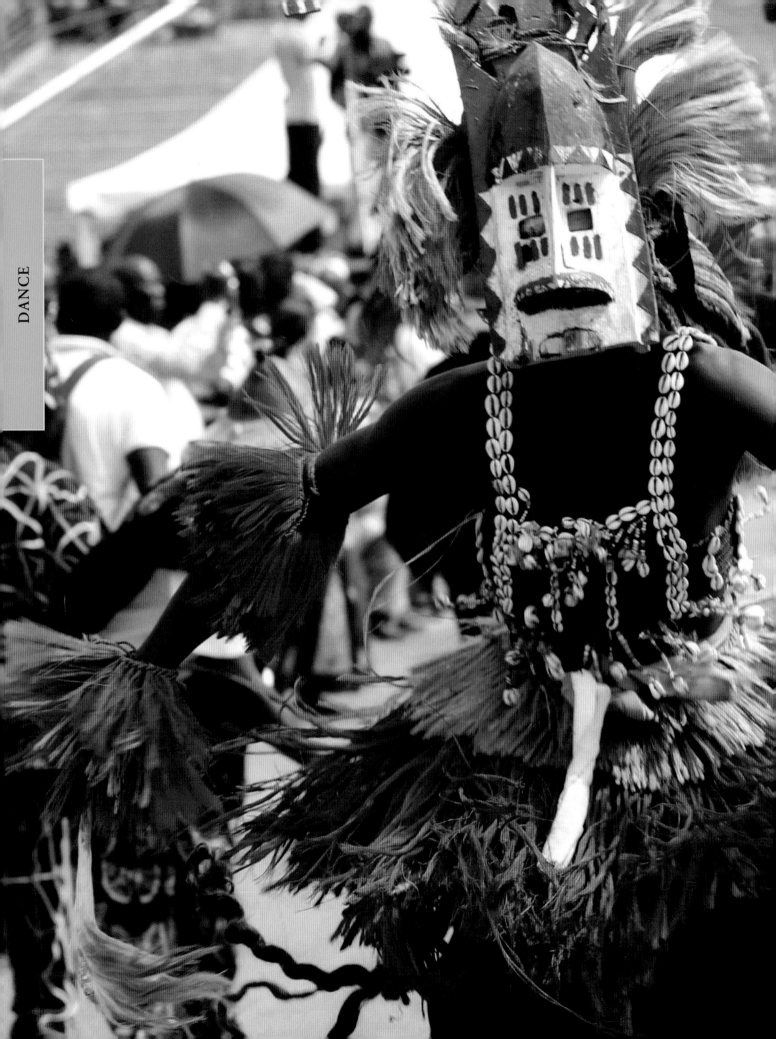

CONTACTING SPIRITS

For some tribal societies, dance is thought to be a way to contact spirits, who are impersonated using masks. The Dogon people of Mali in West Africa hold a ceremony in which they dance wearing masks in order to help the recently deceased to pass over into the spirit world.

Ancient dances

With the rise of the first civilizations, dance took on a new role as an art form. Ancient dance was often religious in origin, performed in temples to please the gods. It later became a popular entertainment. For the first time, highly trained professional performers danced to please audiences.

In the *Dance of the Stars*, Egyptian priests would act out the movements of heavenly bodies.

▼ TOMB OF NEBAMUN
This Egyptian tomb painting from c.1350 BCE shows female dancers and musicians at a banquet.

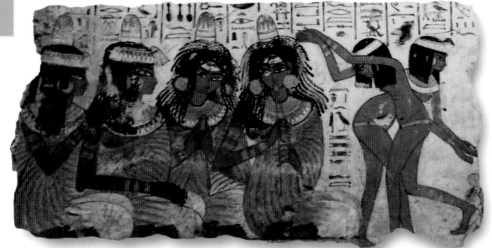

EGYPTIAN PROCESSION

In ancient Egypt, religious festivals were always accompanied by dancing, by both men and women. Even the pharaoh danced to honor the gods. Paintings show female dancers following funeral processions, and also dancing to entertain guests at parties. Egyptian dancing was often acrobatic, and the women would leap and perform backflips.

FRENZIED GREEKS

In Greek mythology, Dionysus, the god of wine and ecstasy, was accompanied by women called Maenads (meaning "the raving ones"), who would dance wildly. The Greeks invented theater to honor Dionysus, and dance was a central element in every Greek play. Euripedes' play *The Bacchae* features dancing Maenads, played on stage by men.

▶ DANCING MAENADS
Greek myths were a popular subject among artists in the 16th century, including Italian Giulio Romano, who depicted dancing Maenads in this fresco.

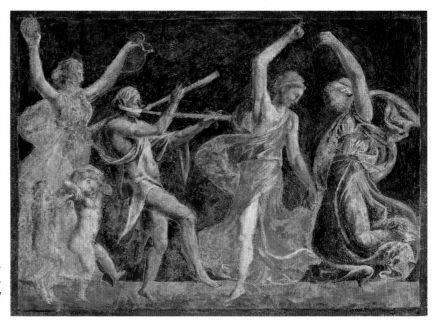

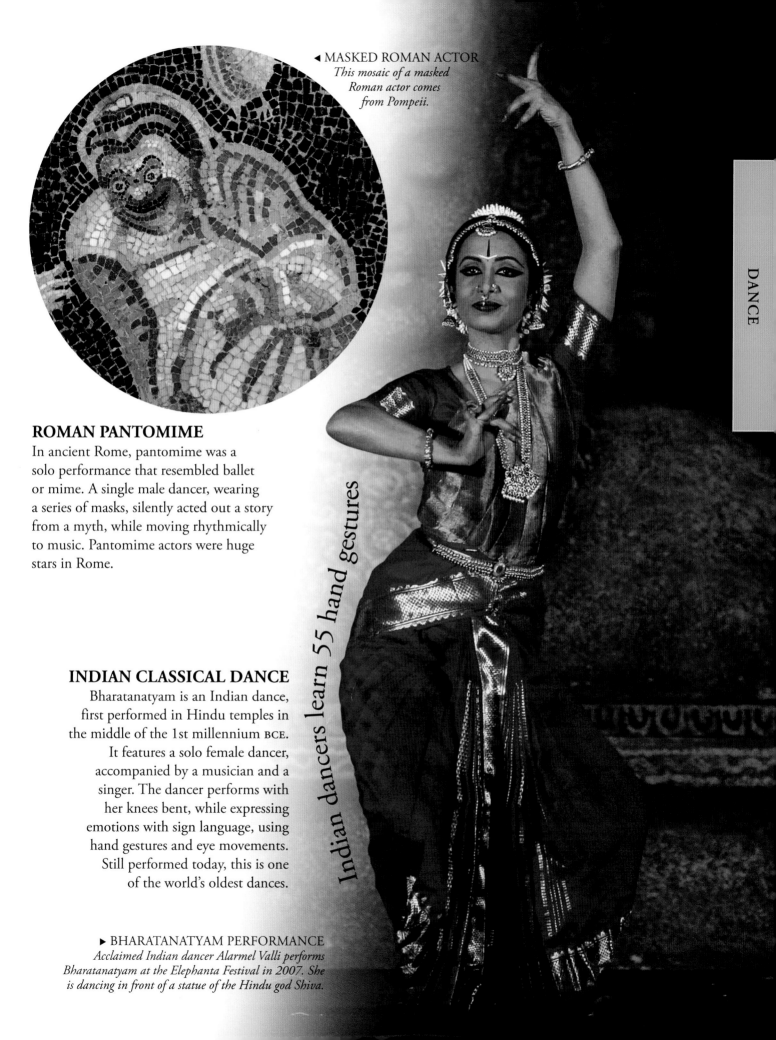

◄ MASKED ROMAN ACTOR
This mosaic of a masked Roman actor comes from Pompeii.

ROMAN PANTOMIME

In ancient Rome, pantomime was a solo performance that resembled ballet or mime. A single male dancer, wearing a series of masks, silently acted out a story from a myth, while moving rhythmically to music. Pantomime actors were huge stars in Rome.

INDIAN CLASSICAL DANCE

Bharatanatyam is an Indian dance, first performed in Hindu temples in the middle of the 1st millennium BCE. It features a solo female dancer, accompanied by a musician and a singer. The dancer performs with her knees bent, while expressing emotions with sign language, using hand gestures and eye movements. Still performed today, this is one of the world's oldest dances.

Indian dancers learn 55 hand gestures

▶ BHARATANATYAM PERFORMANCE
Acclaimed Indian dancer Alarmel Valli performs Bharatanatyam at the Elephanta Festival in 2007. She is dancing in front of a statue of the Hindu god Shiva.

East Asian dance

The civilizations of East Asia have all developed similar styles of classical dance. Like Western ballet, these dances follow strict rules, and require grace, precision, and elaborate formal movements. East Asian classical dancers use exaggerated gestures to express the emotion of the dance.

Chinese opera
Acrobatic song and dance drama

- **Invented** Origins c.350 CE
- **From** China

Invented in the 18th century, but with its roots in much earlier dances, Peking or Beijing opera combines dance, song, martial arts, and acrobatics. From its beginning, this was a popular art form, enjoyed by ordinary people as well as the court. Until the 1920s, only men could perform, but today, women's parts can be played by both sexes.

▶ KABUKI STAR
Nakamura Shido, a leading Kabuki and film star, performs in the Kabuki theater piece Hanakurabe Senbonzakura *in Tokyo in 2016.*

Japanese Kabuki
Dance drama performed by all-male casts

- **Invented** 1603
- **From** Japan

Kabuki is Japanese dance drama. It was performed only by women until 1629, when the shogun (ruler) banned female actors. Men now play all the roles. They wear masklike makeup, whose colors show their character's sex, age, class, and personality. Light blue conveys calm, while brown shows selfishness.

The actor pictured above, playing a supernatural hero, has his face painted with purple lines, which represent nobility.

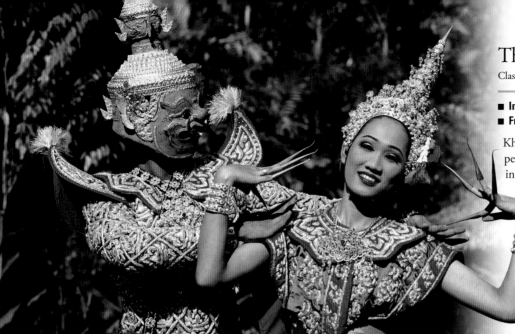

Thai Khon dance
Classical dance once performed by royalty

- **Invented** Unknown
- **From** Thailand

Khon is a type of dance drama originally performed only in the court by men, including members of the Thai royal family. In modern Khon, women can play female roles. The performers in masks have to express emotion only through gestures. They are accompanied by offstage narrators who tell the story. The central role is that of the monkey god, Hanuman, who performs agile leaps and backflips.

Khmer classical dance
Graceful dance performed only by women

- **Invented** Unknown
- **From** Cambodia

Also called the Royal Ballet of Cambodia, Khmer classical dance originated in Cambodian courts, where it was both an entertainment and a religious ritual. It is always performed by women, who make slow, graceful movements. They are accompanied by offstage singers and musicians, who play pipes, drums, gongs, and bamboo xylophones.

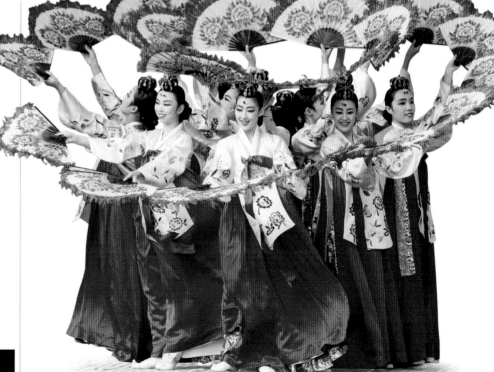

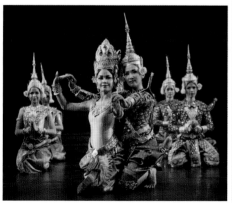

Korean Buchaechum
A celebratory fan dance

- **Invented** 1954
- **From** Korea

Buchaechum is a dance performed by women, who display large fans painted with pink peony blossoms. Moving in harmony with one another, the women create various shapes until they join together as a single, large, fluttering flower. Although this dance is a modern creation, the tradition of dancing with fans is a very old one in Korea.

255

DANCE

Courtly dance

Dance at Renaissance European courts was stately, formal, and dignified. Each dance involved complex steps, which had to be learned from dancing masters. Only nobles could afford to learn to dance, and so dancing was a sign of high status, as was the fine clothing worn by the nobles in this painting.

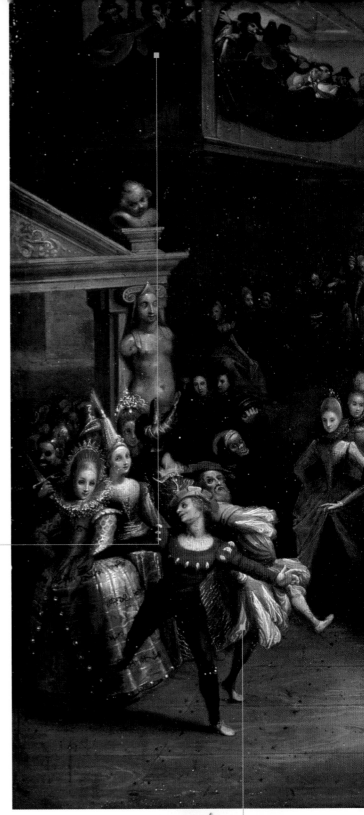

MUSICIANS' GALLERY

In a gallery above the court, musicians play various instruments, including a lute and a viol. Musicians had the status of servants, so they were kept apart from the nobles.

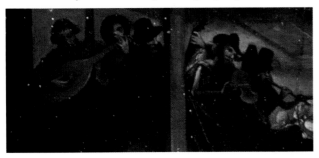

THE BALL AT COURT

There was a wide variety of court dances, from the slow stately pavane to the lively galliard. Many balls began with a processional dance, in which couples moved around the ballroom, hand in hand. A typical processional dance is shown in this 1604 painting, *The Ball at Court*, by the Flemish artist Marten Pepijn.

PAID PERFORMERS

On the left side of the painting, there is a lively dance by men and women in garish costumes. These are probably actors, hired to entertain the court. The bearded man may be a jester.

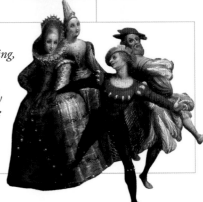

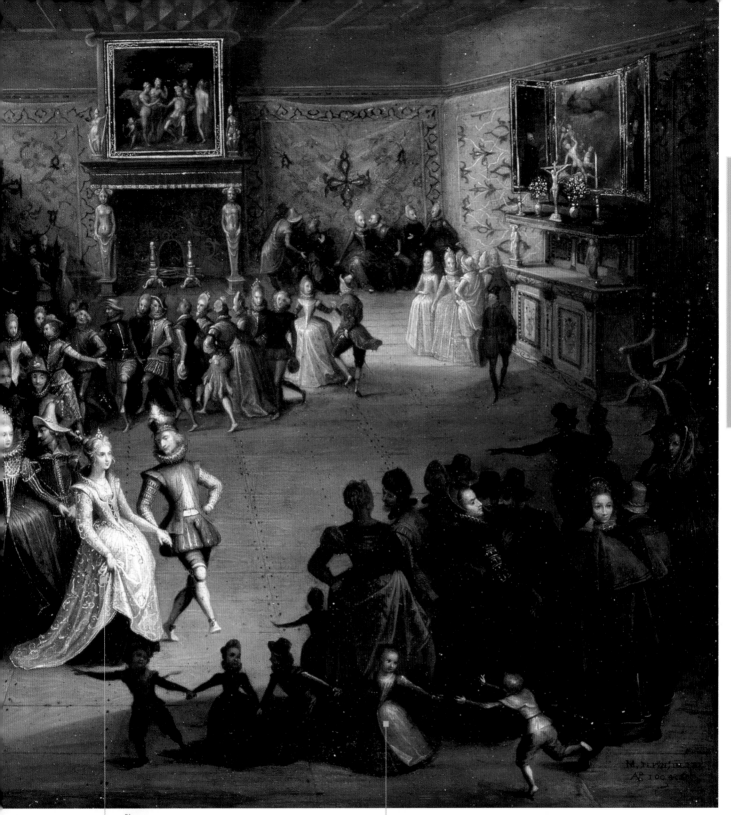

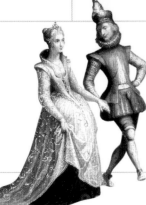

PROCESSION
The nobles dance in a stately procession, moving in an counterclockwise direction around the ballroom. Position in such dances was in order of rank, with the king and queen leading the way.

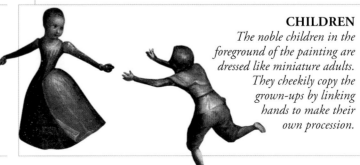

CHILDREN
The noble children in the foreground of the painting are dressed like miniature adults. They cheekily copy the grown-ups by linking hands to make their own procession.

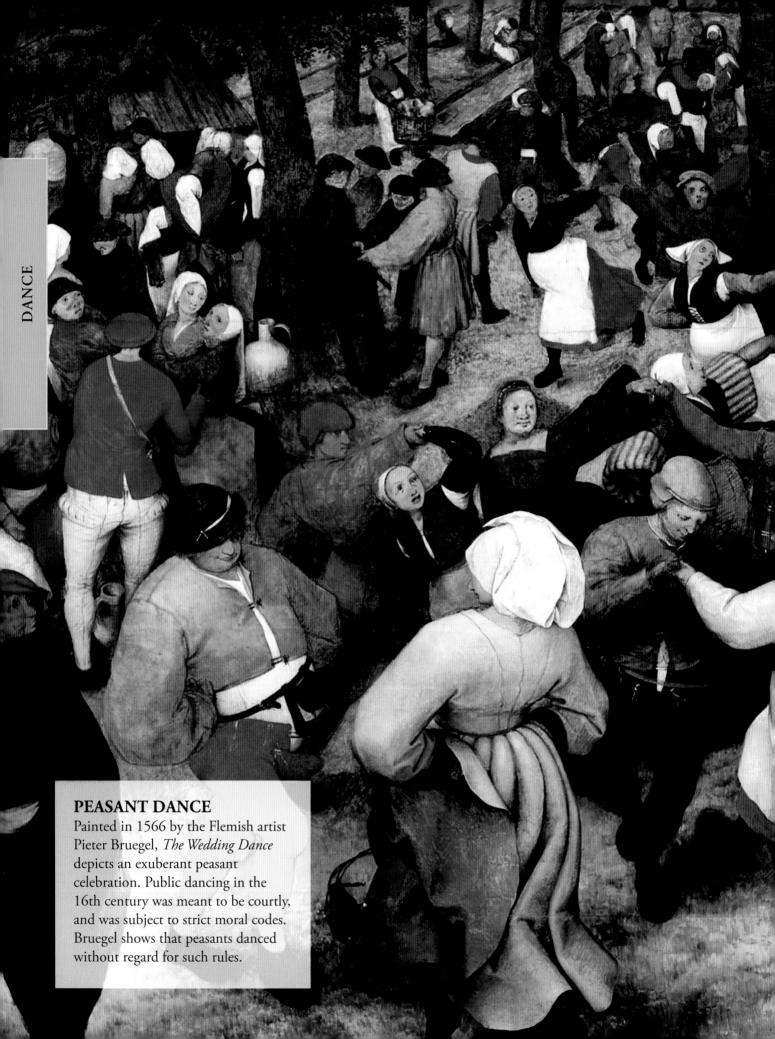

PEASANT DANCE

Painted in 1566 by the Flemish artist
Pieter Bruegel, *The Wedding Dance*
depicts an exuberant peasant
celebration. Public dancing in the
16th century was meant to be courtly,
and was subject to strict moral codes.
Bruegel shows that peasants danced
without regard for such rules.

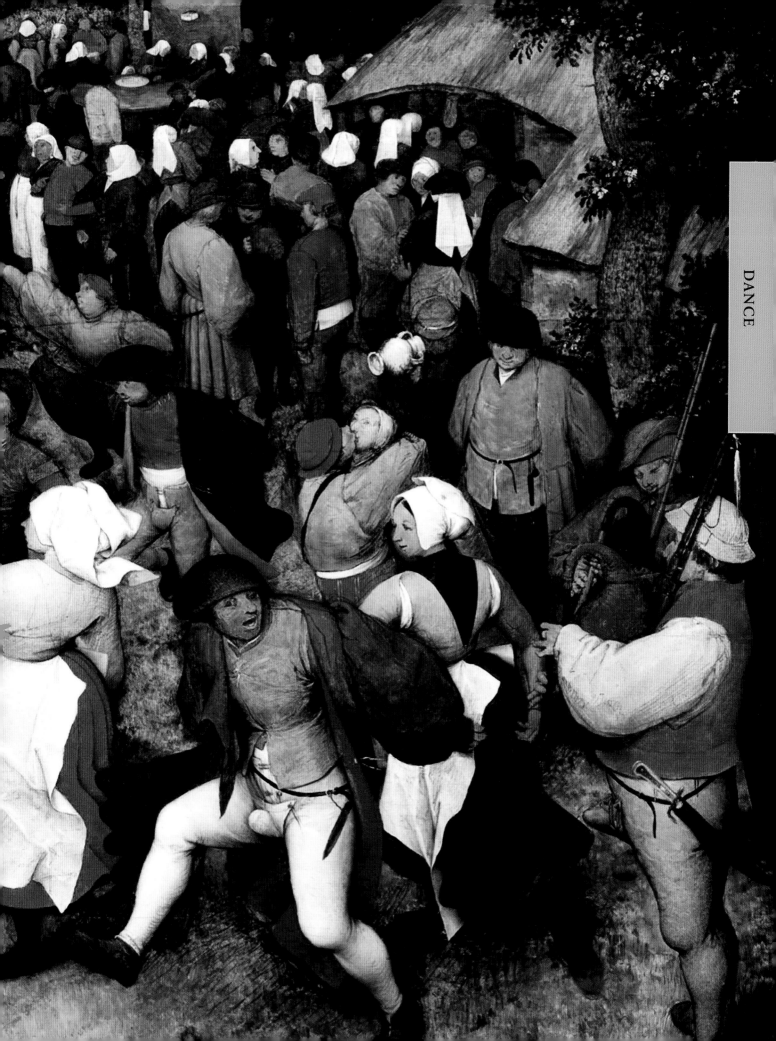

Folk dances

Passed down through generations, folk dancing is a traditional form of dance for ordinary people. In urban Western societies, where the old ways of life have disappeared, folk dancing is a fun way to keep customs alive. In countries where people continue to live traditional lives, dancing is a natural expression of their culture.

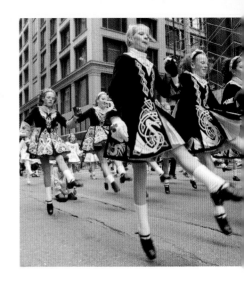

The term "folk dancing" was invented in the late 19th century by scholars of the new science of folklore.

Morris dancers celebrate the brief

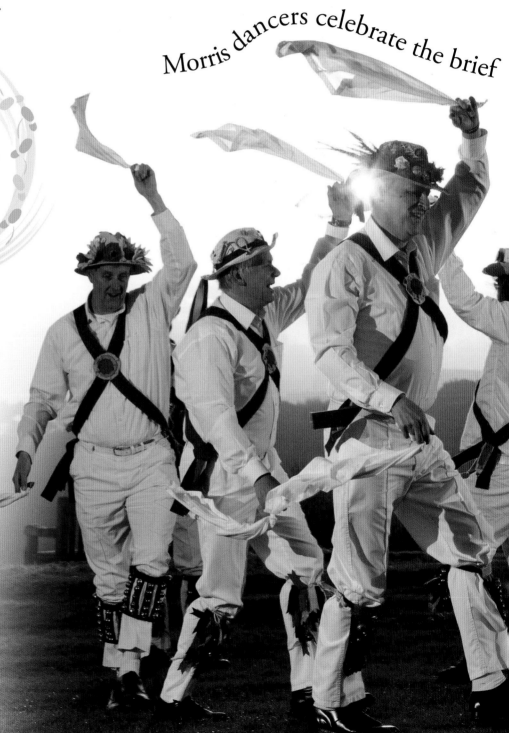

MORRIS DANCING

Every summer, from the start of May onward, English morris dancers can be seen leaping outside pubs and on village greens. They perform a rhythmic step dance, in which dancers—wearing bells on their knees—wave handkerchiefs and clash wooden sticks together. Though morris dancing can be traced back to the 15th century, it had almost disappeared by 1900. It was revived in the early 20th century by folklorists, who learned the dances and passed them on to future generations.

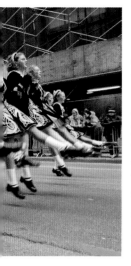

◀ ST PATRICK'S DAY DANCE
*American Irish step dancers in a
St Patrick's Day parade in Chicago.*

IRISH ENERGY

Irish step dancing developed in crowded
rooms and bars, where a lack of space meant
that dancers held their arms to their sides
while performing leaps and kicks. People
of Irish ancestry in many countries, such
as the United States, perform Irish dancing
to stay in touch with their heritage.

◀ DANCERS AT DAWN
*Morris Dancers celebrate sunrise
on May Day, the beginning of
summer and the start of the
dancing season.*

English summer

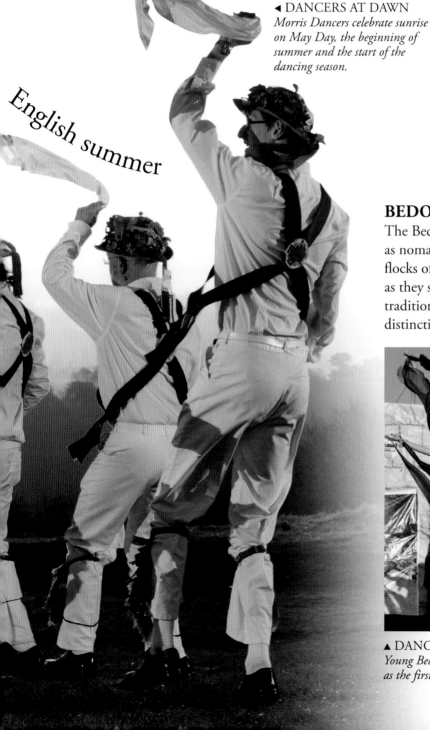

SNAKE DANCE

The Kalbelia are a tribe from northwest
India, related to the Romany of Europe.
Their main source of income in the past was
to catch poisonous snakes, reflected in the
snake-like movements of their dancing.

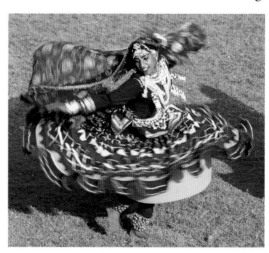

▲ TRADITIONAL DRESS
*A Kalbelia woman performs wearing a
traditional long, colorful skirt.*

BEDOUIN TRADITION

The Bedouin are an Arab people who traditionally lived
as nomads, moving from place to place with tents and
flocks of livestock. In Israel, their way of life is changing,
as they settle down in new towns. By performing
traditional dances, the Bedouin of Israel keep their
distinctive culture alive.

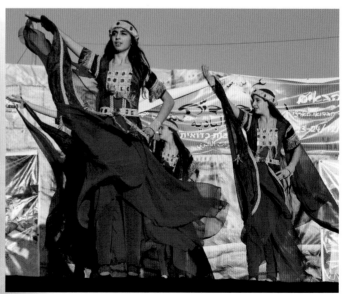

▲ DANCE TROUPE
*Young Bedouins dance at Tel Sheva, founded in 1967
as the first of seven Bedouin townships in Israel.*

National dances

Many nations around the world have a unique and distinctive dance that has come to be identified with them. Some peoples deliberately promote their dances as a way of displaying their cultural identity to other nations. For others, a national dance is simply a good way to entertain tourists.

Hopak
Ukrainian Cossack dance

- **Place** Ukraine
- **Origins** 16th century

The hopak, or Cossack dance, is an energetic dance characterized by kicks from a squatting position and high leaps. The name comes from the Ukrainian word "hopaty," meaning "to jump." It is usually performed by young men as a display of strength and endurance. The dance became famous during the Soviet era, when it was performed on world tours.

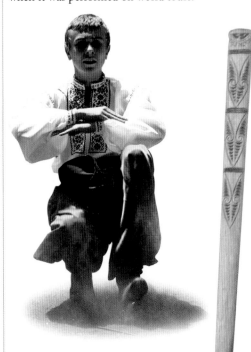

Can-can
French music hall dance

- **Place** France
- **Origins** 1840s

The can-can is an energetic dance for women, with high kicks, splits, and cartwheels, danced to a fast tune called *The Infernal Galop*. It was first performed in Paris music halls in the 1840s, a period when respectable women would not even reveal their ankles. Then, the can-can was considered shocking. Today, a visit to the Moulin Rouge nightclub to see the can-can performed is a spectacle enjoyed by many visitors to Paris.

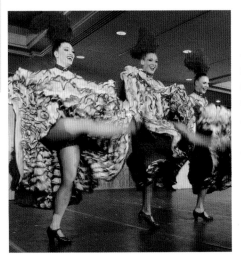

Hula
Traditional dance of Hawaii

- **Place** Hawaii
- **Origins** Unknown

The hula is a graceful Hawaiian dance, accompanied with song and elaborate hand movements, to act out traditional stories. Hula dancing has always been a big tourist attraction in Hawaii. The popular image of a hula dancer is of a woman in a grass skirt, but it is also danced by men. Hula is so important in Hawaii that it is performed as a form of prayer at state functions.

Haka
Maori war dance

- **Place** New Zealand
- **Origins** Unknown

The haka is the war dance of the Maori people of New Zealand. Dancers stamp their feet, slap their bodies, and make terrifying faces, while chanting. Today, it is performed by Maori in traditional costumes, and provides a popular spectacle for tourists to New Zealand. It is also world-famous thanks to performances before matches by New Zealand rugby teams, who dance to motivate themselves and intimidate their opponents.

Dabke

A dance of celebration

- **Place** The Levant
- **Invented** Unknown

Dabke is a circle-and-line dance, performed by men and women at weddings and other celebrations. Though it is performed in several Arab countries, it is especially important to Palestinians living under Israeli occupation. Palestinian companies such as Baraem (right) see the dance as a way of maintaining their national identity and traditional culture, and showing it to the world.

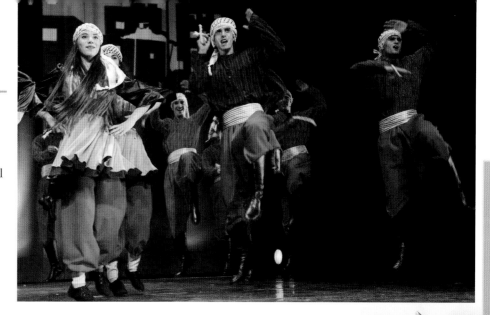

▼ WARRIOR DANCE
Maori dancers perform a haka at Rotorua, the center of Maori tourism in New Zealand.

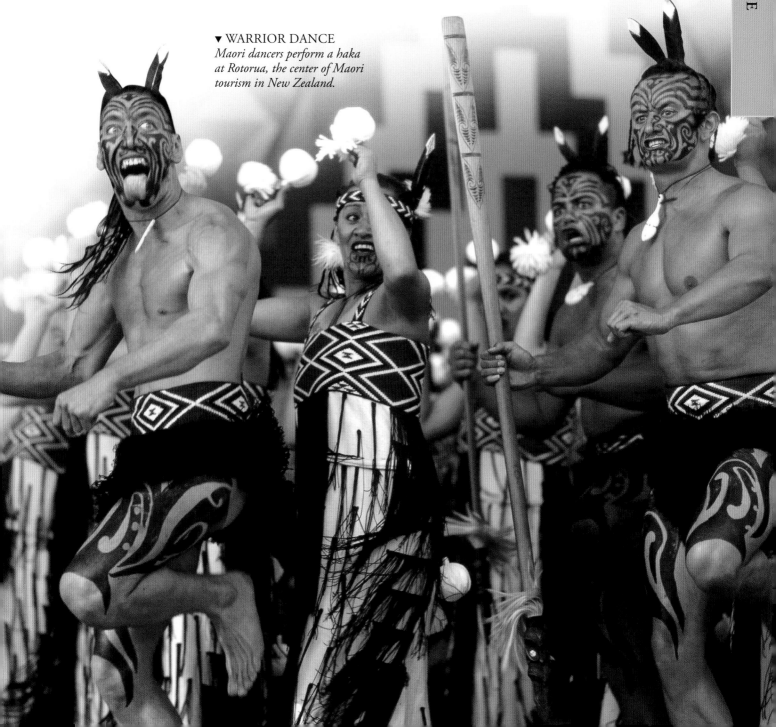

Ballet

One of the most physically demanding forms of dance is ballet, which grew out of 17th-century court dances in Italy and France. Ballet became a fully developed art form in the 19th century, when ballerinas, wearing tutus, began to dance *en pointe* (on the tips of their toes), performing the roles of spirits, fairies, and swans.

A central aim of ballet was to make ballerinas appear weightless, as if flying through the air.

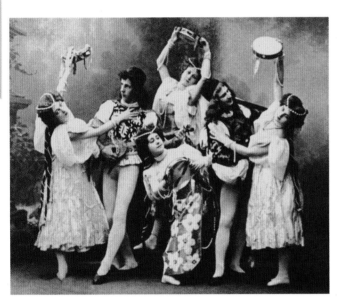

RUSSIAN CLASSICS

Some of the most famous ballets, including *The Sleeping Beauty*, *The Nutcracker*, and *Swan Lake*, were created in late 19th-century Russia. The female ballerinas were the stars. The main role of male dancers was to support the ballerinas, lifting them as they flew through the air.

◀ *SWAN LAKE*
The cast of an 1895 production of Swan Lake *at the Mariinsky Theatre in St Petersburg poses for a photograph.*

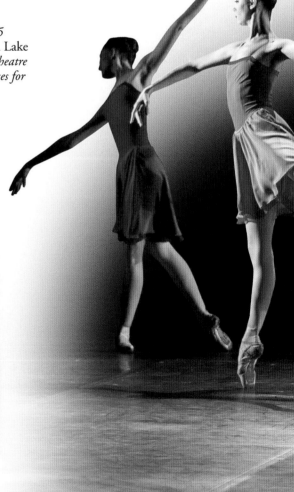

ANNA PAVLOVA

The Russian prima ballerina (star female dancer) Anna Pavlova was the first ballet dancer to tour the world. She became famous for her performance of the dying swan, a solo ballet she created in 1905 and danced throughout her life.

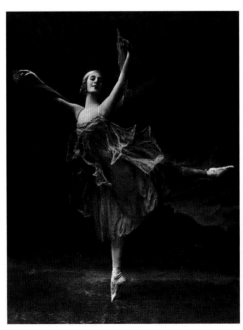

▶ *EN POINTE*
Dancing en pointe, *Anna Pavlova creates the impression of weightlessness.*

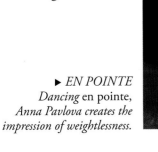

CARLOS ACOSTA

Following the success of Rudolf Nureyev (see p. 266), several male dancers have become ballet stars. Carlos Acosta is a Cuban dancer who began with the National Ballet of Cuba and went on to perform with international companies. He is celebrated for his athleticism and grace, and the joy he exhibits when dancing.

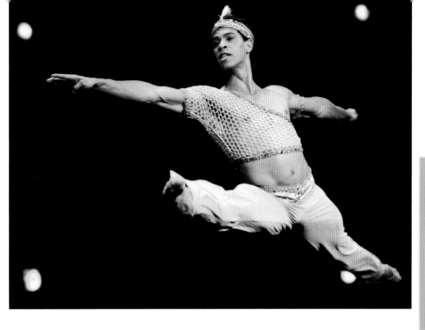

▶ ATHLETIC MOVER
Carlos Acosta executes a leap while dancing in Le Corsaire *(The Pirate), in Havana, Cuba, in 2009.*

MODERN BALLET

Today, new styles of ballet are emerging, influenced by contemporary dance. In 2013, the Russian choreographer Anton Pimonov created the ballet *In the Rhythm of Dreams*, which combines the free movement of contemporary dance with classical ballet techniques. Moving away from formal styles, the ballerinas wear light dresses rather than tutus.

▼ OLD AND NEW
Dancers of St Petersburg's Yakobson Ballet dance en pointe *during a performance of* In the Rhythm of Dreams.

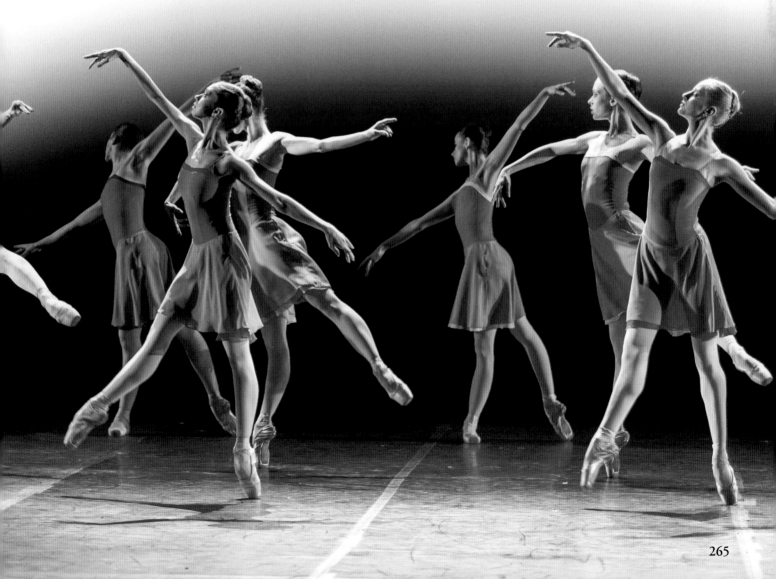

Rudolf Nureyev

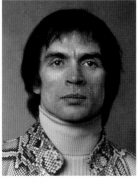

Rudolf Nureyev in 1975

Russian-born Rudolf Nureyev was the most famous ballet dancer of the 20th century. After a long period in which ballerinas had been the stars, Nureyev re-established the importance of the male dancer. His acrobatic dancing made ballet popular with a mass audience, both live and on television.

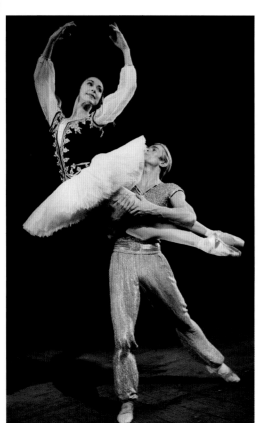

◄ FIRST DANCE
Nureyev and Fonteyn dance in the ballet Giselle, *the first dance they ever performed together, at Covent Garden in London.*

FAMOUS PARTNER

In 1962, Nureyev began a long and successful partnership with the British ballerina Margot Fonteyn. This revived the career of Fonteyn, who, at 42, was already past the age when most ballet dancers retire. Their partnership lasted until 1979, and took them all over the world. Everywhere they performed, they were greeted enthusiastically. At the end of one performance of *Swan Lake,* in Vienna in 1964, they received a record 89 curtain calls.

► LEAPING PRINCE
As the prince in Sleeping Beauty, *Nureyev performs one of his famous leaps.*

MAKING HIS OWN DANCES

Nureyev was a choreographer as well as a dancer. He devised his own versions of classical ballets, such as *Sleeping Beauty*, originally created for the Kirov Ballet in St Petersburg, Russia, in the 1890s. Nureyev would always expand the role of the male lead dancer to give himself the opportunity to display his dazzling dancing.

LIFE STORY

1938	1955–1958	1961	1962
On March 17, Rudolf Nureyev is born during a journey across Russia on the Trans-Siberian Railway.	Nureyev trains at the Kirov Ballet School in Leningrad (now St Petersburg). On graduating, he becomes principal dancer of the Kirov Ballet.	While performing in Paris with the Kirov Ballet, Nureyev renounces his Soviet citizenship and defects to the West.	Nureyev becomes permanent guest artist at the Royal Ballet in Covent Garden, London, where he dances *Giselle* with Margot Fonteyn.

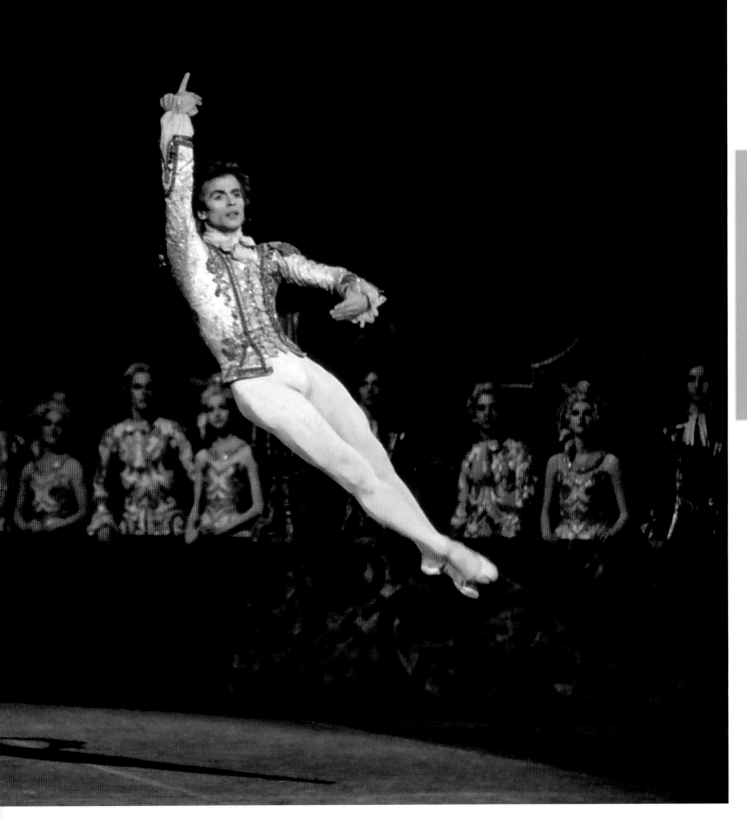

1963	1975	1983–1989	1992–1993
Nureyev and Fonteyn perform *Marguerite and Armand*, a ballet created for the couple by British choreographer Sir Frederick Ashton.	In New York, Nureyev studies modern dance with American choreographer Martha Graham, who creates a dance piece, *Lucifer*, for him.	As artistic director of the Paris Opera, Nureyev leads the company on a series of international tours.	On October 8, 1992, Nureyev, who by then is seriously ill, gives his final performance, in *La Bayadère*, in Paris. He dies on January 6, 1993.

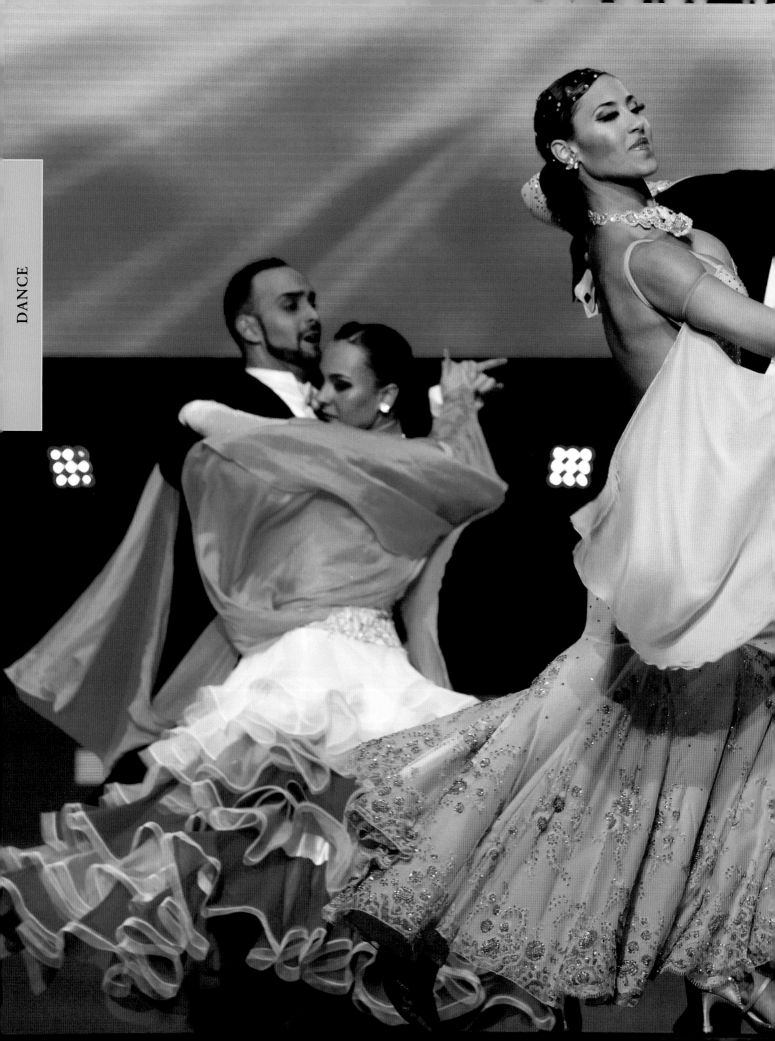

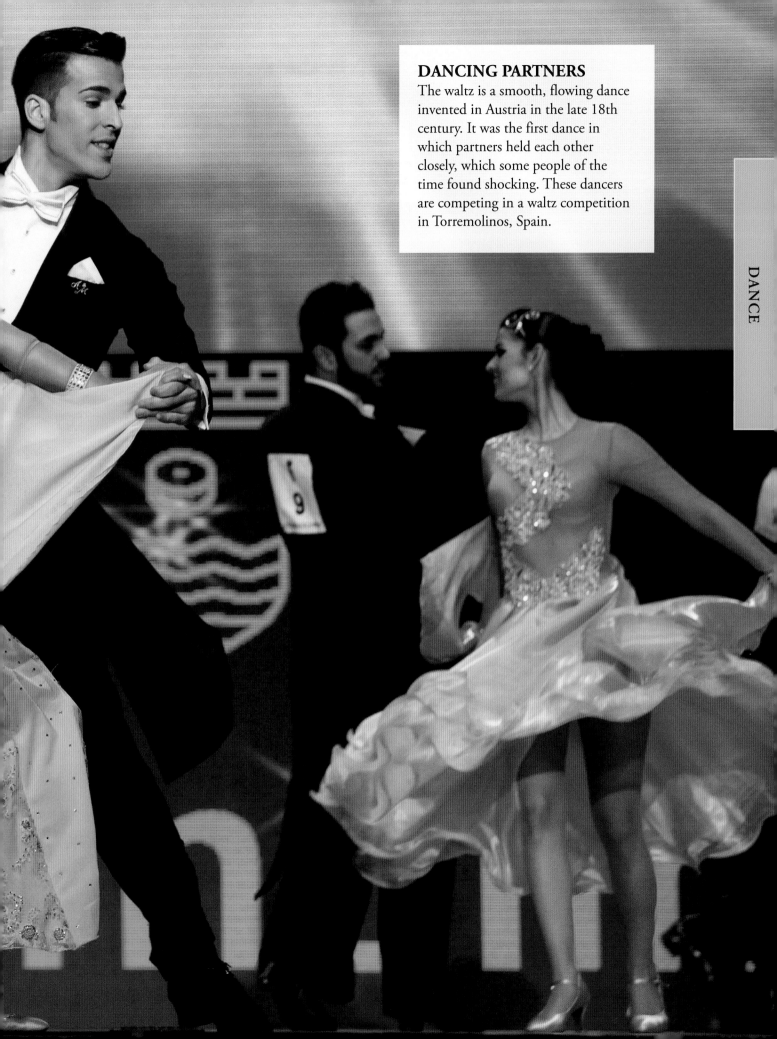

DANCING PARTNERS
The waltz is a smooth, flowing dance invented in Austria in the late 18th century. It was the first dance in which partners held each other closely, which some people of the time found shocking. These dancers are competing in a waltz competition in Torremolinos, Spain.

DANCE

Latin American moves

In Latin America, African rhythms and European music have combined to create a variety of dynamic dances, including the rumba, tango, samba, and salsa. Latin dances were popularized worldwide by Hollywood films, and later adapted to become ballroom dances. Today, they are danced all over the world in clubs and exercise classes.

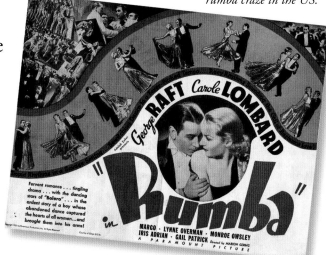

▼ CRAZE STARTED BY THE MOVIES
The 1935 Hollywood film Rumba *helped to create a rumba craze in the US.*

RHYTHMIC RUMBA

The 1930s brought a craze for the rumba, a slinky and smooth Cuban dance with wiggling hips, performed to a slow-quick-quick rhythm. In Cuba, the rumba was originally much wilder and faster.

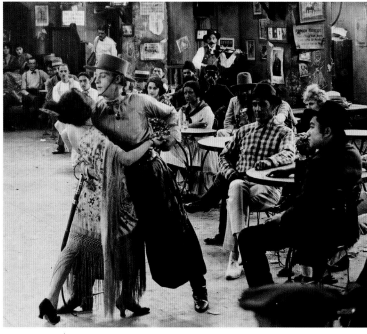

SHOCKING TANGO

The very first Latin American dance craze was for the Argentine tango, which swept Europe and the United States from 1913. This was a passionate dance, performed by a man and woman, chest to chest, and with their heads often pointing to the side. At the time, many people found this intimate way of dancing shocking.

▲ SILENT DANCERS
Rudolph Valentino performs the tango in the 1921 film The Four Horsemen of the Apocalypse, *which was actually a silent movie.*

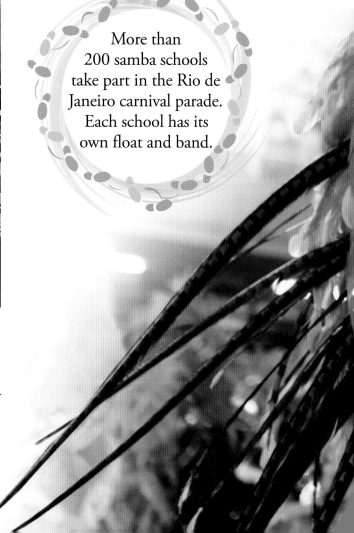

More than 200 samba schools take part in the Rio de Janeiro carnival parade. Each school has its own float and band.

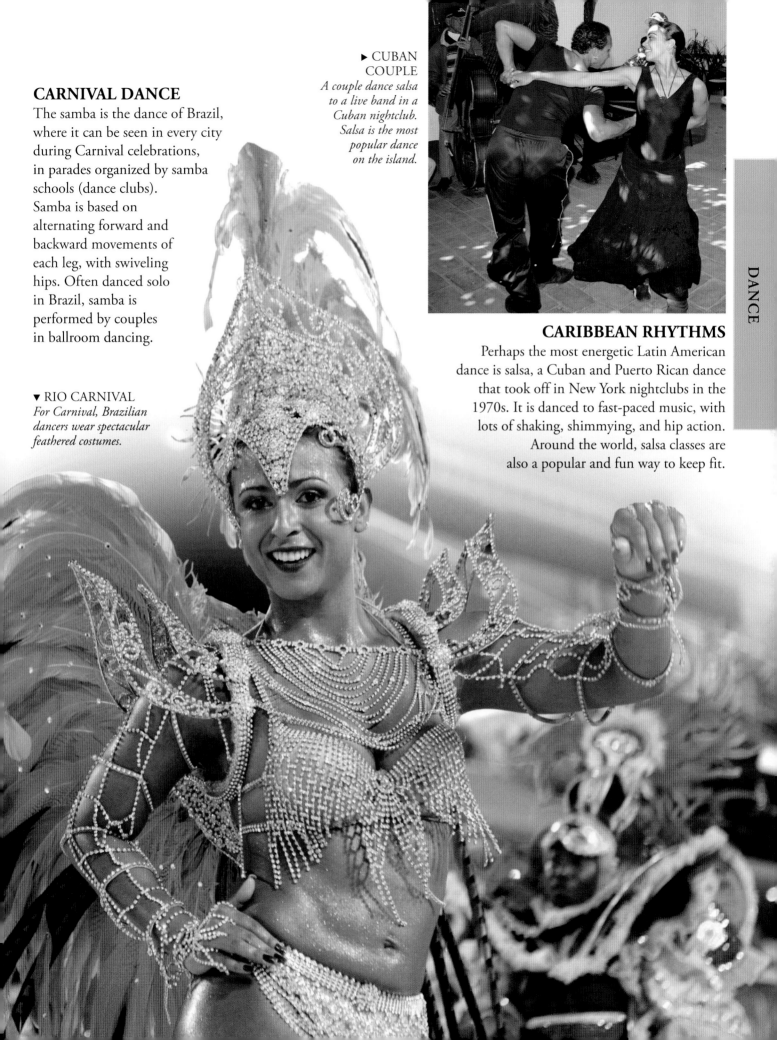

CARNIVAL DANCE

The samba is the dance of Brazil, where it can be seen in every city during Carnival celebrations, in parades organized by samba schools (dance clubs). Samba is based on alternating forward and backward movements of each leg, with swiveling hips. Often danced solo in Brazil, samba is performed by couples in ballroom dancing.

▼ RIO CARNIVAL
For Carnival, Brazilian dancers wear spectacular feathered costumes.

▶ CUBAN COUPLE
A couple dance salsa to a live band in a Cuban nightclub. Salsa is the most popular dance on the island.

CARIBBEAN RHYTHMS

Perhaps the most energetic Latin American dance is salsa, a Cuban and Puerto Rican dance that took off in New York nightclubs in the 1970s. It is danced to fast-paced music, with lots of shaking, shimmying, and hip action. Around the world, salsa classes are also a popular and fun way to keep fit.

SPANISH PASSION
Flamenco is a traditional dance style from Andalusia, Spain. It involves dramatic foot stamping, hand-clapping, finger clicking, and skirt twirling, and is performed to strummed guitar music and singing. Here, Charo Espino performs with the celebrated guitarist and composer Paco Peña (seated left).

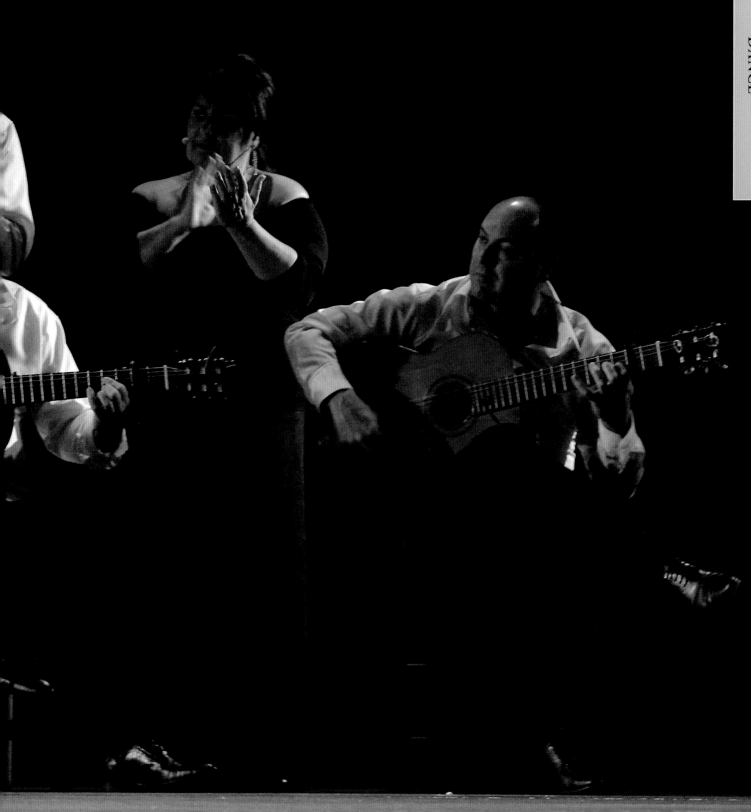

The birth of modern dance

In the early 20th century, dance went through revolutionary changes. Western choreographers, impatient with the narrow rules of ballet, explored different forms of movement. Many of these pioneering choreographers were women, searching for new ways to express emotions through dance.

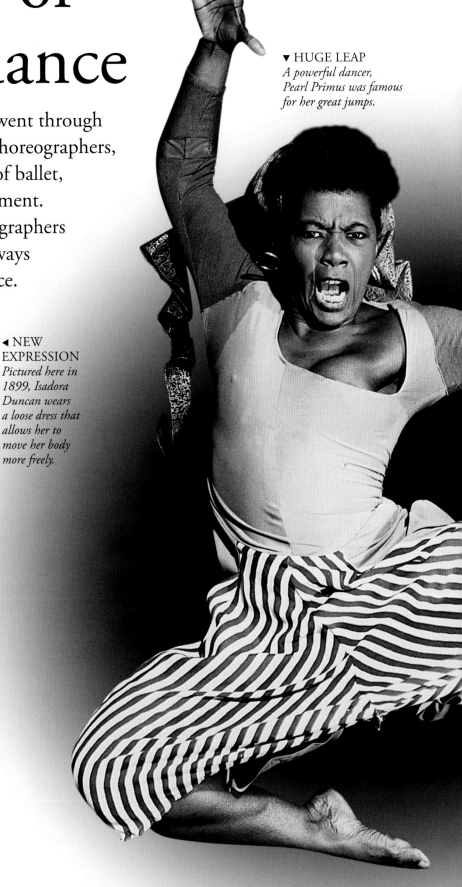

▼ HUGE LEAP
A powerful dancer, Pearl Primus was famous for her great jumps.

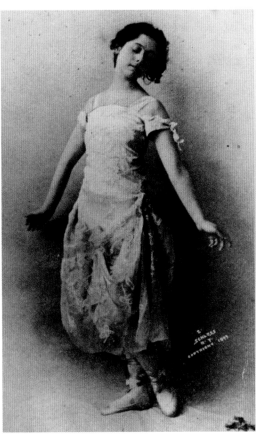

◄ NEW EXPRESSION
Pictured here in 1899, Isadora Duncan wears a loose dress that allows her to move her body more freely.

FREE DANCE

For the American dancer Isadora Duncan, dance was an expression of freedom. She got rid of the tight ballerina tutu and wore loose clothing based on ancient Greek dress. She drew her inspiration from the movement of waves, trees, and clouds.

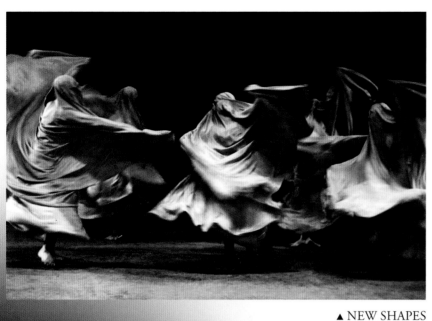

EXPRESSIONIST DANCE

The German dancer Mary Wigman used dance to express emotions, which were often dark and disturbing. Rejecting the prettiness of ballet, she believed that dance should not be afraid to be ugly. Wigman introduced strong movements, with grasping claw-like gestures.

▲ NEW SHAPES
In her 1932 piece, Der Weg *(The Way), Wigman draped her dancers in loose shimmering fabric, creating startling shapes.*

"If I could tell you what it meant, there would be no point in dancing it."
Isadora Duncan

MODERN AFRICAN-AMERICAN DANCE

In the 1940s, American dancer Pearl Primus found inspiration from African and Caribbean dances. She saw dance as way of expressing her African-American identity and fighting racial prejudice. Primus said, "Through dance I have experienced the wordless joy of freedom."

▼ STRANGE MOVES
Pina Bausch's company performs one of her final works, Rough Cut, *in 2008, the year before she died.*

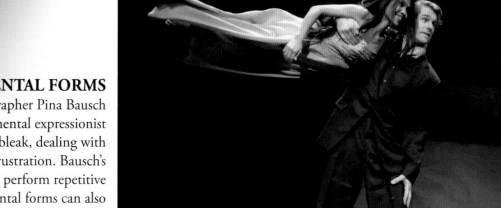

EXPERIMENTAL FORMS

German choreographer Pina Bausch worked within the experimental expressionist tradition. Her pieces are often bleak, dealing with violence, isolation, and frustration. Bausch's dancers scream, sing, and perform repetitive actions. However, experimental forms can also include gentle, fluid movements.

Martha Graham

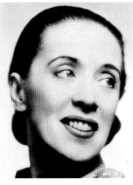

Martha Graham
in 1947

The American choreographer Martha Graham is often called the mother of modern dance. In the 1920s, she invented a new language of movement, using a dancer's whole body to convey emotions. Known as the Graham technique, it is now taught worldwide. In her long career, Graham created 181 dance pieces, many of which are still performed today.

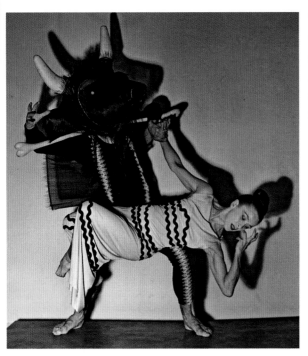

▲ DANCING WITH A MINOTAUR
In her 1947 piece Errand of the Maze, *Graham told the story of the Greek myth of Ariadne and the Minotaur.*

TELLING STORIES

Graham told stories through her dance. In her early ballets, she often chose American themes. Her most famous work, *Appalachian Spring*, which she created in 1944, celebrates early-19th-century frontier life. Other works retold stories from ancient Greek myths.

A LASTING LEGACY

Graham would take the lead role in most of her works, sometimes remaining on stage for the entire performance. After retiring from performance in 1970, she continued to choreograph new works for her dance company right up to 1990, the year before her death. The Martha Graham Dance Company in New York regularly revives her works, while also commissioning new works from contemporary choreographers.

▶ LIFE OF A POET
In her 1940 piece Letter to the World, *Graham portrayed the American poet Emily Dickinson.*

LIFE STORY

1894–1908	1916–1923	1926	1931
Martha Graham is born in Allengheny, Pennsylvania. The family move to California when Martha is 14 years old.	Graham trains at the Denishawn School of Dancing in Los Angeles, and dances with the school's professional company.	She founds the Martha Graham Dance Company and the Martha Graham Center of Contemporary Dance in New York.	Graham creates *Primitive Mysteries*, her first major work, based on Native American ceremonies of the Southwest.

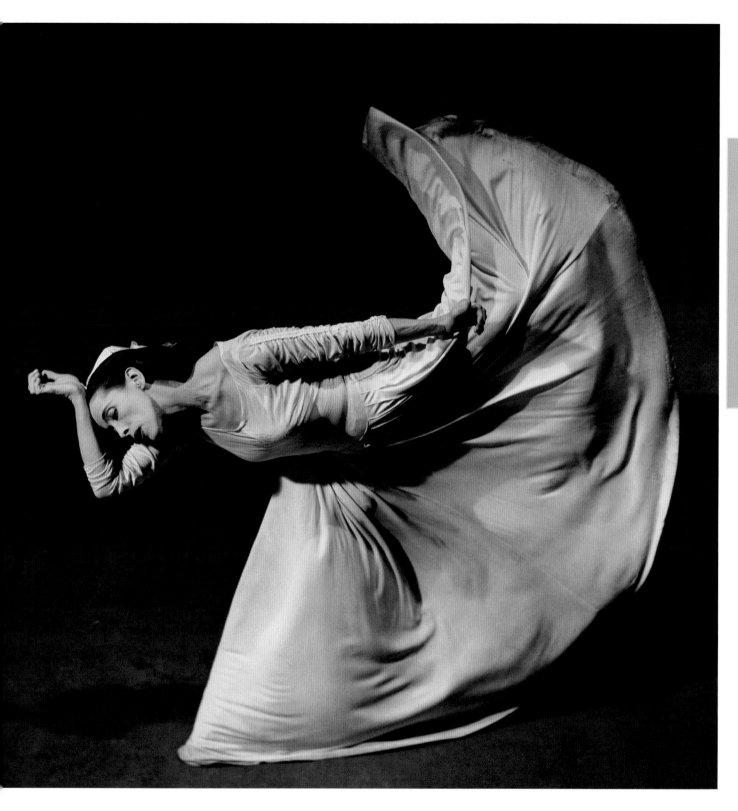

1933–1944	1946–1958	1970–1990	1991
She makes ballets on American themes, including *Frontier* (1935), *American Document* (1938), *El Penitente* (1940), and *Appalachian Spring* (1944).	Graham uses Greek myths as the subject of ballets, including *Cave of the Heart* (1946), *Errand into the Maze* (1947), and *Clytemnestra* (1958).	After making her farewell stage appearance at 76, in *Cortege of Eagles*, Graham goes on to create 10 new ballets.	Graham dies in New York at the age of 96, soon after finishing her autobiography, *Blood Memory*, which is published after her death.

Indian dance

Traditional Indian dance is divided into folk and classical forms. There are eight recognized classical Indian dances that originated in different parts of the Indian subcontinent, and many regional folk dances. Bollywood is the nickname of India's film industry. Its films are famous for their spectacular dance routines, combining Indian and Western styles.

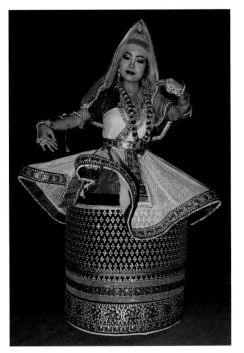

▼ TRADITIONAL MANIPURI DRESS
This Manipuri dancer is wearing a traditional barrel-shaped skirt called a kumil.

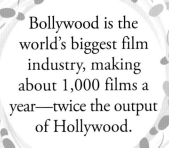

Bollywood is the world's biggest film industry, making about 1,000 films a year—twice the output of Hollywood.

SMOOTH MOVEMENT
One of the oldest Indian classical dance forms, Manipuri is named after the region of Manipur in northeastern India, where it originated. Manipuri is a slow, graceful dance, involving elaborate gestures with the hands and arms, and little lower-body movement.

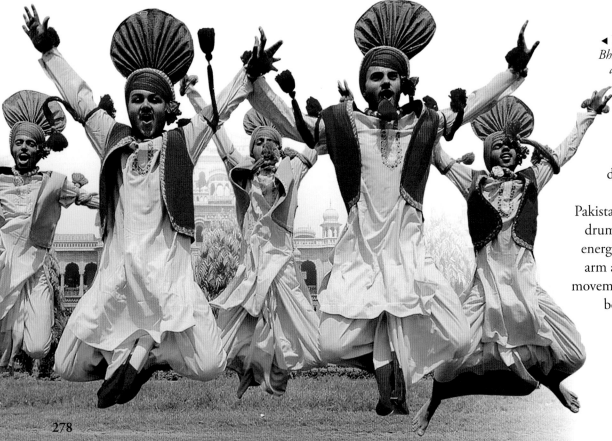

◄ BHANGRA DANCERS
Bhangra dancers leap into the air at a 2007 sports festival in Amritsar, India.

FOLK DANCE
Bhangra is a folk dance from the Punjab region of India and Pakistan. Performed to a fast drum beat, bhangra is very energetic, with many raised arm and leg movements. A movement on one side of the body is always followed by a matching one on the other. Modern bhangra music fuses pop or hip-hop with bhangra drumming.

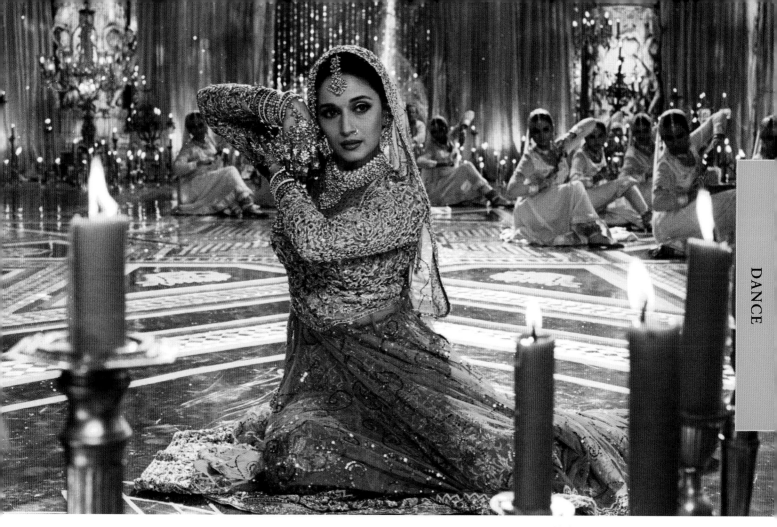

▲ SEDUCTIVE ROUTINE
Madhuri Dixit performs a traditional dance form called mujra in the 2002 film Devdas.

ACTING AND DANCING

Many Bollywood stars are as celebrated for their dancing skills as they are for their acting abilities. Described by colleagues as "a choreographer's delight," Madhuri Dixit is nicknamed the "dhak dhak girl," after a dance she performed to the song *Dhak Dhak Karne Laga* in the 1992 film *Beta*.

◀ SWAN
The hamsasya mudra is a swan's beak.

HAND GESTURES

Taken from Bharatanatyam and other classical Indian dance forms, Bollywood dancers use hand gestures called "mudras" or "hastas." These are used as a sign language, helping to tell a story. There are mudras for events, objects, animals, birds, flowers, and ideas.

▲ LOTUS
The padmakasta mudra is a lotus flower opening.

Ballroom dancing

Ballroom is a set of partner dances with set rules, which are performed for enjoyment and in competitions. Watching ballroom dancing has become hugely popular thanks to television shows in which celebrities compete in various dance styles, such as the tango, foxtrot, or quickstep, before a panel of judges.

Paso doble

Latin ballroom dance based on a bullfight

- **Invented** c.1910
- **Place of origin** Spain and France

The paso doble (two-step) is a Latin ballroom dance based on Spanish flamenco and the movements of a bullfighter. It is a dramatic dance in which the man plays the part of the matador, while the woman plays the matador's cape or the bull. In competition, it calls for acting skills as well as dancing skills.

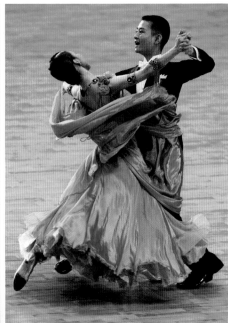

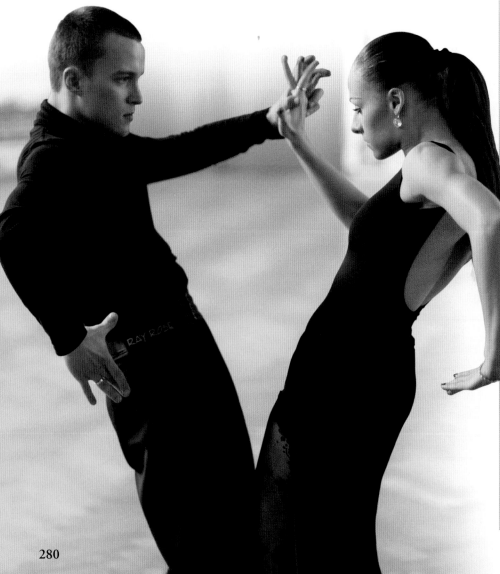

Foxtrot

A graceful, gliding dance

- **Invented** 1914
- **Place of origin** USA

The foxtrot is an elegant dance in which couples sweep around the dance floor in an counterclockwise direction, moving in turns and lines. Foxtrot dancers have to switch between two different rhythms as they dance. One has four beats: "slow slow quick quick;" the other three beats: "slow quick quick." This variety makes the foxtrot the most technically demanding ballroom dance to learn, although many dance professionals say it is their favorite. It was originally named Fox's trot, after Harry Fox, a New York comedian and dancer who popularized it.

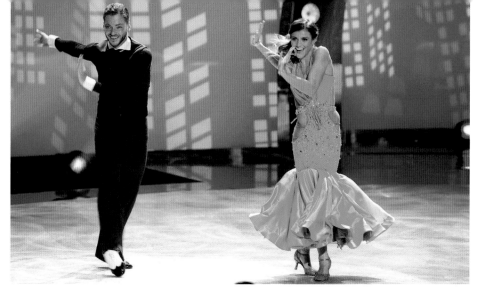

Quickstep
The fastest ballroom dance

- ■ **Invented** 1927
- ■ **Place of origin** USA

The quickstep was invented in New York City jazz clubs by dancers who combined a fast foxtrot with the Charleston, a lively dance with side kicks and arm movements. The quickstep was the perfect dance for the new jazz music of the 1920s. In ballroom, it demands a lot of movement across the floor, with many hops, runs, and rotations.

Ballroom tango
Stylized version of Argentine tango

- ■ **Invented** 1922
- ■ **Place of origin** UK

Ballroom tango is based on the Argentine dance (see p. 270). However, when it was adapted for ballroom dancing in the United Kingdom in 1922, the tango was made less passionate and more aggressive. In competition, it is danced with jerky head flicks from side to side.

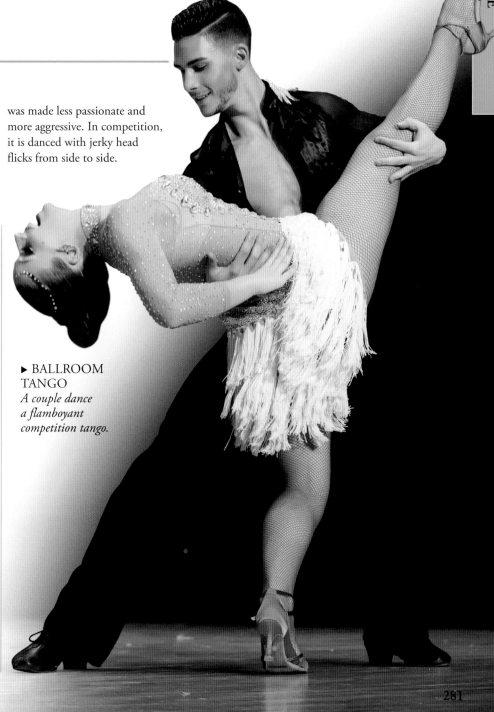

▶ BALLROOM TANGO
A couple dance a flamboyant competition tango.

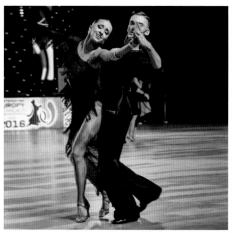

Ballroom rumba
The slowest Latin ballroom dance

- ■ **Invented** 1930s
- ■ **Place of origin** USA

Originally a fast-paced dance, the Cuban-inspired rumba was slowed down when it was adapted for ballroom dancing. In ballroom, it is danced to a slow, pulsating rhythm. Each couple occupies only a small area of the floor, using backward and forward walks and turns.

Tap dancing

To perform tap, dancers use special shoes fitted with metal "taps" on the soles. By combining a variety of rapid toe, heel, and ankle movements, dancers are able to create complex and exciting rhythms. Tap can be danced to music or solo, without musical accompaniment (a cappella). Solo tap dancers make their own music, with their feet.

SHOES FOR SOUND

The first tap dancers wore shoes with heavy wooden soles. In the 1930s, dancers began to fit steel taps to leather shoes. Modern shoes have taps made from aluminium, which is lighter than steel. There are different types of tap shoe, which produce slightly different tones.

▶ METAL TAPS
Taps are fitted to both the heel and toe. Each is used to make sounds.

TAP BEGINNINGS

In the early 19th century, African-American slaves, who were forbidden to play drums, learned to use their own bodies for percussion, slapping their sides and stomping their feet. This style, known as juba dancing, was mixed with Irish clog dancing to create the earliest tap dances. In the 1840s, William Henry Lane (known as "Master Juba") was the first person to perform these moves for a paying audience.

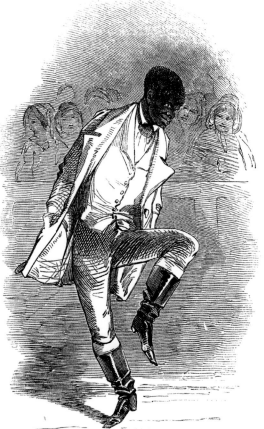

◀ MASTER JUBA
A woodcut of Master Juba, who was described by his promoters as "the dancinest fellow that ever was."

Each tap step has its own name, such as the shimmy, the stomp, the shuffle, the paradiddle, and the cramp roll.

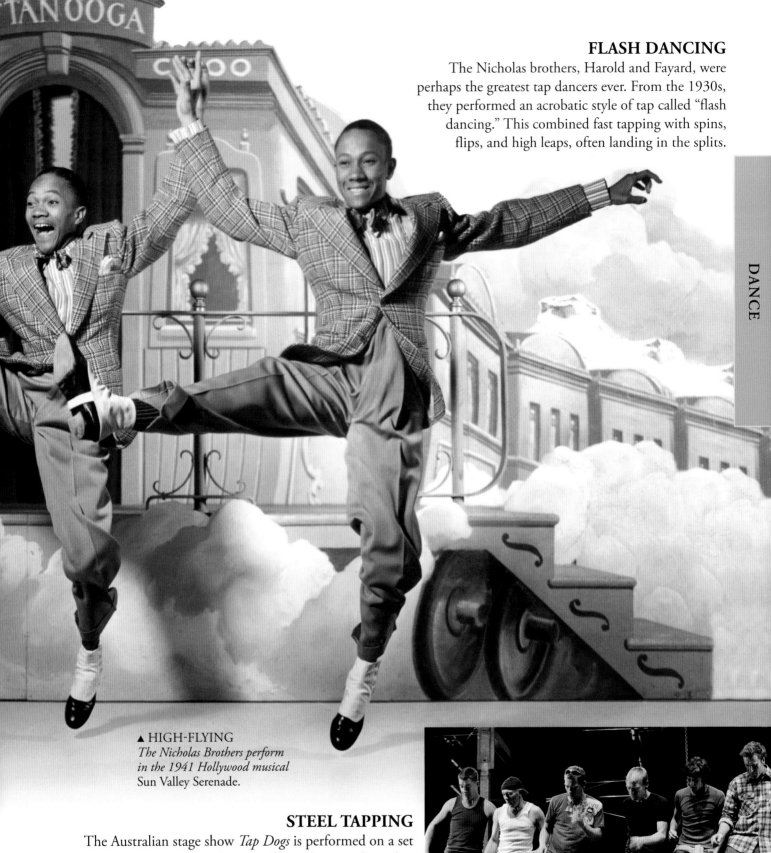

FLASH DANCING

The Nicholas brothers, Harold and Fayard, were perhaps the greatest tap dancers ever. From the 1930s, they performed an acrobatic style of tap called "flash dancing." This combined fast tapping with spins, flips, and high leaps, often landing in the splits.

▲ HIGH-FLYING
The Nicholas Brothers perform in the 1941 Hollywood musical Sun Valley Serenade.

STEEL TAPPING

The Australian stage show *Tap Dogs* is performed on a set resembling a steelworks. Six athletic dancers, dressed as builders, stomp their boots, jump through scaffolding, and even tap upside down. The hugely popular *Tap Dogs* show has been seen by more than 12 million people around the world.

▶ DANCING BUILDERS
The Tap Dogs *show has been continuously touring the world since 1995. This is a performance from 1997.*

283

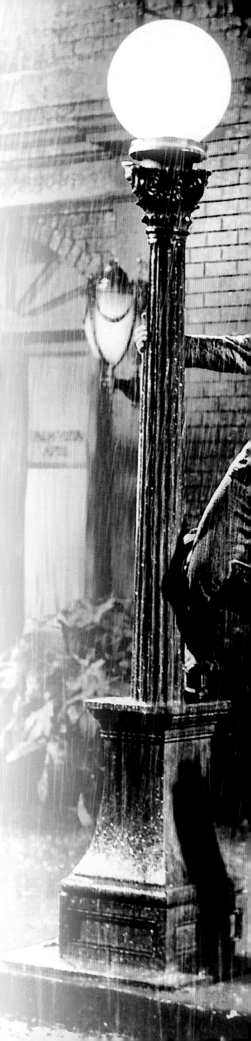

Dance on film

Dance has featured in movies ever since the start of cinema in the 1890s. Each new style of dance, from 1920s tango to modern hip-hop, has inspired hit Hollywood films. Although the dances change, the stories remain similar. Romances between couples who fall in love while dancing continue to be popular.

FRED AND GINGER

Hollywood in the 1930s was dominated by the dance partnership of Fred Astaire and Ginger Rogers. They made 10 romantic comedies, featuring graceful ballroom and tap dancing routines, all choreographed by Astaire. The extremely talented pair made dancing look effortless and natural, but it was the result of much hard work in rehearsals.

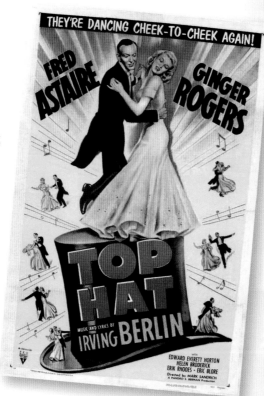

▶ TOP PAIR
Astaire and Rogers' most popular film was Top Hat, *released in 1935.*

Before sound in cinema arrived in 1927, dance films were silent. A cinema pianist provided live musical accompaniment.

SINGIN' IN THE RAIN

In the 1940s, Gene Kelly brought a new acrobatic and athletic style into Hollywood dance. He was an adventurous choreographer, influenced by modern ballet, which he studied with Martha Graham (see p. 276). Kelly is best known for his 1952 film *Singin' in the Rain*, in which he dances with an umbrella, splashing along a rainswept street.

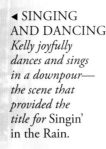

◀ SINGING
AND DANCING
*Kelly joyfully
dances and sings
in a downpour—
the scene that
provided the
title for* Singin'
in the Rain.

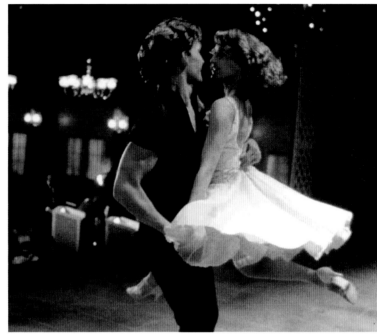

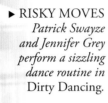

▶ RISKY MOVES
*Patrick Swayze
and Jennifer Grey
perform a sizzling
dance routine in*
Dirty Dancing.

ROCK AND ROLL ERA

Though made in 1987, *Dirty Dancing* is set in 1963, and features the rock and roll music of the period. Jennifer Grey plays a teenage girl spending the summer at a holiday camp. To the horror of her parents, she falls in love with the camp dance instructor, played by Patrick Swayze. Much of the dancing is Latin in style, with elements of rumba, salsa, mambo, and cha cha.

▶ LOVE STORY
Hip-hop moves catch on in the ballet rehearsal room in this dance scene from Step Up, *and romance soon follows.*

DIFFERENT WORLDS

In the 2006 movie *Step Up*, Hollywood showed how different dance forms could be combined. Actor Channing Tatum, playing a troubled hip-hop street dancer, is sentenced to community service in an Arts School. Here he meets an ambitious ballet student, played by Jenna Dewan, and forms a dance partnership with her.

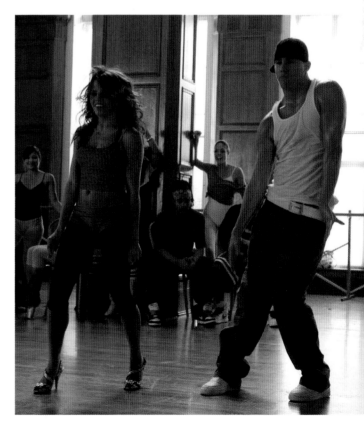

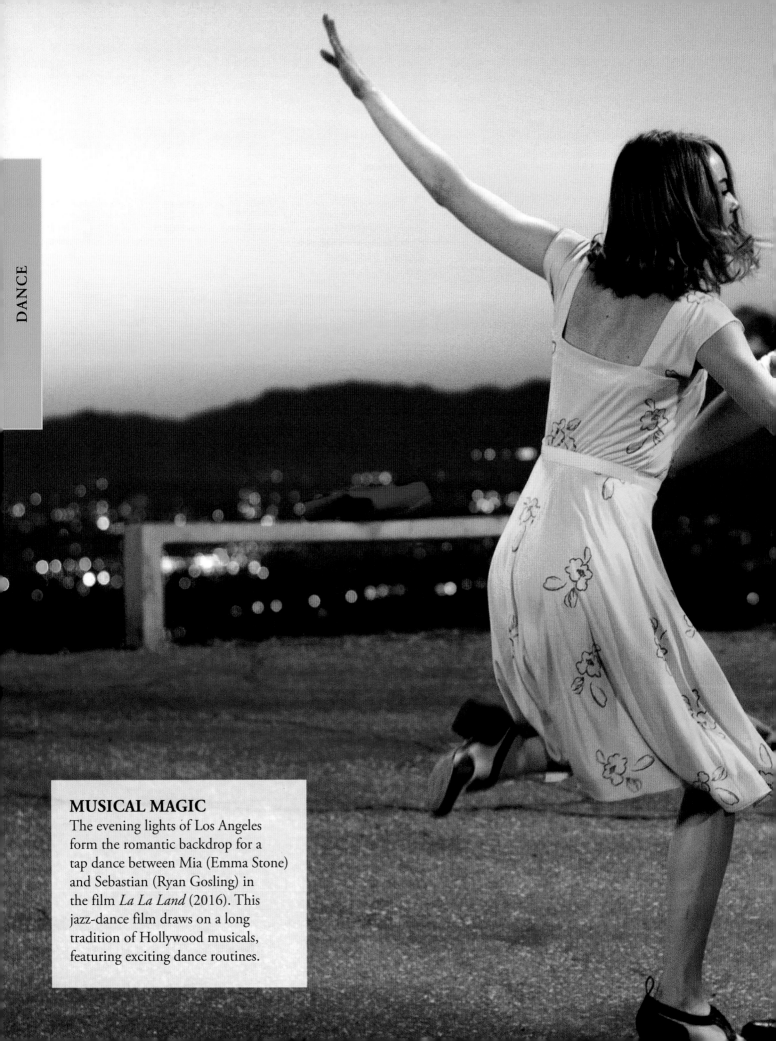

MUSICAL MAGIC
The evening lights of Los Angeles form the romantic backdrop for a tap dance between Mia (Emma Stone) and Sebastian (Ryan Gosling) in the film *La La Land* (2016). This jazz-dance film draws on a long tradition of Hollywood musicals, featuring exciting dance routines.

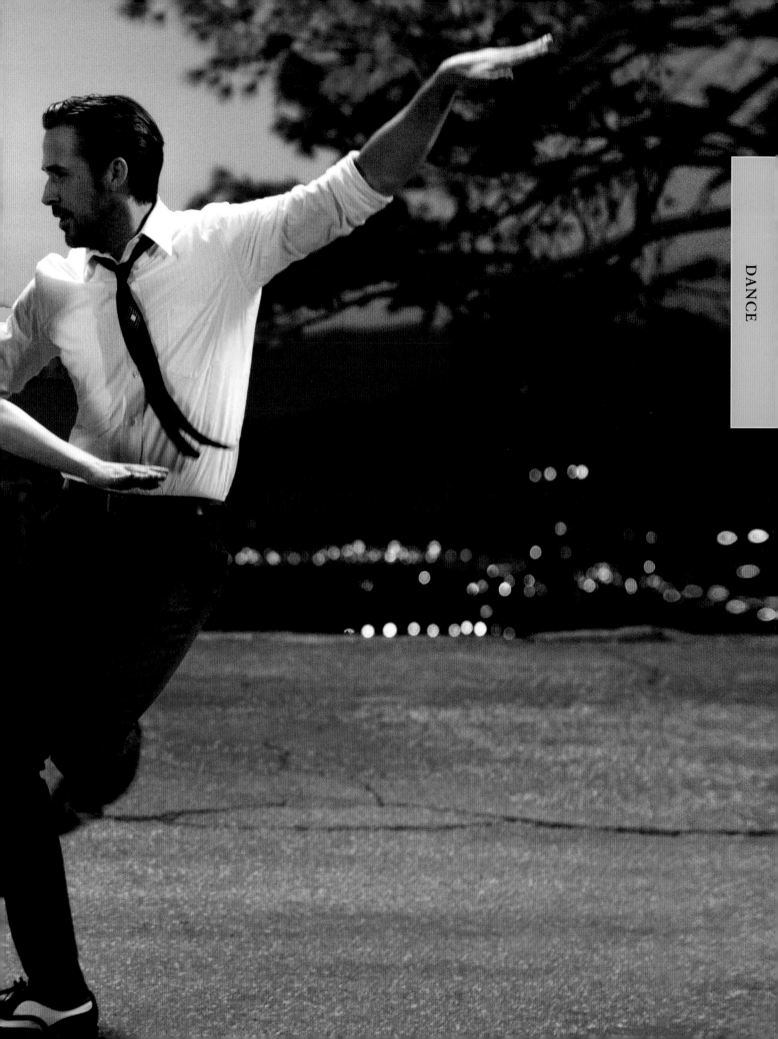

Modern dance crazes

The pop music revolution of the 1950s and 1960s changed the way that young people danced. Couple dances, such as jiving, went out of fashion, as teenagers began to dance solo, performing simple steps such as the twist. New dance crazes changed constantly, as hit records and films spread their popularity worldwide.

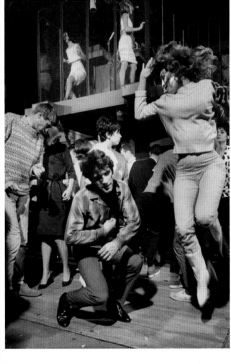

The Twist
The first teenage solo dance

- **Place of origin** USA
- **Invented** 1959
- **Associated song** *The Twist* (Chubby Checker)

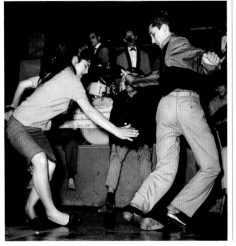

The first big dance craze was the twist, invented by teenagers on the dance floors of Tampa, Florida. Hank Ballard, who saw the dance, celebrated it in a 1959 record, which became a huge hit when it was covered by Chubby Checker in 1960. The twist was danced from a stationary position, with dancers twisting their bodies from side to side.

The Watusi
A style inspired by African tribal dances

- **Place of origin** USA
- **Invented** 1962
- **Associated song** *The Watusi* (The Vibrations)

The Twist was followed by the Watusi, which is the former name of the African Tutsi people. The Watusi craze was inspired by the African tribal dances that appeared in two Hollywood films, *King Solomon's Mines* and *Watusi*. It was more mobile than the Twist, as dancers slid to the left and right. By 1965, when the photo above was taken, the dance had evolved into a free form of self-expression.

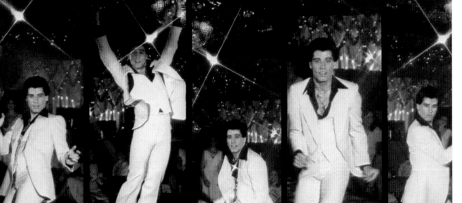

The Hustle
A disco solo and line dance

- **Place of origin** USA
- **Invented** 1975
- **Associated song** *The Hustle* (Van McCoy)

With disco music in the 1970s, there was a return to more demanding steps that required practice. The Hustle was a disco dance that became huge after the actor John Travolta danced it to the song *Night Fever* in his 1977 film, *Saturday Night Fever*. It could be performed solo or as a line dance, and involved a series of steps, turns, hand movements, and poses. The film included a tango version of the dance, which was invented by Travolta himself.

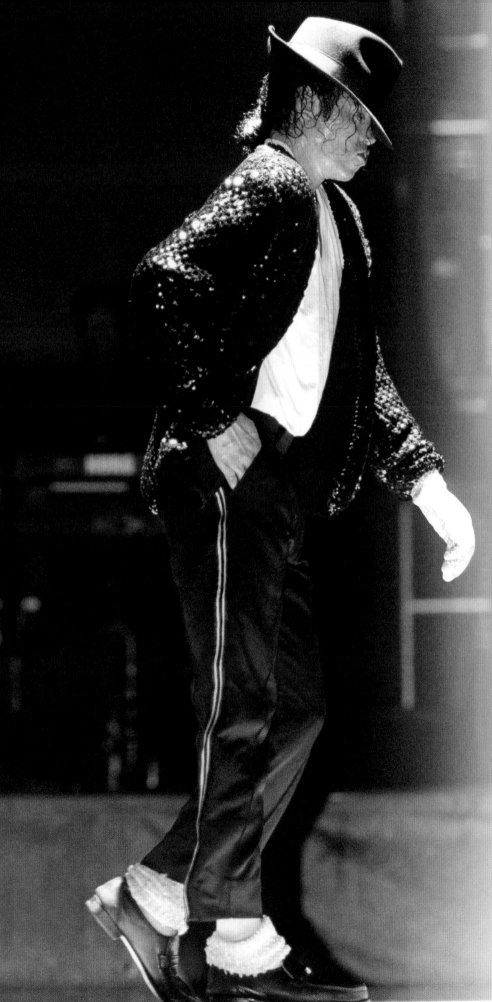

Moonwalking

A dance step popularized by the "King of Pop"

- **Place of origin** USA
- **Invented** Became popular 1983
- **Associated song** *Billie Jean* (Michael Jackson)

The Moonwalk is a dance step in which a performer appears to be walking forward while actually sliding backward. It became popular in 1983 after Michael Jackson moonwalked on television, while singing his hit *Billie Jean*. Jackson did not invent the step, which he had learned from body-poppers (see p. 291). The jazz singer Cab Calloway commented that he had used the same step as far back as 1932, when it was called "the buzz."

◀ A PERFECTED MOVE
Michael Jackson moonwalks during a performance on his 1996 HIStory tour.

DANCE

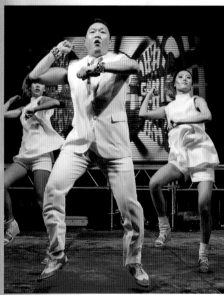

Gangnam Style

Energetic comic dance

- **Place of origin** South Korea
- **Invented** 2012
- **Associated song** *Gagnam Style* (Psy)

Gagnam Style is an East Asian dance that became a global craze. It began with the catchy single *Gagnam Style*, by the South Korean singer Psy (Park Jae-sang). In the video, Psy performs a comical dance in which he pretends to ride an invisible horse while twirling a lasso. The video, shared about 3 billion times on the website YouTube, inspired people all over the world to do the dance.

Dancing in the streets

Invented by young African-Americans and Puerto Ricans, street dancing emerged in the New York City streets in the late 1970s. Wearing loose, comfortable clothes, people would compete with each other by performing athletic, improvised fast moves that required strength and balance.

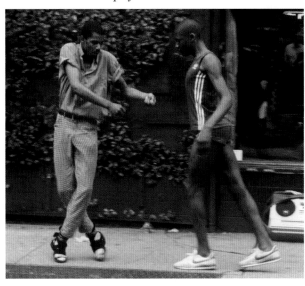

▼ MUSIC IN THE STREETS
Two breakdancers toprock to a boombox, a portable cassette player and radio invented in the 1970s.

UPRIGHT MOVES

Toprocking is breakdancing while standing, with rapid bouncing foot movements. There are various moves, such as the Indian Step, which involves circling and kicking. Dancers spend a long time developing their own individual toprocking style. A dance will often begin with toprocking, before falling to the floor to downrock.

BREAKDANCING

Breakdancing, or b-boying, gets its name from the music of New York DJ Kool Herc. In the 1970s, he began to loop, or repeat, instrumental breaks from records for dancers. He called those who danced to the breaks b-boys (though b-girls later joined in). Breakdancing combines different techniques, such as toprocking, downrocking, and freezes.

▼ DOWNROCKING
In downrocking, breakdancers keep their bodies close to the floor, supporting themselves on their hands, shoulders, or heads.

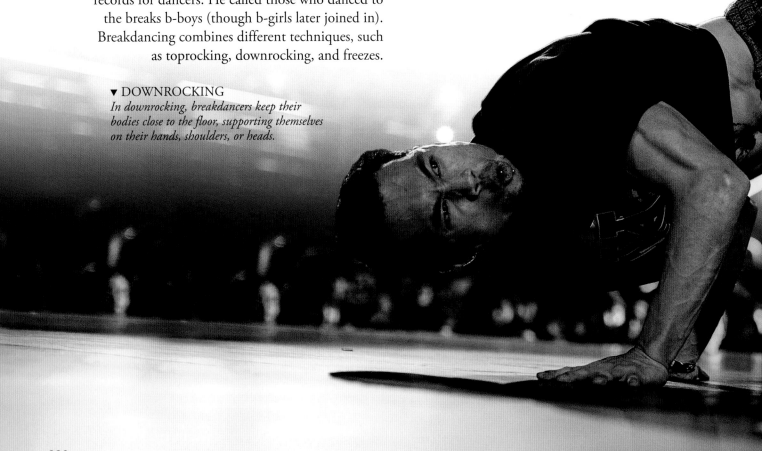

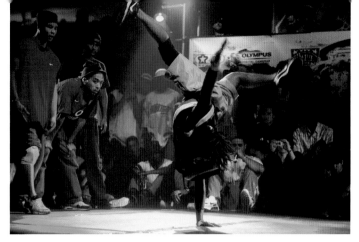

◄ MAKING SHAPES
In the Y-freeze, a dancer balances on one hand while opening his or her legs into the shape of the letter Y.

Body popping is a street dance in which dancers contract and relax their muscles, making their bodies jerk, or pop.

FREEZE FORMS

The trickiest breakdancing move is the freeze, in which the dancer suddenly stops moving and adopts a balancing pose that may be held for several seconds. There are many different kinds of freeze, using various parts of the body, such as the head, to balance on. The freeze acts as a dramatic pause within a dance.

DANCE AS RELEASE

Krumping is an aggressive style of street dance, which began in Los Angeles in the early 2000s. Performed upright to fast-paced music, it combined stillness with intense bursts of movement. Moves include chest pops, foot stomping, and arm flailing. For dancers, it is a way to release aggression in a non-violent way. "Krump" is said to stand for "Kingdom Radically Uplifted Mighty Praise."

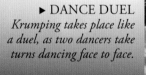

► DANCE DUEL
Krumping takes place like a duel, as two dancers take turns dancing face to face.

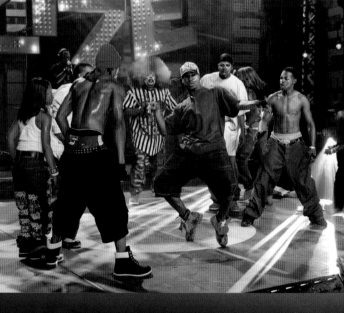

Glossary

Abstract art An artistic style founded in the early 20th century that uses shapes and colors to represent ideas or emotions, rather than depicting people, objects, and scenes in a recognizable way.

Abstract Expressionism This movement began in the 1940s in New York. Art was typically created with strong brushstrokes and industrial paints.

Acrylics A plastic-based, fast-drying paint.

Action painting An artistic technique where the dynamic process of painting itself is as important as the finished work.

Antiquity The distant past, particularly in ancient Egypt, Greece, and Rome.

Art Nouveau A decorative, floral style in art and architecture, popular between the 1890s and early 20th century.

Automatism The technique of creating art in a random way, led by the unconscious mind. This method is often used in Surrealist works.

Ballet A dance form developed from 16th-century French and Italian court dances. The two main styles today are classical ballet and modern ballet.

Baroque A grand and theatrical style of art and architecture popular in 17th-century Europe and Latin America. It also refers to music written during that era.

Brass A family of instruments that includes the trumpet, horn, and tuba.

Calligraphy Decorative or ornamental writing. In East Asia and the Islamic world in particular, artists use brushes and ink to transform script into works of art.

Ceramics Objects, such as pots or bowls made of clay, and the art of making them.

Charcoal Burnt wood used for drawing.

Chiaroscuro A strong, dramatic contrast between light and shade in a painting.

Chord Several notes played on an instrument at the same time, together making a harmonious sound.

Choreography The arrangement of steps, positions, and movements that make up a dance piece. A person who specializes in this is called a choreographer.

Classical A term to describe ancient Greek or Roman art, especially sculpture, as well as later art inspired by it.

Classical music Refers to the type of music composed in the Western world from the Middle Ages to the present. It follows certain rules in terms of notation, melody, harmonies, and style—and does not allow for improvisation. The term can also be used to describe the ancient formal music of a country, such as India or Japan.

Collage An image that is made of a variety of materials stuck onto a flat surface.

Color Field An abstract art style where color is the subject of the painting, and is applied to the canvas in large, flat shapes.

Color wheel A circle that demonstrates the relationship between colors, showing the many hues that can be created by mixing primary and secondary colors.

Complementary colors Colors from opposite sides of the color wheel, such as red and green, which may be used by artists to create a particular impact.

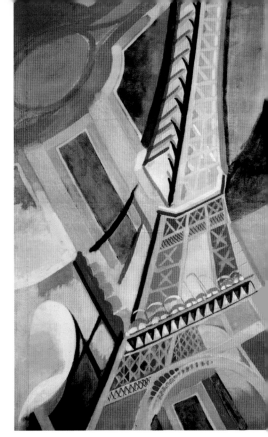

▲ *TOUR EIFFEL*, 1926,
ROBERT DELAUNAY

Composer A person who writes music.

Composition In art, how the artist decides to place things or people in an artwork. In music, it refers to a piece of music that someone has composed (written).

Conceptual art An artistic style where the idea or meaning behind a piece of art is more important than what it looks like.

Concerto A piece of music performed by a soloist accompanied by an orchestra.

Conductor The person who leads an orchestra, showing them when to play soft or loud, and keeping the rhythm.

Cubism Emerging in early 20th-century Europe, this style of painting shows objects or people from many different viewpoints at the same time, breaking them up into odd angles and fragments.

Dada An art movement that led to strange and shocking works of art, born out of the horrors of World War I.

De Stijl This Dutch movement, which encompasses Neoplasticism, emphasized harmonious forms and primary colors.

Diptych A painting that has two parts.

Dutch Golden Age A period spanning most of the 17th century, when the Netherlands was the leading European power in the arts, trade, and science.

En plein air The French expression for painting "in open air," referring to the style of many 19th-century Impressionists who preferred the natural light of the outdoors.

Encaustic In painting and ceramics, a process of mixing pigments with hot wax, widely used in ancient times.

Engraving A picture or design that has been cut into a surface, usually metal or wood, by using a sharp tool.

Exposure In photography, the amount of light that enters the camera lens to take a photograph.

Expressionism This artistic movement emerged in the early 20th century, and emphasized distorted or exaggerated objects, people, and colors to express the inner lives and emotions of artists.

Fauvism This early 20th-century art movement was typified by artists' use of simplified shapes, bold brush strokes, and vibrant color to express a sense of wild, energetic emotion.

Figurative art An artistic style that depicts people, scenes, and objects in a recognizable way.

Foreshortening In painting, a term for making an object or person seem to project forward, toward the observer.

Fresco A technique of painting, usually on a wall, using a mixture of powdered pigments and water on wet plaster.

Futurism An artistic style invented in the early 20th century that celebrated the modern world, including machines.

Genre art Paintings that show people at home or at work, doing everyday things; very popular in the Dutch Golden Age.

Gothic A style of art and architecture that flourished in Western Europe between the 12th and 15th centuries.

Hieroglyphs An ancient Egyptian writing system that used symbols and pictures to convey meaning.

Hymn A religious song, usually praising a god or goddess.

Icon In painting, this term refers to an image that depicts Jesus Christ, the Virgin Mary, a saint, or another holy person.

Illuminated manuscript A handwritten book, usually from the Middle Ages, filled with intricate images and decorated letters.

Impressionism An artistic movement beginning in France in the 1860s. Its painters wanted to create an "impression" of their subjects, recreating effects of light and color with rapid brushstrokes.

Keyboard instrument A family of instruments including the piano, organ, synthesizer, and harpsichord.

Landscape 1. A painting or photograph of natural scenery, like mountains, rivers, or farmland. 2. A format of painting or photograph that is wider than it is tall.

Luminism An American 19th-century style of painting, showing grand, calm landscapes in delicately reflected light.

Mannerism A 16th-century style of painting and sculpture that began in Italy. It typically shows people in poses that are mannered (elegant but exaggerated and not very natural).

Medieval A term that describes European art and music from the Middle Ages.

Medium The type of material an artist uses, or an artistic method, such as drawing, sculpture, music, or dance.

Middle Ages The period in Europe between the 5th and mid-15th centuries.

Modernism A broad term for describing beliefs, attitudes, arts, and architecture from the beginning of the 20th century.

Mosaic The technique of producing images by combining small pieces of glass, stone, and other hard materials.

Mural A big painting made on a wall.

◄ 19TH-CENTURY PLATE CAMERA

Naive art A work of art made by an artist with no formal qualifications or training.

Neoclassicism A style that was inspired by ancient Greek and Roman art and architecture. It became popular in Europe and North America in the late 18th and early 19th centuries.

Neoplasticism An abstract style of painting, using only rectangles, straight lines, and a small number of colors.

Notation A system used to write down music so that others can read and play it, showing the pitch and length of each note.

Oil paint A type of paint that dries very slowly, and is made by mixing pigments of color with oil, such as linseed.

Op Art A form of abstract art that uses certain colors and patterns to create optical illusions, which appear to move in a hypnotic way.

Opera A dramatic performance where specially trained singers act and sing the story, accompanied by an orchestra. It is the classical music version of a musical.

Orchestra A large group of classically trained musicians, such as violinists, trombonists, and percussionists, who play and perform music together.

Percussion A family of instruments that are struck to produce a sound, such as drums, cymbals, maracas, and xylophones.

Peredvizhniki movement A group of 19th-century Russian artists who wanted to paint for "ordinary" people, depicting the beauty of simple country life.

Perspective The technique used to depict something three-dimensional, such as a building or person, on a flat surface.

Petrogram A prehistoric design made on the surface of a rock.

Pigment A colored powder that is mixed with a binder—such as gum, oil, or acrylic—to make paints.

Pitch A term used to describe how high or low a note is perceived to be in relation to other notes on the musical scale.

Plate camera An old-fashioned camera that uses glass or metal plates with a light-sensitive coating, rather than film or a memory disk, to create a photograph.

Pointillism A painting technique that consists of tiny dots of different colors placed close together. Seen from a distance, these dots combine into a complete picture.

Polaroid camera A camera that takes and develops a photograph, after which it produces a print, all within seconds.

Polyphony A musical term describing a combination of different sounds played to create a single unifying tone or mood.

Polyrhythmic Music that has more than one main rhythm going at the same time; it is a common feature in African music.

Pop Art An artistic style from the 1950s and 1960s that is based on modern popular culture, especially using images from comic books and advertisements.

Portrait 1. A painting or photograph of a person or group of people. A self-portrait is a painting or photograph of the artist by him- or herself. 2. Describes an image format that is taller than it is wide.

Post-Impressionism A catchall term encompassing the different types of art movements that followed Impressionism, such as Symbolism.

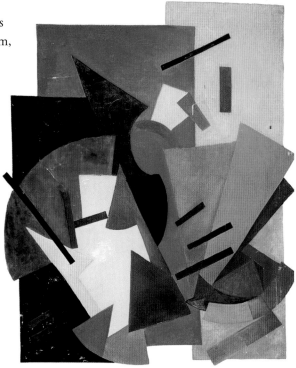

▲ *FLIGHT OF AN AEROPLANE*, 1916, OLGA ROZANOVA

Pre-Raphaelites A group of British painters who formed in 1848 in protest against London's Royal Academy of Art, which favored traditional styles based on the Renaissance artist Raphael.

Primary colors The basic colors (red, yellow, and blue) that can be mixed together to make other colors.

Primitive art A term to describe tribal and folk art from around the world.

Printmaking A method of making many copies of one image.

Realism An art movement that begun in the 1850s, showing life, people and everyday subjects in a realistic way.

Renaissance A movement inspired by the artistic ideals of ancient Greece and Rome, which began in Italy in the 14th century and then spread to other parts of Europe. Also refers to the period between the late 14th and 16th centuries, and the style of classical music written at that time.

Rococo A light, playful art style popular in 18th-century Europe, often featuring idyllic scenes of fashionably dressed pretty women and elegant men.

Romanticism A 19th-century movement in which artists painted in a dramatic, emotional style, often showing a person surrounded by a wild or stormy landscape. Romantic composers wrote music that was moving and sentimental, or nationalistic and inspired by their country's folk music.

Sarcophagus A type of coffin used in ancient times, often decorated.

Score Music written for a ballet or film.

Sculpture Art created by carving, shaping, or molding materials such as marble, clay, or wood into abstract or realistic figures.

Sfumato A method of gradually blending colors in a painting to create blurred, soft outlines.

Sonata A piece written for a solo pianist, or for a solo instrumentalist with or without piano accompaniment.

Stained glass Pieces of colored glass combined to form geometric patterns or images of, for example, biblical characters, flowers, or animals.

Stave The set of five horizontal lines on which music is written, with symbols representing the notes.

Still life A painting of objects, such as fruit or flowers, arranged decoratively.

Subject Something that an artist has decided to paint or photograph.

Suprematism One of the earliest forms of abstract art, created by the Russian artist Kazimir Malevich from 1913. He painted groups of circles, squares, triangles, and other geometric forms.

Surrealism An art style beginning in the 1920s that expressed startling or confusing thoughts of the unconscious mind. Surreal means "more than real."

Symbolism A poetic, mysterious art style appearing in the late 19th century as a reaction to Realism and Impressionism.

Symphony A long piece of classical music consisting of several parts, or movements, and composed for an orchestra.

Syncopation A type of rhythm in which the regular pattern of beats is interrupted by stressing the weak beats.

Tempera A type of paint made by mixing color pigments with egg yolk.

Tenebrism A painting style that produces extreme contrasts between large areas in dark shadow and small, lit-up details.

Tone In music, it is the quality of sound coming from a voice or an instrument, also known as timbre. In art, it describes a darker or lighter shade of a color.

▼ SINGER AND MUSICIAN
LITTLE RICHARD, 1956

Vanishing point Describing perspective in art—especially paintings—this is a specific point in the distance where parallel lines appear to meet, such as where a straight road meets the horizon.

Viewpoint The point of view from which the artist looks at their subject; it also identifies where the horizon is in relation to everything else in the painting.

Watercolor Water-based paint with a light, transparent color quality. Also a painting made with this paint.

Woodblock printing The Asian method of carving an image into a block of wood, covering the uncarved surfaces with ink, and pressing it onto paper.

Woodcut A woodblock print made in Europe or other part of the Western world.

Woodwind A family of instruments that includes flutes and reed instruments such as the saxophone and clarinet.

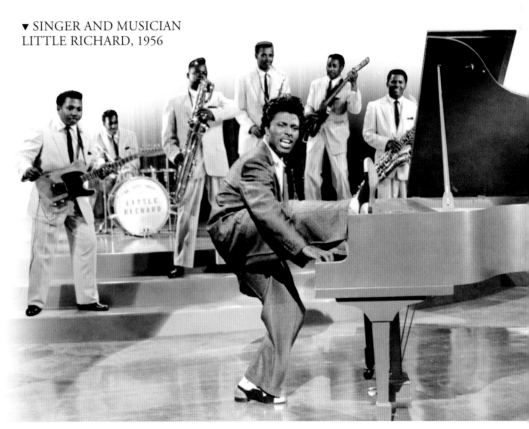

295

Index

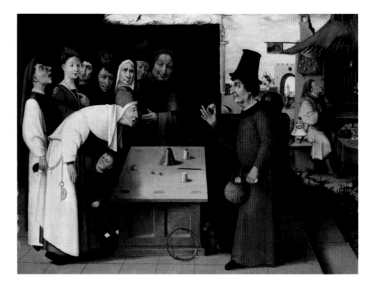

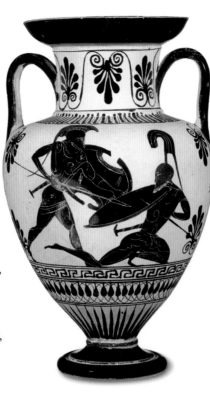

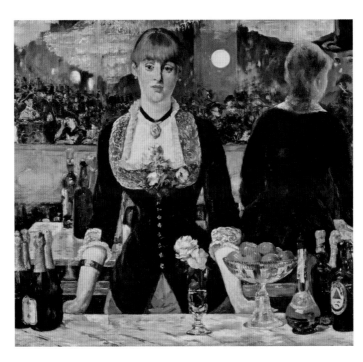

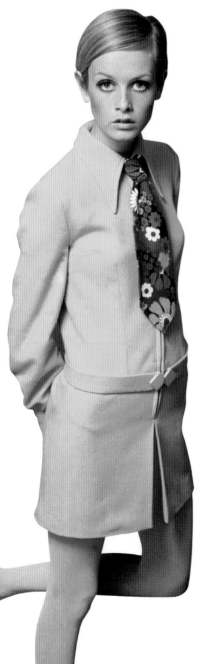

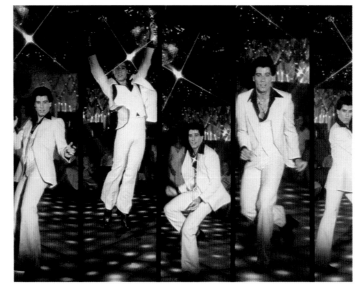

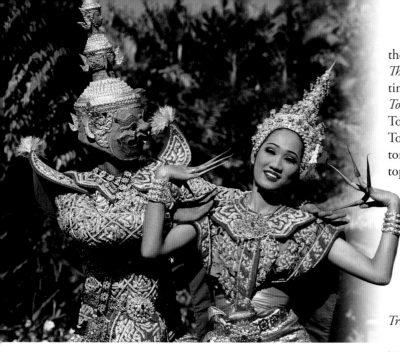

Acknowledgments

DK would like to thank: Alice Bowden for fact-checking; Anna Limerick for editorial help; Chrissy Barnard and Mary Sandberg for design help; Elizabeth Wise for indexing; Kieran Macdonald for proofreading; Jasmin Saunders at DACS.

The publisher would like to thank the following for their kind permission to reproduce their photographs:

(Key: a-above; b-below/bottom; c-center; f-far; l-left; r-right; t-top)

1 akg-images: works by Barbara Hepworth © Bowness / IAM. 2-3 Alamy Stock Photo: FineArt. 4 Alamy Stock Photo: World History Archive (cr/4); Heritage Image Partnership Ltd (tr/1); Granger Historical Picture Archive (cr/1); PAINTING (cr/3); classicpaintings (br/2). Getty Images: DEA / A. DAGLI ORTI (tr/2); The Print Collector / Heritage-Images (cr/2); Buyenlarge (br/1). 5 123RF.com: flaperval (c/4). akg-images: Erich Lessing (tr/1). Alamy Stock Photo: Archivart (ca/1); Stocktrek Images, Inc. (cb/2); World History Archive (c/3); FineArt (ca/2); travelstock44 (cr/4); Semen Lihodeev (br/1). Getty Images: Carl Court (cr/3); Sergey Prokudin-Gorsky / Galerie Bilderwelt (cb/1); Fine Art Images / Heritage Images (c/1); Universal History Archive / UIG (c/2); JACQUES SARRAT / Sygma (tr/2); RB / Redferns (cr/1); Linda Vartoogian (cr/2); Bruno Vincent (br/2). 6-7 Alamy Stock Photo: PAINTING. 7 123RF.com: tannjuska (tl). Alamy Stock Photo: mauritius images GmbH (tr); Granger Historical Picture Archive (tc). 8 Alamy Stock Photo: Heritage Image Partnership Ltd (bl). Getty Images: Universal History Archive (tr). 9 Alamy Stock Photo: Archivart (tr); PAINTING (bc). Dreamstime.com: Pridumala (tl). 10 Alamy Stock Photo: Photo Researchers, Inc (c). 10-11 Alamy Stock Photo: FineArt (t); Lebrecht Music and Arts Photo Library (b). 11 Alamy Stock Photo: SuperStock (c). Dreamstime.com: Pridumala (tr). 12 Alamy Stock Photo: Peter Horree (l). Dreamstime.com: Pridumala (br). 13 Alamy Stock Photo: PAINTING (tl). Dreamstime.com: Albachiaraa (cr). Getty Images: Fine Art Images / Heritage Images (bl). 14 Alamy Stock Photo: blickwinkel (bl); Robert Preston Photography (c). Dreamstime.com: Pridumala (tr). 15 Alamy Stock Photo: age fotostock (br). Dorling Kindersley: Philippe Giraud (tl). 16-17 Alamy Stock Photo: Heritage Image Partnership Ltd. 18 akg-images: Pictures From History (bl). 18-19 Alamy Stock Photo: Peter Barritt (tc). The Trustees of the British Museum: (bc). 19 akg-images: ullstein bild (crb); IAM (br). Alamy Stock Photo: age fotostock (cra); World History Archive (tr). 20-21 Alamy Stock Photo: Granger Historical Picture Archive (bc). 20 Alamy Stock Photo: Heritage Image Partnership Ltd (bl); Granger Historical Picture Archive (tl). 21 Dreamstime.com: Pridumala (cr). Getty Images: ALESSANDRO VANNINI (t). 22-23 Getty Images: DEA / G. SIOEN. 22 Getty Images: DEA / G. SIOEN (cl, tr). 23 Getty Images: DEA / G. SIOEN (tl, tc, tr). 24-25 Alamy Stock Photo: World History Archive. 26-27 Getty Images: Werner Forman / Universal Images Group (b). 26 123RF.com: Lucian Bolca (cr). 27 Dreamstime.com: Pridumala (br). Getty Images: DEA / A. DAGLI ORTI (cr); VCG Wilson (tc). 28-29 Alamy Stock Photo: David South. 30 Getty Images: DEA PICTURE LIBRARY / De Agostini (c); VCG Wilson (bl). 31 123RF.com: Joerg Hackemann (tr). Getty Images: VCG Wilson (cl). Photo Scala, Florence: DeAgostini Picture Library (br). 32-33 Alamy Stock Photo: Peter Horree (tc). 32 Alamy Stock Photo: Sites & Photos / Capture Ltd (br). Getty Images: ALESSANDRO VANNINI (bl). 33 Getty Images: DEA / A. DAGLI ORTI / De Agostini (br); Bettmann (c). 34 Getty Images: Photo12 / UIG (cl). 34-35 Alamy Stock Photo: Beijing Eastphoto stockimages Co.,Ltd (b); Granger Historical Picture Archive (tc). 35 Alamy Stock Photo: ephotocorp (cr). Dreamstime.com: Pridumala (c). 36 Alamy Stock Photo: Granger Historical Picture Archive (cl); Ivy Close Images (br). Dreamstime.com: Pridumala (cr). 37 123RF.com: jorisvo (br). Getty Images: Universal Images Group / Hulton Fine Art (t). 38 Alamy Stock Photo: Peter Horree (bl). 39 Alamy Stock Photo: World History Archive (tl); Poulberin (bl); Anton Starikov (tr). 40-41 Getty Images: DEA / A. Dagli Orti / De Agostini. 42 Alamy Stock Photo: PRISMA ARCHIVO (cr); Classic Image (bl). 42-43 Alamy Stock Photo: Sean Pavone (b). 43 Alamy Stock Photo: V (tr). Dreamstime.com: Pridumala (tl). 44-45 Getty Images: The Print Collector / Heritage-Images (c). 44 Getty Images: Hulton Archive (b). 45 Getty Images: The Print Collector / Heritage-Images (tr, cra, crb, br). 46 Alamy Stock Photo: Artepics (tr); Granger Historical Picture Archive (b). 47 Alamy Stock Photo: Dennis Hallinan (br); World History Archive (tr). Dreamstime.com: Pridumala (cl). 48 Alamy Stock Photo: Peter Barritt (cr, cl). 48-49 Alamy Stock Photo: World History Archive (b). 49 Alamy Stock Photo: David Collingwood (cr); INTERFOTO (br). 50 Alamy Stock Photo: SuperStock (bl). Dreamstime.com: Pridumala (br). Getty Images: DeAgostini (tr). 51 Alamy Stock Photo: The Artchives (br); ACTIVE MUSEUM (tl). 52 Alamy Stock Photo: PAINTING (cl). Dreamstime.com: Pridumala (tr). 52-53 Getty Images: DeAgostini (b). 53 Bridgeman Images: The Birth of Venus, c.1485 (tempera on canvas), Botticelli, Sandro (Alessandro di Mariano di Vanni Filipepi) (1444 / 5-1510) / Galleria degli Uffizi, Florence, Tuscany, Italy (cr); Granger Historical Picture Archive (tl). 54-55 Alamy Stock Photo: Peter Barritt (tc); ART Collection (b). 55 Alamy Stock Photo: FineArt (cr). Getty Images: Leemage / UIG (bc). 56-57 Getty Images: Universal History Archive / UIG. 58-59 Bridgeman Images: Primavera, c.1478, (tempera on panel), Botticelli, Sandro (Alessandro di Mariano di Vanni Filipepi) (1444 / 5-1510) / Galleria degli Uffizi, Florence, Tuscany, Italy (b). 58 Bridgeman Images: Primavera, c.1478, (tempera on panel), Botticelli, Sandro (Alessandro di Mariano di Vanni Filipepi) (1444 / 5-1510) / Galleria degli Uffizi, Florence, Tuscany, Italy (bl, cl, tr). 59 Bridgeman Images: Primavera, c.1478, (tempera on panel), Botticelli, Sandro (Alessandro di Mariano di Vanni Filipepi) (1444 / 5-1510) / Galleria degli Uffizi, Florence, Tuscany, Italy (tl, tr). 60-61 Getty Images: Leemage / Corbis (bc). 60 Alamy Stock Photo: PAINTING (bl). 61 Alamy Stock Photo: INTERFOTO (tr); SuperStock (br). Dreamstime.com: Pridumala (tc). 62 Getty Images: Time Life Pictures / Mansell / The LIFE Picture Collection (cl); DeAgostini (tl). 63 Alamy Stock Photo: World History Archive. 64-65 Alamy Stock Photo: FineArt (tc); INTERFOTO (b). 64 Alamy Stock Photo: ACTIVE MUSEUM (c). Getty Images: VCG Wilson / Corbis (bl). 65 Alamy Stock Photo: Ivy Close Images (cr). 66-67 Getty Images: Leemage / Corbis (t). 66 Getty Images: Leemage / Corbis (cl, br). 67 Getty Images: Leemage / Corbis (bl, br). 68 Dreamstime.com: Pridumala (br). Getty Images: VCG Wilson / Corbis (tr); DeAgostini (bl). 69 Alamy Stock Photo: FineArt (tl). Getty Images: Leemage / Corbis (br). 70 Getty Images: Arte & Immagini srl / Corbis (bl); DeAgostini (c). 70-71 Getty Images: DeAgostini (b). 71 Getty Images: 1993 / Mondadori Portfolio (br). 72-73 Getty Images: Fine Art Images / Heritage Images. 74 Dreamstime.com: Pridumala (tr). Getty Images: Buyenlarge (b). 75 Alamy Stock Photo: Universal Art Archive (tr); Robert Fried (br). Getty Images: DeAgostini (cl). 76 Getty Images: Hulton Archive (tl); INTERFOTO (br). Alamy Stock Photo: SuperStock (bl). Dreamstime.com: Pridumala (br). Getty Images: DeAgostini (tr). Universal History Archive / UIG (cl). 77 Getty Images: DeAgostini (cr); Universal History Archive / UIG (tl). 78-79 Alamy Stock Photo: Heritage Image Partnership Ltd. 80-81 Photo Scala, Florence: Copyright The National Gallery, London (c). 80 Photo Scala, Florence: Copyright The National Gallery, London (tl, cla). 81 Photo Scala, Florence: Copyright The National Gallery, London (crb, tr, cra, ca, cr, bc); Photo Scala, Florence: The National Gallery, London (br). 82 Getty Images: VCG Wilson / Corbis (br); Summerfield Press / Corbis (l). 83 Dreamstime.com: Pridumala (cl). Getty Images: Imagno / Austrian Archives (tr); VCG Wilson / Corbis / Fine Art (bl). 84 Alamy Stock Photo: PAINTING (br). Dreamstime.com: Pridumala (bl). Getty Images: Imagno / Austrian Archives (cl). 85 Alamy Stock Photo: FineArt (r); ACTIVE MUSEUM (t). 86 Getty Images: Hulton Archive (tl); Fine Art Images / Heritage Images (cl). 87 Getty Images: DeAgostini. 88-89 Alamy Stock Photo: Granger Historical Picture Archive (b). 88 Alamy Stock Photo: PAINTING (bl); Bridgeman Images: The Laughing Cavalier, 1624 (oil on canvas), Hals, Frans (1582 / 3-1666) / Wallace Collection, London, UK (tr). 89 Bridgeman Images: National Gallery, London, UK (tr). Getty Images: VCG Wilson / Corbis (cl). 90-91 Getty Images: 2004 / Remo Bardazzi / Electa / Mondadori Portfolio (b). 90 Getty Images: 2004 / Remo Bardazzi / Electa / Mondadori Portfolio (bl, c, tr). 91 Getty Images: 2004 / Remo Bardazzi / Electa / Mondadori Portfolio (tl, tr). 92 Alamy Stock Photo: Archivart (cl); PAINTING (bc). 92-93 Alamy Stock Photo: Dennis Hallinan (tc). 93 Alamy Stock Photo: classicpaintings (tr). Getty Images: DeAgostini (br). 94 Dreamstime.com: Pridumala (tr). Getty Images: Leemage / Corbis (cl). 94-95 Alamy Stock Photo: Artepics (b). 95 Alamy Stock Photo: Artepics (cr); World History Archive (tl). 96 Alamy Stock Photo: GL Archive (tl); FineArt (bl). 97 Alamy Stock Photo: Ian Dagnall. 98 Alamy Stock Photo: Peter Horree (cr); Peter van Evert (b). 99 Alamy Stock Photo: Art Collection 2 (br); FineArt (cr); The Print Collector (tl). 100 Alamy Stock Photo: Artokoloro Quint Lox Limited (cl); Peter van Evert (tl). 101 Getty Images: Universal History Archive / UIG. 102-103 Alamy Stock Photo: Heritage Image Partnership Ltd. 104-105 Alamy Stock Photo: Artepics (tc). 104 Alamy Stock Photo: Heritage Image Partnership Ltd (c). Dreamstime.com: Pridumala (bl). 105 Alamy Stock Photo: classicpaintings (br). Getty Images: Fine Art Images / Heritage Images (tr). 106

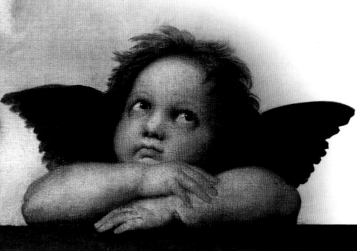

REFERENCE